ANNUAL REVIEW OF BEHAVIOR THERAPY

ANNUAL REVIEW OF
BEHAVIOR THERAPY

THEORY AND PRACTICE

VOLUME 10

CYRIL M. FRANKS
*Carrier Foundation and
Rutgers University*

G. TERENCE WILSON
Rutgers University

PHILIP C. KENDALL
Temple University

KELLY D. BROWNELL
University of Pennsylvania

THE GUILFORD PRESS
New York   London

Imagination is useless without knowledge; nature gives in vain the power of combination, unless study and observation supply materials to be combined.

SAMUEL JOHNSON

©1984 Cyril M. Franks, G. Terence Wilson, Philip C. Kendall, and Kelly D. Brownell

Published by The Guilford Press
A Division of Guilford Publications, Inc.
200 Park Avenue South, New York, N.Y. 10003

Printed in the United States of America

Library of Congress Catalog Card No. 76-126864
ISBN 0-89862-750-8
ISSN 0091-6595

PREFACE

Volume 10 in any series seems an appropriate milestone to pause, reflect, and engage in a little stock taking. This is all the more so when drastic changes have occurred along the way. The first *Annual Review of Behavior Therapy* was characterized by some 10% or less commentary by Franks and Wilson and 90% reprinted articles. With successive years, this ratio increased steadily until it was approximately 50–50 by Volume 8. It was at this stage that major changes took place. Beginning with Volume 9 and a new publisher, there were no reprinted articles, and the nature of the critical commentaries took on a different format and perspective.

With the addition of Philip C. Kendall and Kelly D. Brownell, the *Annual Review* took on its present format. Each of us was committed to the writing of two chapters and independent responsibility for the same subject areas from year to year, thereby ensuring continuous and integrated commentary that took up annually where the previous volume left off. Unlike most annual reviews, continuity of subject matter and perspective was maintained by this simple device of retaining the same team of authors from year to year. How effective this new format is and whether the reprinting of articles is missed at all is a matter for our readers to decide.

There is another matter to which we draw attention at this stage. It is becoming increasingly evident that, if the aim of the *Annual Review* is to draw attention to substantive developments, the behavior therapy literature may not warrant intensive, critical appraisal on an annual basis. Indeed, more than one reviewer—including such seasoned campaigners as Rachman himself—have drawn attention to this possibility. Commencing with Volume II, it is our intent therefore, at least for the next three issues, to publish our *Review* biennially rather than annually. In so doing, the present format, especially that of ensuring continuity by having the same author cover the same subject area for three consecutive volumes, will remain essentially unchanged. It is our hope that a biennial rather than annual review of the literature will lead to a more readily documentable chronicle of change. As a side benefit (and so far none of us has voiced any regret in this respect), we will no longer spend a significant portion of time each year working under pressure to process a vast pool of literature in a short time in a determined attempt to demonstrate progress or lack thereof.

The behavior therapy of the mid-1980s is no longer the simplistic infant of the 1960s, or even the fledgling entrepreneur of the 1970s. If not yet a mature adult, it is well beyond the stress and storm of adolescence. The signs of maturation are evidenced in the increasing sense of responsibility. Claims are made with caution, and the emphasis is upon evaluative research.

A striking feature of our field in the 1980s is the rapid rate of expansion. The domain of behavior therapy now extends into virtually every point on the social, clinical, and professional compass. In particular, we note the attention now given to the roles of cognitive variables and therapist–client relationships in producing behavior change, and, albeit on a much smaller scale, the attempt to contend with the problem of affect in behavioral terms.

But when all is said, if not done, it is hard to refute the accusation that events in the behavioral arena are characterized more by expansion than by conceptual advance. A behavioral model of man and woman is still absent, and individuals seeking guidance with respect to the existential problems of life are forced to look elsewhere. Finally, we draw attention to the relative absence of theory in contemporary behavior therapy. Regrettably, the pragmatic demands and exigencies of daily living seem to take preference over the need for theory and research-based intervention that triggered off behavior therapy as an independent movement in the first place.

It is these developments that we have attempted to chronicle and place in perspective over the years, and it is our hope that the present volume continues in this tradition. In so doing, our fundamental acknowledgment must be to the many researchers and clinicians who provide the data and informed opinions upon which we draw from year to year.

At the more personal level, we acknowledge those individuals who continue to provide that invaluable secretarial assistance without which this volume would not have appeared at all. GTW is much indebted this year, as in the past, to Barbara Honig of the Rutgers Alcohol Behavior Research Laboratory. PCK acknowledges with gratitude the able assistance of Janet Peterson, his former secretary at the University of Minnesota Department of Psychology. As always, CMF is deeply grateful to the indomitable Alleen Pusey, to Carol Martin, and to Gloria Johnson for their timeless efforts. Once again, we are especially grateful to our wives, Violet, Elaine, Sue, and Mary Jo for their forbearance and support throughout the preparation of this volume.

Cyril M. Franks
G. Terence Wilson
Philip C. Kendall
Kelly D. Brownell

CONTENTS

BEHAVIOR THERAPY: AN OVERVIEW

CYRIL M. FRANKS

INTRODUCTION

World congresses are appropriate occasions for reflection and stock taking. It is therefore apposite that this overview be written upon my return from Washington, D.C., the venue for the Second (1983) World Congress on Behavior Therapy. A world congress that is held once every 3 years serves as a marker within a discipline, and it is by this yardstick that I attempt to document progress in behavior therapy.

Many publications have appeared, numerous conferences and workshops have occurred, and probably hundreds of more or less well-designed studies are in progress. What is less certain is whether this activity heralds any significant conceptual, theoretical, or even techno-logical development, and it is to this issue that I return more than once in the coming pages.

While cognition is still very much in the behavioral air, less talk and less print is now dedicated to the proposition that we are in the throes of a major conceptual revolution, a paradigm shift from an outmoded conditioning to the brave new world of cognition. Present concerns are more with the development of a sophisticated method-ology that satisfies both those who seek to adorn themselves with the elusive garb of cognition and those whose cloth is cut to the measure of the traditional behavioral scientist.

As part of the increasing dissatisfaction with the unfulfilled prom-ise of learning theory as an adequate foundation for behavior therapy (e.g., Cullen, 1982), a small but influential group of research-oriented clinicians has become vocal. This past year has seen three such leaders compellingly argue the case for the failure of S-R learning theory. In a recently edited volume by Boulougouris (1982), Wilson, Barlow, and, from a somewhat different vantage point, Marks all point out the limitations of traditional learning theory formulations in understanding, for example, the neuroses. Systematically, the various conditioning-based theories of neurosis are examined and found wanting: classical fear theory, including Mowrer's two-factor theory; operant conditioning; self-efficacy theory; learned helplessness; Eysenck's revised conditioning theory; and more. But, on the other side, there are those who defend conditioning and modeling as at least temporarily adequate bases for the practice of behavior therapy (e.g., Stampfl, 1983). In the laboratory, well-designed studies continue to demonstrate the relatively minor roles of cognition, thought, and expectation in eyeblink conditioning (e.g., Frcka, Beyts, Levey, & Martin, 1983). Irrespective of the roles played by cognition, awareness, set, and the like, dismissal of conditioning may be premature. Classical conditioning still has its uses, and a case can even be made for a Pavlovian contribution to social psychology (Eysenck, 1983b).

Turning to a different topic, this year has seen a plethora of how-to manuals, practitioner's guides, and introductions to behavior therapy whose critical appraisal is outside the domain of this chapter. At a more scholarly level, one still lively topic is the integration of psychoanalytic and behavior therapy. But here, too, while a small number of edited volumes have recently appeared (e.g., Goldfried, 1982) and special issues or new volumes are "in the works," little of significance has surfaced during the past year or so.

A notable exception is Wachtel's (1982a) *Resistance: Psychodynamic and Behavioral Approaches*, in which leading behavior and psychoanalytic therapists contribute original chapters on client resistance in therapy and comment on the opinions of their fellow authors in the rival camp. What is of particular interest is Wachtel's gradual realization that his hoped-for integration is not to be. It would seem that the more thoughtful proponents of either position recognize the impossibility of integration at anything more than a superficial level.

"Resistance" provides a striking example of one word with two different meanings. As George Bernard Shaw long ago noted with respect to the United Kingdom and the United States, we are divided by a common tongue. For the behavior therapist, "resistance" refers to undesired, noncompliant behavior that the therapist has to understand and cope with as best he or she can so that the business of therapy can proceed without further encumbrance. For the analyst, resistance is a desirable and usable component of therapy which is at the core of the treatment process.

Social skills training is also on the upsurge, and a barrage of publications and workshops assails us from all directions. The book singled out for comment here (Spence & Shepherd, 1983) is of significance on one major account. It points to the different direction that social skills training is taking in the United Kingdom. In the United States, the link is primarily with assertion training and the empirical studies arising out of this movement. In the United Kingdom, social skills training has emerged mainly out of the work of such theoretical psychologists as Argyle and his colleagues at Oxford University. The essential feature of this model is an analogy between social interactions and the performance of a motor skill such as driving a car. In both instances, what the person actually does is continually being adjusted by means of a feedback loop dependent upon effectiveness in achieving a particular goal. Social interactions are similar to motor skills, and the analysis and correction of social difficulties is to be formulated in terms stemming from social psychology rather than behavior therapy alone.

As far as traditional assertion training is concerned, the United Kingdom is beginning to discover and apply what has been "old hat" in the United States for years. For example, Fry's (1983) discussion of social skills training within women's groups is technically competent but hardly novel—at least not on this side of the Atlantic.

While many popular articles and books geared toward the application of behavioral principles in industry have appeared, few have achieved the scholarship and level of comprehensiveness enjoyed by Frederiksen's (1982) *Handbook of Organizational Behavior Management*. It brings together under one cover the ideas, techniques, experiences and thinking of leaders in the field of OBM: Scott, Latham, Gilbert, Luthans, Sulzer-Azaroff, and, of course, Frederiksen himself. If no written rather than edited treatise has as yet appeared, this probably reflects the newness of the field more than anything else.

Maturity includes the ability to engage in objective self-evaluation. In the 1960s, behavior therapists were surrounded by a professional environment that was at best indifferent and at worst hostile. Understandably, behavior therapists reacted defensively, and boasts about quick cures and 90% success rates were commonplace. In the 1970s, behavior therapy became increasingly part of the establishment, and emphasis more properly turned to methodological strengths. In the 1980s, this encouraging trend continues apace, and it is now sober appraisal that is the order of the day. Even so, outcome evaluation is still inclined to focus upon successes, and it is only a few small voices within behavior therapy that raise the disquieting notes of clinical failure. But carefully documented failure—if not a delight—is something to be used to advantage. (See Goldfried, 1982, 1983, for further discussion of this point.)

Foa, Grayson, Steketee, Doppelt, Turner, and Latimer (1983a) use this notion to construct a model for the prediction of success and failure in the behavioral treatment of obsessive–compulsives. Almost two decades ago, Paul (1967) urged us to abandon a simplistic attitude of "Does psychotherapy work?" and investigate instead the more complex issue of which therapeutic intervention applied by which therapist to which patient under what circumstances is more likely to lead to what results. In so doing, systematic study of failure as well as success would seem to be mandatory. What is surprising is that it has taken as long as it has for this seemingly elementary point to gain recognition.

To the best of my knowledge, Foa and Emmelkamp's (1983) *Failures in Behavior Therapy* is the only book of its kind. The various contributors to this edited text delineate well "failure to benefit" in behavior therapy. What is given shorter shrift is the possibility that clients sometimes get worse in the course of treatment and that the circumstances surrounding this process also merit investigation.

As yet, there is an absence of solid evidence bearing on the occurrence of treatment failure, and the Foa and Emmelkamp volume reflects this lacuna. This might account in part for the inconsistent attention given to data in the various chapters. For example, both Foa, Steketee, Grayson, and Doppelt (1938b) and Dubbert and Wilson (1983) are careful to document the occurence of treatment failures and to identify possible predictive or mediating variables. Other contributors, such as Marshall and Gauthier (1983), rely primarily on plausible speculation.

It is always tempting to focus upon success and present only collaborative data. Commendably, this volume avoids such a pitfall. Graziano and Bythell (1983) contribute to the understanding of failure by their detailed discussion of the manner in which failures can be classified into contextual or technical failures. All therapy is inevitably carried out within a context that is necessarily larger than the immediate goals or procedures of behavior change. This context includes the physical and social setting in which the treatment is carried out, as well as the divergent values, beliefs, and goals of clients, supporting staff, the agency, and the community at large. When the therapist is insensitive to these matters, failure is more likely to occur. The more obvious examples of conceptual failure pointed out both by Graziano and Bythell and by Foa occur in situations whereby treatment is disrupted because of conflict with the surrounding value systems.

Other types of conceptual failure pertain to the subverting of values by context. For example, behavioral studies can be geared toward reduction of what the school, home, or other powers that be consider disruptive rather than enriching from the perspective of the child.

Technical failures are more straightforward to conceptualize. The processes involved in behavior therapy are complex, and there are many points at which procedural error can be made. Technical failures are conceptualized by Graziano and Bythell as failures made by behavior therapists themselves and thereby less dependent on the surrounding context. For example, successfully bringing about behavior change without systematic attention to procedures for generalization across setting and maintenance over time is viewed by Graziano and Bythell as technical failure. Even if the change is large, generalized, and maintained, it is of little value if it does not meaningfully improve the quality of life.

Finally, Graziano and Bythell's chapter is one of the few to draw attention to the negative effects of treatment. Clients could, and occasionally do, become worse as a result of treatment, and such unattended negative effects constitute another much-neglected category of failure in behavior therapy. This failure is even more deleterious when negative effects occur without the therapist's awareness.

Another new book of more ephemeral significance is the *International Handbook of Behavior Modification and Therapy* (Bellack, Hersen, & Kazdin, 1982). Leaders in the field contribute over 1,000 pages of double-columned commentary to what is literally and figuratively a weighty tome. The opening chapter, Kazdin's (1982a) "History of Behavior Modification," is a disappointment. It is little more than an encapsulated version of his splendid 1978 text (Kazdin, 1978b). It is time for Kazdin to bring the history of behavior modification up to date.

Perspectives on Behavior Therapy in the Eighties (Rosenbaum, Franks, & Jaffe, 1983) arose out of the First World Congress in Behaviour Therapy, but it is in no sense a rehash of papers submitted. Rather, some 22 participants were invited to present current thinking and new developments in a particular area. At the same time, to the extent that this was possible, contributions were selected to represent world behavior therapy. For obvious reasons, this is both a strength and a weakness of the volume. In their introductory chapter, Franks and Rosenbaum (1983) trace the origins of the Association for Advancement of Behavior Therapy (AABT), the birth pains of the World Congress, and the developmental history of the book.

Contemporary Behavior Therapy (Wilson & Franks, 1982) is one of the few volumes that attempt to place behavior therapy in conceptual and theoretical context. Without doubt, there have been remarkable technological and methodological advances within the past decade. This has led to a proliferation of demonstrably effective intervention strategies spanning an impressive range of psychological, educational, sociological, and medical modalities. But, as pointed out in Volume 9 of the *Annual Review of Behavior Therapy*, last year, this rapid advance may contain within it the seeds of its own destruction. The development of theory and the explicit testing of formalized models have been neglected. The basic question addressed by Wilson, Franks, and their invited contributors is as follows: What is the relationship between theory and practice in behavior therapy, and what does this augur for the future? Two decades ago, the gap between theory and application was small, perhaps because theory was rudimentary and application limited. With application growing exponentially and theory largely ignored, the gap is widening. If the Wilson and Franks volume does not close or even appreciably reduce the gap, it does help to place salient issues in perspective.

Punishment is a sensitive and much maligned topic. Technical and popular attributions are blurred and inconsistent. Many practitioners themselves remain unclear with respect to basic issues. This year sees the appearance of two books devoted exclusively to punishment (Axelrod & Apsche, 1983; Matson & DiLorenzo, 1984). While far from the "last words" on the subject, both serve as timely re-evaluations of issues that await resolution. Both books are reviewed elsewhere in this chapter.

The technology of behavior therapy generates curious alliances. Consider, for example, Krapfl and Gasparotto's (1982) "behavioral systems analysis." What is behavioral systems analysis? It is "the analysis of behavior that occurs in complex and organized social environments!" Complex environments can be analyzed to determine how various behavioral combinations interact to make an organization function, develop, and change. Systems theory is based on the proposition that no system or organization can be analyzed without taking into account the interactions of its various subsystems. The problem is that behavior therapy and most systems theory models operate within different conceptual and methodological frameworks, and, so far, Krapfl and Gasparotto have not shown how integration is to occur.

Krasner and Houts (1984) address themselves to the now outmoded "value-free" conceptualization of science captured in the once fashionable phrase, "Science is about facts, not values." The histories of both science and behavior therapy reflect this seemingly futile struggle toward an abstract knowledge free of worldly constraints and human bias. The "value-laden" conceptualization of science that is beginning to take its place rests on somewhat different assumptions, and it is the study of these assumptions that forms the basis of Krasner and Houts's new discipline. Psychology is well suited to the systematic study of the values of scientists, and Krasner and Houts see a new field, the "psychology of science," beginning to emerge.

To make their point, Krasner and Houts report an investigation of value systems in two groups of psychologists: behavioral scientists who launched a behavior modification movement in the 30-year era following World War II; and a comparison group of nonbehavioral psychologists from the same period. A total of 82 behavioral scientists and 100 randomly selected nonbehavioral psychologists were identified in terms of various demographic characteristics and asked to respond to three value-oriented questionnaires. Not surprisingly, the behavioral group endorsed factual, quantitative, empirical, and objectivist approaches to the study of human behavior. In contrast, the comparison group was characterized by a more "humanistic" and subjectivist approach. Of more interest, the two groups did not differ with respect to personal or sociocultural values, as early critics of behavior therapy had assumed. The values that characterize behavior modification are not necessarily associated with any particular sociopolitical value system. Behavior modification can encompass a diversity of viewpoints across a spectrum of cultural values.

"Behavioral economics," another relatively new term, was coined by Winkler and others to denote the theoretical and technicological linkages between reinforcement theory and economics. In his most recent formulation, Winkler (1983) spells out this relationship in detail. All behavioral interventions take place within some economic system. Failure to place the behavior change process within an economic context is at best a limitation and at worst a distortion of what is going on.

Another newcomer is "behavioral toxicology." Behavioral toxicology came into being only in the present decade and, although now established, is still in the consolidation phase (B. Weiss, 1983). The adverse health impact of environmental chemicals needs to be gauged by how people feel and function, in addition to the more customary physiological indicators of disease. This offers a new field for behavior therapists in terms of the investigation of the behavioral affects of chemical pollutants and the mechanics of administrative and societal change.

Finally, I draw attention to O'Leary's (1984) presidential address to the AABT, entitled "The Image of Behavior Therapy: It Is Time to Take a Stand." O'Leary asks these questions: How prevalent are behavior therapists? How has our influence been professionally? What is our image in the public arena? What have been our treatment successes? And last, what should we do next?

The AABT now has over 3,500 members, a growth that has occurred largely within the past decade. In 1982, a survey of clinical child psychologists by Tuma and Pratt revealed the major orientation of respondents to be psychodynamic or behavioral. A similar survey of pediatric psychologists by Tuma and Cohen in 1981 indicated that behavioral psychology was the primary orientation of some 60% of the sample. In the 1982 survey of the American Psychological Association (APA) Division of Psychotherapy by Norcross and Prochaska, psychodynamic and eclectic orientations were the most frequent (each 30%), followed by behavior therapy (14%). In a more recent survey of counseling psychologists, a behavioral or cognitive–behavioral orientation accounted for 17% of the sample, with psychoanalysis a poor second (D. Smith, 1983). As O'Leary (1984) concludes, behavior therapy is emerging as one of the top three preferences in professional psychology.

So much for the prevalence of the behavior therapist, but before proceeding to a discussion of O'Leary's second question, attention can usefully be drawn to Norcross and Wogan's (1983) study of the relationships between the personalities of behavior therapists and clinical practice. According to Norcross and Wogan, "behavior therapy" can denote either a set of techniques, a consortium of theoretical principles, or the application of a methodological style. This, to my way of thinking, misguided portrayal of behavior therapy as a series of techniques led Norcross and Wogan to the conclusion that personality, training, experience, and background might be largely irrelevant to the practice of behavior therapy. To explore this unacceptable conclusion, Norcross and Wogan surveyed members of the AABT and came up with the finding that technique usage varies with setting and type of client. Behavior therapists selectively employ interventions deemed appropriate to the environment and the problems encountered. Furthermore, personal characteristics as well as professional training appear to influence therapy. As with theory, there is more to clinical practice than the impersonal application of principles.

To answer his second question, O'Leary (1984) surveyed the 1983 journals of the three major mental health organizations in the United States with core disciplines of psychology, psychiatry, and social work, respectively. Some form of behavioral intervention was preponderant in the psychological literature, well represented in nonpharmacological treatment studies in the psychiatric literature, and totally absent in that of social work. As far as the influence of behavior therapy in treatment research supported by the National Institute of Mental Health (NIMH) is concerned, O'Leary (1984) cites a report prepared for the Psychosocial Treatments Research Branch of NIMH and its conclusion that "behavior therapy treatment makes up nearly 74% of the treatment efficacy studies supported by this branch" (O'Leary, 1984, p. 222).

To assess the image of behavior therapy in the public arena,

O'Leary surveyed all references to behavior therapy, behavior modification, or behaviorism that appeared in the *New York Times* between 1965 and 1983. Independent analyses of "impact ratings" by O'Leary and his assistant indicated that behavior modification and behavior therapy were generally described in negative terms up to 1978. However, most of the articles dealt with specific and limited subject matter, references to Skinner being the most numerous. These ranged from very negative to quite positive, with a generally somewhat negative view. References to the use of behavior modification in prisons were almost uniformly negative. References to the controlled drinking controversy of 1982 were fairly objective or neutral in tone. The depiction of behavior therapy with depressed or fearful individuals was favorable.

Although not mentioned by O'Leary, a 5-year follow-up by Carey, Carey, and Turkat (1983) of data uncovered by Turkat and Feuerstein (1978) revealed essentially similar findings. Once again, the *New York Times* was surveyed, this time from January 1977 to December 1981. According to Carey *et al.* (1983), several changes have occurred over the past decade. First, fewer articles on the subject of behavior modification now appear in the media, a surprising finding in view of the rapid growth of the field. Second, the media representation of behavior modification has become more accurate, with a smaller percentage of inaccurate, negatively toned reporting. Nevertheless, the legacy remains sufficiently strong for Carey *et al.* to warn their readership that "negative media presentations of behavior modification continue to haunt its professional image" (1983, p. 500).

As far as treatment successes are concerned, O'Leary (1984) is cautiously positive in the areas of autism, aggression, hyperactivity, agoraphobia, marital discord, and depression. His sober appraisal is very different from the aggressive success parades of less than two decades ago. Regrettably, not all behavior therapists have abandoned this particular battlefield. Giles (1983a, 1983b), for example, is still determined to demonstrate the superiority of behavioral interventions and concludes from a survey of five major research areas that "all comparisons favored behavior therapy. Though methodological quality of the studies ranged from poor to excellent, behavior therapy was found superior regardless of methodological quality, experience of therapists, degree of subject approximation to 'real' clinical patients or type of disorder!" (1983b, p. 192).

In the rest of this chapter, I try to make an objective appraisal of behavior therapy in various areas. To the extent that this is appropriate, themes developed in Volume 9 of the *Annual Review* are maintained. O'Leary's final question—What should we do next?—is examined at the end of this chapter.

BEHAVIOR THERAPY IN THE INTEREST OF
THE CONSUMER

Despite best efforts and progress made, public disquiet about behavior therapy remains strong. It is not difficult to understand how this came about. Behavior therapy is effective, and, for complex reasons, this effectiveness tends to be exaggerated by society. Even some professionals still confuse behavior modification with a diversity of procedures for changing behavior, ranging from contingency management to electroshock therapy and psychosurgery. It is hardly surprising that the public is confused. Sometimes behavior therapists themselves contribute to this confusion by ill-chosen terminology and rash statements. Sometimes the programs designed, endorsed, or carried out by behavior therapists are questionable. (For a detailed exposition of these problems and their implications, the reader is referred to previous commentary throughout this series.)

The needs to protect both clients and behavior therapy are closely related. Unfortunately, as Feldman and Peay (1982) point out, it is easier to talk about the need to avoid consumer abuse than to do anything about it. It is this attempt to protect the consumer at all levels, ranging from direct therapy contact to the impact upon society at large, that is the primary concern of this section. It is because behavior therapy is readily exploitable that behavior therapists must question the directions of their research and the uses to which their findings may be put. As indicated, science is far from value-free, and there may upon occasion be cogent arguments in favor of not undertaking certain investigations.

Feldman and Peay draw further attention to the insufficiency of reliance upon legal regulation alone. Behavior therapists as a professional body need to look to more than the law for guidance in the establishment of standards. The primary control may have to come from within the profession.

Accountability is one of the main tenets of contemporary behavior therapy, and its impact is spilling over into the mental health profession at large. If accountability is now at least one of the orders of the day in general psychiatry, it was behavior therapists who spearheaded the trend.

Consumer satisfaction is rapidly becoming a popular slogan, and at least lip service is given to this phrase in most clinical investigations. Sometimes the in-words are "social validation," but it comes to the same thing. Most institutions now have human rights and peer review committees, mechanisms whereby the right to effective treatment and the right to be free from harm are balanced (Sheldon-Wildgen & Risley,

1982). While general principles can perhaps be formulated, cut-and-dried rules and regulations remain elusive. As Sheldon-Wildgen and Risley note, what such committees can do is address the issue of providing professionally justified and ethically appropriate treatment. In addition to monitoring client interests, these committees also help to protect programs that otherwise might be subjected to premature and unwanted termination. This, too, is a means of protecting the interests of the consumer.

Peer review, now a firmly established policy of the AABT, is another consumer protection mechanism. Christian (1983b) describes two forms of professional peer review: case consultation and program review. Case consultation involves review of programming for a particular client and is designed to protect client, therapist, and program from limitations inherent in virtually all human service delivery. Program review is more comprehensive than case consultation. Typically, it involves off-site examination of written material followed by on-site review.

Consumer protection has to take place at all levels, ranging from the mundane and specific (e.g., the provision of data to help clinicians choose self-help manuals at a reading level appropriate to their clients' educational attainments; see Dentch, O'Farrell, & Cutter, 1980, and O'Farrell & Keuthen, 1983) to the determination of policy and strategy at high levels. Also important, because of the greater potential for influencing a large number of people, is the reward system of psychotherapy itself and the implications for the consumer.

In a now-classic study, Hollingshead and Redlich (1958) demonstrated that where and how an individual was treated for psychological disorders was determined in large part by his or her location in the class structure. A follow-up by Link and Milcarek (1980) suggests that, although class differences have narrowed over time, lower-class persons are still less likely to receive professional attention. Mental health resources seem to be preferentially delivered to those who are seen as the more desirable patients rather than to those who are most in need. And this is surely not in the interest of the consumer. Younger, more motivated, more communicative, and more competent patients are still more likely to receive most of the attention. Even more recently, Link (1983) adduced data to suggest that providers who treat "advantaged" as opposed to disadvantaged patients tend to be evaluated more positively by their peers. Inequities in the delivery of mental health services are directly related to the reward structure in which mental health professionals conduct their activities. Once again, this can hardly be construed as being in the interest of the consumer.

Correction would necessitate social change beyond the domain of even a grandiose behavior therapy. Nevertheless, there is much that can be done to protect the consumer at more down-to-earth levels. Christian (1983a), for example, describes the various strategies that go into managing the performance of the human service consultant. Obtaining and managing the services of a consultant in the interest of the consumer requires careful planning and, like everything else in behavior therapy, must be programmed rather than lamented when it does not occur. Similarly, Yeaton and Sechrest (1981) stress for the need for practicing clinicians to develop explicit criteria for exercising good judgment in choosing optimal treatments for their patients. Unfortunately, it is easier to spell out criteria for good judgments in treatment than to implement them. Regrettably but understandably, professionals are more likely to be reinforced by the "peer acclaim" values underscored in the preceding paragraph.

Attempts to protect the interest of the institutionalized consumer have met with more success. But here the problem is complicated by the need to protect the interest of the public at large. For society to achieve maximum benefit from the facilities provided for the consumer, the institution concerned must function at optimal efficiency. If society is called upon to pay for therapy, self-enhancement, or education, then it has the obligation and the right to help determine how the needs for these services are arrived at, who is qualified to receive them, and who should provide those services. Just as it is the therapist's and the client's right between them to determine what needs treating, so—argues Parloff (1983)—it is the right of society to determine for what it will pay. As important as consumer satisfaction is the evidence that the service provided enhances patient effectiveness and thereby reduces the burden on society.

The most widely referenced cost-effectiveness plan to date is probably that of Fishman (1981). If two programs are equally effective, clearly it is the more costly that will be eliminated. But the demonstration of equal effectiveness may be more complicated than many such plans have anticipated, and it is the delineation of a precise decision recommending strategy that makes Fishman's plan attractive. (See Sacco, 1982, for a more extended discussion of this point.)

Of late, public debate has focused on the use of demonstrable effectiveness as one criterion for approving certain treatments for reimbursement. But this may serve only to increase costs, inhibit innovation, and interfere with clinical practice (McGuire & Frisman, 1983). Somehow, cost and effectiveness have to be incorporated into the overall model if the direct interests of the consumer and the interests of society at large (the indirect interests of the consumer) are to be equitably balanced. It is this that may be the fundamental task for those who seek to develop appropriate models of quality assurance. Hetherington (1982), for example, has developed a problem-solving model that identifies four problem areas: goal attainment, engendering maximal bureaucratic responsibility; integration, which serves to increase motivation on the part of the professionals involved; adaptation, which leads to containment of costs and the maximum utilization of valid resources; and pattern maintenance, the preservation of societal values that take into account both the needs of the professional and bureaucratic accountability. We have come a long way from the "earlier" days, less than half a decade ago, when direct consumer satisfaction was the primary data base

The miniseries on consumer satisfaction that appeared in *Behavior Therapy* in 1983 under the general editorship of Forehand is probably unique to the behavior therapy literature. It might even be the forerunner of yet another journal! In their introductory article, Bornstein and Rychtarik (1983) set the scene by reviewing "procedures, problems and future perspectives" for the role of consumer satisfaction in adult behavior therapy. They attribute part of the traditional professional lack of interest in consumer satisfaction to the model of clinical practice that has been dominant until very recently. Psychoanalytic therapy has always been skeptical of patient reports, and its legacy remains (e.g., Auerbach & Luborsky, 1968).

The gradual change with respect to the acceptance of consumer satisfaction measures is attributed to a variety of factors. There is a small but significant body of research to suggest that, when clients and therapists fail to agree about improvement, it is often client ratings that are more congruent with external evaluations than the ratings of those providing the service (e.g., Horenstein, Houston, & Holmes 1973). In a somewhat related development, several states are now attempting to mandate some form of direct consumer involvement in the evaluation of mental health services.

Unfortunately, according to Bornstein and Rychtarik (1983), behavior therapists still remain insufficiently attuned either to basic issues or to the need for a sophisticated research methodology. Lebow (1982) concludes that consumer satisfaction research in the mental health field in general is primitive, and Bornstein and Rychtarik echo these sentiments with respect to behavior therapy. Assessment procedures tend to be poorly described, results are vaguely reported, and the purposes of most evaluations remain unclear.

Bornstein and Rychtarik's first corrective recommendation is that consumer satisfaction measures should be an integral component of all outcome evaluations. Second, evaluation of consumer satisfaction should be multidimensional and should include direct measures, unsolicited comments, unobtrusive observation procedures, self-report, overt observation, and more. Third, the Consumer Satisfaction Questionnaire of Larson, Attkisson, Hargreaves, and Nguyen (1979) is the most sophisticated instrument developed to date, and Bornstein and Rychtarik advocate its use as a standard part of consumer satisfaction evaluation in behavior therapy. Fourth, they stress the need for component evaluation to determine which procedures are most satisfactory to which clients under what circumstances. Fifth, alternative treatments are not equally acceptable to all clients (see Kazdin, 1981). Satisfaction has many dimensions, and relationships among satisfaction, involvement, and maintenance in treatment can be complex. Bornstein and Rychtarik's sixth point pertains to the neglect of psychometrics in consumer evaluation research—a deficit common to much of behavior therapy, alas.

The next three recommendations made by Bornstein and Rychtarik are methodological, ranging from such seemingly obvious matters as assurances of anonymity in the cross-sectional sampling of clients (i.e., a particular period of time is chosen, and all clients who receive services during that period are used to generate data with respect to their levels of satisfaction). Finally, Bornstein and Rychtarik draw attention to practical considerations. The collection of information needs to be kept simple and inexpensive, yet meaningful, and to be grounded in careful program design.

In the next article in this miniseries, McMahon and Forehand (1983) critically review consumer satisfaction in the treatment of children. Although a relatively greater proportion of child behavior therapy studies include some measure of consumer satisfaction than their counterparts in the adult world, the same limitations still obtain. What is most disturbing to McMahon and Forehand is the failure to assess satisfaction from the immediate and direct perspective of the child. Children have the right to participate in treatment decisions and activities at levels commensurate with their maturity and the complexities of the issues involved. Inquiry addressed directly to a child may be more meaningful than the customary exclusive reliance upon the evaluations of parents or teachers (Ross, 1980). For example, Kirigin, Braukmann, Atwater, and Wolf (1982) found that youth evaluations of satisfaction with their Achievement Place program were more highly related to reductions in future legal offenses than ratings by group home parents, teachers, or even the parents themselves.

Kiesler's (1983) contribution to this miniseries is atypical, in that he approaches the problem from the perspective of an experimental social psychologist. For Kiesler, consumer satisfaction research is, in essence, a study of attitudes and attitude change. Behavior therapists tend to emphasize categorizations of behavior, single-subject designs with repeated measures, the establishment of proper baselines, the development of statistics specific to multiple measurements, threats to external validity, and the like. Social psychologists are more likely to emphasize theory and alternative explanations, threats to internal validity, factorial designs that include single measurements (or single times of measurement), and problems in measuring change in general and attitude change in particular. The two technologies rest on different metatheory and different metamethodology. According to Kiesler, a more formal use of attitude change and attitude measurement technology would serve behavior therapists well in their evaluation of consumer satisfaction.

It is of probable significance that it has taken a decade for consumer satisfaction to achieve sectional status in this overview, and it will be of interest to see what lies ahead.

PROFESSIONAL TRAINING IN BEHAVIOR THERAPY

One would expect behavior therapists to be very concerned with the training of future clinicians and researchers. Unfortunately, behavior therapists seem to have been too busy doing and creating to think much about training. But without proper training, it is difficult to see how behavior therapy can become established as a teachable discipline with a sense of continuity and tradition. What constitutes proper training is another matter. With a certain eminent exception who shall be nameless, no one has had the temerity to proclaim what "proper" training is or how this is to be accomplished.

There is little that is new to report. Bernstein (in press) has compiled a bibliography on training, which contains nearly 700 references. Nearly half of these are concerned with the somewhat specialized and relatively well-developed area of parent training. Of the remainder, many are anecdotal descriptions that contain no data whatsoever. The lack of methodological sophistication or adequate design makes it difficult, if not impossible, to draw meaningful conclusions. (Bernstein's bibliography may be obtained on request to the author, at the Center for Child Development, University of Colorado Health Sciences Center, Denver, Colorado, for the cost of photocopying and a stamp.)

There are some interesting new training proposals, but, for the most part, these are not adequately translated into action. For example, Willems (1983) makes a plea for training in "ecobehavioral technology," the study of the complex systems-oriented interrelationships between behavior and the environment. But, as yet, he has not explained how the promise is to become a working reality.

In terms of specifics, Bernstein's interactive ecobehavioral framework, reported in this chapter last year, is now further developed, and attention is drawn to the need for training programs to consider what to teach, how to teach it, and how to insure generalization of skills taught. For maximal generalization to occur, process and analytic skills rather than the specific procedures should be taught. Rule-governed behaviors, so it is argued, are less likely to be adaptable and responsive to new situations. According to Bernstein (in press), this issue is unlikely to be resolved while researchers teach either analytic skills *or* techniques. Both types of behavior can occur at a wide variety of stimulus conditions, and, while the teaching of operational discriptions and techniques is usually adequate, the teaching of analytic skills is less well developed. Systematic long-term investigations of both types of teaching are needed (see also Bernstein & Ziarnik, 1982).

Bernstein's perspective goes beyond the classroom. For example, she questions the ethics of training without provision for concomitant environmental support for the newly acquired behavior change skills. In training, argues Bernstein, the system is as important as the training program per se. Bernstein's suggestion that those who design training programs address themselves to the development of models for deciding when the training of behavior change agents is appropriate to a given situation and when it is not is reminiscent of Blechman's (1981) decision model for deciding whether or not to use parent training (see Volume 9 of the *Annual Review*). Relevant questions include: Is the organization capable of providing support for the use of these newly acquired skills? Can it provide any kind of positive consequences for use of these skills? Are there institutional barriers that might make these skills difficult if not impossible, to implement? Students need to learn how to utilize and maintain the behavioral skills of organizations that may not necessarily support the continuing use of these behaviors: They have to be trained to act behaviorally in nonbehavioral places.

On a more limited scale, there are a few recent, not highly significant, studies of specific facets of behavioral training. For example, Jason (1984) describes a program designed to train undergraduates in certain circumscribed phases of behavioral clinical and community psychology at the practical level. And Milne (1982) reports a study of two alternative forms of nurse training in behavior modification, regrettably limited to questionnaire and self-report measures. Follow-up was not attempted, and nothing is known about the subsequent behavior of either nurses or patients other than what was gleaned from a structured trainee interview some 6 months later.

While unfortunately confined to only three undergraduates, the well-designed study of Borck, Fawcett, and Lichtenberg (1982) sheds methodological light in a poorly illuminated area. The identification of relevant behaviors involved in counseling and problem solving was used to develop leaders for the teaching of these skills. Based on experience with behavioral approaches to skills training, instructional procedures for teaching identified counseling and problem-solving behaviors were prepared, field-tested, and revised. Behavioral specification, description of relevant conditions, rationales for the behaviors, situational examples of the behaviors, study guides, and practice plus feedback and performance were used to develop appropriate training procedures. Following training, the occurrence of counseling and problem-solving behavior increased to 89%. Generalization data with actual clients, together with expert ratings of the overall quality of the counseling, provided further evidence of generalization to other settings and other situations. A staggered introduction of training across the three students demonstrated that increases occurred only after training and were therefore directly attributable to the training received.

While other forms of parent training have been well studied (see Chapter 7), behavioral programs remain relatively neglected. Furtkamp, Giffort, and Schiers's (1982) evaluation of a curriculum designed to teach behavior modification skills to direct care staff is one of the few recent examples of investigations in this area. Because all training had to be confined to a limited number of classroom sessions, little time was left for trainee evaluation.

In 1979, O'Dell, Tarler-Benlolo, and Flynn developed a 50-item multiple-choice procedure for assessing how well respondents understood the application of behavior modification principles with children in a residential setting. They called this the knowledge of Behavioral Principles as Applied to Children (KBPAC) Test. Unfortunately, it requires 30 to 60 minutes of classroom time, which prohibits its use in most in-service training programs. Fortunately, evaluation of two specially developed 14-item versions of the same test, carried out with 111 trainees, led to the conclusion that reducing the length had little psychometric impact. Unfortunately, the use of this revision is not described, and there is no way of knowing about relationships among test scores, trainee performance, and changes in the children being trained.

Turning next to a very different level of training, Temple University Medical School's annual June Institute offers an intensive 1-month program in behavior therapy. The first of these Institutes was held in 1965. In 1972, six Institutes later, Ascher and Edwards (1972) formulated two main goals for this annual event and proposed that they be evaluated at subsequent meetings. The goals were instruction and proselytization—instruction in the theory and practice of "correct" behavior therapy; and the motivation of trainees to add behavior therapy techniques to their clinical repertoires, as well as encouragement of active teaching of behavioral strategies to other mental health professionals.

This proposal was ignored until 1980, when O'Farrell, Sewitch, and Cutter reported an evaluation of the 1976 Institute. (It should be noted that O'Farrell was a trainee at this Institute.) Pre- to post-Institute changes and the durability of these changes at 24-month follow-up were evaluated statistically, and participant reports were used to assess goal attainment. As one might perhaps expect, the reported results were highly favorable.

Unfortunately, this study suffers from major methodological deficits and meaningful conclusions are not possible. O'Farrell et al. themselves draw attention to their inadequate self-report coverage, the lack of reliability and validity data with respect to the questionnaires used, and the fact that respondents reported pre-institute ratings retrospectively at the end of the Institute.

Paraprofessionals offer certain advantages, or so the claim is made. Based on impression rather than evidence, it is commonly believed that, because paraprofessionals are more like their clients, rapport is more readily established. In addition, paraprofessionals themselves benefit from being in the "helper" role. Starting with the premise that such arguments rest upon mostly unexplored assumptions, Graziano and Katz (1982) review the history of paraprofessionalism and the more recent emergence of behaviorally based training programs.

Gartner (1971) points to three distinct categories of paraprofessionals that have emerged over the years. Hospital-based workers, such as psychiatric aides, comprise the traditional group. These "old paraprofessionals" perform relatively routine patient care duties; they are generally minimally educated; and they are not recruited from the groups they serve. The "indigenous paraprofessionals" come from the target population they serve. Also limited in formal education, their alleged strength is the sense of identification with the groups they serve. Finally, there are the "new middle-class paraprofessionals," frequently female, often well educated, and sharing values and beliefs with the professionals with whom they work. To Gartner's three groups Graziano and Katz (1982) add a fourth, parents as mental health professionals (to be discussed shortly), and reject a possible fifth, teachers.

Teachers trained in mental health procedures should not be regarded as paraprofessionals. They are professionals in their own right who have been taught some of the technology of a related profession to enable them to carry out adjunctive therapeutic activities in addition to their educational functions.

Parents trained to work as paraprofessionals with their own children form a unique group. Unlike other paraprofessionals, they seek training not to enhance occupational skills or status, or to help individuals with whom they have had little prior contact. Rather, the training is intended exclusively to help their children. Parent training is perhaps the most systematically explored area in the behavioral training movement. It has been repeatedly demonstrated that mothers can be trained to bring about improvements in their children and their interactions with their children. Nevertheless, much remains to be investigated. For example, little is known about the characteristics of successful as compared with unsuccessful mother trainees, the generalizability and permanence of the observed changes, or the "personal" values of these changes to the parents and children concerned. Furthermore, as Graziano and Katz note, parent training has been limited largely to mothers. (This topic is further discussed in Chapter 7.)

The training of behavioral aides typically involves instruction, modeling, role playing, and videotape feedback, and much of the discussion about training centers on comparisons of the effectiveness of different training procedures. In 1972, Gardner claimed a close relationship between knowledge of behavioral principles and the ability to apply behavior modification procedures. Graziano and Katz's (1982) rather different conclusion better reflects the complexities involved: Different training strategies lead to different gains, depending upon whether principles or applications are stressed. Formal training for behavioral aides has to be chosen with care and instituted in terms of the types of improvement desired.

Is the attendant's actual behavior different as a result of the training? In one study cited by Graziano and Katz, behaviorally trained aides tended to focus primarily on behavior considered likely to produce adaptive patient behavior (Gardner & Giampa, 1971). Unfortunately, because of serious methodological inadequacies in the reported research, Graziano and Katz are unable to answer this question. In addition to poor research design, lack of control groups, and small samples, few studies report outcome data, and most of those that do so use measures that are not directly related to behavioral change in their patients.

The use of undergraduates is sometimes cited as one means of relieving personnel shortages. Once again, as Graziano and Katz pessimistically note, it is difficult to draw conclusions about the effectiveness of students as paraprofessionals from the research literature. Most studies are concerned with benefits accruing to the students rather than the clients, and serious methodological limitations characterize those studies that do focus upon the training program and its effects upon the clients rather than the students. What is surprising is Graziano and Katz's observation—and there is no reason to doubt them—that, despite the inadequacies of the data, it is still generally contended that college students are as good as, if not better than, professionals in developing beneficial working relationships with patients.

It seems evident that, with the exception of behavioral parent training, behavior therapists have failed to give systematic and sustained consideration to the problems involved in training. Since training is a major vehicle in the transmission, development, and preservation of an evolving system, this is unfortunate.

WHAT'S NEW IN MENTAL RETARDATION?

From the point of view of behavior therapy, the answer to the question "What's new in mental retardation?" is "Very little." Most developments in mental retardation stem from the mainstream of mental retardation research rather than from the activities of behavior therapists.

Defining mental retardation is, in itself, complicated. "Retardation" is a diagnostic term that identifies a category of people rather than a specific set of behaviors. And from a behavioral perspective, it is behaviors rather than individuals that are retarded. How, then, can behavior therapists feel comfortable with the term "mental retardation"? Rather than replace the term "mental" with some such prefix as "developmental" or "behavioral," as is sometimes the practice, Neisworth and Madle (1982) favor the use of the single word "retardation" to refer to a condition characterized by generalized delay across a wide range of behavioral domains.

While consistent with the increasingly accepted term "developmental disabilities," the definition given above does not permit differentiation of those individuals traditionally regarded as mentally retarded from those suffering from some form of autism, for example. However, it is highly consistent with Neisworth and Madle's behavioral model. As originally advanced by Bijou (1963), instead of being viewed as either a theoretical construct or a biological phenomenon, "retardation" is conceived of as a behavioral deficiency brought about by adverse reinforcement histories or by a failure of S-R functions. This leads naturally into the functional analysis of study of pertinent learning variables in an individual's life. Since such variables as reinforcement, punishment, and satiation are all amenable to objective definition and manipulation, they lend themselves nicely to a behavioral approach. Best of all, this approach requires not so much a special theory of retardation as an extension of known principles of learning to the study of behavioral retardation.

A matter of importance to all who work in this area is that of mechanisms for protecting the rights of the institutionalized. Legal, ethical, professional, and scientific issues are all involved (see Morris & Brown, 1983, for further discussion of these matters). As populations of the large state institutions for the mentally retarded decline in accordance with prevailing policies of deinstitutionalization, those who remain tend to fall increasingly into the category of the severely and profoundly retarded. Such individuals are quite unable to protect their rights and frequently have no relative or guardian available or capable of doing so for them. To meet this need, a variety of mechanisms have been developed. These include individual advocates, state-wide advocacy agencies, interest group organizations, institutional resident advocates, and human rights committees (HRCs).

Kemp (1983) surveyed 74 state residential committees concerning their HRC functioning. The most commonly reported HRC activity involved behavior modification programs, followed closely by the use of psychotropic medication to control behavior. Three-quarters of the respondents reported problems with the expertise of the committees appointed to cope with the problems involved. Behavior therapists working in such institutions might do well to apply their skills to the development and performance of HRCs.

Until recently, behavioral psychologists working in institutions for the retarded expended most of their energies on traditional studies geared toward increasing not very relevant bits of performance. The present trend is toward the generation of more socially meaningful activities (e.g., Mansell, Felce, De Kock, & Jenkins, 1982). But many of these studies remain "traditional" in the sense that they focus in a one-to-one fashion upon the patients rather than upon the infrastructure of the institution (Cuvo, Leaf, & Borakove, 1978).

Woods and Cullen (1983) are on the right track when they address themselves to failures and successes in achieving desired changes in long-term institutions by asking pertinent "How?" and "Why?" questions. In contrast to prevailing belief, they found little evidence of deliberately produced meaningful changes in staff behavior. In 1975,

Quilitch concluded that there was no relationship between institutional effectiveness and in-service training, and, 6 years later, Ivanic, Reid, Iwata, Faw, and Page (1981) came to much the same conclusion.

Presumably, the main reason for trying to change staff behaviors is that such changes somehow bring direct benefit to the residents. To address themselves to this question, Woods and Cullen (1983) reviewed the few studies that attempted to measure the value of staff training in terms of changes in resident behavior. Mostly, the dependent variables consisted of changes in staff attitudes, number of training sessions attended, the ability of the staff to talk or write in behavioral terms, and, very occasionally, changes in performance as measured by role-play sessions. As yet, no convincing relationship between such variables and either staff performance or the behavior of the residents has been demonstrated.

Participants often report the in-service workshop to be pleasurable; this may act as positive reinforcement for the smooth and continued maintenance of the workshop, but there is little reason to believe that there will be much beneficial effect accruing to the residents. Most studies focus on direct, short-term staff changes, and long-term maintenance of ward–staff interactions is rarely examined. The reversion of residents and staff to their original states soon after the investigator's departure is all too familiar. If the interest is in long-term behavior change, the time scale has to be in years rather than weeks.

To illustrate this point, Woods and Cullen (1983) review several seemingly impressive studies of training the institutionalized mentally retarded. Toilet training the profoundly retarded is a serious and difficult problem in most long-stay institutions. When Woods and Guest (1980) attempted to increase the frequency of appropriate urination behavior, improvement was so slow and imperceptible over the short term that several of the nurses asked if the procedure could be abandoned. The procedure was, however, maintained with at least one resident for over 5 years. So, as Woods and Cullen note, whatever was responsible for maintaining that nurse's behavior, it was not perceived positive effects on residents' behavior. Similarly, in a study of room management behavior cited by Woods and Cullen, there was a dramatic initial improvement in behavior. Nevertheless, after a period of time, precise application of the procedure drifted, and the behavior of the residents deteriorated noticeably. Positive changes in behavior are not sufficient in themselves to maintain staff behavior.

In three of four studies reviewed by Woods and Cullen (1983), staff behavior was maintained in the absence of noticeable change, and in the fourth it was not maintained even though there was apparent change. The situation is complex, and contingencies cannot be described in a simple or straightforward manner. Woods and Cullen's conclusions may be summarized as follows: (1) Simple, single manipulations rarely result in permanent behavior change for either residents or staff; (2) there is no readily apparent simple relationship between staff and resident behavior; (3) when change occurs, it is unlikely that there will be a simple explanation for it.

What Woods and Cullen (1983) term the "misguided search for simplicity" has been noted in one way or another by many an investigator, only to be disregarded by those who search for facile solutions. It may be that reinforcement is but one of the many ways in which behavior can be influenced by the environment. As Michael (1980) points out, "[M]any human situations are often tossed off as examples of this or that simple concept, when in fact such analyses are quite superficial and easily spotted as such by critics of the behavioral approach" (p. 14).

Brophy (1981) arrives at much the same conclusion in his analysis of studies predicated upon such statements as "The child's behavior was reinforced with praise." As Brophy notes, depending on the setting, praise may have a variety of functions in addition to direct reinforcement. Thus, for those who work in long-stay institutions, the situation is more complex than had been imagined. For Woods and Cullen (1983), solutions probably lie in a closer examination of currently occurring complex contingencies within the institution. It is, after all, these contingencies that maintain both staff and resident behavior, even if it is not always the positive or adaptive behavior that the staff desires. (See Cullen, Burton, Watts, and Thomas, 1983, for further discussion of institutional interactions from this perspective.)

The situation is not quite as bleak as Cullen and his associates present it. Much research has been directed toward the improvement of work performance by direct care personnel in institutional settings; Prue, Frederiksen, and Bacon (1978) provide a fairly up-to-date annotated bibliography, and Reid and Whitman (1983) give a critical review of behavioral staff management strategies in such facilities.

Four categories of management programs are discussed by Reid and Whitman (1983): antecedent, contingency management, self-control, and multifaceted interventions. Antecedent approaches appear to be the least successful in improving staff performance and contingency management, particularly performance feedback systems, while multifaceted programs appear to be the most successful. While noting progress in the design and implementation of behavioral staff management programs, Reid and Whitman draw attention to certain issues that require research resolution before behavioral management practices can be considered valid and ready for general use.

First, investigators have tended to focus on restricted areas of staff performance, and it is not clear whether procedures can be applied effectively at any given time to the total set of attendant job duties. It may be that behavioral approaches are effective in staff management, but that the demands required of supervisors prohibit proficient intervention in several areas at once. Second, it is important to determine the acceptability of behavioral staff management intervention programs to direct care workers and their supervisors. Increasingly, even limited self-care studies are beginning to include measures of staff and general institutional acceptability (e.g., Augustine & Cipani, 1982). The third issue, punishment, is to be reviewed shortly.

A final area of staff management that seems to warrant attention pertains to the analysis of the contingencies that control attendant performance on a day-to-day basis. Specific questions suggested by Reid and Whitman (1983) for investigation include the following: (1) What are the effects of peer models (e.g., older and more experienced staff members) and/or peer interactions on the performance of new direct care staff members? (2) What is the optimum number of job responsibilities for which attendant personnel should be held accountable? (3) What effect does management's application of traditional civil service regulations have on attendant job performance?

A number of recent well-designed studies shed light upon these issues, and I will cite two to make the point. Most programs for managing the work performance of the direct care staff in institutions for the mentally retarded require intensive involvement by supervisory staff. Despite reported successes, such programs suffer from serious limitations in terms of efficiency and cost–benefit analysis. It has therefore been suggested on more than one occasion that, if the direct care staff members could acquire the necessary skills to manage their own work-related behaviors effectively without direct supervision, then less professional time and financial investment might be required to bring about the desired behavior changes. To this end, it has been further suggested that the staff members themselves might be the most effective agents for changing performance, since they have more immediate and continued access to their own behavior than would any external supervisory agent. Furthermore, direct participant management training could provide a set of skills that could be applied to future programs.

Burgio, Whitman, and Reid (1983) developed and evaluated a program exclusively for line staff rather than supervisors in an institution for the severely retarded, teaching them how to use self-monitoring, standard setting, self-evaluation, and self-reinforcement procedures with minimal supervision. The readily evident significant increase in staff interactions was contingent on appropriate resident behavior. This increase, in its turn, was followed by an increase in appropriate

resident behavior, setting up a positive spiral. Follow-up and acceptability data were equally encouraging.

The second study was concerned with improvement in cost–benefit
ratios in a residential facility for the mentally disabled. To prevent
harm to residents, caretakers must be well versed in certain safety-
related skills. Such skills are typically performed at a low frequency,
with limited opportunity for practice and reinforcement. How, then,
are these emergency skills to be maintained? One possibility involves a
peer training system in which staff members train other staff members.
It is this "pyramid" effect that was the subject of an investigation by
Van Den Pol, Reid, and Fuqua (1983).

A multiple-baseline design was used to assess three sets of safety-
related skills in simulated emergency situations: responding to facility
fires, managing aggressive attacks by residents, and assisting residents
during convulsive seizures. The peer training program was found to be
effective in the transfer of all three emergency skills to new direct care
staff members. The program also seemed to be effective in improving
the skills of the peer trainers. Proficiency declined in emergency skills
for which peers did not act as trainers. Social validity and other acceptability measures collected over a 24-month period indicated that
the program was both effective and acceptable to the staff members
concerned. While their program suffers from certain methodological
limitations, such as the artificiality of the situation, their findings
point to the advisability of further research.

Neisworth and Madle (1982) compared the pre-1973 behavioral
literature with the approximately 100 articles that appeared between
1976 and 1978. Several trends are evident. First, the setting in which the
intervention occurs has been gradually shifting from institution to
home and community, a finding that is in line with the prevailing
Zeitgeist. Consistent with this trend, it is the mild retardate who is more
likely to be placed in the community and therefore to become a subject
for community-oriented research. Second, with the exception of overcorrection, there is some reduction in the use of punishment techniques. (For a timely assessment of the use of overcorrection with the
mentally retarded, see Ferretti & Cavalier, 1983.) Third, for those who
remain institutionalized, there seems to be a preoccupation with techniques geared toward behavioral reduction or elimination. While
recognizing institutional needs to maintain order and nondisruption,
Neisworth and Madle (1982) rightly lament this devotion to "custodial
behavior modification," the contemporary substitute for chains and
drugs.

Next, Neisworth and Madle draw brief attention to the need for
validated, easily learned, and easily applied training packages for use
by parents and paraprofessionals. Their final concern is with the

hapless practitioner confronted with the problem of what technique to select for dealing with a specific target area for a specific individual. At the present time, most applications of behavioral technology to the retarded have been derived from one of three sources: (1) the filtering through of behavioral programs from other areas, as in systematic social skills training; (2) fads in behavioral technology, "something new that has not been tried with the retarded"; and (3) trial and error. What to do about this unfortunate situation, what should be done, and what will be done must await a future overview.

COMMUNITY BEHAVIOR THERAPY: FROM INSTITUTION TO COMMUNITY

Each year sees the usual parade of inconsequential studies of trivia in a field where so much of significance is happening, and this year is no exception.

As indicated, for those individuals for whom institutionalization is unavoidable, such as the severely mentally handicapped, efforts are being extended to make both the institution per se and the experience more palatable. The era of the token economy as an agent of the establishment is now past. (For a thought-provoking and knowledge-able update of the changing token economy scene, see Fernandez, 1983.) But even sophisticated token economy programs tend to de-emphasize the development of cognitive coping skills. (For the development of alternatives and additives to the token economy within the institutional setting, see Levendusky, Berglas, Dooley, & Landau, 1983.)

For most individuals, the ultimate goal should be some form of deinstitutionalization. Talbott and the other contributors to his volume (Talbott, 1981) illustrate well the advantages of returning or introducing the mentally ill and handicapped to the community. Along the way, they introduce the notion of a model service system or network of programs, each contributing a specific service. Disregarding for the moment the lack of consensus about virtually every facet of rehabilitation, this is still an important contribution in the sense that it places at least some of the responsibility upon the community at large. But, as Levine (1983) points out, the belief that deinstitutionalization is the only viable program for the chronically mentally ill is unfounded. A significant number of individuals are not appropriate for rehabilitation. As Levine suggests, rather than simply replacing one ineffective public policy, hospitalization on a large scale, with another, massive deinstitutionalization, we could improve the institution. Before institutionalization or any aftercare program becomes public policy, it might be advisable to begin rehabilitation within the institution—and it is for this reason, among others, that the developments noted in the preceding section are encouraging. But this is not an either–or situation. It is possible to develop and evaluate innovative programs within and without the walls of the institution simultaneously.

The economic advantages of deinstitutionalization, at least in the short term, have been pointed out by numerous individuals (e.g., Kiesler, 1982). But a word or two of caution is in order. The trend toward deinstitutionalization is too readily influenced by economic rather than humane considerations. Rosenzweig (1983) recommends the halting of this trend toward deinstitutionalization until outcome data have been accrued. Meanwhile, rehabilitation within the institution might smooth the way for eventual transition to the community at large.

Mansell, Jenkins, Felce, and De Kock (1984) report a program of first-stage rehabilitation within an ordinary housing sheltered care community facility. But, as Schutz, Vogelsberg, and Rusch (1980) note, the deinstitutionalization process involves more than physical removal from one setting to another. Preparation for each transition necessitates planning in terms of the personal needs of the individual and an assessment of factors deemed important for integration into that particular community. Clients, family, friends, employers, and the general public should all find the program acceptable. And follow-through programs to insure continued integration of client and community needs are essential.

What we need fewer of are projects geared directly and exclusively toward narrow-band problems, such as litter control or the conservation of energy by turning off unnecessary house lights. Encouraging signs of the times are the concerns and second thoughts beginning to creep into the behavioral community literature. For example, Jason and Glenwick (in press) generate a thought-provoking "No" to this question: Are the behavioral preventive and community programs and projects instituted by behavior therapists maintained once the formal studies have been concluded? Designing more cost-effective and cost-efficient technologies is not necessarily the best solution. Without effective programs to smooth the diffusion of these innovations and make them acceptable, failure is likely. For example, despite the demonstrable advantages of home weather insulation, and the virtual certainty of an investment payback time of less than 5 years, most people remain reluctant to take advantage of such innovations. According to Yates and Aronson (1983), this is because human behavior is too complex for existing economic models. The failure is more than a problem in technology and economics; it is a people problem. As Winett, Hatcher, Fort, Leckliter, Love, Riley, and Fishback (1982a) note, we know little beyond the short-term benefits brought about by behavioral procedures in the modification of energy-related practices.

The era of simple reliance upon self-report or even direct behavioral observation, considered adequate by early investigators, is coming to an end (see Geller, 1981). Jason and Glenwick (in press) speculate that it is the absence of layperson involvement and community ownership that may be contributing to the moribund status of our interventions once the data have been collected and our interests are directed elsewhere. The possibility is raised that it is our training that pushes us inexorably toward the exertion of excessive control of community affairs. Citizens and consumers who are already feeling alienated, frustrated, and powerless may not respond favorably to such tactics.

Jason and Glenwick (in press) draw further attention to the gnawing doubts raised by perceptive researchers. Fawcett, Mathews, and Fletcher (1980), for example, suggest that our technology is overly expensive and "inflexible" in the eyes of the community. Too many behavioral programs implicitly encourage the belief that in the "real world," good behaviors are generally rewarded. Investigators are beginning to question the manner in which our policies reinforce the status quo and emphasize behavior change rather than the need to modify society (e.g., Whang, Fletcher, & Fawcett, 1982).

For some, a solution lies in an alliance or interface with those disciplines that are already involved with the community and its problems, such as economics, urban planning, environmental engineering, and any group that is concerned with the public interest. For example, Greene and Neistat (1983) report the emergence of a working alliance between community behavioral psychologists and consumer action groups. Public interest research groups (PIRGs) are organized networks of university-based consumer action groups established originally by Ralph Nader in the 1960s. According to Greene and Neistat, approximately 175 such PIRGs now exist. Their primary purpose is to sponsor a range of decision-influencing programs pertaining to important social issues, such as pollution control, health care, and education. To illustrate the many areas of potential collaboration between PIRGs and behavior therapists, Green and Neistat report a controlled study of an attempt to encourage dental professionals to reduce exposure to radiation during diagnostic X-rays. Perhaps, when the so-called "therapeutic alliance" is re-examined, it is links such as these that will become one basis of community behavior therapy.

The "quality of life" has many determinants—more than the behavioral settings of Schoggen (1983), more than the behavioral economics of Winkler and Winett (1982), more than the social network theory of Greenblatt, Becerra, and Serafetinides (1982)—and yet all of these are relevant to the multilevel paradigm that is beginning to emerge as community behavior therapy broadens its perspectives (see O'Donnell & Tharp, 1982).

Psychiatry as well as clinical psychology is beginning to be influenced by these trends. For example, a recent American Psychiatric Association Task Force suggests that the term "ecopsychiatrist" be adopted to describe the complexity of biological, physical, and psychosocial person–environment interactions that determine mental health and illness (Wilkinson & O'Connor, 1982). The individual is viewed as intertwining within several larger systems, each of which has to be understood within its own determinants. Even here, or perhaps especially here, caution has to be expressed. It cannot, for example, be assumed that social networks are inevitably advantageous. As recent data attest, they can be sources of stress as well as support (Fiore, Becker, & Coppel, 1983).

BEHAVIOR MODIFICATION IN INDUSTRY AND BUSINESS

"Unless we solve the problem of productivity, our children will be the first generation in the history of the United States to live worse than their parents." This is the challenge, and, according to Perloff and Nelson (1983), psychology has much to contribute to the solution. When Katzell and Guzzo (1983) examined some 207 fairly recent field experiments to test the effects of diverse psychological programs on employee productivity, 87% were found to improve productivity in at least some respect. Even more encouraging, they report a mutually reinforcing, hand-in-hand relationship between enhanced quality of work life and improvements in productivity.

Two edited texts, noted briefly last year, warrant further mention, since both adopt a forward-looking approach to this problem (Frederiksen, 1982; O'Brien, Dickinson, & Rosnow, 1982). Both are broad rather than deep, and neither would seem appropriate for the line managers to whom they are directed. Low- to middle-level managers are unlikely to have the time, the necessary training, or the inclination to read the many hundreds of detailed pages presented in these two volumes. The short-term needs of the working manager are more likely to be met by such crisp and well-organized practical guides as Brown's (1982) *Managing Behavior on the Job*. The eventual need is for a written rather than edited text that reviews conceptual and practical problems, asks the necessary questions, examines prevailing assumptions, explores pertinent theoretical issues—and does all of this within a contemporary behavioral perspective that spans the range of biological, behavioral, cognitive, systems, and other determinants. Whether the time is ripe for such a formidable undertaking is another matter.

In tracing the origins of OBM back to Skinnerian operant and respondent behavior, Crowell and Anderson (1982) argue that the too-close alignment of behavior management with a reinforcement-based technology of behavior change has led to a perspective that is inappropriately narrow for our times: It is the general methodological characteristics of behavior modification that are of primary significance, rather than commitment to specific variables. The point is well taken, but Crowell and Anderson may be overstating their case. The contemporary literature offers numerous examples of behaviorally sound approaches that transcend the limitations of a sterile reinforcement technology (e.g., Durand, 1983; Sajwaj, Schnelle, McNees, & McConnell, 1983).

The cognitive trend in behavior modification has unfortunately given rise to concepts and procedures that lack objectivity and methodological rigor. Self-efficacy theory, a relatively recent outgrowth of Bandura's social learning theory, is an outstanding exception. Self-efficacy beliefs can serve as cognitive mechanisms for behavior change. Furthermore, these beliefs can be distinguished from response–outcome expectations (Bandura, 1977). A self-efficacy belief is an expectation of personal mastery, the belief that successful performance will follow if sufficient effort is expended. Response–outcome expectations are beliefs about long-term consequences of behavior, with the expectation that specific outcomes will follow successful performance.

Self-efficacy beliefs have been investigated in a variety of situations across a broad range of determinants, but never in a work setting. Insurance sales performance lends itself readily to such an investigation on two accounts: the past successes of cognitive theorists in similar areas, and the need for persistence and skill as demonstrations of the personal mastery that characterizes successful insurance salesmanship. Recognizing this opportunity, Barling and Beattie (1983) used 200 insurance sales representatives to develop a questionnaire measure of self-efficacy beliefs and response–outcome expectations. The questionnaire was then given to a different sample of 97 insurance sales representatives, and four criterion measures of performance (calls per week; number of policies sold; sales revenue; and a composite performance index on which actual sales commissions were based) were used to complete a regression analysis. A correlational relationship, which tells nothing about causality, was demonstrated between self-efficacy beliefs and sales performance.

Frederiksen, Richter, Johnson, and Solomon's (1982) study of the effects of individualized performance feedback on the maintenance of clinic charts is another example of sophisticated behavioral application. An A-B-A design was used to track four types of charting errors. Feedback modified only those components of the overall task for which it was given, a finding systematically replicated on a second group of subjects.

While recognizing the possibility that different behaviors, different feedback systems, different settings, and different subjects might yield different findings, two related implications for those who design feedback systems in organizational settings were drawn. First, there must be careful attention to the selection of target behaviors for the provision of feedback. The behavior targeted for feedback should be functionally related to the desired organizational outcome. Feedback can be extremely narrow in its effects, and generalization to other behaviors or desired organizational outcomes has to be assessed rather than assumed. Second, in situations where generalization to other behavior is desired, it must be planned. Such planning may include attempts to alter social contingencies and other aspects of the supervisor's behavior, or to extend feedback to a wider range of behaviors. In essence, the major conclusion from the Frederiksen *et al.* (1982) study is that the effects of feedback can be quite specific. Generality of feedback effects cannot be assumed, and this is a finding that has important ramifications across the entire performance spectrum, regardless of the setting in which it is carried out.

The value of individual accountability is widely acknowledged in American business and industry. But until recently, the focus has been primarily on production employees. Management accountability, other than at the highest level (where it is considered synonymous with overall organizational success), has been studiously neglected. As the organizational ladder is ascended, the job becomes more diffuse and less routine. This makes effective performance measurement correspondingly more elusive.

Bourdon's (1982) schema for the evaluation of top-level management has seven main components. The first six are as follows: (1) an analysis of what the organization expects from each particular management position; (2) the delineation of performance goals for management in quantitative, explicit terms; (3) the development of an objective, valid, and reliable system of performance measurement; (4) formalized feedback in terms of hard data measured against specific goals; (5) the delivery of differential consequences for variable performance (particularly difficult for industrial and business management, where attention is traditionally given to what is wrong rather than to what is right); and (6) systematic data-based individual performance appraisal (this requirement is also a consequence). To be constructive, performance appraisal must help determine where the performer is at present and what aids can be mustered to help improve performance; these determinations lead to the seventh step, which is career action based on performance data and data-based performance appraisal. All that remains now is for some brave OBM psychologist to mandate Bourdon's effective seven-point schema in the setting of his or her choice!

The management team system developed by Foxworthy, Ellis, and McLeod (1982) to integrate performance management with current management practices is more applicable to middle management. Left to their own devices, managers typically apply behavior management training to a limited set of problems and make use of circumscribed techniques. Foxworthy *et al.*'s team system would seem to be an effective way of encouraging across-the-board, behaviorally sound practices on a daily basis. In their initial study, some 46 managers from a large tobacco company participated in a three-phase program; this included formal classroom training in the principles of behavior management, the development of performance improvement projects based on this training, and, finally, integration with routine management activities. While short-term data indicate that the system contributed to improvement within the organizational structure, it is long-term maintenance that really matters, and about this little is known. Dramatic initial results are not likely, in themselves, to maintain the necessary effort. As noted, this requires the development of an effective accountability structure to keep individuals practicing the skills they have learned.

The third illustration of behavioral management at work pertains to the reactions of corporate managers to identical assertive responses made by females as contrasted with those made by males. Managers within a large *Fortune* 500 East Coast corporation were presented by Soloman, Brehony, Rothblum, and Kelly (1982) with taped vignettes showing either a male or a female model handling several work-related conflicts in an assertive manner. The interactions were presented as directly assertive, assertive but moderating assertion with an emphatic comment to the antagonist, or assertive but tempering the response with a self-effacing comment. Self-effacing assertive models of either sex were rated unfavorably, relative to both directly assertive and emphatic–assertive models. On virtually all measures, assertive behavior exhibited by females was evaluated as positively as the same behavior exhibited by males, a finding contrary both to previous research and to what might be expected from research on sex-role stereotypes. Conclusions are limited by the use of audiotapes rather than real-life situations.

Much has been written about the application of behavioral principles at the other end of the employment spectrum, job-seeking behavior. How assertive should the job applicant be? Under what circumstances and along what dimensions? How should this behavior relate to the sex of the applicant as contrasted with that of the individual responsible for doing the hiring? When Cianni-Surridge and Horan (1983) analyzed questionnaire ratings pertaining to 16 frequently advocated assertive job-seeking behaviors in terms of whether or not each would enhance or diminish the applicant's chances for being offered employment, they found the situation to be more complex than expected. As the authors imply, direct behavioral observation, difficult as this is to accomplish, is likely to yield more valid results than questionnaires relying upon what potential employers say they do about assertive behavior. This limits the value of their study.

Hiring practices are also dependent upon the overall labels attached to job applicants. Employers often prefer not to hire ex-psychiatric patients, and they tend to be less friendly to such individuals in the interview. A psychiatric label can also impair the ability of ex-patients to obtain jobs and earn income by influencing their sense of what others think of them. Under these circumstances, it is not surprising that such patients act defensively in the interview situation and thereby reduce their chances of employment (Link, 1982).

Threlkeld and DeJong (1983) were interested in a somewhat related problem—the value of a media presentation in influencing attitudes and behavior of health professionals toward disabled persons seeking employment in hospital settings. The relationship between expressed attitudes and actual behavior is complex, and the assumption that changes in attitudes produce changes in behavior is precarious at best. Behavioral intentions—what people say they are going to do, rather than attitudes expressed—might be a better starting point for attempts to change behavior. According to Threlkeld and DeJong, statements of intent are highly correlated with actual behavior, and a strong predictor of behavioral intent is the set of beliefs people hold about the consequences of that behavior (i.e., whether they believe that performing the behavior in question will produce positive or negative outcomes for them). To change behavioral intentions, and hence behavior, it is these beliefs that need to be addressed.

To identify the beliefs of health professionals regarding the consequences of hiring disabled workers, Threlkeld and DeJong conducted a pilot study. A total of 199 hospital employees in 10 facilities were shown a 20-minute slide–tape presentation of interviews with three wheelchair-confined hospital workers, in which basic misconceptions were addressed and corrected. The tone of the presentation was informational and understanding rather than moralistic. A second media presentation, consisting of a 20-minute filmograph (a slide–tape show transferred to film) that showed a series of still photographs of wheelchair-confined and nonhandicapped people interacting together in a variety of settings, served as a control. Appropriate attitudinal and behavioral intention measures were used to measure changes. A similar procedure was later utilized with 99 state-employed vocational rehabilitation counselors.

In both studies, there was a professed willingness by health professionals to hire disabled workers following showings of the specially designed slide–tape presentation. But what is most interesting about the study is the relationship of these data to various attitudinal measures about the films seen: There appeared to be no clear link between expressed attitudes toward the disabled and stated intention to consider hiring them.

Whether these findings would be replicated with a more general employer group, presumably less rehabilitation-oriented, is a matter for further investigation. Furthermore, each of these media presentations has to be targeted toward specific behaviors and audiences, and their development is consequently time-consuming and costly. It may be that less expensive alternatives, such as lectures or workshops, would serve the purpose as well.

As noted, behavior therapists are becoming increasingly consumer-conscious, and it was only a matter of time before behavior analysts became enmeshed in consumer affairs. Food is fundamental to survival, yet most citizens exercise little or no control over its production, distribution, or cost. While the prospects for major change would seem to be dismal, a variety of consumer groups and even some government agencies have attempted to bring about change by sponsoring comparative food price information programs whose purposes are to maximize retail competition and appraise consumers of alternatives. These two beliefs—that such programs promote competition among stores and lead to more informed comparative shopping—are largely untested. The idealists who generate or foster these beliefs rarely entertain the possibility that either assumption is erroneous or, worse, that such strategies promote price collusion among retailers.

To examine these possibilities systematically, Greene, Rouse, Green, and Clay (1984) carried out a protracted 2-year controlled study of the effects of food price information procedures as applied to the supermarkets of two Midwestern cities. Prices of carefully selected

232-item market baskets were monitored in the supermarkets of both the target city and its control. In the target stores, price levels were publicized. In the control stores, price levels were recorded but never publicized. Following a lengthy baseline period, the prices of items in only one of the market baskets at stores in the target city were published in the local newspaper on five different occasions. Presumably as a consequence, there were reductions in price inflation for both market baskets at the independently operated target stores. Corporate chain stores were not similarly affected.

To the extent that such programs bring about price reductions or reductions in inflation, consumers benefit. In the present study, a number of consumers reported that their shopping decisions were based upon this program and that the program would be worth purchasing. Not surprisingly, the responses of at least some of the store managers were strikingly different. One store manager went so far as to threaten to have the senior author fired from the university!

The prospect of greater consumer control over the production, processing, and shipping of food is exciting. In the present study, the focus was exclusively on the cost of food at its final retail outlet. As Greene et al. (1984) suggest, equally intensive analyses at successive links of the chain along which the food is produced and consumed could heighten the ability of consumers to control one of their most critical reinforcers.

CRIME AND PUNISHMENT REVISITED

Regrettably, no new behavioral theory of crime or delinquency has surfaced during the past year. Perhaps the most interesting development is the revival of interest in punishment, a sensitive area coming back into fashion. This year's discussion will be confined to two areas: (1) crime and delinquency and (2) punishment.

Crime and Delinquency

The most comprehensive overview of the behavior therapy of crime and delinquency to appear within the past two years is probably that of Burchard and Lane (1982). Their primary concern is with long-term effectiveness. Program effectiveness would appear to depend on such variables as the settings in which they are applied, the nature of the behaviors that are being modified, and the characteristics of service providers and recipients.

Burchard and Lane extrapolate certain tentative conclusions from the limited outcome data available to date. While behavior modification procedures have repeatedly been shown to be highly effective in the more immediate and direct improvement of maintenance and educational functions, the evidence that either is related to recidivism is lacking. Part of the problem stems from the failure to report adequate follow-up data. This is particularly true for delinquents requiring mental health treatment while institutionalized. With the notable exception of the Patuxent Program, which uses an incentive system together with group therapy and milieu support (Hodges, 1971), virtually no follow-up data for patients released from behaviorally based treatment centers have been provided.

McNamara and Andrasik (1982) report one of the few outcome evaluation studies of parolees to date. In August 1973, a behavior modification program was initiated at a semirural, forensic psychiatry facility with a 110-inmate maximum capacity, operated within the State of Ohio's Department of Mental Health and Mental Retardation. The volunteer participants were all convicted male felons with mental health or adjustment problems. The behavior change program, terminated some 3 years later for reasons unstated, consisted of a graduated five-step privilege system in effect 24 hours a day.

Progress through the system was dependent upon performance in three areas: self-maintenance behavior (taking care of oneself and one's personal belongings); self-improvement behavior (participating in employment, educational, and other activities); and appropriate behavior (refraining from engaging in various behaviors, ranging from dress code violation to physical aggression). Prior to entry into the program, most applicants were given the Minnesota Multiphasic Personality Inventory (MMPI).

Follow-up information was made available for 64 of the 71 parolled during the 3-year period of the study. Of these, 18 either committed a technical parole violation or a new crime leading to further sentencing within 28 months following release. Neither MMPI scores nor numerous institution adjustment measures collected at the facility were predictive of recidivism.

Small numbers and lack of controls make it difficult to draw more than tentative impressions from these findings. To abandon the search for behavioral indicants of institutional adjustment as predictors of success in the community on the basis of present knowledge would be premature. Meanwhile, in the absence of extensive data, McNamara and Andrasik (1982) speculate that a more meaningful approach to the prediction of recidivism would be to try to identify those situational variables in the postrelease environment that occasion crime. Knowledge of the environment in which the parolee lives, together with an assessment of the parolee's perception of the situation and his or her reactions to the situation, would seem more suited to recidivism prediction than most of the procedures hitherto employed. As an example of this strategy, McNamara and Andrasik cite the promising development of an operational methodology known as Behavioral Evaluation, Treatment, and Analysis (BETA) (Jenkins, DeValera, & Mueller, 1977).

As far as residential community-based programs are concerned, Burchard and Lane (1982) are more encouraging. The teaching-family home would seem to be more effective than an institutional program, as effective as a non-teaching-family group home, but possibly less effective than other community-based alternatives. As far as nonresidential community-based behavioral programs are concerned, the outcome depends on the setting. Family-based programs would seem to be the most effective as long as the families are relatively intact, the target youths are in early rather than late adolescence, and the emphasis is upon the training of communication and negotiation skills.

Burchard and Lane conclude their review on a note of caution. Most of the data about nonresidential community based programs pertain to older youths, experienced offenders, and programs with a strong job-training and placement component. Regardless of age, Burchard and Lane suggest that the emphasis be on ties within normal family, school, and work settings, rather than placement in aggregate contingency-contracting programs that might serve primarily to increase offender contact.

Behavioral programs are most likely to be effective when used with rehabilitation service providers who have a high degree of positive regard for their clients and are thereby in a position to establish relationships in which they themselves function as positive reinforcers. In so doing, it is important that the needs of the service providers themselves not be neglected. Working closely with delinquents on a day-to-day basis is a taxing occupation calculated to induce stress reactions in even the most resilient. The role of the correctional officer, for example, is particularly demanding, and there is increasing evidence that such individuals experience difficulties in coping (Cheek & Miller, 1980). Correctional institutions have not, as yet, developed adequate programs for the reduction of occupational stress in their correctional officers (Stalgaitis, Meyers, & Krisak, 1982).

"Dangerousness" is an elusive concept that is of relevance to all whose concerns are with crime and delinquency. One of the more extraordinary yet still prevalent beliefs is that those who are trained in medicine somehow have special expertise in the prediction of dangerousness. As Crawford (1983) notes, the medical model of dangerousness implies the existence of some enduring personal trait awaiting detection if only more sophisticated measurement methods could be developed. For the behavior therapist, dangerousness is better conceptualized in terms of the future likelihood of the person seriously harming others. "Dangerousness" then becomes synonymous with future dangerous behavior, and attempts to assess it can only be as good as the ability to predict it. Having developed an appropriate measure, and this remains for the future, what to do about it then becomes a moral rather than a behavioral issue. The balance between individual rights and social protection is delicate and possibly beyond the province of behavior therapists to resolve. (For an extended discussion of the semantics and ethics of dangerousness, see Petrunik, 1982.)

Punishment

"Punishment" is a particularly unfortunate word that has different meanings, depending on whether it is used by members of the lay community or by professionals (Routh & Perlman, 1982). Attitudes toward the purpose of punishment are as diverse as its various definitions. Several recent studies have attempted to shed light on these matters, but major methodological deficits limit their value. Contrived studies involving questionnaire responses of college students or district judges to hypothetical situations add little to the pool of useful knowledge (e.g., McFatter, 1982; Viney, Waldman, & Barchilon, 1982).

For the behavior therapist, "punishment" has a clearly articulated meaning in terms of contingent relationships between behavior and the events that follow this behavior, and it is to be contrasted precisely with both positive and negative reinforcements. Other professionals use the term in a vague fashion more akin to lay usage, which thinks in terms of pain, coercion, retribution, or "just payment" for a misdemeanor (Franks, 1984a). The two new books devoted exclusively to what behavior therapists have to say about punishment place these issues in perspective. In the first, Matson and DiLorenzo (1984) review in detail the therapeutic applications of punishment. They pay particular attention to ethical and legal issues and point to future trends as well as current status. Some will argue that Matson and DiLorenzo are not as exacting or rigorous in their criticisms of punishment as they could have been, and others will view their examination of the literature as superficial.

Axelrod and Apsche's (1983) edited text is broader in scope. A related article by Balsam and Bondy (1983), discussing reward in terms of possible negative side effects, is also illuminating. Reinforcers are not invariably beneficial, and punishers are not always bad (Yulevich,

1981). It is the negative side effects of adversive control that receive all the attention in the literature, rather than reinforcement and its problems (e.g., Bitgood, Crowe, Suarez, & Peters, 1980; Kazdin, 1980a, 1982c).

Balsam and Bondy (1983) argue persuasively that similar mechanisms underlie appetitive and aversive controls. Both influence responses other than the target behavior, and the effects on behavior are symmetrical. But while a case can be made for certain negative side effects of reward, to infer some form of parallelism with aversive control and its side effects is more questionable. Balsam and Bondy's thesis warrants not only direct forensic and laboratory investigation, but consideration in terms of possible legal and ethical ramifications. (See Griffith, 1983, and Moffitt, 1983, for discussion of the rights of both the punished and the punisher.)

BEHAVIOR THERAPY AND THE AGING PROCESS

Aging is a complex mix of biological, psychological, and social processes, with psychology in the middle to bridge the gap between the basic biological organism and the social contexts within which the aging occurs (Storandt, 1983). Between them, physiological, social, and clinical psychologists, together with other mental health and biomedical professionals, possess the knowledge and skills to investigate the parameters of aging on a multilevel basis. Why, then, has the systematic study of aging been relatively neglected until recently by the professional community?

Few clinicians work with clients over the age of 65; doctoral students tend to resist the arduous demands of working with the elderly impaired; researchers exclude older clients from their treatment groups because they do not conform to criteria or because positive results are less likely to occur; and many university programs prefer to train students to work with children or young adults—and all of this is happening while the population of older adults increases dramatically (Birren, 1983; Haley, 1983).

Despite mounting evidence to the contrary, the belief that aging individuals derive little benefit from psychological intervention persists. Nursing home administrators tend to be less than enthusiastic when it comes to hiring psychologists, and licensing and other regulatory agencies offer little incentive for them to do so. Finally, aging individuals are themselves disinclined to seek out or accept help from mental health professionals. A youth-oriented society provides few reinforcers for those who seek to work with the elderly. And finally, professionals themselves may be reluctant to confront the inevitable reality of personal aging and death (MacDonald, 1983).

On a more encouraging note, Skinner—the dean of operant behavior theory—offers a personal essay in self-management from a behavioral perspective that is the epitome of forward-looking but cautious counsel (Skinner, 1983). Old age is only partly a biological condition, and old dogs can be taught new tricks (Skinner & Vaughan, 1983). As Montagu (1983) puts it, old age is a bad habit—a "psychosclerosis" of the advancing years that can be avoided by appropriate attitudes and retention into later years of certain physical and behavioral traits most commonly associated with childhood. For Montagu, the goal of life is to die young as late as possible! While Montagu's vocabulary is not behavioral, what he advocates is. For both Skinner and Montagu, the emphasis is on a world in which the behavior of old people as well as that of those still young or in middle adulthood continues to be reinforced.

To bring this about, behavior therapists might have to extend their domain beyond traditional S-R learning theory. Two recent examples will suffice to make this point, the first from experimental psychology and the second from social psychology. Quattrochi-Tubin and Jason (1983) have developed differential predications for the specific reactions of the elderly to various aging processes, according to their positions on the relatively stable dimension of introversion–extraversion. Sixty elderly nursing home residents were given the Eysenck Personality Inventory and assigned at random to one of two experimental groups. As predicted, elderly extraverts reported maximum satisfaction when the levels of activity were high, whereas introverts were more satisfied with a lower-activity, noninterpersonal type of manipulation. From this, Quattrochi-Tubin and Jason (1983) conclude that "the personality dimension of Introversion–Extraversion operates in effecting the activity level preference and satisfaction of the elderly" (p. 22) and advocate diversified leisure–activity programs that appeal differentially to introverts and extraverts.

While Quattrochi-Tubin and Jason's methodology is adequate and their recommendation commendable, one cannot but take issue with their logic. To assume causal relationships between either activity level or satisfaction and introversion–extraversion is unwarranted from their data. An equally tenable conclusion is that whatever brings about the personality characteristics of introverts and extraverts is also responsible for their differential activity level preferences and satisfactions.

The second example, from social psychology, pertains to the assumption of age stratification theorists that expectation and prestige vary according to age. This raises the question of how people respond when age-related expectations are violated. According to role theory, behavior consistent with that expected for a person's age role is likely to be more favorably received than behavior considered more appropriate to other ages. Adults who act childishly in serious situations, children who are extremely independent, and older individuals who attempt to take full responsibilities are all in danger of receiving disapproval if their actions violate socially accepted expectations. But as Feinman and Coon (1983) point out in their report of a questionnaire study carried out with undergraduates, role theory prediction fails to take into account the differential distributions of status among role positions and the tendency of social roles to be ranked. Age is associated with prestige in a nonlinear fashion. In the Feinman and Coon study, adults in their so-called prime received highest prestige, and the elderly and children were ranked at much lower status levels. An interesting finding was that elderly individuals who engaged in adult behavior lost less approval than adults who exhibited elderly behavior. Once again, applicability is limited by lack of behavioral data pertaining to "real-life" situations.

According to Atchley (1977), breakdown of the social support system is the primary reason for institutionalization of the elderly. But self-care and social support are strongly interactive in more ways than one. Individuals who do not take good care of themselves are able to survive more effectively in the community if there are others available to care for them. Whether or not others are available depends in part on the social skills of the elderly person concerned. Extending this line of argument, Patterson and Eberly (1983) postulate that the maintenance of self-care and social functioning in older people depends in part upon the retention of regular reinforcing relationships with others. People become less socially desirable if, for example, they fail to practice good hygiene and fail to maintain their residences adequately. This can set up a vicious spiral of degeneration leading eventually to institutionalization.

Data reviewed by Patterson and his associates have highlighted the prevalence of social and self-care deficits among the elderly in institution and community alike (Patterson, 1982; Patterson & Eberly, 1983). It was also noted that many old people who might benefit from other forms of treatment were being referred to state hospitals where they received medical and custodial care but little else. To remedy this situation, the Florida Mental Health Institute developed a program of alternative treatments for two groups of elderly: those already residing in state facilities for whom the goal of return to a noninstitutional community placement was realistic; and those currently residing within the local community who seemed to be in danger of institutionalization if not helped.

Behavior therapy clearly has much to offer the elderly (see Patterson & Jackson, 1981, for a recent review). Yet, until recently, most programs for this segment of society have evolved within a medical or social framework. The medical model looks at physiological changes, many of which are not currently reversible, and the social model focuses on broad changes affecting large numbers of people and requiring years of massive intervention to bring about change. Understandably, the behavioral approach, with its readily observable behaviors and more directly and immediately applicable interventions within a specific environment, seemed more suitable to the needs of the Florida Mental Health Institute.

The program finally developed contains six models—three geared toward activities of daily living (ADL) and three toward social skills. ADL I teaches those basic self-care and eating behaviors needed for any noncustodial setting. Persons completing only ADL I could be placed with families or in boarding homes that would provide for all other aspects of self-care. ADL II stresses care of clothing and room, managing small amounts of money, and using the telephone. With some assistance, persons completing ADL I and II would be prepared for life in most foster homes. ADL III teaches such skills as budgeting, meal planning, the utilization of community resources, and preparation for independent living.

The social skills series consists of three models and an optional social problem-solving training procedure: Conversational training helps develop casual social interactions, communication training develops the expression of basic affects, and self-esteem training develops the recognition of personal positive characteristics. The overall program is incorporated into a traditional token economy system coupled with an individualized behavioral approach to the resolution of specific problems.

According to Garfield (1978), age is unrelated to therapeutic outcome, at least up to age 60 when Garfield's survey ceased—presumably because he could not find a sufficient number of competent studies at the elderly age levels. Much as we might wish it to be so, it will not be known whether Garfield's conclusions are applicable to older individuals until further data are obtained.

It is important to know something about the parameters of the population concerned. When O'Farrell, Keuthen, Connors, and Upper (1983) surveyed some 304 elderly patients in a large Veterans Administration psychiatric hospital, numerous age-related differences emerged. Findings were consistent with expectations: Older patients tended to have been hospitalized longer, to have fewer plans for discharge, to have more medical problems, and to require more help with daily living. They were also more likely to be diagnosed as having an organic brain syndrome or affective disorder, and less likely to be diagnosed as schizophrenic. In terms of daily management, the elderly were more likely to manifest problems with fire setting and careless smoking than the younger patients, and less likely to engage in self-injurious behavior.

Several promising new skills-training programs for the institutionalized elderly have recently been reported (e.g., Klein, Frank, & Jacobs, 1980). In contrast to the innovative but uncontrolled project of Klein *et al.*, Kleitsch, Whitman, and Santos (1983) report a well-designed study of the effectiveness of a group language-training procedure for directly increasing and generalizing rates of verbal interaction among four elderly socially isolated, moderately retarded men who had been institutionalized for over 20 years. A withdrawal-of-treatment design was used to examine the effects of verbal prompt, behavioral rehearsal, and contingent social praise. Changes in behavior were examined in two generalization settings, one similar to the training environment and the other a living area kitchenette with 12 other residents present. At baseline, there was no verbal interaction among the subjects. The rates of verbal interaction increased during training and in the two generalization settings. These increases were maintained 4 months after training had ceased. While the number of subjects was small and nothing is known about long-term effects, the fact that the study was carried out at all with this typically neglected population is encouraging.

A recent study by Schnelle, Traughber, Morgan, Embry, Binion, and Coleman (1983) offers similar cause for optimism. These authors report a behavioral system designed to reduce urinary incontinence in two nursing homes by the introduction of simple time-efficient staff management procedures. A pretest–posttest control-group design with repeated measures involving prompting and contingent social approval was used to demonstrate an increase in correct toileting for the experimental subjects of approximately 45%. Incontinence is a serious problem among the institutionalized elderly, many of whom have physical deficits that preclude independent toileting. The demonstration that, at least under these circumstances, incontinence is largely a management problem is of particular significance, in light of the fact that incontinence in nursing home residents is usually attributed in totality to psychological and physical problems that originate with the patients.

Effective adjustment to institutional living rests upon more than a sophisticated monitoring technology and the behavioral skills of the OBM psychologist (see Schnelle & Traughber, 1983). The stringent cost-conscious budgeting considerations that dominate the thinking and value systems of most nursing home administrators has to be taken into account. Frank, Klein, and Jacobs (1982) report one of the few studies in this area that included cost-effectiveness measures in the design.

Two hypotheses were tested: first, that significant behavior change can be observed in a geriatric inpatient population treated in a broad-based behavior change program; second, that significant cost–benefit ratios can be demonstrated despite the relatively brief life expectancies of the patients. Frank *et al.*'s program included three basic elements: a token economy, a therapeutic community, and a transitional care facility or halfway house. Residents progressed through four phases, beginning in a basic token economy program and ending up at a halfway house. Two-year outcome data demonstrated that the program was successful in decreasing the average length of hospital stay, decreasing the percentage of patients discharged to more dependent settings than those from which they were admitted, and increasing placement in independent living environments. Favorable cost–benefit ratios confirmed the financial robustness of the program.

CONCLUSIONS

It is not implausible to posit four major turning points in the march toward mental health. First, there was Pinel and the emphasis upon humane treatment for the mentally ill, a novel thought in its time. Then came Freud, bringing a radically new perspective to the psychology of all people. Much more recently, there was psychopharmacology and its promise of psychotropic agents as the royal road to mental health. Finally came behavior therapy, which likewise offered to pave the way to a brave new world if only we applied ourselves diligently with the correct methodology. Over the years, it has become clear that, if behavior therapy is to produce lasting change, it will probably be by detailed attention to specifics rather than by any fanciful "breakthrough."

It has been said, somewhat facetiously, that there are two kinds of people in the world: those who believe there are two kinds of people in the world and those who do not. What may be said, with more clarity, is that there are two kinds of behavior therapists in the world: those who specialize in methodological rigor and painstaking investigation of neatly packaged problems, and those whose conceptual boundaries seem to know few limits. What is called behavior therapy in the 1980s encompasses a lot of things that could not have been included some two decades ago (London, 1983).

As we move away from one-to-one interventions and the laboratories of academia, social and political forces begin to loom more prominently on the horizon of behavior therapy. Technology is little more than the tip of the iceberg. Beneath the surface lies a consortium of social and political forces that are sometimes beyond our control, but never beyond our capacities for developing control if we can but learn how to apply behavioral principles to these broader issues (see also Goodman, 1983; Liberman, 1979, 1980).

Winett (1983) takes Matarazzo (1982) to task for focusing upon individual life style and responsibilities without giving sufficient attention to the role of political and economic antecedents of health and ill health. As psychologists, argues Winett, we rightly recognize the impact of environment on behavior. Should we not also be addressing the broader institutional, legal, political, and economic constraints that contribute to the development and maintenance of health-detrimental behavior? Does the behavioral health movement over-emphasize individual responsibility at the expense of social and contextual factors as determinants of human well-being, as Winett claims? In essence, what Winett is arguing for, if in a slightly different context, is the preservation of that delicate balance between the two faces of behavior therapy.

In his 1983 presidential address to the AABT, O'Leary urges behavior therapists to enter the political and social arena. The AABT's Media Watch Committee (Keane, 1983) does all it can to place pertinent material in the local press. A standing Committee on Legislative Affairs monitors state and federal policy matters that may be of concern to our discipline, with the hope that such actions will lead to the development of a national AABT Social Policy Information Network (Jones, Czyzewski, Otis, & Hannah, 1983).

On the one hand, critics still accuse contemporary behavior therapists of being simplistic and trivia-oriented. On the other hand, those who appeal to broader issues (e.g., Goodman, 1983; Willems, 1983; Winett, 1983) are accused of trafficking in vague generalities. Once again, it becomes a matter of preserving that delicate balance—or, to mix metaphors, bridging the theoretical and technological gap between the micro and macro levels.

To end this overview on an encouraging note, brief attention is drawn to one thoughtful attempt to accomplish just this. Abrams, Elder, Carleton, and Artz (1983) bring together ideas derived from social learning theory and certain sociological and educational disciplines to develop a framework for organizational health promotion that pays equal attention to these two seemingly divergent strategies. While still in its formative stages, what Abrams and Artz have to offer could be the beginning of a synthesis between the two faces of behavior therapy.

CHAPTER

2

BEHAVIORAL ASSESSMENT AND METHODOLOGY

PHILIP C. KENDALL

BEHAVIORAL ASSESSMENT

The present examination of the current status of behavioral assessment has an advantage over prior discussions. The advantage is based on the fact that the 1982 Association for Advancement of Behavior Therapy (AABT) presidential address, given by Rosemery Nelson, focused on "Behavioral Assessment: Past, Present, and Future." Using Nelson's address as a starting block, we can anticipate a lively and informative consideration of the life and times of the behavioral approach to psychological assessment.

Nelson's address, and the subsequent published version appearing in *Behavioral Assessment* (Nelson, 1983), began with an accurate account of the initial influences leading to the development and advancement of behavioral assessment. At the time of its early development, the combination of the perceived weaknesses of traditional assessment and the need for assessments of behavioral frequencies for evaluating behavioral therapy spurred a rapid growth. Incidentally, Nelson was accurate in noting that behavioral observations for counting specific behaviors had appeared much earlier in child development research.

The time line drawn by Nelson leads naturally to behavioral assessment's honeymoon period. It was during this time, largely bounded by the decade of the 1970s, that the lists of behavioral assessment techniques appeared and grew. As Nelson stated, "[T]his list included direct observation of behavior in naturalistic or analogue situations, self-monitoring, participant observation, self-report in the forms of questionnaires or interviews, physiological measures, and some standardized tests" (1983, p. 197).

Despite the rapid expanse of the techniques of behavioral assessment, Nelson (1983) saw the techniques, as opposed to the approach, of behavioral assessment, as the source of the current disillusionment. The *techniques* have been somewhat unsatisfying and have bred discontent. The general *approach* of behavioral assessment, however, in Nelson's position, remains acceptable and potent in terms of its impact.

Nelson's sources of disillusionment included the imperfection of current behavioral assessment techniques, the impracticality of current behavioral assessment techniques, and the lack of progress toward standardized behavioral assessment techniques. A closer examination of Nelson's three sources of disillusionment proves valuable. I might add at the outset that I see and will discuss a fourth source of discontent that Nelson did not address.

Imperfection can be discouraging. Indeed, as noted by the numerous researchers employing behavioral observation systems (coding systems), judges do not always agree on the proper response category. Even when the systems have been carefully developed, used by other researchers, honed and shaped, and optimally operationalized, inconsistencies persist. Fortunately, as both humans and psychologists, we have come to be accustomed to less than perfection. Most, if not all, assessments spend a greater percentage of their time being imperfect than being perfect. I grant Nelson the accuracy of her observation that two observers may not always agree (although we do agree in observations in this case), yet I opt to continue by arguing that this alone is not a major source of discontent. Behavioral assessors have achieved and published agreements in the 80% range and seem to be unabashed. Indeed, they are no less a source of imperfection than other assessment methodologies. This does not mean that there should not be more effort and greater conern among all assessors, but rather that imperfection itself is not the major source of decreased interest in behavioral assessment.

I am much more in agreement with Nelson's second source of disillusionment: the impracticality of behavioral assessments. Perhaps more than any other single factor, the lack of "do-ability" interferes with the successful implementation of behavioral assessments at the level of general clinical practice (e.g., private practice, community mental health centers). It is a rare investigator who, when trying to implement a large-scale behavioral program, including assessments, does not run into a marked lack of support from the staff because they are being asked to do additional work. In the occasional cases when observers are available, a more typical event in university-supported programs, there remains a wide range of additional attendant difficulties. Conducting a behavioral assessment of an extremely low-rate behavior (e.g., fire setting), of a very personal behavior (e.g., sexuality), or of an easily faked behavior (e.g., sexual arousal) also makes behavioral assessments impractical. The time and expense of comprehensive behavioral assessment are nearly prohibitive.

The lack of progress toward a standardized behavioral assessment was suggested by Nelson as the third source of disillusionment. Here, as with imperfection, I can only agree that such a concern exists and that it contributes to a degree to the current lack of enthusiasm, but that standardization was never really promised (nor, I think, expected) undermines the negative effect of its present absence. Lack of a standardized behavioral battery has contributed to, but accounts for a slim portion of the variance in, the disenchantment.

Nelson's overall perspective on behavioral assessment is to be applauded. That is, she was able to take a balanced look at the field in which she is a major figure. That she recognized and identified several sources of concern pleases me and identifies her as a trustworthy commentator on the history of behavioral assessment. I would, however, add that there is probably a fourth source of disillusionment (and perhaps a fifth and sixth as well). It is my view that the lack of a conceptual framework has hindered the advance of behavioral assessment. This lack has had several effects. For instance, due to the lack of a theoretically rich network of interrelationships, the thoughtful and theoretical talents of many researchers and clinicians have not been challenged. We have not done theory testing; we have simply been using the observations as part of demonstration studies. Correspondingly, the influx of the concern with cognitive factors has offered a more challenging conceptual systems and captured the interest of many assessment researchers. The need for additional complex conceptualizations has prompted some of the disillusionment that Nelson so accurately identified.

Following her analysis of the sources of discontent, Nelson (1983) turned to a recounting of the contributions of behavioral assessment. These contributions include (1) that behaviors are important to measure in and of themselves; (2) that assessment must frequently occur at the level of the individual; (3) that situational specificity must be applied to behavioral assessment devices; and (4) that behavioral assessment devices should be evaluated functionally. Each point is worthy of additional consideration.

That behaviors are important to be measured in and of themselves is indeed a valid statement. In addition, it is valid to credit the behavioral assessment movement with the infiltration of this position into mainstream psychological inquiry. In the therapy outcome literature, for example, there has been an increased appearance of and demand for some form of observational (behavioral) assessment of outcome.

Individualized assessment is valuable, and behavioral assessment implemented as part of intervention evaluation does involve individualization. What might be a trifle misleading, however, is the implication that only behavioral assessment is individualized and that only individualized assessments are to be encouraged. Idiographic as well as nomothetic approaches have a legitimate place in psychological assessment.

That behavioral assessment has contributed to the understanding and buttressing of the position of situational specificity is a fact that few would contend with, including myself. I disagree, however, with Nelson's (1983) position that questions of interrater agreement and inquiries into the predictive validity of role plays are meaningless (p. 202). Situational specificity has made many, if not most, psychologists recognize a major source of limitations in traditional assessment procedures. Situational specificity has helped clinicians seek to identify factors within social environments that are functionally related to aberrant behaviors, but the questions noted above remain meaningful. To dismiss all assessment variance to the situation is to ignore the consistency that *does* exist in human behavior. True, behavioral assessment deserves credit for magnifying the relevance of situational variability, but it does not mean that consistency does not contribute to some degree. Questions of the concurrent validity of role-play assessments might be framed as follows: "To how many situations, of varying degrees of similarity, can I make predictions based upon samples of behavior taken in this single situation?" Or, "What situation produces a sample of behavior that predicts best across other situations?" Perhaps a taxonomy of situations is a misleading direction, but there may be certain classes of situations in which the behavior can be predicted from a sample in a single situation. Consistencies and situations are an interactive force in behavioral predictions, and the identification of similar situations (classes of situations) would enhance our understanding of the role of situational factors (Kendall, 1978).

The last contribution ascribed to behavioral assessment by Nelson (1983) pertains to functional evaluation. While I would not see this as a contribution already made as much as a position that Nelson sees great merit in, this is an ancillary concern at this point. The main concern is whether or not certain of the traditional and time-honored notions of psychometrics can be meaningfully applied to the evaluation of behavioral assessment strategies. That test–retest reliability should not be expected because behaviors can vary from situation to situation begs the question. Certainly, if two situations are readily viewed as similar, then some degree of reliability is a scientific necessity. Nelson stated, "Given the assumption that behavior is modifiable, test–retest reliability should not be expected" (1983, p. 199). There is some truth here, but clarification is required. If behavior is modifiable, and if an intervention occurs between the two test assessments, then one does expect change on the assessment measures. If an intervention does *not* occur in the interassessment interval, then retest reliability is to be expected. Even those who design and develop intelligence tests (and the American Psychological Association [APA] standards for psychological tests) acknowledge that the meaningfulness of test–retest correlations pertain when there is no intertrial intervention. I do see merit in psychometric evaluation of behavioral assessments, and I would urge that we consider the criteria we would employ for publication of research reports if we were to abandon such concepts as reliability and validity. Adding Nelson's concept of functionally evaluating the "treatment validity" of the assessments can be accomplished without disavowing interest in or the value of other means of evaluating the utility of assessments.

To Role-Play or Not to Role-Play?

The Simulated Social Interaction Test (SSIT) is a role-play test of social skills. Wallander, Curran, and Myers (1983) conducted a social calibration of this measure of social competence by having judges provide ratings and comparing them to community standards of social competence. The outcome was that the SSIT responses were socially calibrated, in terms of both overall and situation-specific item performance. The social calibration means that when clients are rated as a result of behavior in the SSIT as having appropriate social skills, these judgments of appropriateness would be agreed to by members of the community.

This is an example of a positive enhancement brought to the coding of role-play assessments, but it must be contrasted with a series of studies where the validity of role plays remains somewhat in question. As I indicate, some features of the role play can be employed to improve validity, but unequivocal support for the validity of role plays is not a reality.

Kern (1982a) examined brief, extended, and replication role plays and assessed their concurrent validity. For all role plays, the subjects were instructed to behave as if they were actually in the presented situations. The brief-response role-play subjects responded to confederate prompts. The extended role play involved a 3.5-minute interaction. The replication role play asked subjects to "behave as they had" during a prior waiting-room interaction. Analyses focused on the relationship between the role-play tests and the criterion (the prior, unobtrusive, waiting-room interaction). The replication role play provided a moderate to highly valid representation of the naturalistically obtained behavior.

Three role-play assessments were compared to an unobtrusive criterion situation by Kern, Miller, and Eggers (1983): typical, replication, and specification. In the typical role play, subjects were asked to simulate behavior in a situation described by the examiner. In the replication role play, recent relevant interactions (for the subject) were staged, and the client was instructed to replicate his or her behavior. In the specification role play, subjects were told to replicate a recent behavioral interaction, but they were also told specific behaviors that were important to try to replicate. The criterion situation involved an interaction that took place during a waiting period prior to the start of the project.

The authors' interest was in the identification of the best role-play procedure as determined by relationships with behavior in the unobtrusive criterion situation. Results indicated that the specification role play yielded stronger relationships between role play and criterion than the other two assessments. This conclusion offers some encouragement to role-play assessments, but it must be tempered with the question: What are we really assessing if we ask the subject to pick the situation and repeat earlier behavior, and to do so after we tell him or her what is important? Kern and colleagues (see also Kern, 1982a) have made meaningful contributions, but some challenging questions remain.

Role-played and naturalistic behavior were compared in a study by Higgins, Frisch, and Smith (1983). In the context of waiting, subjects engaged in conversation with a confederate. Role-play subjects were either informed or uninformed as to the focus of the assessment (i.e., assertiveness). Both role-play groups were found to behave more assertively than did actual (naturalistic) subjects, with the informed role-play subjects responding most assertively.

These findings, like others before them, suggest that role plays may be sufficiently obtrusive to alter typical responding. Implicit demands and knowledge of the target of the assessment can unwittingly detract from the effort to secure accurate behavioral assessments.

Recent concern with the validity of role-play assessments of interpersonal skills has led to an apparent decrease in researchers' sole reliance on such measures. Looking at the value of role-play assessments from a different vantage point, that of the lack of consistency across studies, M. M. Mahoney and Kern (1983) point to the lack of standardization as a shortcoming. These authors found that varying one aspect of the role play altered the absolute difficulty of the test. The authors go on to speculate that the attractiveness of the confederate in the role play should be standardized, using confederates seen as moderately attractive. Another strategy that I see as worthwhile would be to require subjects to rate the attractiveness of confederates and then to use statistical analytic methods to control for attractiveness as perceived by individual subjects. In this manner, the large variation in what people view as attractive could be controlled. Moreover, the "rate and analyze for" method can be used in many other contexts to remedy numerous concerns.

A further practical weakness of role-play tests is that the confederate who provides the prompts is not consistent across studies, and the behaviors that are produced by subjects may be a function of this nonstandardized aspect of the role play. Indeed, Mahoney and Kern (1983) have reported that varying one aspect of the confederate's prompt, the prompt latency, had meaningful effects on the role plays. For instance, prompt latency affected the ability of the role-play tests to differentiate between criterion groups (i.e., high- and low-frequency daters).

Children have also been used as subjects in investigations of the validity of role plays. For example, role-play assessments of children's social skills were compared to a naturalistic assessment. Twenty-four youngsters participated, 12 popular and 12 unpopular (half boys and half girls) fourth- and fifth-graders. S. Beck, Forehand, Neeper, and Baskin (1982) reported that the frequency of behavior was different for the two types of assessments. There were more behaviors in the role play and fewer in the naturalistic setting. Also, judges rated the children in the role-play scene as more likeable than those in the naturalistic scene. The findings indicate that the method of assessment may affect the rate of the observed behavior and that any decisions about the most appropriate type of treatment must take into account the type of assessment that was employed.

Michelson, DiLorenzo, Calpin, and Ollendick (1982) employed assertiveness role plays in their examination of situational determinants of child behavior. Child psychiatry patients responded to different types of role-play scenes: negative assertion, accepting help, giving compliments, and accepting compliments. Videotaped responses were then rated (six categories of verbal behavior; four ratings of nonverbal behavior; general rating). The findings documented that positive and negative scores predicted significantly different interpersonal behavior. The fact that the prompts for the assertiveness role plays were performed by adults makes the interaction an adult–child and not a child–child one, and this feature of the study might require that we at least rethink whether or not assertiveness best describes the behavior of children in a child–adult situation. As the authors note, further efforts might address other situational factors, such as child–child interactions.

The low correlation between specific role-play behaviors and measures of social competence in children was again reported in a recent paper by Williamson, Moody, Granberry, Lethernon, and Blouin (1983). Thirty role-play scenes, with prompts for five categories of behavior, were used for behavioral assessments; two peer ratings, teacher ratings, and self-report were used for measures of social competence. Again, the prompter was not a child, making the role-play situation an adult–child as opposed to a child–child interaction.

In a review of role plays to assess social competence, McNamara and Blumer (1982) discussed issues of ecological validity. Their survey indicates that whereas role plays are increasingly being used in the literature, and whereas the role-play data do seem to differentiate treatment and control groups, as well as groups of high and low social competence, there is limited support for the ability of role plays to accurately represent naturally occurring social behavior. Moreover, the modest correspondence between role plays and natural behavior occurs at the molar and not at the molecular behavioral level.

There is consistency in the reporting of findings relating role-play tests to criterion behaviors. Unfortunately, the consistency is evident in the low-magnitude relationships that are reported. I queried in Volume 9 of the *Annual Review* (Kendall, 1984a), "Can we expect that a person will display 'key' (predictive) behaviors in the brief role plays we create?" (p. 44). My present response also parallels that noted in Volume 9. We can learn a great deal from our psychological colleagues in personnel selection, where role-play tests as part of a hiring process are undertaken for extended periods of time over several days. As McFall (1982) noted, neither role-play nor molar measures of social behavior are sufficient to independently assess the richness of children's competence or social skill. Indeed, the richness of the behavior we are seeking to measure dictates the need for larger samples and more complicated assessments.

Selected Topics

As is customary, not all of the reported research can be reviewed. Several areas have been selected and are considered here. The rationale for including each topic is different, but each has made an important point worthy of mention in this *Annual Review*.

PAIN

Many observational systems are available for the assessment of institutional and classroom behavior, for example, but little has been done until recently in the area of the behavioral assessment of pain. In a mini-series on the behavioral assessment of chronic pain (*Behavior Therapy*, 1982, *13*, 363–437) edited by Francis J. Keefe, a series of four studies involving an observation system for pain behaviors is reported (Keefe & Block, 1982). The behavioral codes that were employed concerned two categories: mutually exclusive and concomitant behaviors. The mutually exclusive codes included sitting, reclining, standing, walking, and shifting. Concomitant behaviors included guarding, bracing, rubbing, grimacing, and sighing. The first study demonstrated that these behaviors could be reliably observed and that the frequency of the behaviors was positively related to ratings of pain.

In the second study, the frequency of concomitant behaviors decreased due to treatment. The relationship between untrained observers' estimates of pain and patients' actual pain intensity was evaluated in the third study. If naive observers judged patients to be in pain based on concomitant actions, and the patients were indeed in pain, this would add to the validity of the coded behaviors. The results supported the guarding and grimacing codes, in particular. Bracing and rubbing were not related to pain. In the fourth and last study, it was found that low-back-pain patients displayed much higher frequencies of behavior on almost all codes that did normal and depressed controls. Given this systematic and encouraging trial, the suggestion that these assessments may prove beneficial to practitioners seems warranted. However, one must keep in mind that the assessments were quite brief, and that there may well be variations due to the type of pain being studied (low back pain). There is a need for replication and extension.

COUPLES

The Marital Interaction Coding System (MICS) continues to be employed as an indicant of outcome in behavioral marital therapy. For example, Mehlman, Baucom, and Anderson (1983) included a revised MICS in their evaluation of cotherapists versus single therapists and immediate versus delayed treatment for distressed couples. The 29 MICS behavior categories were combined into two larger categories (positive behavior and negative behavior). In this study, the MICS was used to code the behavioral interactions between spouses in two problem-solving situations. In the first situation, couples chose a medium-difficulty problem and tried to solve it during a 5-minute period. In the second situation, the couple worked on solving a hypothetical problem for a similar amount of time. Two problems were enacted, and the interactions were videotaped for later coding. Reliabilities reported for the two larger categories (.90, .91) were achieved after 40 hours of training.

Reliability of spouse observation was addressed by Elwood and Jacobson (1982). These researchers noted that earlier data sets, using volunteer subjects, suggested that spouses agreed on an observation checklist only about 50% of the time. They speculated that the low agreement might be the result of the low motivation of volunteers, so the agreement of 10 couples beginning marital therapy was studied. While one might assume that the clinic cases were more motivated, their overall agreement rate was 38.6%. The highest consensus rate for a single couple was 53.1% and for a single category of behavior was 61.2%. Elwood and Jacobson (1982) commented that clinic couples are particularly inaccurate reporters of their own behavior. The need for pretraining is apparent, but it would also be of interest to try to isolate the types of distortions or errors that contribute to the low reliability and the causes of these distortions. For instance, could self-serving biases be contributing? Given that there are two people involved and that each may be biased toward serving a different self, the bias potential increases dramatically. I cannot help but wonder what would happen if the couple knew that a third party was recording behaviors as well. Knowledge of an outside observer who would provide a more objective criterion might alter the reliabilities meaningfully.

"Reactivity," as described by Jacobson and colleagues (Jacobson, Follette, & McDonald, 1982), refers to the tendency for marital satisfaction to vary according to the frequency of recently occurring positive or negative events. Distressed couples appear more reactive to recent events, whereas nondistressed couples' day-to-day satisfaction is relatively independent of recent positive and negative frequencies. Findings based on 21 nondistressed couples and 20 couples seeking marital therapy supported the reactivity hypothesis. Distressed couples reported lower rates of positive behavior and higher rates of negative behavior, and were more reactive to recent events (in subjects' satisfaction with the relationship) than nondistressed couples. It should be noted that although the frequencies differ, these differences do not explain nor account for the reactivity effects. Jacobson *et al.* go on to suggest that it is more than a negative event that makes a couple distressed; it is the spouses' reaction to the meaning of the event. Certain cognitive/perceptual processes play an important role in the reactivity of the distressed couple.

SEXUAL AROUSAL

Perhaps the most troubling exposé of current times is the discovery of the extent of the problem of child molestation. This topic, which rarely appeared on a school board agenda until recently, now captures the time and attention of numerous school and community officials. The impetus for the attention is the uncovering of school teachers and principals who are being accused of having sexually molested children, many of whom are now young adults. But what does the sexual abuse of children have to do with behavioral assessment, one might ask?

One manner of resolving an accusation of child sexual abuse is for the offending adult to resign his or her position. Some school boards will not, however, accept such a resignation, since it often provides financial benefits to the individual. Court cases can and do result. One argument that has been raised in court cases is the "treatability" of the offender. That is, if the offender successfully completes a treatment program, might he or she be able to return to the place of employment and not be a threat to others? (See the review by Kelly, 1982.) Recent reports of the ability of subjects to "fake" sexual arousal responses call into question the confidence that we might otherwise have in the effectiveness of treatment protocols.

One such study, reported by Alford, Wedding, and Jones (1983), identified how sexual arousal information assessed via a penile strain gauge can be confounded. The patient used aversive scenes to block his arousal in the assessment sessions. It was also found that the patient could achieve 90% or greater erection by covertly attending to sexually evocative imagery. In both instances, when the experimenters were intending for the patient to use one type of covert image to produce the desired response, the client could substitute an opposing covert image and fool the researchers.

Similarly, Laws and Holmen (1978) reported that clients used firm shafts, such as a ballpoint pen, to help "strain" the strain gauge. These authors concluded that it was clear that clients had the capability of generating erection reponses to stimuli that were not erotic to them, as well as the ability to prevent their erection responses to sexual stimuli to which they were typically aroused. The upshot of these reports and concerns is that strain gauge and other behavioral assessments of sexual arousal are being questioned as indices of successful treatment outcome.

Cognitive–Behavioral Assessments

The simplistic conceptualization of the role of self-statements in psychological disorders might be stated as "You'll be anxious if you say anxiety-producing things to yourself." Perhaps this statement has merit at the level of introducing the concept to a nonpsychologically minded client, but it does not represent a psychologically sophisticated understanding of the issues. Indeed, numerous investigators and theoreticians have identified a more complex role for self-referent speech (e.g., Arnkoff & Glass, 1982; Bandura, 1981; Kendall & Hollon, 1981; Meichenbaum, 1977). For instance, data suggest that in some situations, it is not the presence of positive thinking but the absence of negative thinking that is associated with adjustment (e.g., see Volume 9 of the *Annual Review*).

Huber and Altmaier (1983) provide interesting data suggesting that the organization of the self-statement system is the important aspect of avoidance behavior. These authors studied the self-statements of phobic and nonphobic college students performing the behavioral avoidance test. The self-statements, gathered by the thought-listing method, were rated on degree of threat, salience of threat, and time orientation. Interrater reliability of .94 was reached. Interestingly, there were no significant group differences for the amount of threat seen in subjects' self-statements, but there were meaningful differences for the average *salience* of threat. Salience, as measured by Huber and Altmaier, took threat and intensity of threat into account. The personal meaning of self-talk (Arnkoff & Glass, 1982; Kendall & Hollon, 1981) seems to be an important factor and deserves further investigation.

What are the physiological effects of self-critical thought? This complex question was given initial examination by Schuele and Wiesenfeld (1983). These authors selected females who were high on interpersonal anxiety and asked them to rehearse neutral and negative self-referent statements while polygraph recordings were taking physiological data. Some of the subjects anticipated an interpersonal interaction following the self-statement rehearsal, while others had no such expectation. Negative self-statements were more arousing (i.e., led to higher cardiac level and respiration rates) than neutral ones, and the effect was greater when the self-referent thoughts were relevant to the anticipated interpersonal encounter.

The specificity of certain self-statements in determining certain physiological effects was reported by Orton, Beiman, LaPointe, and Lankford (1983). These researchers randomly assigned 60 females to one of three conditions: anxiety, depression, and neutral. The subjects in each condition were instructed to read lists of 50 self-statements relevant to the condition to which they were assigned. The main findings were that the anxiety-inducing self-statements led to significant increases in tonic cardiovascular response and greater increases in reported state anxiety than did the depressive or neutral self-statements. Interestingly, the increases in induced anxiety were produced by the anxious self-talk, whereas earlier studies had reported increases in anxiety from less specific types of self-referent speech. These results suggest the negative effects, assuming that state anxiety is nondesirable, resulting from rehearsal of negative-affect sentences.

Using self-referent statements as experimental stimuli, Finkel, Glass, and Merluzzi (1982) tested the self-monitoring skills of depressed and nondepressed subjects. Depressed subjects estimated having seen fewer positive statements when they occurred at a high rate than did nondepressive subjects. No differences were found on neutral statements.

It seems appropriate at this juncture to call attention to the need for studies of the discriminant and incremental validity of cognitive assessment devices. Traditional measures of personality may not be the best criteria, but we should be willing to test and demonstrate that cognitive assessments add meaningfully to assessments that are already available. Behavioral observations might serve best as the index against which the incremental validity of cognitive assessments could be judged. This type of research should recognize the influence of the assessment method, the varieties of subjects studied, and the types of criteria against which validity can be determined.

IRRATIONAL BELIEFS

Given the rarity of outcome evaluations of rational–emotive therapy (RET), it is not surprising that the one report of the effects of RET with a clinical sample (Lipsky, Kassinove, & Miller, 1980) has received additional analysis (for discussion of the Lipsky *et al.* study, see Volume 8 of the *Annual Review*—Kendall, 1982a). T. W. Smith (1983) identified that the RET model holds that changes in irrational beliefs mediate the effects of RET. Thus, changes in irrational beliefs should be correlated with changes in the problems for which clients were receiving therapy. Smith's analyses of the Lipsky *et al.* data indicated that changes in the endorsement of irrational beliefs were correlated with changes in each outcome measure. Smith proceeded to add the needed cautions to his conclusions by pointing out the shared method variance of the self-report measures used as outcome indices and the fact that the often-used measure of irrational beliefs has questionable validity. I would add to this list by underscoring a concern that emerges from a consideration of subjects' lack of self-awareness. Basically, the assessment of irrational beliefs, especially when accomplished by asking subjects to endorse (or not to endorse) each of Ellis's irrational beliefs, is plagued by subjects' (patients') lack of self-awareness. The lists of irrational beliefs are typically worded in so strong a fashion that subjects who are even moderately self-aware do not endorse them in the irrational direction. The bias at pretreatment assessment is for the subjects (clients) to state that they do not hold such irrational beliefs. At posttreatment, after sessions of focusing upon irrationality, subjects gain self-knowledge and come to see that while they did not recognize their own irrational thinking, their behavior betrayed certain of their irrational beliefs. If and when this occurs, scores on measures of irrationality go from low to high as a result of treatment—not from high to low.

The assessment of irrational beliefs, despite the identified problems, remains an important topic. The IBT (Irrational Beliefs Test; R. G. Jones, 1968) continues to be examined as a measure of irrationality. For example, Lohr and Bonge (1982) measured assertive deficits and irrationality; they reported that assertiveness deficits were associated with the Demand for Approval, High Self-Expectations, and Problem Avoidance factor scores, and with the total irrational belief score of the IBT.

Dysfunctional beliefs as related to distress in close relationships were investigated by Eidelson and Epstein (1982). These authors developed a scale, the Relationship Belief Inventory (RBI), to assess five dysfunctional beliefs about intimate relationships: (1) Disagreement is destructive, (2) mind reading is expected, (3) partners cannot change, (4) sexual perfectionism, and (5) the sexes are different. Data were reported to show that four of the five scales were related to the IBT and that internal consistency coefficients were in the .72 to .81 range. Using clinical and nonclinical couples, RBI scores were significantly and negatively correlated with scores on the Marital Adjustment Scale. One concern, however, is that the clinical participants' scores on the RBI were not particularly high. As Eidelson and Epstein (1982) wrote, this raises the question of whether people actually hold these dysfunctional beliefs to any significant degree. Continued validation of the RBI is needed, with behavioral data and treatment-effects analyses being of particular interest.

Eidelson and Epstein (1982) are not to be singled out, but the assessment of irrationality can be said to suffer from the generally simplistic methods employed. It is as if the developers of the instruments to assess irrational thinking believe that all respondents will be sufficiently self-aware to know what beliefs they in fact hold. More sophisticated assessments, based upon more conceptually challenging but necessary operationalizations of irrationality, will be required (see Arnkoff & Glass, 1982, for a related discussion).

In a less typical and more creative enterprise, Linehan, Goodstein,

Nielsen, and Chiles (1983) developed a measure of beliefs that are potentially important as reasons for staying alive. With the thrust of data on depression, and its association to suicide, the measurement of those beliefs that might foster nonsuicidal behavior is much needed. Linehan *et al.*'s inventory is entitled the Reasons for Living (RFL) Inventory. The scale requires that subjects rate how important each of 48 reasons would be for living if suicide were being considered. Factor analyses identified six factors within the 38-item scale: Survival and Coping Beliefs (24 items, e.g., "I believe I can find other solutions to my problems"); Responsibility to Family (7 items, e.g., "It would hurt my family too much and I would not want them to suffer"); Child Related Concerns (3 items, e.g., "The effect on my children could ["would" is used on p. 278, "could" on p. 279] be harmful"); Fear of Suicide (7 items, e.g., "I am a coward and do not have the guts to do it"); Fear of Social Disapproval (3 items, e.g., "I would not want people to think that I did not have control over my life"); and Moral Objections (4 items, e.g., "My religious beliefs would forbid it").

The RFL (along with an information sheet and a suicidal behavior questionnaire) was given both to shoppers in a community mall and to inpatients in a psychiatric hospital. Background information, including any past suicide attempts, was also gathered. Based on the suicidal behavior questionnaire, shoppers were classified as never considering suicide, briefly considered suicide, seriously considered suicide, and attempted suicide. Inpatients were classified (according to the suicidal behavior questionnaire and interviews) along two dimensions describing their level of suicidal involvement. In both samples of subjects, the RFL reliably differentiated suicidal from non-suicidal individuals. Also in both samples, the factors labeled as Survival and Coping, Responsibility to Family, and Child-Related Concerns were most useful in differentiating the groups. The Child-Related Concerns factor contains only three items and was related to the number of actual children in the family of respondents. Thus, this factor may have less psychological meaning than the other dimensions of the reasons for staying alive. The RFL–suicidal behavior relationship is particularly meaningful, since the endorsement of various suicidal beliefs was not related to psychopathology in general, nor was it related to recent life stress. Measurement of the different reasons for living may prove helpful in remedial endeavors with suicidal subjects: Efforts directed toward training of those beliefs most predictive of not attempting suicide may be likely to foster nonsuicidal action. Correspondingly, following assessment and identification of low scores on RFL factors, patients could be trained to recognize some additional reasons for living. The specific focus of this effort to assess beliefs may prove valuable, since the measurement instruments and their underlying rationale were focused and directed toward meaningful interventions.

DEPRESSIVE CONDITIONS AND SELF-TALK

Working largely from A. T. Beck's cognitive model of depression, several researchers have sought to develop measures of the cognitions and self-talk that specifically characterize depressive subjects. One such scale, the Automatic Thoughts Questionnaire (ATQ; Hollon & Kendall, 1980), consists of 30 self-statements that differentiated psychometrically depressed from nondepressed subjects. In a study that sought to replicate the relationship found by Hollon and Kendall (1980), Ross and Gott-fredson (1983) examined the ATQ, MMPI D, and Beck Depression Inventory (BDI) scores of various clinically defined samples. According to the authors, the means, standard deviations, and intercorrelations obtained in their study were very similar to those reported in the initial study using mild to moderately depressed college students.

Also using the ATQ, Ross, Todt, and Rindflesh (1983) examined the relationship among measures of binge-eating severity, depression, and depressive cognitions. Subjects were classified as anorexic, bulimic, or bulimic–anorexic. As expected, anorexics scored lower than bulimics on binge eating, and anorexic subjects scored higher on a measure of dieting efficacy. Interestingly, the bulimic group had significantly more depressive cognitions than the other two groups.

Three cognitive assessment measures pertinent to depression were studied by Dobson and Breiter (1983). These researchers undertook a psychometric study of the ATQ, the Dysfunctional Attitude Scale (DAS), and the Interpretation Inventory. Based on a large sample, all measures showed good internal reliability (alpha coefficients), with the ATQ evidencing notably high internal reliability. Also, the relationship between the ATQ and the BDI was significantly stronger than the BDI's correlation with the other two scales. Although the sample consisted of college students and the measures that were contrasted did not include all possible measures, the ATQ received empirical support for its psychometric credibility.

Assessing the clinical validity of the ATQ, Harrell and Ryon (1983) administered the 30-item scale to clinical populations. Mental health patients who met criteria for depression were found to have higher ATQ scores than mental health patients who were not depressed and nondepressed medical patients. Also, the ATQ was found to be significantly correlated with therapist ratings of depression, the MMPI D scale, and the BDI. Harrell and Ryon suggested that the ATQ demonstrated "considerable specifity for depressive cognitions, as score elevations were not evidenced by nondepressed individuals with diagnosed syndrome psychopathologies or by medical outpatients" (1983, p. 724).

Based on this burst of published research suggesting that the ATQ has acceptable features of reliability and validity, continued research seems warranted. Indeed, there are more challenging tests remaining for the ATQ. For instance, to what degree of specifity can the ATQ predict level of depression as opposed to other psychiatric disorders? Does the scale offer incremental validity to predictions of treatment outcome? These questions aside, the existing psychometric information offers some confidence to the outcome reseacher seeking an instrument to use to study the types and mechanisms of change that result from treatments of depression.

In an important study of the mechanisms of change in cognitive and pharmacotherapy, Simons, Garfield, and Murphy (1984) employed three cognitive measures: the DAS to assess the basic schemata of depression, the Cognitive Response Test to assess ongoing information processing and certain distortions, and the ATQ to measure the specific thoughts occurring to depressed persons as a result of their faulty thinking. The patients were clinical cases randomly assigned to cognitive therapy (12 weeks) or pharmacotherapy (12 weeks; Aventyl). Using the BDI and the Hamilton ratings, the authors pointed out that both groups showed positive treatment outcome. Using the cognitive measures, and despite a different prediction, the two groups also evidenced nearly identical improvements. Despite the fact that these are two very different focuses of treatment, the observed outcomes were remarkably similar.

Simons *et al.* (1984) make an interesting point when they comment that their results do not question the efficacy of cognitive therapy, nor do they question the ideas that changing cognition (as in cognitive therapy) can change depression. What these data do challenge is the idea that only cognitive therapy would change cognition. As the authors continue, what is important is that a "radically different form of treatment based on an entirely different set of assumptions secures almost identical results in terms of cognitive changes" (1984, p. 49).

One would, no doubt, be curious to know whether other forms of treatment also result in parallel changes in cognition. Recalling the work and findings of Zeiss, Lewinsohn, and Muñoz (1979), we might respond affirmatively, since their three treatments (a variant of cognitive therapy, interpersonal skills training, and pleasant events scheduling) produced comparable changes on the criterion measures specific to each type of treatment. However, these authors did not assess dysfunctional attitudes or negative automatic thinking. Thus, comparability of change was seen, but the instruments measuring change were not directly tapping depressive cognition. Simons *et al.* have opened an interesting and important topic for further inquiry.

One note is in order: Skeptics might suspect that patients in the pharmacotherapy condition somehow received some therapy in the course of their medication clinic contacts. However, Simons *et al.* audiotaped and examined the medication-only contacts to insure the absence of other interventions.

An international perspective on the role of self-talk in depression was provided by Missel and Sommer (1983). Depressed subjects were inpatients in a West German clinic with BDI scores greater than or equal to 20 and rated by their therapists as depressed. The nondepressed subjects, also from the clinic, scored less than 19 on the BDI and were rated as nondepressed. Missel and Sommer created a 38-item questionnaire to assess self-verbalizations. Situations were presented with positive and negative outcomes, and the subject had to choose one of these self-statements. These options included positive self-talk, negative self-talk, and an external attribution. These clinicians agreed 97.3% that the items and self-statements measured the concepts intended. Analyses confirmed that the depressed clients showed less positive and more negative self-verbalization, as well as more negative-balance (positive minus negative self-talk) self-verbalization.

Hammen and Krantz (1976; Krantz & Hammen, 1979) developed the Cognitive Bias Questionnaire (CBQ) and reported, along with moderate test–retest reliability, that the CBQ differentiates depressed and nondepressed individuals. The CBQ consists of four stories with multiple-choice questions that are coded (1) depressed–nondepressed in tone and mood, and (2) distorted–nondistorted in terms of logical inference. In a study by Norman, Miller, and Klee (1983), 30 primary depressives, 30 secondary depressives, and 30 nondepressed/nonschizophrenic patients were administered a test battery. Research Diagnostic Criteria were used for diagnoses. The depressed patients selected significantly more depressed distortions on the CBQ than did the nondepressed patients. On the CBQ, primary and secondary depressives did not differ. Nevertheless, patients who had endorsed high levels of depressed distortion on the CBQ revealed significantly more cognitive symptoms of depression on self-report and inventory measures.

An alternate measure of the cognitions associated with depression was developed and reported by Crandell and Chambless (1981). The scale is referred to as the Crandell Cognitions Inventory, and is composed of 100 items. Subjects are asked to rate how frequently they think each of the self-statements on a scale from 1 to 5. The total score is the sum of the 81 negative self-statements. The scale significantly discriminates clinically depressed persons from nondepressed subjects, psychiatric controls, and normal controls. Internal consistency is high, and the scale shows a strong relationship to depth of depression and little relationship to a measure of intelligence.

OTHER ASSESSMENTS RELATED TO DEPRESSION

Depressives are typically reported to show selective memory that favors the recall of negative information about themselves. Zuroff, Colussy, and Wielgus (1983) conducted a signal detection–analysis of the recall and recognition performance of depressed, formerly depressed, and nondepressed female college students presented with positive and negative adjectives. Two criteria were used in subject selection: cutoff score on the BDI and upper 20% on a postdepression measure. As reported by Zuroff et al., the depressed subjects recalled more negative adjectives correctly, produced more negative intrusions in recall, and produced more negative false alarms in recognition. While these findings seem to provide support for the notion that depressives have a selective memory for negative events, Zuroff et al. further suggest that the recognition differences for negative adjectives were shown to be due to differences in beta; in terms of d', the depressives did not differ from the other groups. These findings, using signal detection methodology, suggest that the "depressed subjects might have been more willing than nondepressed subjects to report remembering negative self-relevant words" (1983, p. 229). The authors illustrate the employment of the methodology of experimental psychology and the examination of differences associated with psychopathology—a worthy cross-fertilization.

The development of the Attributional Style Questionnaire (ASQ), intended for use in the study of attributions in depression, was described by Peterson, Semmel, von Baeyer, Abramson, Metalsky, and Seligman (1982). The ASQ contains 12 different hypothetical events (6 "good" and 6 "bad" events; half of each are interpersonal/affiliative and half are achievement-related) to which subjects provide responses. Subjects are asked to "imagine yourself in the situation" and, "if it happened to you, what would you feel would have caused it? Pick the one major cause and write it down." Next, subjects are asked to rate the cause along three attributional dimensions and the importance of the event.

As the authors point out, the scale allows for the derivation of 20 different subscales, each subscale based on different composites of items. The multiplicity of scoring methods is a solid idea, but one must recall that the scale consists of only 12 situations. I have elsewhere (Kendall, 1983; Kendall & Braswell, 1982) speculated that individual behaviors are followed by individual attributions, and that it takes many behavioral events across many situations before one can ascribe an attributional style to an individual. The ASQ, as a measure of an attributional style, could have benefited from a wider range of situations and a larger number of items. The limited numbers of items per subscale could also have affected the psychometric characteristics of the scale. In this regard, it is not surprising that the six-item subscale reliabilities (internal consistency) averaged .54 and the three-item sub-scales averaged only .38. The authors suggest that the achievement–affiliation distinction did not emerge as meaningful and that it not be scored separately in future work. However, the good–bad outcome distinction did evidence meaningful differences. Test–retest reliabilities for the subscale ranged from .57 to .70. The average test–retest reliability was determined to be .63. For a measure purported to be assessing a style or characteristic that is stable over time, this reliability estimate seems a bit low. It is pleasing to see that Peterson *et al.* (1982), in their discussion section, speak to the need for future research to determine whether the attributional *style* is truly a style.

The potential role of social desirability in the assessment of hopelessness, and, correspondingly, in determining the relationship between hopelessness and suicidal behavior, was discussed by Linehan and Nielsen (1981). Nevid (1983) responded to the original 1981 paper by questioning the true merit of the concern with social desirability. He argued that social desirability should not be a concern, for instance, unless the scales overlap to such a degree as to be redundant. He also expressed concern about the sample used—a group of shoppers assessed while in a mall area. Linehan and Nielsen (1983) replied, including a report of data from a sample of inpatients. Again, there was a substantial correlation (negative) between hopelessness and social desirability. The predictions of suicidal behavior (a positive relationship between hopelessness scores and patients' estimates of future behavior) dropped from .33 to .26 when social desirability was controlled. Although these findings do point to the need to consider social desirability, and although the concepts of suicide and hopelessness are clearly susceptible to bias by subjects wishing to distort their true feelings, the magnitude of the moderating influence of social desirability is less striking than might be expected. Nevertheless, the consistency seen in both shoppers and inpatients adds to the generality of the findings.

The Hamilton Rating Scale for Depression (HRS) (Hamilton, 1960) is an often-used clinician rating scale for the assessment of the severity of depression. The scale is often employed in evaluations of the effects of various treatments for depressive disorders. In such cases, at least two clinician ratings are seen as needed. O'Hara and Rehm (1983) sought to determine whether trained students could be used for HRS ratings; if students are found to be reliable, they would offer a less expensive alternative to two clinicians. Using four expert clinical raters, 20 depressed clients, and three trained students, O'Hara and Rehm found comparable reliabilities and very acceptable criterion validities. Apparently, not only will the HRS continue to be a widely used instrument, but the employment of trained student raters may facilitate the use of the scale.

Of ancillary interest is the fact that the various measures of depression have been subjected to analysis of their readability (Berndt, Swartz, & Kaiser, 1983). Two readability indices suggested that the scales were readable by ninth-grade-educated individuals. The Kovacs Children Scale (Kovacs, 1980) was easiest, with a fifth-grade reading level, and the General Behavior Inventory (Depue, Slater, Wolfstetter-Kausch, Klein, Goplerud, & Farr, 1981) scored a twelfth-grade reading level.

Of prime importance, in my opinion, is the need for researchers to be concerned with discriminant validity when assessing depression. In particular, the oft-found .60 to .70 correlation between anxiety and depression would suggest that depression is not an independent affective state. Anxiety shares some of the unwanted affect that is associated with depression. Indeed, in a study conducted with my colleague Rick Ingram, we had to screen over 2,000 undergraduates to be able to investigate a small sample of subjects who were depressed but not anxious, anxious but not depressed, both anxious and depressed, or neither anxious nor depressed. It was the task of filling the first two cells that required the extensive assessments. The potential for clarity justifies the extensive screening. That is, to discern that something is true of depression and not true of anxiety informs us in a more convincing fashion that we have learned something about depression than when we learn that something is true of depression but no other disorders (e.g., anxiety) are eliminated. Further investigations of the *specificity* of findings associated with depression are warranted at this time.

SELECTED TOPICS

Expectancies. Expectancies have been examined by Christiansen and Goldman (1983) as a mediational factor in the development of alcohol problems among adolescents. According to the authors, demographic variables are often said to be the best predictors of alcohol consumption among adolescents. Using a large number of subjects ($n = 1,580$), Christiansen and Goldman compared the predictive validity of demographics to that of expectations. First, the authors derived three adolescent drinking styles (based on factor analysis). Next, they sought to predict drinking using the demographic data and then using the expectational data. It was found that "expectancies at least equalled and even added to the predictive power of the background variables" (1983, p. 249). Two of the three drinking styles were seen as particularly important: "frequent social drinking" and "problem drinking." In relation to these two drinking styles, it was found that adolescents who drank in a frequent social manner expected alcohol to enhance their social behavior, whereas adolescents who reported alcohol-related problems expected an improvement in their cognitive and motor functioning. Given these marked expectational differences, it may be wise for preventive efforts to work toward the correction of expectational errors, as opposed to the current use of what Christiansen and Goldman have called "scare tactics." The examination of adolescents' expectations about the effects of alcohol have special meaning when one considers that the expectations exist before the individual has any meaningful degree of experience with alcohol. While I would not want to be misread as stating that all of the effects of alcohol are expectational, I do think that this line of inquiry promises to inform us in many ways about the nature and role of expectations within the array of alcohol effects.

Actor–Observer Differences. Attributional researchers have found the pattern of actor–observer differences described by E. E. Jones and Nisbett (1972) to be robust. In a recent clinically related study, Compas and colleagues (Compas, Adelman, Freundl, Nelson, & Taylor, 1982) examined the attributional patterns of parents and children regarding problem characteristics of the children. When interviewed individually, parents and children differed in their attributions about the causes of the children's problems. As the actor–observer hypothesis would predict, parents made more attributions to characteristics of their children than did the children themselves. However, the attributional differences were not evident when the family was interviewed together.

Self-Efficacy. While the concept of self-efficacy (Bandura, 1977) continues to generate a large number of research and conceptual papers, it also receives its share of critical commentary. For instance, Kirsch and Wickless (1983) examined the "microanalysis" method employed by Bandura and colleagues and suggested that the concordance rates between efficacy and behavior on behavioral avoidance tests are redundant. On the positive side, Barling and Abel (1983) reported positive and significant correlations between self-efficacy expectations and tennis performance. Also, one of the early studies of self-efficacy and the maintenance of behavior change (Condiotte & Lichtenstein, 1981) was replicated and extended by K. O. McIntyre, Lichtenstein, and

Mermelstein (1983). These authors reported that self-efficacy scores were associated with smoking cessation and smoking status at 3-month follow-up and 6-month follow-up, but not at one year (see also DiClemente, 1981).

The Power of Nonnegative Thinking. I like the ring that the phrase "power of nonnegative thinking" engenders. It implies that the person himself or herself has some control, and it avoids the simplicity of such self-supporting directives as "I think I can." Moreover, the notion behind the phrase is consistent with much of cognitive theory related to psychopathology: It is the person with disturbed thinking, such as irrational or illogical thinking, who is likely to suffer from psychological disturbances. Healthy persons do not have the negative thinking. The enthusiasm for the phrase must be tempered somewhat, however, in light of the data suggesting that some disturbed subjects, such as depressed subjects, are more accurate in recall than normals, since the normals recall more positive information than what actually took place (e.g., Alloy & Abramson, 1979; Kuiper & MacDonald, 1983).

Kuiper and MacDonald found that mildly depressed individuals recalled equal amounts of positive and negative personality information about themselves, whereas normals displayed a preference for the recall of positive personality information about themselves. One must, therefore, ask, "Is it the disturbed group that is showing the inaccuracy?" Perhaps not. A source of concern, however, is the extent to which the subjects were depressed. Perhaps clinically depressed patients would show a more negative self-schema than the mildly depressed sample. To return to the "power of nonnegative thinking," it may be the case that a resolution is possible. Consider, for example, that nondisturbed people do have a bias or preference for nonnegative thinking. While this could be seen in the absence of negative thinking in some cases, it may also be viewed as an abundance of positive thinking in others. That is, nondepressed persons do not have a negative view of themselves, and this is their nonnegative thinking—but they seem, at times, to go further and to evidence not only nonnegative thinking but a wealth of positive thinking as well.

Evidence from outcome studies (see also Volume 9 of this series) continues to suggest that treatment gains are differentially evident in positive and negative thinking. Studying coping imagery in the removal of test anxiety, G. M. Harris and Johnson (1983) reported that the reduction in negative coping statements was more dramatic than the increase in positive coping statements and drew attention to Wine's (1971, 1980) theoretical position, which emphasized negative cognitions as primary factions in the performance problems of text-anxious clients. Accepting the notion that the dimension of self-talk that focuses on positive and negative poles is a potent strategy for assessors, it is likely that more research analyses will be reported and a more comprehensive review provided in the near furture.

Cognitive Assessment and Methodology. How can we come to learn about the cognitive events, processes, and structures that we theorize to be so central to adjustment and conditions of psychological pathology? As evident in the reviews of cognitive–behavioral assessment in Volume 8 and 9 of the *Annual Review* (Kendall, 1982a, 1984a), the methods used to assess and study cognitive phenomena, such as self-verbalization, are quite varied. Self-statement inventories, thought-listing methods, videotape reconstruction, thought diaries, self-monitoring of thoughts, and thought sampling are illustrative.

Envisioning merit in the thoughts that individuals would articulate during controlled situations, Davison, Robins, and Johnson (1983) present a paradigm not surprisingly entitled "Articulated Thoughts during Simulated Situations." In an initial experiment reported by these authors, the situational variations introduced as part of the study were found to have an effect on the types of self-statements articulated by subjects. More specifically, the authors proposed that the factor of *personal involvement* in the situations influenced the ways in which the participants were thinking. That the "articulated thoughts" procedure was successful means that it too must be included among the methods to assess cognition. While this is not troublesome, the important task of comparing the different methodologies becomes further complicated.

Concerns have been raised about the potential confounding effects of method variance in the assessment of cognition (Kendall, 1983). The essential concern is that data can be more influenced by the method used to collect them than by variations in the topic being assessed. Unless the target cognitions are measured by several different procedures, one cannot isolate and remove from the total variability that which is attributable to method variance. In Volume 9 of the *Annual Review*, several studies were discussed in relation to this question (e.g., Chiauzzi & Heimberg, 1982; Galassi, Frierson, & Sharer, 1981). Being cognizant of method variance issues, Houston, Fox, and Forbes (in press) employed both "think aloud" and questionnaire methods of assessment. The correlations between the two methods of measuring the cognitive behaviors were found to be significant and ranged from .22 to .48 for five of the seven cognitive-behavior categories that were assessed. Only these five somewhat convergently validated categories were retained for further analysis. One must keep in mind, however, that the strength of the convergent validity coefficients is moderate at best.

Methods are being developed and refined, and will, no doubt, be tested against one another. Nevertheless, we may still be perplexed by the illusiveness of an outside criteria against which to judge the relative merits of assessments. The validity process must involve the elimination of rival hypotheses, the reporting of replications, and the usefulness of the data for proper interventions and productive evaluation.

Assessments with Children

With reluctance from some, and with some reluctance from many, the need to report information about the DSM-III status of research subjects has increased. APA journals, and others, evidence an increase in the reporting of DSM-III-diagnosed research subjects. To a degree, this is also true among behaviorally oriented researchers. In the case of children, diagnostic interviews have received increased attention. Though typically not from a behavioristic vantage point, the interview schedules rely heavily on reports of behavior. Studies of attention deficit disorder, depression, or separation anxiety (school phobia), for example, will probably evidence an increase in diagnostic interviewing.

The interview schedules, typically structured, that are gaining in interest in the assessment of children's disorders are designed to produce diagnostic information (e.g., Herjanic & Reich, 1982; Hodges, Kline, Stern, Cytryn, & McKnew, 1982). Questions addressed in these studies involve the assessment of reliability and the types of symptoms reported by parents and children (Herjanic & Reich, 1982) and agreement on diagnoses, based on child and parent interviews (Reich, Herjanic, Welner, & Gandhy, 1982). Hodges *et al.* (1982) also report on an assessment interview for children. DSM-III diagnoses are targeted by the structured interview procedures. Unfortunately, while the structured interview approach has merit, insufficient effort has been directed toward the type of assessment that would provide increased predictiveness of treatment of choice and treatment effect.

Although the question of whether or not depression, as a true syndrome, exists in childhood remains, there are an ever-increasing number of studies designed to evaluate various methods of assessing depression in children. In one study, Kazdin, French, Unis, Esveldt-Dawson, and Sherick (1983) examined the hopelessness, depression, and suicidal intent of children in an inpatient psychiatric facility. The Hopelessness Scale used for adults (Beck, Weissman, Lester, & Trexler, 1974) was modified for use with children. The revised Hopelessness Scale contained 17 items to which the child respondents answered true or false. Children scoring high on hopelessness showed more severe depression and lower self-esteem than low-hopelessness children. In regard to suicidal ideation (which was assessed independently at an initial intake), hopelessness was a better predictor than depression. As the authors noted, the findings suggest that negative expectations about oneself and the future can be assessed in children and that these features are related to suicidal intention.

As mentioned in Volume 9 of the *Annual Review*, the cognitions of adults in evaluative contexts are predictive. That is, adults high and low in test anxiety differ in their self-referent speech. An examination of the cognitions of test-anxious children (Zatz & Chassin, 1983) reported findings similar to those found in adult samples. The children ($n = 294$) were screened using the Test Anxiety Scale for Children (Sarason, Davidson, Lighthall, Waite, & Ruebush, 1960) and divided into groups high, medium, and low in test anxiety. Children's cognitions were assessed using the Children's Cognitive Assessment Questionnaire, a 40-item yes–no scale developed for this study. Items were phrased "I thought . . ." and included Negative Evaluations, Positive Evaluations, Off-Task Thoughts, and On-Task Thoughts subscales. Those children who were highly test-anxious reported more task-debilitating thoughts and fewer positive evaluations. Subjects low in anxiety approached the task with more thoughts of mastery and competence. Interestingly, the moderately and highly test-anxious children evidenced a greater number of on-task thoughts than the low-anxiety children. While this might have suggested that these children were working toward coping and successful performance, task performance scores were not related to on-task thoughts for boys and only slightly for girls. Other sex differerences were also reported. For example, girls did not evidence a relationship between cognitions and performance when ability was partialed out, whereas boys did. For boys, task-debilitating thoughts were associated with poorer performance, while positive evaluations were associated with better performance.

Some findings have focused on the consistency between adults and children. For example, Kazdin *et al.* (1983) reported that hopelessness was more related to suicidal intention than depression in their young adolescent sample, a finding that parallels that found in adults. Correspondingly, Zatz and Chassin (1983) reported that the cognitions of test-anxious children resembled those of test-anxious adults: High-anxiety children reported more task-debilitating thoughts, while low-anxiety children approaching the task with more thoughts of mastery and competence. Methodologically, the question of consistency between child and adult disorders is a longitudinal one.

Resemblances between relationships found in children and in adult samples can suggest that the concepts being examined are equally important for both age groups. However, consistency over the life span and factors associated with the processes involved at the different age levels requires an examination of the same individuals over an extended period of time. This approach, however, is not as simple as it sounds. The problem that emerges is measurement equivalence (e.g., Baltes, Reese, & Nesselroade, 1977). Long-term assessment studies must ask and attempt to answer this question: "Should the same assessment device be used for children, adolescents, and adults, or should a different but age-appropriate measure be used to measure the identical concept?" One solution would be to use both identical measures (which may or may not be age-appropriate) and age-appropriate measures (which may or may not be identical), and to look for consistency across the measurement methods (see Kendall, Lerner, & Craighead, 1984).

METHODOLOGY

Use of Normative Data

The description of normative comparisons as a method for evaluating the normalizing effects of therapy was covered in Volume 9 of the *Annual Review*. Normative comparisons (Kendall & Norton-Ford, 1982) provide clinical significance to tests of statistical significance and can be employed across behavioral observations, ratings, test and task performances, and self-report measures of therapy outcome. Indeed, outcome data can be buttressed by evidence that formly deviant clients are, at posttreatment, no longer outside normative limits on the dependent measures.

Additional recommendations for the use of normative data have appeared. For instance, the use of normative data was recommended by Hops for the assessment of childhood social competence. Considerable data exist to indicate changes in both quality and quantity of social behavior with increasing age (e.g., Greenwood, Walker, Todd, & Hops, 1981). Using age-related normative data, the clinical researcher will be likely to make more reasoned decisions about whether or not to include a child in treatment and how to evaluate the treatment results.

A slightly different use of normative information was provided by Wallander *et al.* (1983). As part of their social calibration of the SSIT, they used the ratings of social skills behavior provided by community members to create a community, or normative, standard. Thus, the use of community members as raters allowed the researchers to calibrate their role-play test such that role-play ratings were representative of what people in real life consider appropriate. The use of normative data relates to social validation. Interestingly, normative comparisons have also been recommended as useful evaluative tools for assessing the effectiveness of alcohol treatment programs (Moos & Finney, 1983).

Follow-Ups

Follow-ups are recognized as important sources of data in the comprehensive evaluation of the effects of an intervention. Recent efforts include a 5-year follow-up of a behavioral weight loss program (Graham, Taylor, Hovell, & Siegel, 1983), a 2½- to 3-year follow-up of the treatment of children's night fears (Graziano & Mooney, 1982), a 2-year follow-up of the treatment of tension headache (Holroyd & Andrasik, 1982b), and a 6-month follow-up of a social problem-solving project with preschoolers (Rickel, Eshelman, & Loigman, 1983). The range of length of follow-up periods reported from 1960 to 1979 was 1 month to several years, with an average of 8 months (Nicholson & Berman, 1983).

In the weight loss follow-up, a surprising 97% of subjects participated. Successful maintainers of weight loss were adhering to behavioral procedures and being physically active. Can these facts be assessed to be responsible for the maintained loss of an average of 4.5 kg (10 lb)? As noted in Volume 9 of the *Annual Review* (Kendall, 1984a), follow-ups can be undermined by participants' involvement in other programs. Programs for weight loss may be particularly susceptible— participants may have enjoyed the program and sought to be in another. Indeed, Graham *et al.* (1983) reported that clients pursued an average of three different types of treatments after their weight loss program. Interestingly, a significant relationship existed between maintenance and additional/alternate treatments. The more successful subjects were in maintaining weight loss, the more they had been involved in the additional programs.

In the follow-up of the treatment of night fears, 34 of the 40 original families were located. Of these, 31 were seen as having maintained their significant improvements. These data are limited by their self-report nature and by the absence of any way to eliminate the rival hypothesis of additional treatment.

Holroyd and Andrasik's (1982b) data indicated that the coping strategies taught to tension headache sufferers produced lasting gains that were superior to those produced by biofeedback. The suggestion that cognitive changes mediate reductions in tension headaches was discussed by Holroyd and Andrasik (1982a) and given additional support by their 3-year follow-up (Andrasik & Holroyd, 1983). In contrast,

Rickel *et al.* (1983) found initial support for their cognitive problem-solving training, but there were no significant behavioral training effects at the follow-up assessment.

Follow-up studies must attend to a methodological note of caution. It is likely that only a sample of the original group will be retrievable for the follow-up assessments. In such cases, the remainers and the defectors may be different in meaningful ways. To eliminate rival explanations of the data, it is methodologically sound to contrast the remainers and the defectors based on the initial data set. If it is found that the sample of remainers is not different from the defectors and that they are a representative subgroup of the initial sample, then it is sound to proceed to draw conclusions based on those who were participants in the follow-up. For instance, Holroyd and Andrasik's contacted clients did not differ from the noncontacted clients on demographics, personality features, or headache symptoms.

Is follow-up necessary in evaluating psychotherapy? This question serves as the title for a paper by Nicholson and Berman (1983). In addressing the question, the authors state that "the emphasis on follow-up is understandable" (p. 621), since improvements during therapy may not persist afterwards, there may be deterioration, or desired effects may not appear until after a "sleeper" period. However, these needs must be balanced against the costs of time, finance, and resources, the authors add. Nicholson and Berman proceeded to review outcomes and follow-ups to see whether the results differ at posttreatment as opposed to at follow-up.

The 67 reviewed studies involved individual adult therapy (or marital therapy) outcome reports published between 1960 and 1979 in which posttreatment and follow-up assessments were conducted. Nicholson and Berman also selected patient samples traditionally labeled as neurotic. (It would have been preferable that contemporary descriptors of the behavioral problems be employed.) Studies where subjects were paid for participation or recruited (for an experiment or from college classes) were not included.

Nicholson and Berman (1983) conducted a quantitative review of posttreatment and follow-up outcomes, using an assessment of effect size; they reported that follow-up data often add little to what is learned at the end of treatment and that, therefore, follow-up designs need not be used routinely. This suggestion was based on the findings that (1) outcome at posttreatment was correlated with outcome at follow-up, but unrelated to the length of the follow-up period; (2) differences between treated and control conditions did not change reliably over time for any of the types of therapy; and (3) there were no meaningful variations across types of disorders or types of dependent measures.

The data do support the fact that psychological therapies, for the studies of "neurotic" samples reviewed, produce durable gains. Much of the anxiety about the effects of therapy can be reduced by such supportive evidence. However, is it appropriate to go on to suggest that follow-up assessments may not be as essential as once thought? I think not. The prediction of a client's follow-up status, while predictable from gains at posttreatment, is not perfectly predictable. Might it not be exciting and worthwhile to seek to identify the features of patients, the treatment, the therapists, and other factors that can moderate this prediction? That is, what types of clients, therapists, or problems evidence strong posttreatment follow-up relationships, and which evidence weak or no relationships? These and other empirical questions require that continued attention be given to follow-up data.

Given the limited range of disorders examined ("neurotic"), the conclusions, as the authors acknowledge, must be restrained. This is true, but continued use of follow-up assessments will be necessary to determine at a later date that some disorders are not as likely as others to experience durable therapeutic outcomes. Since psychotic, antisocial, and addictive problems were not addressed, follow-ups in these areas will be needed for the data base for future investigations. A theme from developmental psychology has pertinence here: namely, cohort effects. Studies done during one decade may produce results different from studies done in another decade. For instance, studies of sex roles, family life styles, and perhaps the effects of therapy can vary due to cohort effects. A dramatic change in society toward a 100% genetic view of human behavior might precipitate unmotivated, non-therapy-seeking clients—and outcomes would be affected. Comparisons of the follow-up durability across types of disorders would necessitate that the data were derived from a similar cohort. New and (one hopes) improved treatments will be examined to test their efficacy against controls and against other already-documented therapies. Part of this comparison of relative effects must involve maintenance data, which are, of course, gathered via follow-ups.

Theoretically, we can stand to profit from comparisons of the processes and mechanisms that are involved in change during therapy and change during maintenance periods. Are change and persistence of change theoretically comparable? Can we, at this juncture, state with any confidence that theories of behavior change are equally compelling as explanations of the durability of behavior change? We do not want to overemphasize durability to the exclusion of other pressing questions, but we cannot afford not to mine the maintenance period as a source of interesting hypotheses and data related to theories, processes, and mechanisms of change. What I am arguing here is that we need not lessen the interest in follow-up, lest we decide prematurely that therapy effects are permanent effects. Follow-ups have provided the necessary data for the determination of the durability of therapy with "neurotic" cases, and we will, not doubt, be able to learn more with continued follow-up assessment.

Meta-Analyses

The interest in the debate about the statistical tool referred to as "meta-analysis" is evident in the "special topics" status that it has been assigned in two journals: The *Journal of Consulting and Clinical Psychology* (1983, *51*, 4–75) has set aside a large portion of its archival space, and the *Clinical Psychology Review* is offering an entire issue (in press) on the topic. Outside clinical psychology, in areas such as social and educational psychology, program evaluation, and methodology and measurement, there is parallel interest in the proper procedures and appropriate applications of meta-analytic techniques (e.g., Glass, McGaw, & Smith, 1981; Hedges, 1982; Rosenthal, 1983b).

In Volume 9's commentary, the second wave of meta-analytic studies was reviewed. The "second wave" refers to those studies that followed M. L. Smith and Glass (1977) but sought to refine and/or replicate their earlier conclusions. A third wave, although not a new wave, seems to be focusing on the application of meta-analytic methods using more circumscribed collections of studies (e.g., studies of self-statement modification with adults instead of all studies of psychotherapy). Associated with the present examination of this third wave is a consideration of the future of meta-analysis as applied in clinical psychology.

THE THIRD WAVE

Meta-analyses of more specific forms of clinical intervention have begun to appear as individual reports. That is, rather than examining the effect sizes of different types of therapy and coding the type of treatment to determine whether this feature moderates the size of the treatment effect, researchers have taken a more microscopic perspective and have begun to look for moderating influences *within* types of therapy. Two such studies have appeared in the recent literature, and both, probably due to the dominant interest in cognitive–behavioral therapy (both as a content area and as a treatment that receives much of the research evaluation), have examined some version of cognitive–behavioral intervention. In the report by Miller and Berman (1983),

48 studies using cognitive–behavioral treatments were examined. In Dush, Hirt, and Schroeder (1983), 69 studies that included some form of self-statement modification were included in the meta-analysis. Conclusions drawn from these studies, as well as the methodological features that affect the conclusions, are discussed here.

Miller and Berman (1983) were intrigued by the speculation of several theorists and clinicians that cognitive–behavioral therapies were superior to the behavioral (alone) therapies. Because these authors felt they were able to identify 48 studies with sufficient variability in the degree to which behavioral and cognitive–behavioral procedures were employed, they addressed the question. In addition, the authors compared the cognitive–behavioral treatments to other types of therapy, compared individual to group treatment, and considered the effects of drugs. According to Miller and Berman, they selected treatments in which "at least one component of the therapy specifically focused on the patient's maladaptive beliefs" (1983, p. 42). While it is true that modification of maladaptive beliefs can be seen as central to cognitive–behavioral therapy, one must point out and argue that other foci must be included within the cognitive–behavioral realm. However, it is perhaps the restrictions on journal space, as opposed to a rigid selection of studies based on treatment of beliefs, that led the authors to their qualifying statements. For instance, the authors add later that studies seeking an active restructuring approach were included. Effect sizes were estimated in terms of a comparison between cognitive–behavioral therapy and either a no-treatment control group or another form of treatment. Unlike the meta-analytic methods of M. L. Smith and Glass, these authors used the pooled within-group standard deviation, as opposed to the control-group standard deviation, as the "best estimate" of the population standard deviation (within the formula for calculating effect sizes).

According to the reported findings, the efficacy of the cognitive–behavioral therapies was greatest when the effect sizes were compared to those produced by no-treatment controls. Patients receiving cognitive–behavioral treatments also had better outcomes than patients receiving other treatments, though the effects were less differentiating when compared to other treatments than when compared to the no-treatment controls.

Of particular interest in this study was the extent to which therapies emphasizing behavioral techniques were more or less effective than techniques that were primarily cognitive. Pertinent results indicated that the cognitive–behavioral therapies with more or less emphasis on behavioral techniques produced comparable and nonsignificantly different effect sizes. In a similar vein, Miller and Berman also reported that in a subset of 13 studies in which cognitive–behavioral treatments were contrasted with systematic desensitization, the two treatments were not reliably different at posttreatment or follow-up. According to analyses of different types of disorders (i.e., depression, anxiety, somatic problems) and individual versus group administration of the treatment, the size of the treatment effect was not reliably different. The authors also reported no meaningful differences according to whether the subject sample consisted of either clinical cases or community/student respondents. (Such a conclusion carries with it the implication that studies with volunteer patients provide a reasonable test of the effects of the treatments with clinical cases.)

The readily apparent criticism that lumping cognitive–behavioral therapies together obfuscates the potentially meaningful differences between the several types of cognitive behavioral treatment is aptly directed at the Miller and Berman study. Yet, the authors themselves noted this concern and addressed it by pointing out that there are, to date, simply too few studies of each type of treatment for that to be a meaningfully coded characteristic of the analysis. Nevertheless, we must be cautious so as not to assume that all cognitive–behaioral therapies are alike; there are conceptual differences (see Kendall & Bemis, 1983; Kendall & Kriss, 1983).

Studies of "self-statement modification" were the specific target for the meta-analysis reported by Dush et al. (1983). These authors sought to examine the outcomes of cognitive–behavioral therapies reported in controlled clinical outcome trials. The question of inclusion-exclusion criteria was handled differently by Dush et al. than by some others. That is, Dush et al., like the initial M. L. Smith and Glass (1977) report, included all studies not selecting out those with methodological or design inadequacies. As noted elsewhere (e.g., Kendall & Norton-Ford, 1982; Mintz, 1983; Wilson & Rachman, 1983), meta-analysts have been criticized for including unsound studies in a cumulative report. Thus, Dush et al. may be equally culpable. However, these authors did code the methodological features of the studies and sought to determine whether such methodological features had a meaningful influence on the obtained effect size. The effort to evaluate methodological variability and its effect or outcome is satisfactory, but some studies may be so unsound as to be impotent in contributing to conclusions either in support of or in refutation of the outcomes of various psychotherapies.

Given the recent interest, it was not surprising that the matter of drugs versus psychotherapy for the treatment of depression has become the sole topic for a meta-analytic review. What is surprising, however, is that there are a sufficient number of good-quality studies on this question to qualify for a meta-analysis. Surprise aside, such a report was published by Steinbrueck, Maxwell, and Howard (1983). These authors sought to gather a comprehensive list of studies dealing with "psychotherapy," "drug therapy," and "depression." Several exclusion criteria narrowed the literature to studies of unipolar depression in adults. Some methodological exclusions were also made, such as the exclusion of studies without some type of control group. Studies where the treatment was a combination of a drug therapy and psychotherapy were not included. A total of 56 studies were examined, producing 31 psychotherapy effect sizes and 79 drug effect sizes.

Being aware of the early and accurate criticisms of meta-analyses, such as the evaluation of overly broad categories, Steinbrueck *et al.* (1983) coded 15 characteristics of the studies and correlated these characteristics with the effect sizes. The psychotherapies were coded (see Steinbrueck *et al.*, 1983, p. 857) into (1) cognitive, (2) behavioral, (3) marital, and (4) other. Thirty-five different pharmacological agents were among the medication treatments. The results produced effect sizes for drugs that averaged .61. The mean effect size for the psychotherapies was 1.22. This difference is statistically significant. To remove criticism that the drug group was overly broad, the authors examined the effect size for the subsample of studies employing tricyclics. This mean effect was .67, again significantly less than the effect size for the psychotherapies (see also p. 47 of Miller & Berman, 1983). Unfortunately, no more specific analysis of the psychotherapies was reported except for a multiple-regression analysis in which "type of therapy" produced the largest standardized regression weight, but it was nonsignificant.

Steinbrueck *et al.* (1983) concluded that studies of psychotherapy evidence greater treatment effect sizes that drug therapy studies in the treatment of unipolar depression in adults. Appropriately, the authors qualify their findings by noting, for example, that the conclusions drawn from the meta-analysis are only as good as the data presented in the original studies. Inadequacies in the initial studies cannot be overcome. However, the authors did not code the different types of dependent variables, and thus we are uninformed as to whether or not the effect sizes vary with regard to self-report versus clinician ratings. This information would be worthwhile in future reports.

ON THE FUTURE OF META-ANALYSIS

In any consideration of the future applications of a controversial methodology, there is obvious merit in first describing, even if at a rudimentary level, the procedures involved in the actual use of meta-analysis. Following this discussion, recommendations for future applications are offered (after Kendall & Maruyama, in press).

A Look at Procedures. Why is meta-analysis referred to as a "tool" for review of a body of literature? After all, aren't there already existing reviews that are nothing but meta-analyses? The answer is no. Meta-analysis is analogous to the methods and results sections of an empirical study. Without a good theoretical framework (i.e., an introduction) to guide an empirical study, and without a cogent discussion to interpret the findings, the value of the study decreases markedly. Similarly, before conducting a meta-analysis, one must develop a solid understanding of the studies to be included and a strong theoretical framework. In meta-analysis, studies (or dependent measures of studies) become observations; thus, in the way that in an empirical study one must decide how to "run" subjects, in meta-analysis one must decide how to analyze each study that is reviewed. In the same way that an experimenter would not run different types of subjects in different conditions, in meta-analysis the studies must be conceptually similar in order for them to be combined. In other words, unless the independent and dependent variables of the studies to be reviewed tap the same conceptual processes, meta-analysis is not appropriate. How broadly or narrowly "same conceptual processes" is defined is subject to interpretation, and there is some disagreement about how widely meta-analysis can be applied. Additionally, it is important to remember that meta-analysis reviews virtually never can claim random assignment of observations to conditions; it is difficult to imagine a body of literature in which studies are randomly selected from all studies that could conceivably be done. Findings from meta-analysis, therefore, can never be truly causal. Meta-analysis is a correlation–regression technique in which the selection of independent variables comes from theory and in which relations between independent and dependent variables at best suggest plausible patterns of causality. Meta-analysis is not an acceptable replacement for a traditional review. It can, however, be seen as a means of quantifying variables thought to be important conceptually in order to see whether those variables display expected relations with the dependent measures. If one decides to perform a meta-analysis, the following steps are involved (adapted from Kendall & Maruyama, in press; for a fuller description, see Glass, McGaw, & Smith, 1981).

1. A traditional review of all relevant studies is a necessary prerequisite. It provides the researcher with information about the methodological and conceptual variables that could be important. Such a review typically addresses a major research issue: For example, what are the effects of a certain therapy for treating a specific disorder?

The coding of and subsequent analysis of the relationship of "type of therapy" to the magnitude of the effect size is both laudable and laced with lunacy. On the praiseworthy side, *accurately* coding types of therapy is the only method available at this time to disaggregate the therapy effect size into meaningful units. However, inaccurate coding may be responsible for excessive and misleading conclusions. If a treatment is included as an indexed case of cognitive–behavioral therapy (typically based only on the title or brief description provided by the author in the space-restricted journal article), but in fact did not adhere to recognized procedures embraced by cognitive–behavioral therapists, then we have a very misleading mislabeling. A meta-analyst who knows only the effect sizes could proceed unwittingly toward producing inaccurate conclusions. A reader of the literature who has accomplished a careful examination of the target studies and who is aware of the accuracy or inaccuracy of treatment titles will, with access to effect size formulas and procedures, produce the more rewarding and meaningful conclusions.

Typically, questions are stated as "main-effect" predictions. Answers to these questions are quite interesting in their own right, but they tend to go against fundamental notions that the world is complex, and, in practice, there are virtually always a number of variables that have been conceptualized as qualifying such questions. For example, in assessing therapy outcomes, we are typically interested in different outcomes for different types of clients. Such "moderating" factors can be extracted, for example, from the introductory or discussion sections (and be based upon speculation or specification of others), or from the methods section (and be based upon the meta-analyst's interpretation of what is done) of articles, or from overall patterns that seem to emerge as the studies are reviewed. In the way that general research questions can be viewed as producing "main-effect" variables, these ancillary variables can be thought of as "control" variables or "interaction" variables. Finally, there is a third set of variables, which might be called the "Campbell and Stanley" variables (Campbell & Stanley, 1963). These are methodological weaknesses (sources of internal invalidity) that could affect findings of particular studies. For meta-analysis, these variables can be used as selection criteria or analyzed along with the "interaction" and "control" variables to define limits on the main-effect conclusions.

2. Once the variables to be recorded are selected (the features of studies that will be coded for disaggregation of the overall effect), one must review each study appropriately coding as many of the variables as possible. At this stage, reviewers should/may choose to exclude studies that they believe are methodologically faulty. The potential

predictor variables are coded as in any questionnaire or survey study, with different "levels" representing various values. The criterion or dependent measures can be coded in any of several ways (e.g., Hunter, Schmidt, & Jackson, 1982). Most simply, one can record whether or not there are significant differences, and, if so, the direction of the differences. This is often referred to as the "voting method," for each study or measure casts its vote as to the true nature of the effect. There have long been available formulas for pooling probabilities of independent events. As applied to research synthesis, this approach is called the "z-score method" (Stouffer's z scores; e.g., see Mosteller & Bush, 1954). It uses the probability level of each study to estimate overall probability of the studies reviewed. Finally, there is the method most commonly used, the "effect size." An effect size is a measure of the differences between the means of the various treatments expressed in standard deviation units. For example, an effect size of 1.0 would show that one condition exceeded another by one standard deviation. The effect size measure is affected less than the voting or z-score methods by sample size fluctuations, and yields a finding that is simple to interpret.

3. Following the coding of the studies, the researcher computes overall effects in the same way that any correlational data set is analyzed. One difference from most empirical studies is the importance of the grand mean test (which frequently is trivial, since departures of means from 0 are meaningless). The grand mean is the overall effect size. Researchers should report both overall findings (earlier referred to as main effects) and relations of all the predictor (interaction, control, and methodological) variables with the dependent measures—the effect size, z-score, or voting method measures (e.g., Johnson, Maruyama, Johnson, Nelson, & Skon, 1981).

4. The interpretation of the findings is the final step. Meta-analytic findings are correlational, so caution in interpretation is necessary. Findings are only suggestive, both because they may be artifactual (insofar as many study characteristics are interrelated and regression approaches cannot distinguish between predictors that are truly causal and predictors that are effects), and because findings may not hold true for future studies.

Recommendations. Researchers have become aware of the limitations of the meta-analytic methodology and improvements, refinements, and replications have appeared (e.g., see Volume 9 of the *Annual Review* for an overview and discussion). As the claims are tempered and the procedures enhanced, meta-analytic studies may contribute meaningfully to the future understanding of cumulative literatures. The following recommendations are offered to assist future meta-analytic efforts.

Quality Selection. Commentaries on the value and accuracy of meta-analytic reports have evidenced markedly different points of view. Two points of view can be contrasted.

"Garbage in, garbage out" describes the end of the continuum where studies with questionable or inferior methodology should simply be excluded from cumulative summaries. There is no substitute for good research, and one cannot mend, post hoc, methodological inadequacies. A study that is methodologically weak cannot contribute to the confirmation or refutation of a hypothesis. The number of studies available for a meta-analysis would be reduced by quality selection, but additional quality research will eventually provide answers.

"Let's test it and see" might describe the opposite end of the quality selection continuum. Here, it is argued that it is not necessarily clear that studies have flaws so damning as to require exclusion. In at least some cases, study weaknesses may only represent weaknesses from one vantage point but not from another. The "let's test it" position also contends that there may be some subjectivity in the exclusion of studies, whereas a nonexclusive stance would allow for an empirical evaluation of whether or not issues of quality are associated with variations in effect size. That is, specific methodological weaknesses (e.g., inappropriate control group) can be coded and examined. Any hypotheses the experimenter has about the consequences of methodological weaknesses ought to be made explicit. Once the information about quality is recorded, the quality variables can be used to see whether outcomes of "flawed" studies differ from outcomes of "sound" studies.

Recommendation 1: The future will perhaps best be served where major weaknesses are used to eliminate studies (basic flaws cannot be overcome), and where variations in other, less critical, methodological features are coded and their relationships to effect sizes examined.

Critical Features of the Study. Although the space crunch has forced journal editors to ask authors to condense methods and results sections, features of an individual study that have been carefully measured and quantified should be included so as to make them available to potential literature reviewers, meta-analytic or otherwise.

Not all of the critical features of a study are assessed. For example, consider variations in the *quality* of the therapy that is provided in the outcome study (quality of the therapy, not quality of the study's methodology as considered before). Quality has suffered from non-benign neglect. It is a dimension of therapy that requires assessment, quantification, and evaluation (Kendall & Hollon, 1983). If therapy, as provided as part of outcome research, can be taped and archived, then analyses of the tapes in terms of the quality of therapy can be accomplished. However, until some form of quantification of the quality of treatment is presented in the literature, the importance of this dimension in clinical outcomes cannot be estimated, and, consequently, its importance cannot be evaluated by meta-analytic techniques. It is quite paradoxical that the single dimension that may account for a substantial portion of variance in outcome, the quality dimension, has not been sufficiently quantified or evaluated.

Recommendation 2: Anticipate potent moderator variables, and assess and report them along with other data in therapy outcome research. Assess quality of therapy, and, perhaps, conduct evaluations of the effects of manipulations of treatment quality.

Clinical Significance. Meta-analysis, as is true for most outcome analyses in individual studies, concerns itself with change due to treatment in relation to change seen in controls. Comparisons employ statistical tests to examine significance, and change that is beyond chance levels is considered significant. Clinical significance focuses on the extent to which clients who are distressed before treatment emerge as nondistressed after treatment. "Nondistressed" refers to the fact that the disturbed subjects are no longer outside normal limits. Statistical evidence that change is beyond chance levels remains essential, but clinical significance adds new meaning to outcome reports. From this "clinical significance" perspective, it helps little to know that therapy improved patients one standard deviation or one-half of one standard deviation on the primary dependent measure. The data base for these measures of variability should be based on a representative sample of the full range of subjects. Meta-analysis can provide information about the clinical effectiveness of treatment, provided that norms exist on criterion measures. That is, if there is available a normed instrument that can be used to assess the targeted facet of adjustment, the logic of meta-analysis can be used to compare the client population with normals. Meta-analysis typically uses the effect size measure to contrast treatment and control-group means. The difference between these means is assessed in terms of standard deviation units, either of the control group or of the two groups pooled. If norms are available, however, the "normal" population norms can be used as the comparison group. One could compare the treated sample mean with the "normal" mean, expressed in normal standard deviation units. Similarly, the study control-group mean could be compared with the "normal" mean. This approach would involve computations such as $(\bar{x}_e - \bar{x}_n)/SD_n$, and $(\bar{x}_c - \bar{x}_n)/SD_n$, where $\bar{x}_c$ = control-group mean, $\bar{x}_e$ = treatment-group mean, $\bar{x}_n$ = normal population mean, and SD_n = normal population standard deviation.

Recommendation 3: Include consideration of the degree of change produced relative to normative distributions of scores on the dependent measures.

ON THE MEANING OF META-ANALYSIS

The phrase "meta-analysis" deserves some attention. Admittedly, this is an aside; I am nevertheless compelled to examine what this new phrase means. "Meta-," often seen as related to metaphysics, can mean "after," "beyond," "behind," or "change," as in "metamorphosis." In the case of "meta-analysis," the term means "beyond analysis." In a sense, this is misleading, since meta-analysis is not beyond analysis, but itself includes analysis and may be seen as a method of analysis. Perhaps "mega-analysis" is more felicitous, since it implies a vast and overriding analysis.

For psychologists, the meaning of meta-analysis may not have been seen as confusing. Perhaps, we were prepared by "metacommunication" and "metacognition." Nevertheless, "metanalysis" means something entirely different to William Safire, the reader-educated language specialist. Safire (1981) refers to meta-analyses as "simple misdivision of words" (p. 168). With good humor and clear image, Safire states, "The most saluted man in America is Richard Stans. Legions of school children place their hands over their hearts to pledge allegiance to the flag, and to the republic for Richard Stans" (p. 168). Safire adds other examples of wrong cuttings, such as the coveted journalistic award, the Pullet Surprise. I was immediately reminded of two different students who, on different writing tasks, unwittingly informed me of their lack of text reading when they cited Van Dura and Mike Enbaum.

FEAR REDUCTION METHODS AND THE TREATMENT OF ANXIETY DISORDERS

G. TERENCE WILSON

The literature on the behavioral treatment of anxiety disorders continues to burgeon. As in previous years, most of the research and the theoretical analysis focused on phobic disorders, especially agoraphobia, and, to a much lesser degree, obsessive–compulsive disorders. A particularly prominent theme this past year was the evaluation of the comparative efficacy of behavioral and pharmacological treatments of agoraphobia. The results of these different investigations bear importantly not only on the type of treatment that should be provided, but also on our understanding of the nature of agoraphobic disorders, as discussed below. Discussion of the applicability of controlled clinical outcome studies to general clinical practice, and of the overall clinical management of anxiety disorders in service delivery settings, has been a welcome feature of the behavioral literature during this past year. And on another positive note, the theoretical mechanisms in fear reduction have continued to receive critical attention.

PHOBIC DISORDERS

Evaluation of Treatment Outcome

Meta-analysis first appeared upon the treatment evaluation scene in 1977, when M. L. Smith and Glass published their widely cited evaluation of the effects of all forms of psychotherapy applied to a bewildering range of diverse problems. Meta-analysis is a statistical technique for summarizing and integrating a large number of different studies. According to M. L. Smith and Glass (1977) and other apologists of meta-analysis (e.g., Landman & Dawes, 1982; Rosenthal, 1983a; Shapiro & Shapiro, 1983), this statistical technique is said to be inherently superior to traditional, qualitative literature reviews. A consensually validated statistical method, meta-analysis aims to eliminate or at least to minimize the subjectivity and reviewer bias to which traditional "literary reviews" of the evidence are susceptible. It is argued not only that meta-analysis is fairer and more objective, but that it is more thorough and comprehensive than other methods of reviewing diverse studies. In sharp contrast to these ambitious and uncritical claims, meta-analysis in the evaluation of the effects of psychological therapies has not gone unchallenged (e.g., Erwin, 1984; Eysenck, 1983a; Wilson, 1982c; Wilson & Rachman, 1983). Despite these criticisms of the limitations and liabilities of meta-analysis, the technique has been increasingly employed in the evaluation of treatment outcome. Not surprisingly, given the large number of related studies, one area of application has been treatment outcome studies of agoraphobia (Andrews, Moran, & Hall, 1983).

Andrews et al. (1983) based their meta-analysis on 26 outcome studies that were published between 1956 and 1982, 1975 being the median year. These studies involved the treatment of some 850 agoraphobics, most of whom were women, most of whom had been treated as outpatients, and who had received an median of 17 hours of therapy over 4½ weeks and were assessed a median of 3 months later. The designs used in the 26 studies varied from retrospective examinations of case material to randomized controlled trials against patients on placebo or on a waiting list. The majority of studies were pre–post designs, subjects being measured before and at various times after treatment. A standard measure of improvement, or effect size, was calculated for each measure in each study following the procedure advocated by M. L. Smith, Glass, and Miller (1980).

Andrews et al. (1983) employed two strategies in an attempt to improve upon the inadequacies of the M. L. Smith et al. (1980) meta-analysis. First, they tried to correct for studies reporting several dependent measures having a disproportionate influence on the results of the meta-analysis: When multiple measures were reported, an upper limit of one effect size per 10 subjects or part thereof was imposed, in order that studies measuring large number of variables on small numbers of subjects did not have a disproportionate influence on the outcome of the meta-analysis. When calculating effect sizes from studies with multiple measures, preference was given to the most reliable measure taken at the longest times after the end of treatment. These rules of procedure resulted in a total of 79 effect sizes based on the outcome of 44 treatment groups. Second, in response to criticisms (e.g., Wilson & Rachman, 1983) that M. L. Smith *et al.*'s (1980) meta-analysis ignored the methodological quality of studies, Andrews *et al.* tried to code the methodological quality of their 26 studies and assess the effects of quality in an empirical (statistical) fashion. To this end they constructed a probity score for each group by summing scores across five variables deemed to relate to the probity of the study design: a clear description of method, less than 15% patient attrition between treatment and assessment, a treatment-to-assessment interval greater than 3 months, blind assessment of outcome, and judged validity of design. The mean effect sizes for the different measures were then weighted by these probity scores.

Most of the 26 studies evaluated the effects of some form of graded *in vivo* exposure treatment. Three studies evaluated the efficacy of pharmacotherapy (Sheehan, Ballenger, & Jacobsen, 1980; Zitrin, Klein, & Woerner, 1978, 1980). Parenthetically, Andrews *et al.* (1983) note their surprise at finding no trials of benzodiazepines, since "in our clinical experience virtually all the agoraphobics we have seen had been given benzodiazepines for their panic attacks. Furthermore, many had developed a mild, but chronic, dependence on these drugs which is difficult to treat." The clinical experience of these Australian investigators is no different from that of their counterparts in the United States. For example, Sheehan (1982) comments,

> [98% of the] patients seen in our unit for spontaneous panic attacks and multiple phobias had already received minor tranquilizers (benzodiazepines). Some had been taking these medications for many years, and almost 40 per cent had received major tranquilizers (antipsychotics, such as phenothiazines) before consulting us. Yet there is no published evidence that any of the widely used benzodiazepines are effective in the relief of panic disorder with phobias. (p. 158)

The results of this meta-analysis suggest that graded exposure was significantly more effective than placebo or waiting-list control groups. Similarly, the use of antidepressant medication appeared to be more effective than the control groups in these studies. A direct comparison of graded exposure and drug treatments at 1 to 12 months posttreatment, with the patients still receiving medication, indicated no difference. Since patients treated with antidepressant drugs usually relapse upon being taken off medication, as discussed below, this finding can provide little comfort to advocates of pharmacological treatment. Finally, strictly verbal forms of psychotherapy seemed no different from control conditions. Andrews *et al.* (1983) arrive at the following conclusion:

> On balance, therefore, it would appear that the graded exposure techniques are the treatments of choice, with the use of antidepressants being reserved for those unable or unwilling to confront their fears or for when behavior therapy is unavailable. Certainly, both treatments seem to offer better results than the symptomatic management of panic attacks by anxiolytics, treatment which has no support in the literature, but which is very commonly used.

Andrews *et al.*'s meta-analysis would, at face value, appear to provide support for the efficacy of graded exposure as the treatment of choice for agoraphobia. Indeed, the results of existing meta-analyses of the effects of psychological treatments consistently and unequivocally support the superiority of behavior therapy compared to alternative treatments such as psychodynamic therapies (Wilson, in press-b). Yet the inevitable difficulties that attach to this sort of meta-analysis make it difficult to interpret these findings. The behavioral treatments included in this analysis were a mixed bag. Why even bother with outdated and severely flawed retrospective studies (e.g., Marks & Gelder, 1965) when exemplary, well-controlled clinical studies (e.g., Gelder, Bancroft, Gath, Johnston, Mathews, & Shaw, 1973) were subsequently carried out? Even Andrews *et al.*'s (1983) commendable attempt to take account of the varying quality of different studies does not overcome the inherent problems of meta-analysis in this respect (see Wilson & Rachman, 1983).

Treatment Outcome Studies

LONG-TERM FOLLOW-UP OF
BEHAVIORAL TREATMENT OF AGORAPHOBIA

In volume 8 of this series, I summarized the results of four long-term (a minimum of 4 years) follow-ups of the treatment of agoraphobics in Britain and Holland (Wilson, 1982b). Another recently completed British study describes an 8-year follow-up of agoraphobics treated with behavioral methods, such as systematic desensitization and graded *in vivo* exposure (Burns, Thorpe, & Cavallaro, 1983). Of the 34 patients who were treated, 20 participated in the 8-year follow-up, which included a tape-recorded interview, questionnaires, and a standardized behavioral test. This careful and comprehensive assessment of outcome at long-term follow-up is an improvement over all previous studies.

The interviewer was one of the original therapists. Independent ratings of these interviews by an independent assessor yielded an interrater reliability coefficient of .74. The results are consistent with previous studies (e.g., Munby & Johnston, 1980). Treatment-produced improvement was maintained, although few patients "felt completely relieved of handicap." There was no evidence of symptom substitution; specifically, the interviews did not reveal evidence of emergent marital problems. To illustrate the level of functioning of these former patients, the mean rating of current anxiety and phobic avoidance on a 9-point scale (0 = no problem, 8 = severe pathology) was 2.65. Impairment in work, family roles, and leisure was rated as 2.25.

It is difficult to place much confidence in these results, in that they are based on just over half of these agoraphobics who had been treated. Although Burns et al. (1983) note that subjects who returned for the 8-year follow-up did not differ from the rest of the sample, the fact remains that the missing subjects might have fared more poorly and therefore might have eschewed further contact.

BEHAVIOR THERAPY VERSUS SUPPORTIVE PSYCHOTHERAPY

Several reviews of the literature have concluded that behavior therapy (based on some form of *in vivo* exposure) is the most effective psychological treatment for phobic disorders (Barlow & Wolfe, 1981; Mathews, Gelder, & Johnston, 1981; O'Leary & Wilson, in press). Klein, Zitrin, Woerner, and Ross (1983) have challenged this conclusion. They report the final results of a study comparing behavior therapy with supportive psychotherapy in the treatment of agoraphobics, mixed phobics, and simple phobics. (Preliminary results from this study [Zitrin et al., 1978] have long been reviewed in the behavior therapy literature, and the methodological criticisms that have been made need not be rehashed here.) All subjects in each of these conditions also received treatment with either imipramine or a placebo. This drug treatment comparison is analyzed in a later section in this chapter.

The major finding of this study, for present purposes, was that behavior therapy was not significantly superior to supportive psychotherapy on clinical ratings of phobic anxiety and avoidance. The authors point out that this was not because behavior therapy was ineffective; rather, it was because patients in the supportive psychotherapy condition did "unexpectedly well." The behavior therapy treatment in this study was mainly imaginal systematic desensitization. In addition, other techniques were used, such as relaxation and assertion training. Behavior therapists have been quick to argue that imaginal desensitization has been shown to be less effective than *in vivo* exposure. Had the more effective method been used, the argument goes, behavior therapy would have been more effective. Klein *et al.* consider and then reject this objection. They state that studies showing that the superior efficacy of *in vivo* over imaginal exposure methods have all been short-term, and "it remains to be determined whether any supposed superiority is qualitative or simply an acceleration of a comparable degree of effectiveness" (1983, p. 144). Furthermore, they cite their own earlier study, in which they retrospectively compared a group *in vivo* exposure treatment with a matched control group of agoraphobics who received imaginal systematic desensitization. Klein *et al.* claim that "Our results indicated that ten weeks of real-life exposure led to more rapid improvement, but that during 26 weeks the patients given individual treatment caught up and were entirely equivalent, in both proportion of patients whose conditions improved and degree of improvement" (1983, p. 144).

Behavior therapists have also argued that the supportive psychotherapy group might have been far more directive than intended. In other words, this instance of nonbehavioral supportive psychotherapy cannot be taken as representative of this approach as it is usually conceptualized. The absence of appropriate process measures makes it impossible to resolve this issue. The point does, however, underscore the importance of collecting data that will allow assessment of the integrity of the independent variables—namely, the degree to which treatments are implemented in accordance with their formal specifications (Kazdin & Wilson, 1978).

In their thoughtful commentary on their findings, Klein *et al.* (1983) consider the possibility that their particular treatment was dissimilar to supportive psychotherapy as it is customarily employed. They note that the same therapists conducted both treatments and that this "may well have engendered in them a more sympathetic, tolerant attitude toward the patients' self-initiated changes than might be the case for some dynamically oriented therapists, although the therapists were carefully briefed to avoid contaminating the supportive therapy with behavioral techniques" (p. 142). The likelihood that something along these lines occurred is increased by virtue of the fact that the patients knew that they were attending a prestigious clinic specializing in phobia treatment. Klein *et al.* comment that "It was our distinct impression that regardless of the specifically nondirective nature of the [supportive therapy], many patients approached their treatment with an obviously activist attitude. Conceivably, our patients may have been favorably impressed by the setting to the degree that even simple, nondirective supportive methods led to effective real-life attempts to confront the phobic situation repeatedly" (p. 144). Klein *et al.* also acknowledge the well-known proclivity of psychodynamic therapists to discourage *in vivo* exposure, since it is construed as "counterphobic acting out," or a "flight into health."

Klein *et al.* (1983) conclude that the results of their study are consistent with the therapy outcome literature in showing that there are no significant differences among psychological treatments. For phobic patients, they all achieve their effect by instigating "corrective activity" between therapy sessions in the form of *in vivo* exposure. If there are differences among treatments, they reduce to the theoretically uninteresting matter of rapidity of change. Undoubtedly, Klein *et al.* are right in observing that many forms of nonbehavioral therapies serve the instigating function they describe. But there are both practical and theoretical limitations to this analysis.

The first point that must be made is that not all psychological therapies, either deliberately or unwittingly, encourage or instigate some form of *in vivo* exposure. Klein *et al.* themselves note that such a tactic is often proscribed in the more traditional psychodynamic therapies. (This issue of whether there exists a genuine commonality among diverse therapeutic approaches with respect to instigating outside learning is taken up more fully in Volume 8 of this series; see Wilson, 1982a.) To the extent that nonbehavioral therapies ignore or even discourage *in vivo* exposure, they will be relatively ineffective at best, counterproductive at worst. On a practical level, this would appear to be an obviously important dimension for differentiating among effective and ineffective therapies.

A second point that can be made in connection with Klein *et al.*'s analysis raises a more fundamental issue. Since it is agreed that some form of corrective activity (*in vivo* exposure) is central to overcoming phobic disorders, surely it then makes sense to use the most efficient (behavioral) methods for accomplishing this task. Moreover, these methods would ideally be those that follow logically from theoretically sound conceptualization of the effective ingredients in exposure treatment. Klein *et al.* correctly reject an explanation of exposure in terms of reciprocal inhibition. But they fail to acknowledge that current conceptualizations of fear reduction processes and exposure treatment are quite different (Bandura, 1977; O'Leary & Wilson, in press). They err in dismissing behavioral treatments as mere "persuasive devices" that are fundamentally no different from the persuasive devices of other forms of therapies. In contemporary behavior therapy, exposure methods are used within a systematic theoretical framework. A social learning or cognitive–behavioral conceptualization provides guidelines for how exposure treatment might be optimally implemented. Moreover, these guiding considerations differ from those that follow from alternative views (e.g., a simple habituation model). This last point was discussed in greater detail in Chapter 3 of Volume 9 in this series (Wilson, 1984b).

For example, the social learning perspective (one that includes but also goes beyond self-efficacy theory) recognizes that there is no isomorphic relationship between behavioral accomplishments, as during *in vivo* exposure practice, and the cognitive processing of these events. Clients with emotional disorders typically show distortions in the way in which they process personally relevant events. These cognitive distortions might undermine the therapeutic effects of exposure. A social learning approach provides a framework for understanding and correcting the problems produced by self-defeating cognitive processing. Explicit therapeutic attention to clients' subjective interpretations of success and failure experiences during *in vivo* exposure practice is often necessary in sustaining motivation and preventing relapse following treatment. If behavioral techniques are only persuasive devices, they seem to be devices that are usually effective in addressing these therapeutic concerns.

BROADENING THE TREATMENT BASE

Although it can be concluded that systematic exposure methods are superior to alternative forms of psychological treatment, behavior therapists are well aware of the limitations of existing methods. For example, Barlow, O'Brien, Last, and Holden (1983c) estimate that roughly 25% of agoraphobics fail to benefit from exposure treatment. And of the remaining 75%, many make only limited improvements, and few ever reach the stage where they are completely free of at least periodic anxiety symptoms. This latter point is made clear by long-term follow-ups, as noted above in regard to Burns *et al.*'s (1983) results.

One approach to improve upon our current rate of success is to broaden the range of behavioral treatment for agoraphobics. Indeed, it is clear that behavioral practitioners have long been using a multifaceted approach in treating agoraphobia, in which *in vivo* exposure is usually only one component (Lazarus, 1981; O'Leary & Wilson, in press). Estimates of therapeutic success such as Barlow *et al.*'s (1983c) are based on controlled outcome studies that mainly evaluated the effects of some form of exposure treatment. Does a broader treatment approach produce better results, as Lazarus (1981) and others have long asserted? If Goldstein's (1982) results are any indication, the answer would seem to be yes.

Goldstein (1982) has reported the outcome of 34 successive agoraphobics treated at his phobia clinic at Temple University Medical School. Treatment, using the approach described by Chambless and

Goldstein (1982), involved an intensive 2-week program that included 10 daily travel groups of 3 hours each, four 1½-hour group psychotherapy sessions, two 1½-hour "significant other" groups, two 2-hour couples group sessions, and four 1-hour individual sessions. Each 2-week program group was composed of six to eight clients. Aside from the intensive exposure sessions, treatment included cognitive restructuring, teaching of anxiety-coping skills, breath control for hyperventilation symptoms, and "Gestalt techniques, to use the highly charged exposure circumstances to facilitate the process of forming associations from anxiety states to whatever antecedent events might be connected to the fears" (Goldstein, 1982, p. 191). No drugs were used. Several clients availed themselves of additional individual and group treatment following the 2-week program.

At posttreatment (the end of the 2-week program), only two clients (6.25%) failed to show any improvement. Another 22% were completely free of agoraphobic symptoms (including no panic attacks). This proportion increased at the succeeding follow-ups as follows: 34.9% at 3 months; 58.9% at 6 months; and 71.4% at 1 year. All other subjects were rated as moderately to much improved at each assessment period following treatment. The number of clients assessed at these last three follow-ups were 26, 19, and 7, respectively. Goldstein also reports significant improvement in other areas of the clients' functioning, such as depression and obsessive thinking. The apparent elimination of panic attacks in the majority of clients without any medication is noteworthy.

The usual reservations about an uncontrolled clinical series apply to Goldstein's (1982) results. As he is quick to caution, the small number of clients at the longer follow-up points (due to the preliminary nature of this report rather than to confirmed dropouts) is especially limiting. Nonetheless, this report does suggest that the findings of controlled studies of briefer and more limited interventions may provide too conservative an estimate of the actual clinical success that can be obtained with a multifaceted treatment program that is largely but not exclusively behavioral in composition.

Among the more common methods behavior therapists use to complement *in vivo* exposure in the treatment of complex phobic disorders are assertion training and different forms of cognitive restructuring. Emmelkamp, van der Hout, and de Vries (1983) assigned 21 unassertive agoraphobic patients to one of three treatments: (1) prolonged exposure *in vivo*, (2) assertiveness training, and (3) a combination of assertiveness training and prolonged exposure *in vivo*. Treatment-specific effects were found, with exposure reducing phobic anxiety and avoidance and assertion training improving assertiveness at posttreatment and a 1-month follow-up. Since agoraphobics tend to be unassertive (Chambless, Hunter, & Jackson, 1982; Fisher & Wilson, in press), assertion training might be a useful component of behavioral treatment programs.

As reviewed in Volumes 8 and 9 of this series (Wilson, 1982b, 1984b), several studies have failed to show any benefit of adding self-instructional training or rational restructuring to *in vivo* exposure in the treatment of phobic disorders. Yet another study failing to show the value of self-instructional training was reported by Ladouceur (1983). He showed, predictably by now, that participant modeling was more effective than a placebo condition in treating simple phobics. Combining self-instructional training with participant modeling did nothing to enhance outcome at posttreatment. And at a 1-month follow-up, this combined group showed significantly more phobic avoidance and less self-efficacy than the group that received participant modeling alone. Ladouceur suggests that self-instructional training might have distracted subjects and interfered with the cognitive processing. It is not clear how this might have occurred, but this result is in line with the observation that I have made before in this series (e.g., Franks & Wilson, 1977) that combining two treatments in a controlled outcome study often results in inferior results to those obtained with either treatment alone.

A more positive note about adding cognitive methods to exposure treatment was struck by Mavissakalian, Michelson, Greenwald, Kornblith, and Greenwald (1983b). They assigned 26 agoraphobics to either a self-instructional training or a paradoxical intention treatment that consisted of 12 weekly 90-minute group sessions. All subjects were also instructed to practice self-directed, prolonged exposure *in vivo* between sessions. Both treatments were carried out by the same therapist.

At the end of treatment, the paradoxical intention group showed greater improvement on some measures of agoraphobia than the self-instructional group. This difference disappeared at the 6-month follow-up, due to the continuing improvement of the self-instructional group. The tendency for phobics treated with cognitive restructuring to continue improvement after the end of therapy was also noted by Emmelkamp and Mersch (1982; see Volume 9 of this series).

Since both cognitive treatments were confounded with instructions for self-directed exposure, an effective intervention in its own right, it is difficult to interpret the success of both groups as evidence for cognitive methods. Nevertheless, Mavissakalian *et al.* (1983b) make the plausible argument that the different rates of improvement between the two treatments indicate a specific cognitive effect. Paradoxical intention produced the more rapid change, and effect Mavissakalian *et al.* (1983b) suggest is consistent with its logic of being a confrontative experiential technique that immediately focuses clients' attention on the most feared consequences. Self-instructional training, they argue, is more rational and deliberate, and requires time to practice and master.

A useful methodological feature of this study was the recording of subjects' verbalizations as they participated in a standardized behavioral avoidance test at each assessment period. Both treatments produced similar reductions in verbalizations that were coded as self-defeating. However, neither treatment resulted in an increase in positive, coping statements. Mavissakalian *et al.* (1983b) stress the importance in future studies of direct assessment of cognitive changes if conclusions are to be drawn about the putative effects of specific cognitive strategies.

As a final comment, one can question the designation of paradoxical intention as a "cognitive–behavioral" technique. Of course, labeling treatment techniques always involves some arbitrary decision, and this frequently complicates evaluation of therapy outcome (see Rachman & Wilson, 1980). Paradoxical intention would seem to involve an important affective dimension and could be said to be aimed directly at a primary emotional change in a way that differs from the hypothesized indirect action of self-instructional training on emotional responding. What is important is the systematic evaluation of a promising technique, such as Mavissakalian *et al.* (1983b) have provided.

MARITAL ADJUSTMENT IN THE TREATMENT OF AGORAPHOBIA

The effects of marital adjustment on response to treatment in agoraphobics, as well as the reciprocal interaction (see Wilson, 1984b) continue to be an important focus of investigation. The most detailed and systematic research program on this topic has been that of Barlow and his group at the Phobia and Anxiety Disorders Clinic at the State University of New York in Albany. Barlow *et al.* (1983c) have reported the initial results of a study in which women agoraphobics were treated alone or with their husbands. The program consisted of 12 weekly 60- to 90-minute group sessions of what the authors describe as "self-initiated, graduated, exposure treatment combined with instruction in panic management procedures, as well as cognitive restructuring combining the use of coping self-statements, paradoxical intention, and, in general, methods that obviated cognitive avoidance of fear" (p. 110). In the couples training group, each husband was asked to attend all sessions and to accompany his wife at least once, but no more than twice, during the week on the assigned practice.

On the usual 9-point rating scale, the mean improvement for the 28 patients, based on an average of the therapist and independent assessor's clinical ratings, was 2.36. Barlow *et al.* (1983c) point out that this represents the usual improvement registered by behavioral studies. Of the subjects, 68% were said to have shown substantial clinical improvement, as defined by a change in at least 2 points on this scale. Barlow *et al.* (1983c) note that this success was achieved without therapist-aided exposure, making the treatment more cost-effective. However, it should be stressed that this self-directed exposure was carried out under the intensive and weekly supervision of therapists. The same research group has shown that simply providing clients with a treatment manual without regular therapist contact is ineffective (Holden, O'Brien, Barlow, Stetson, & Infantino, 1983).

Although the differences were not always statistically significant, there was a clear and consistent trend for the couples training group to show superior improvement across a wide variety of measures, compared to the group that did not involve spouses in treatment. Effects of treatment showed little change in well-adjusted marriages (defined by a score above 100 on the Locke–Wallace questionnaire), but marked increases in marital satisfaction in the couples training treatment if the marriages were poor to begin with. An intriguing finding shows that in well-adjusted marriages, patterns of improvement (clinicians' rating of phobia) were the same. However, in the poorly adjusted marriages, the group that did not involve spouses showed less improvement than the couples training group. Barlow *et al.* (1983c) conclude that the inclusion of the husbands in treatment appeared to override the negative effect of bad marriages.

The latter finding must be viewed cautiously, as it is based on small numbers and a single outcome (clinical rating) measure. Nonetheless, the results as a whole argue strongly for the desirability of couples training for agoraphobics. Explanation of how it is that couples training exerts a beneficial effect, especially in poorly adjusted marriages, must await studies of detailed interactions between spouses on an ongoing basis.

Among the most methodologically deficient and consistently criticized studies on marital adjustment and the behavioral treatment of agoraphobics have been Hafner's (1976, 1977). In a reanalysis of Hafner's 1977 study, Hafner and Ross (1983) use statistical techniques to identify predictors of outcome. Of relevance here is Hafner's conclusion that husbands' questionnaire scores at posttreatment were the major predictors of their wives' outcome over the next 6 months. Specifically, the more vigorous and friendly the husbands were, the less well their wives fared. In a manner characteristic of Hafner's previous idiosyncratic analyses of this study, Hafner and Ross are able to interpret the husbands' friendliness and vigor as a reflection of their "capacity . . . to deny aspects of their negative feelings" (1983, p. 381). One wonders how these ill-fated husbands would have been viewed had they been unfriendly and passive. Beyond these uninformative data, Hafner and Ross offer their clinical observation that husbands who acknowledge the impact of their wives' changes on themselves are most likely to facilitate the maintenance of improvement. Most therapists would presumably concur with this sentiment.

BEHAVIORAL VERSUS PHARMACOLOGICAL TREATMENTS

Increasingly, there appears to be a consensus that behavior therapy (*in vivo* exposure) and pharmacotherapy (imipramine) are the two most effective approaches for treating agoraphobics. Several controlled studies evaluating the separate and combined effects of these two types of treatment have been recently published. One of the major research centers in this regard is the Phobia Clinic at the University of Pittsburgh School of Medicine. In one report, Mavissakalian and Michelson (1983a) compared the effects of four different methods in the treatment of agoraphobics. *in vivo* flooding; imipramine; a combined flooding and imipramine method; and a control condition, consisting of therapeutic rationale and instructions for self-directed *in vivo* exposure between treatment sessions, that was common to all therapeutic groups. The self-directed exposure condition produced marked improvement in 33% of the cases, but was inferior to the other three treatments, which, in turn, did not differ among themselves. The latter treatments produced overall improvement rates ranging from 66% to 84%. Although imipramine had a significantly greater effect on mood (e.g., depression, panic, anxiety) earlier in treatment, at posttreatment the flooding and imipramine treatments did not significantly differ on measures of either mood or agoraphobic outcome.

In a second report, Mavissakalian and Michelson (1983b) analyzed the behavioral diary data from the 49 agoraphobic subjects in the study described above. Contrary to the authors' expectations that the control condition would show the poorest record of self-directed exposure between sessions, neither the number nor the duration of weekly homework activities discriminated among the four treatment groups. Nor was there any difference in terms of these self-recorded homework activities between the most and the least successful patients. (The latter distinction was made in terms of a composite score comprising severity as judged by clinician and patient, clinical ratings of phobic anxiety and avoidance, and behavioral avoidance measures.) Subjective ratings of anxiety during homework activities did discriminate among the treatments and the most and least successful groups. In other words, this pattern of findings suggests that therapist-directed flooding and imipramine, respectively, enhance the therapeutic improvement produced by the same amount of self-directed exposure between sessions.

Mavissakalian and Michelson (1983) report that they obtained reassuringly high rates of compliance with instructions for self-directed exposure in their subjects. It is always possible, however, that these self-ratings are unreliable. Such inaccuracy might militate against showing differences among treatments or between successful and unsuccessful patients. Assuming, however, that the data are reliable, how does one explain the action of therapist-directed flooding and imipramine in decreasing subjective anxiety during self-directed exposure, which was significantly associated with greater therapeutic improvement? Mavissakalian and Michelson (1983b) appeal to Lader and Mathews's (1968) notion that habituation of anxiety reactions is facilitated by lowered levels of autonomic arousal. Imipramine has been shown to block panic reactions (Liebowitz & Klein, 1982), and Mavissakalian and Michelson (1983) suggest that the drug might lower autonomic arousal so as to promote habituation. As for therapist-directed flooding, the authors suggest that the therapist's presence provides a "more favorable cognitive set" and thereby enhances emotional processing (habituation?) of fear. They fail to indicate exactly what this cognitive set might be and how such a set would facilitate emotional processing. As discussed below, Telch, Teaman, and Taylor (1983) suggest that such a cognitive mechanism might be.

In a third study by the Pittsburgh group, Mavissakalian, Michelson, and Dealy (1983a) randomly assigned 18 agoraphobics to treatment with imipramine alone or imipramine plus programmed *in vivo* exposure. The behavioral component of the combined treatment method entailed sessions with a clinical psychologist for detailed, systematic instructions and reinforcement for self-directed *in vivo* exposure practice. Treatment lasted for 12 weeks. Results at posttreatment clearly showed the significant superiority of the combined treatment over imipramine only. These differences were evident on the Marks and Mathews (1979) fear questionnaire, as well as on clinician and patient ratings of severity of disorder, the Hamilton Depression Ratings Scale, and mean ratings of panic. As the authors conclude, these data support the "clinical argument that agoraphobics treated with imipramine require additional behavioral treatment for phobic avoidance and anxiety" (p. 352).

The question that must be asked of this set of studies is whether they provide support for the use of imipramine in the treatment of agoraphobia. Mavissakalian *et al.* (1983a) emphasize that "clinical research has clearly established the usefulness of both MAO [mono-

amine oxidase] inhibitors and tricyclic antidepressants in the treatment
of agoraphobia" (p. 348). This assertion is questionable (see below)—
and at odds with the conclusions of other reviewers of this literature
(e.g., Emmelkamp, 1982; Marks, 1981). Moreover, these authors' own
results pose problems for such a bald assertion of imipramine's efficacy.
In the Mavissakalian and Michelson (1983a) study, imipramine did
enhance the effects of self-directed *in vivo* exposure. While this finding
does support the value of the drug, it should be recalled that flooding
produced comparable results. More specifically, imipramine did not
produce greater changes in measures of mood at posttreatment than
strictly psychological treatment (flooding). The rationale for using
imipramine is that it has specific "antiphobic" properties. As such it is
said to reduce the primary problem in agoraphobia—namely, spontaneous panic attacks (Klein *et al.*, 1983). Phobic anxiety and avoidance
are allegedly secondary reactions that may then be treated with behavioral methods. Mavissakalian and Michelson's (1983a) failure to
find differences in measures of mood at posttreatment is inconsistent
with this explanation of the drug's effects.

The problem identified above is even more evident in the Mavissakalian *et al.* (1983a) study. One of the considerable strengths of this
group's research program has been the comprehensive and detailed
process and outcome measures they have reported. For example, they
directly assessed panic, as defined in DSM-III, through detailed patient
self-reports. Although analyses of within-treatment change showed
significant reductions in measures of panic for both groups, the combined imipramine plus behavioral treatment produced the most improvement. Assuming that their measure of panic is valid, and previous
studies of pharmacotherapy have failed to provide a better measure, this
finding is problematic for the theory that imipramine has a unique or
specific effect on panic. The authors themselves comment that

> the fact that 60–70 percent of agoraphobics are treated successfully with
> exposure methods indicates that pharmacological suppression of panic
> attacks is not necessary in the majority of patients. Furthermore, successful
> elimination of panic attacks in agoraphobics treated with behavioural
> methods poses a serious problem for the conceptualization of panic as
> primary and phobic anxiety or avoidance as secondary. Indeed, one can,
> from a strictly behavioural perspective, consider the so-called "spontane-
> ous" panic attacks as n^{th} order generalization of phobic anxiety to
> internal, cognitive stimuli. (p. 352)

This last point must be underscored. It is simply false to declare, as
Sheehan (1982) does, that behavioral treatments affect only avoidance
behavior and do not change "other sectors of the symptom cluster (e.g.,

spontaneous anxiety attacks)" (p. 157). Several well-controlled studies (see below), as well as the results of clinical practice (e.g., Goldstein, 1982), clearly show that broad behavioral treatments reduce most dimensions of the agoraphobic's problems, including panic attacks.

Perhaps the most frequently cited findings in support of the efficacy of imipramine are those obtained by the New York group of Klein and Zitrin and their colleagues. Zitrin, Klein, Woerner, and Ross (1983) have recently published the final data from their study that had previously been reported in part (Zitrin, 1981; Zitrin et al., 1978). This most recent publication confirms previously reported results and reaffirms the authors' conclusions about the efficacy of imipramine. Briefly, imipramine was found to be significantly more effective than a placebo in the treatment of those phobic patients (agoraphobics and so-called mixed phobics) who suffered from spontaneous panic attacks. There was no difference between the drug and placebo in simple phobics who did not experience panic attacks.

Analyses of the strengths and weaknesses of this study have also previously appeared in the literature (e.g., Marks, 1981; Mathews et al., 1981; Wilson, 1982b), and the latest publication by the New York group does little to alter the implications of these past critiques. A major limitation of the Zitrin et al. (1983) study, as previously pointed out by Marks (1981) and others, and particularly relevant to the discussion of the Mavissakalian et al. (1983a) study above, is the absence of a direct measure of panic attacks. More recently, Emmelkamp (1982) has criticized the New York group's conclusions. He suggests that with "218 patients involved in the study, it is not surprising to find statistically significant differences between groups" (p. 15). Emmelkamp then proceeds to make the case that while they were statistically significant, the differences between the imipramine and placebo groups were "clinically unimpressive." In redrawn graphs of the data, Emmelkamp argues that "both placebo and imipramine groups improve along the same line and that the statistical difference found between both conditions is far from clinically significant" (p. 150). This particular criticism is all the more relevant, in that Zitrin et al. (1983) defend their choice of dependent measures for statistical analysis in terms of their presumed clinical significance.

A well-controlled, data-rich study by Marks, Gray, Cohen, Hill, Mawson, Ramm, and Stern (1983), which improves greatly on the methodology used by Zitrin et al. (1983), provides a searching evaluation of the relative merits of imipramine and in vivo exposure in the treatment of agoraphobics. A total of 72 agoraphobics were randomly assigned to imipramine or placebo treatment conditions for 28 weeks. All patients also received systematic self-exposure homework with an instruction manual. In addition, half of each drug group had therapist-aided exposure and half had therapist-aided relaxation, each totaling 3 hours. Of the initial sample of 72 subjects, 45 completed the treatment and a follow-up at the end of 1 year. Multiple measures of outcome and drug effects were taken throughout treatment and at weeks 35 and 52.

Agoraphobics in both the imipramine and placebo conditions improved substantially and maintained this improvement at week 52. Improvement was observed on measures (ratings) of agoraphobia; self-ratings of anxiety and panic; and ratings of global improvement, depression, and spontaneous panic attacks. Therapist-aided exposure significantly increased the effects of instructions for self-directed exposure. Not a single significant therapeutic effect of imipramine was found, including direct measures or self-rating of spontaneous panic. The impact of these strongly negative findings is underscored by Marks et al.'s demonstration that satisfactory plasma levels of imipramine were obtained, together with significantly greater side effects in the imipramine condition. Furthermore, the vast majority of these patients had experienced spontaneous panic attacks during the week before treatment began, indicating that they were a suitable sample for demonstrating putative pharmacological effects.

Several factors might explain the striking discrepancy between the results of the Marks et al. (1983) study and that of Zitrin et al. (1983). Beyond such methodological issues as the nature and method of measurements (in terms of which the Marks et al. study is superior and arguably more credible scientifically), the obvious variables in evaluation of pharmacotherapy involve the dose and the schedule of administration of the drug. In their commentary on the London and New York studies, Matuzas and Glass (1983) make a number of relevant observations. Both studies used a flexible dose schedule. Marks et al. (1983) increased the dose to a mean high of 158 mg daily at week 14; at week 26 the mean dose was 110 mg daily. In contrast, Zitrin et al. (1983) increased the dose more quickly to 150 mg and increased it further to 300 mg if panic attacks continued. The maximum dose in the London study was 200 mg. At week 26, at posttreatment in the New York study, the mean dose was 204 mg daily for the agoraphobics and slightly higher for the mixed phobics. It is impossible to rule out the possibility that the higher doses in the Zitrin et al. (1983) study might have contributed to the different outcomes. In view of other lines of evidence that are inconsistent with the argument for tricyclic treatment of agoraphobia, the view taken here is that the onus is on proponents of this approach to demonstrate that a specific variable, such as dose, can account for the negative outcomes obtained by Marks et al. (1983) and others (see below).

In another comment, Matuzas and Glass (1983) point out that in the London study, imipramine patients were evaluated at week 14 when treatment was still ongoing, and then again at week 28 when the drug had been discontinued. In contrast, Zitrin *et al.* assessed their patients at posttreatment (26 weeks), at an optimal time for showing maximal drug effects. This would seem to be a weak attempt to account for the negative findings in the London study, for a couple of reasons. Marks *et al.* anticipated such an objection by emphasizing that their patients showed "no trace" of drug-produced improvement at week 14:

> We think it unlikely that such effects would have occurred by week 26 even had we been able to persuade them to take higher doses of imipramine beyond week 14. Their reluctance to take the medication is a drawback to such treatment. Furthermore, we question the value of a drug that might take four months or more to start showing its effects when effective exposure treatment for the same condition requires merely three to eight sessions spread over one to eight weeks. (1983, p. 160)

Marks *et al.* suggest that imipramine might be effective in the treatment of those agoraphobics who are also depressed. This postulated mechanism of action of the drug is indirect. It reduces depression, an outcome that, in turn, has favorable effects on agoraphobic problems. This is the pattern of findings that Marks, Stern, Mawson, Cobb, and McDonald (1980) found with obsessive–compulsive disorders (see Wilson, 1982b, for a summary of this research). Given the current evidence, it would be difficult to sustain this explanation of imipramine's effects. Zitrin *et al.* (1983) argue against it, noting that there was an inverse correlation between depression and outcome in their drug study. Furthermore, both Sheehan *et al.* (1980) and McNair and Kahn (1981) reported that the antiphobic effects they obtained were independent of their patients' levels of depression.

One final comment on the Marks *et al.* (1983) study is in order. These investigators report that during the 26 weeks following the end of therapy, 15 (33%) of the patients received additional treatment. Of these 15, 7 had been treated with imipramine; 8, with placebo; 8, with therapist-aided exposure; and 7, with relaxation. Five received further therapist-aided *in vivo* exposure, while the other 10 received treatment with imipramine. That agoraphobics who have improved significantly during behavioral treatment seek and receive additional treatment during long-term follow-up appears to be commonplace (e.g., Munby & Johnston, 1980) and must be taken into consideration not only in evaluating the results of controlled clinical outcome studies, but also in actual clinical practice (Wilson, 1983).

Of the drug versus behavioral treatment studies discussed above, only the Mavissakalian *et al.* (1983a) investigation evaluated the effects of imipramine without some form of *in vivo* exposure treatment. In the Mavissakalian *et al.* (1983a) study, for agoraphobics treated with imipramine only, a within-group analysis showed clinical improvement across almost all of the measures, yet this improvement was substantially less than that observed in the imipramine plus *in vivo* exposure treatment. And, in the absence of a placebo control condition, the improvement of the imipramine-only group cannot be unequivocally attributed to the drug itself. (Parenthetically, the authors of this study attempt to justify the exclusion of such a control group on the unacceptable grounds that it is unnecessary, since the efficacy of imipramine is established.) Fortunately, Telch (1982) has completed a comparative outcome study that does permit evaluation of the independent effects of imipramine. Thirty-seven agoraphobics were randomly assigned to the following conditions: (1) imipramine alone, (2) imipramine plus *in vivo* exposure, and (3) placebo plus *in vivo* exposure. To control for the effects of exposure, subjects in the imipramine-alone condition were given counterpractice instructions, which emphasized the importance of refraining from entering phobic situations for the first 8 weeks so that the medication would have time to take effect. The *in vivo* exposure treatment consisted of a total of 9 hours of therapist-assisted group exposure spread over 3 consecutive days, followed by a partner-assisted home-based exposure method described by Mathews *et al.* (1981). Subjects and their partners were provided with slightly modified versions of the Mathews *et al.* treatment manuals and were required to meet in small groups with their partners for four 90-minute weekly sessions to discuss their progress with home practice. Particular emphasis was given to helping couples overcome obstacles for home practice.

Multiple behavioral, self-report, and physiological measures of outcome showed that the imipramine-only treatment produced no improvement on any index of phobic anxiety or avoidance. Imipramine did, however, reduce depression. In contrast, the two exposure groups resulted in marked improvements on measures of phobic anxiety, phobic avoidance, self-efficacy, panic, and depression. Comparisons between the combined imipramine–exposure and placebo–exposure conditions revealed a slight advantage for the combined imipramine–exposure group, although these differences reached statistical significance only for phobic anxiety. These data indicate that impraine, in the absence of some form of exposure treatment, has little therapeutic effect for agoraphobics. The drug may act to facilitate exposure, as previously suggested by Mavissakalian and Michelson (1983b). The finding that imipramine significantly decreased depression without any observable influence on phobic anxiety or avoidance provides additional evidence against the hypothesis that the drug has a therapeutic effect with agoraphobics who are depressed.

Telch *et al.* (1983) provide an incisive critical review of the use of antidepressant drugs in the treatment of agoraphobia that will prove useful to both the researcher and the clinician. Rejecting the theory that imipramine has a specific antiphobic action, Telch *et al.* propose another mechanism of action of the apparent facilitative interactive effect of imipramine and exposure treatment. (It should be emphasized that the therapeutic effect of imipramine, where it has been empirically demonstrated, is, as Marks *et al.* [1983] put it, "globally patholytic rather than merely antiphobic" [p. 161]. Anxiety, depression, and other related psychopathology seem to be altered. Proposed theoretical mechanisms of imipramine's action must be addressed to this global effect.) Telch *et al.* (1983) assume that the therapeutic action of imipramine is mediated through its effects on depressed mood. They then suggest two ways in which depression might hinder treatment. The first would involve depression's well-known effect in decreasing compliance with homework assignments (see Marks *et al.*, 1980). The second is what Telch *et al.* call the "dysphoria-induced efficacy inhibitory hypothesis." They speculate that depressed mood will interfere with the cognitive appraisal of behavioral accomplishments in a manner that undermines the development of self-efficacy *à la* Bandura's (1977) social learning theory. The problem with this position, however, at the outset, is that the available evidence, including Telch *et al.*'s own study as indicated above, simply does not encourage such a view. These authors fail to address this obvious and troubling inconsistency in their review.

Leaving aside Telch *et al.*'s attempt to explain imipramine's putative effects via a reduction of depressed mood, their suggestion about the inhibitory influence of depressed mood on the cognitive processing of efficacy information raises interesting possibilities about understanding the interaction between depression and the treatment of phobic disorders. They argue that the negative self-statements that accompany depression undermine processing of efficacy information. Rather than specific self-statements, it is more likely that depressed mood creates an emotional state that is relatively inaccessible to mood-incongruent input (e.g., successful accomplishment of therapeutic tasks; see Bower, 1981, Rachman, 1983c, and Teasdale, 1983, for details and therapeutic implications of the role of mood in cognitive processing). Most of the literature on this topic has focused on the difficulty of accessing mood states with verbal (rational) therapies. It is commonly assumed that one of the reasons for the greater efficacy of performance-based treatments is that this type of experience does access mood states and then alter them through emotional processing (e.g., Rachman 1983c). Although performance-based information is more effective than verbal persuasion in affecting emotional processing, it is reasonable to suppose that even information derived from this level of experience will be less effective in modifying the central mediating states underlying fear and fear reduction. This seems particularly true of self-efficacy theory, with its critical emphasis on cognitive appraisal of events.

Telch *et al.* (1983) conclude their review with some cautions regarding the clinical use of imipramine. First, they reiterate the reality that many agoraphobics dislike—and avoid—pharmacotherapy. For example, Telch (1982) found that almost 20% of all agoraphobics who contacted the clinic expressed an unwillingness to take medication and thus were not accepted into the study. Further evidence for this limitation of drug treatment comes from Norton, Allen, and Hilton's (1983) study of the social validity of treatments for agoraphobia. Both a nonpatient group and a group of agoraphobics rated psychological procedures as more acceptable, and perceived them to be more effective, than drug treatment. Graduated *in vivo* exposure received the highest ratings on both dimensions. Antidepressant medication was rated as the least acceptable treatment. Although the implications of social validity studies of therapies for actual clinical practice are necessarily limited, Norton *et al.*'s findings, together with Telch's clinical experience, must be seriously considered in planning treatment services for the full spectrum of agoraphobic patients.

Second, adverse physical side effects of drug treatment must be taken into account. These side effects are undoubtedly a cause of the relatively high rates of attrition associated with drug treatment. According to Telch *et al.* (1983), "drop-out rates from the antidepressant trials published to date consistently average between 35 and 40%, well above the mean of 10% for drug-free behavioral treatments" (p. 516). (Marks *et al.*, 1983, report an attrition rate of 36%; the comparable figure for behavioral treatment studies conducted by this group is 16%.) This phenomenon, together with the refusal of many agoraphobics to enter into pharmacotherapy in the first place, means that a nontrivial number of agoraphobics must necessarily be treated with psychological methods. It also means that the success rates of pharmacotherapy with agoraphobics, whatever they are, are based on a somewhat select sample of patients.

The third caveat that must be issued about the use of antidepressant medication with agoraphobics concerns the problem of relapse. Relapse rates when patients are withdrawn from imipramine are unacceptably high and predictable. Telch *et al.* (1983) estimate that this relapse rate ranges from 27% to 50%, and Jansson and Ost (1982) use the figure of 40%. It is important to realize that assertions of the utility of imipramine in the treatment of agoraphobia (e.g., Klein *et al.*, 1983; Mavissakalian *et al.*, 1983a; Sheehan, 1982) are all based on immediate posttreatment evaluations. Empirical data on the lasting value of pharmacotherapy for agoraphobia do not exist. Clinical guidelines about how long medication should be continued appear to be unacceptably vague. Sheehan (1982) recommends that "If a patient has had a satisfactory period of stability, the drug may be discontinued after six months to a year" (p. 158). Matuzas and Glass (1983) refer to continuation of medication "for a period of time after the initial control of symptoms" (p. 221). Compare this unsatisfactory state of affairs with the mounting evidence that the therapeutic benefits of behavioral treatment are maintained 4 to 9 years after termination of treatment (Munby & Johnston, 1980; see Volume 8 of this series). Moreover, the durable—albeit the less than optimal—effects of behavioral treatment are not achieved at the expense of an initial treatment effect that falls short of that obtained with imipramine, as Matuzas and Glass (1983) erroneously suggest. As discussed above, the better-controlled studies have thus far failed to show that imipramine produces improvement on phobic anxiety, panic, or avoidance that is not at least matched by behavioral methods.

To summarize this section, a clear pattern has emerged. In general, studies indicating that antidepressant drugs are effective in the treatment of agoraphobia have been completed by avowed proponents of this approach (e.g., Klein *et al.*, 1983; Sheehan *et al.*, 1980). Behavioral researchers have found mainly negative results, and behavioral reviewers of the literature have arrived at far more negative evaluations of the evidence (e.g., Mathews *et al.*, 1981; Telch *et al.*, 1983). Emmelkamp (1982), in his recent book, has added yet another negative assessment of pharmacotherapy. Aside from underscoring the problems of side effects, attrition, and high relapse rates with imipramine, Emmelkamp claims that the drug effects that have been shown are small and clinically insignificant. He also points out a potential methodological problem with these drug studies that has not received much attention:

> . . . although most studies were double-blind, it is questionable whether patient and assessor were really unaware which drug the patient received. The side effects associated with this drug were more often reported in the drug condition as compared with the placebo condition. Several studies demonstrate that "blind" raters could correctly guess which drug the subject received 63–100% of the time (Solomon & Hart, 1978). The only

study that checked whether the assessor was truly "blind" found no significant difference between tricyclic and placebo (Marks *et al.*, [1983]). (Emmelkamp, 1982, p. 154)

Proponents of pharmacotherapy will not be persuaded by Emmelkamp's (1982) critical review any more than they have by previous negative evaluations of the existing literature. Future studies, which ideally will incorporate the methodological rigor of the better behavioral investigations and respond to the clinical concerns of pharmacotherapists, will be necessary to take us beyond the present situation.

Theoretical Mechanisms

IS EXPOSURE A NECESSARY CONDITION FOR FEAR REDUCTION?

In the parallel chapter to the present in Volume 8 of this series (Wilson, 1982b), I discussed de Silva and Rachman's (1981) paper that non-reinforced exposure to fear-eliciting stimuli may be a sufficient but not a necessary condition for the elimination of fear and phobic reactions. In response, Boyd and Levis (1983) have argued that this conclusion is premature and unwarranted. They claim that to heed de Silva and Rachman's call for systematic investigation of the factors responsible for fear reduction in the absence of exposure amounts to abandoning conditioning principles. de Silva and Rachman do not advocate the abandonment of conditioning principles, but they do point out that acceptance of the view that exposure is not a necessary condition for fear reduction would call for an extension or modification of conditioning theory. As I have noted previously, this would not be that novel, since social learning theory, with its particular emphasis on cognitive mediating processes, explicitly predicts that fear reduction can be achieved through both exposure and nonexposure methods (Wilson & O'Leary, 1980).

But what of Boyd and Levis's rebuttals to de Silva and Rachman's six sources of evidence in support of their thesis? Two major points they make are unhelpful. The first is that critics of the "exposure is necessary" position must demonstrate not only the absence of exposure to CSs, but also of "any external or internally elicited CS exposure both within and outside the experimental setting" (Boyd & Levis, 1983, p. 144). As de Silva and Rachman (1983) observe in their rejoinder, this demand has the effect of making conditioning theory incapable of disproof and hence of little value. The second defense marshaled by Boyd and Levis is the expansion of the concept of "exposure." Here it would be well to define what is reasonably described by this increasingly popular term. It refers to "planned, sustained and repetitive evocations of images/image sequences of the stimuli in question. Mere thoughts or fleeting images do not constitute imaginal exposure in this sense" (de Silva & Rachman, 1981, p. 227). Boyd and Levis assert that exposure incorporates "mediated generalization" from other fears, unidentified "internally elicited CS," self-verbalizations, "relabeling of past threatening situations," and even becoming aware of repressed impulses. At this degree of dilution, it is hard to disagree with de Silva and Rachman's contention that the concept has lost much of its utility. What is needed is both the continuing analysis of the extinction process, as Boyd and Levis note, and increasing research on nonexposure means of fear reduction.

One of the studies that called for the recognition of nonexposure methods was that of Jannoun, Munby, Catalan, and Gelder (1980), as discussed in Volume 8 (Wilson, 1982b). This group found that a problem-solving treatment, involving no identifiable exposure to fear-producing stimuli, was as effective as *in vivo* exposure in treating agoraphobics. More recently, however, Cullington, Butler, Hibbert, and Gelder (in press) have reported a failure to replicate this finding. Contrary to Jannoun *et al.* (1980), Cullington *et al.* (in press) conclude that problem solving is not as effective as planned *in vivo* exposure, and that "the hypothesis that exposure is a necessary condition for the treatment of agoraphobia still stands."

SELF-EFFICACY THEORY

Bandura's (1977) self-efficacy theory continues to generate both research and debate. An unusually thorough and thoughtful analysis of this theory has been completed by Lee (1983a). Among the issues she has addressed in the course of a series of logically related studies are those of the differential accuracy of efficacy expectations and behavior as predictors of subsequent performance, and the respective roles of efficacy and outcome expectations in predicting behavior.

A critical assumption of the theory is that efficacy expectations are better proximal predictors of future performance than overt behavior. Bandura has reported several studies that provide evidence for his position (e.g., Bandura, Adams, Hardy, & Howells, 1980; Bandura, Reese, & Adams, 1982), but Lee (1983a) argues that they can all be criticized on methodological grounds. More specifically, she suggests that Bandura's microanalytic technique is statistically inappropriate and that a correlational analysis is called for (see also Kirsch & Wickless, 1983). A study of the effects of assertion training (Lee, 1983b) showed that both self-efficacy and previous tests of assertive behavior were accurate predictors of assertiveness, but that behavior was superior.

Lee attributes this result to the influence of other variables that impinge on the relationship between efficacy and behavior. As Bandura (1977) has made clear from the outset, self-efficacy is said to determine behavior, given adequate skills (ability) and sufficient motivation to perform. Lee discusses how difficult it is to ensure that the latter two conditions are satisfied when one is working with the interpersonal phemonena involved in assertiveness. In addition, she states, "Although Bandura does not specifically mention the accuracy of feedback in his analysis of the development of efficacy, it seems clear that learning about one's ability through performance accomplishments and vicarious experience, and developing efficacy expectations on that basis, requires accurate and consistent feedback" (1983a, p. 173). Indeed, Bandura and Cervone (1982) have since stressed the importance of goals and feedback about performance in developing accurate efficacy expectations. Feedback on the effects of assertiveness, as well as its desirability, is likely to be variable. In a second study (Lee, 1983a) using a nonsocial target behavior in which skill level, motivation, and feedback could all be determined, efficacy expectations were superior to past behavior as predicted by the theory.

Several critics have argued that it is difficult if not impossible to separate efficacy from outcome expectations in Bandura's scheme of things (e.g., Teasdale, 1978). Others have claimed that outcome expectations alone might predict behavior without the need to invoke the construct of self-efficacy (Kazdin, 1978a). Carver and Scheier (1981) take the position that outcome expectations are more important in determining behavior, and that what Bandura refers to as "efficacy" is one component of outcome expectations. In two experiments, one on assertiveness and the other on fear of snakes, Lee (in press-a, in press-b) found that efficacy and outcome expectations were correlated, but that efficacy expectations alone were better predictors of outcome than were outcome expectations alone or an additive or multiplicative combination of the two. The view that outcome expectations might predict behavior either better than or independently from efficacy expectations received no support.

Lee (1983a) points out that since outcome expectations were highly correlated with performance, therapeutic methods should be designed to alter both efficacy and outcome expectations. Fear reduction methods such as participant modeling do just this. She adds that it would "be interesting to compare the effects of different behaviour change techniques on efficacy expectations, outcome expectations, and behaviour to examine further the roles played by these cognitions" (1983a, p. 209).

Rachman (1983d) has suggested what he describes as fresh possibilities for the modification of agoraphobic avoidance behavior. Two of these possibilities are a self-efficacy analysis, for which evidence already exists (Bandura *et al.*, 1980), and "therapy by disconfirmation." By the latter, Rachman refers to Seligman and Johnston's (1973) analysis of the extinction of avoidance behavior in terms of disconfirmation of outcome expectations. This emphasis on outcome expectations can, as Lee's (1983a) results show, be profitably incorporated into the general framework of self-efficacy theory.

Barrios (1983) obtained mixed evidence for self-efficacy theory in the treatment of heterosexual anxiety. The absence of the predicted relationship between efficacy expectations and changes in physiological arousal could, as Barrios explains, be attributed to measurement considerations rather than the theory itself. Rachman (1983b), in the course of his program of research on fear and courage among military bomb disposal operators, also reports limited support for self-efficacy theory in predicting levels of fear.

COGNITIVE PROCESSES IN ANXIETY

The importance of cognitive processes in anxiety and its modification is, of course, fundamental to Bandura's social learning theory and other cognitive–behavioral conceptualizations of anxiety disorders (e.g., Beck, 1976). Butler and Mathews (1983) have reported the results of an investigation of cognitive processes in anxiety that was guided by previous research on depression. The influence of cognitive structures (schemata) on depressed moods is a major topic in both experimental and clinical approaches to depression (e.g., Beck, 1976; Bower, 1981; Teasdale, 1983). And the research of Tversky and Kahneman on judgmental heuristics and their impact on assessment of risk and outcome (see Nisbett & Ross, 1980, for the extension of this pioneering research to social cognition and personality) has begun to filter into the behavior therapy literature (e.g., Meichenbaum & Cameron, 1982; Rachman, 1983c; Wilson, 1984a). Butler and Mathews looked for the possible role of danger schemata in anxiety.

Consistent with the view that judgments of the risk of an event are thought to be influenced by judgmental heuristics such as availability of cognitive representations of such events, Butler and Mathews found that anxious patients were more likely than nonanxious controls to interpret ambiguous material as threatening. They also rated the subjective cost of threatening events as higher than did controls. Also, anxious patients have a higher subjective probability for negative threatening events, if those events are predicted for themselves rather than for someone else. Less consistent with their hypothesis of a distinct "danger schema" was the finding that depressed patients showed the same reactions as anxious patients, with the exception that the former indicated less discrepancy between ratings for self and others than did the latter.

The clinical implications of this line of thinking are clear. Activation of "danger schemata" will make the retrieval of previous anxiety-eliciting events more probable and will increase the probability that anxiety will be aroused, due to the relatively strong link between the cognitive representations of emotional states and mood-congruent events. These schemata will also be less accessible to the more objective, rational interpretations (verbal persuasion) of therapists—or even the feedback from actual *in vivo* exposure, as mentioned earlier in this chapter. A clinical example of this phenomenon would be the agoraphobic who vividly remembers the details of a previous panic attack in a particular setting while "ignoring" (being less able to access memories discrepant with the danger schemata?) other occasions on which no panic occurred (Wilson, 1983). These schemata would also be consistent with other clinical phenomena, such as agoraphobics' discounting positive experiences in the manner of depressed patients.

Given the operation of these cognitive processes in anxiety disorders, Butler and Mathews suggest that coping strategies must be taught in a way that "links them with the cognitions concerning danger and anxiety. One solution would thus be to deliberately invoke anxiety during treatment and then teach cognitive coping methods under these conditions" (1983, pp. 61–62). One can go further in speculating that the operation of such hypothesized danger schemata makes the full rationale and procedures of Beck's cognitive–behavioral approach as directly applicable to anxiety disorders as they are to depression.

Although this research on cognitive processes in anxiety is discussed here in the section on phobic disorders, the issues involved are directly relevant to all of the anxiety disorders, and may be especially useful with respect to developing more effective methods for treating generalized anxiety disorders.

Clinical Considerations

The Royal Australian and New Zealand College of Psychiatrists has initiated a project to develop treatment outlines for various psychiatric disorders. They recently published a treatment outline for agoraphobia, an outline that was developed by a project team and an expert committee on agoraphobia (Andrews, 1982). Although the outline has not yet been accepted by the College, it is likely to have an important influence on continuing education and peer review in these two countries. It is also important in another sense. Currently, the American Psychiatric Association has charged several task forces with evaluating the treatment of specific disorders. One of these task forces is on phobic and anxiety disorders. It is likely that this publication will have significant impact on peer and possibly third-party review in the United States. It is worth examining the Australian and New Zealand document to see what can be learned from such a process.

As part of the project, practicing psychiatrists in Australia were surveyed. They were asked to indicate preferred treatment for agoraphobia and to provide treatment plans for three cases of varying complexity. Of the 193 psychiatrists who were approached, an impressive number of 165 (85%) responded. Verbal psychotherapies and graded exposure were ranked first as recommended treatments; tricyclic antidepressants were ranked last. This latter finding is surprising, in view of the popularity antidepressant drugs appear to have with psychiatrists in the United States. The Australian psychiatrists, however, seem to concur with evaluations of the public in North America, as described in a preceding section.

Based upon the results of this survey, a review of the empirical literature (the Andrews *et al.*, 1983, meta-analysis discussed in the beginning of this chapter), and the views of the expert committee, the treatment outline shown in Figure 3-1 was developed. This outline should prove useful to practitioners, and it is notable for the extent to which it is based on the use of behavioral and cognitive–behavioral methods. As for MAO inhibitors and imipramine, the outline states, "Although not at present a treatment of first choice they can be important in the treatment of difficult cases and in the treatment of people who do not wish to participate in a behaviour therapy program" (Andrews, 1982, p. 31).

Several chapters of Foa and Emmelkamp's (1983) book on treatment failures in behavior therapy are relevant to anxiety disorders. With respect to agoraphobia, Emmelkamp and van der Hout (1983) looked at reasons for clients' either refusing treatment or dropping out of therapy. Of 25 consecutive referrals who declined treatment, 16 responded to a questionnaire. The answers were not especially informative, particularly in view of the small, possibly unrepresentative sample. Roughly half of these clients reported that they had already improved, suggesting less than candid responses. Others expressed a fear of treatment. As in the rest of Emmelkamp and van der Hout's investigation, their findings are based on clients response to their

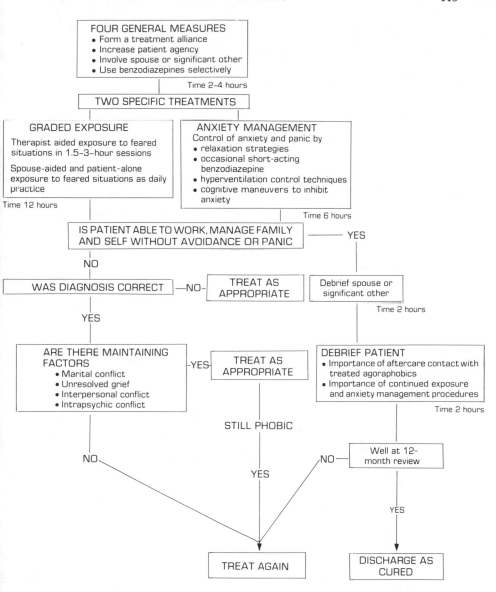

FIG. 3-1.

Flow chart of steps in the treatment of agoraphobia. (From "A treatment outline for agoraphobia" by G. Andrews, 1982, *Australian and New Zealand Journal of Psychiatry, 16,* 25–33. Copyright 1982, Royal Australian and New Zealand College of Psychiatrists. Reprinted by permission.)

particular treatment approach—mainly a standardized, group, prolonged exposure treatment, sometimes preceded by cognitive restructuring. The extent to which their results apply to other methods can only be guessed at.

Of the 15 clients who had dropped out of the treatment program, only 8 responded to a questionnaire. The authors' conclusion that more attention should be paid to individualizing treatment stands, regardless of these sketchy post hoc enquiries. In a third study, 16 agoraphobics were classified as treatment successes or failures. The 5 failures had changed by less than 3 points of the 9-point clinical rating scale of improvement (see above). Neither assertiveness nor depression was related to outcome. With such a small sample, and without knowing the range of depression and lack of assertion involved, these results cannot be easily interpreted. Clients' complaints of marital problems were related to treatment failure.

Another conclusion Emmelkamp and van der Hout reach is that the therapist–patient relationship is of paramount importance. This question is discussed more fully in Chapter 8. If suffices to state here that while this might be the case, it certainly does not follow from the data the authors present in this connection.

In their chapters on flooding and the treatment of social anxiety respectively, Marshall and Gauthier (1983) and Marzillier and Winter (1983) stress the importance of an adequate assessment of the presenting problem and the need to tailor treatments to individuals' needs. There is nothing new or surprising here. Marshall and Gauthier indicate that they try to involve a spouse or family member in flooding treatment. They also engagingly describe an example of the failure of adequately preparing a client (a spider phobic) and the therapist for flooding: "As soon as [the client] saw the insect she began to scream very loudly and fled from the room, much to the dismay of those in the building who witnessed the episode, not to mention the embarrassment we experienced or the distress of our hapless client" (1983, pp. 89–90).

OBSESSIVE–COMPULSIVE DISORDERS

From Research to Clinical Practice

A perennial theme in the behavior therapy literature has been the debate over the clinical value of analogue research (e.g., Borkovec & Rachman, 1979; Kazdin, 1980b; Rachman & Wilson, 1980). Although analogue research is invaluable in its own right, particularly in elucidating theoretical mechanisms in fear and fear reduction, there is a clear consensus that we need studies of clinical populations that address the concerns of practitioners (Barlow & Wolfe, 1981). Largely overlooked in this debate over laboratory versus clinical research has been the crucial question of generalizability of the findings of controlled clinical research to actual clinical practice in service delivery situations. In terms of the framework outlined elsewhere (Wilson, 1982a), this is the problem of moving from level 3 research to level 4 clinical practice.

The problem can be stated quite simply. Most controlled clinical studies are conducted in medical school or university settings that differ from routine service delivery settings in many important ways. The clients might be "real patients" in that they seek help for severe clinical disorders. But they are often screened for one purpose or another, and some are excluded from the study. Naturally the extent of selection varies from one study to another, but the fact that some selection takes place places obvious limitations on the external validity of the results. Too many outcome studies have not made clear exactly what screening procedures have been employed, making it all the more difficult to know how representative the subjects were of the broader patient population.

The therapists are usually highly trained or under constant supervision. They and the primary investigators are committed to completing the project successfully; they are enthusiastic and optimistic. The research "team" provides social support, guidance, and help in troubleshooting the inevitable problems that arise. There is not the time urgency most practitioners confront. Then there is the potentially reactive effect of the various assessment and measurement procedures in enhancing the so-called "nonspecifics" of therapy. The average therapist in routine clinical practice typically cannot count on any of these advantages. How effective, then, are the methods evaluated in controlled clinical studies when they are applied in routine clinical practice under conditions that are far less than optimal?

Some clinical outcome studies are designed with the goal of generalizing the findings to routine clinical practice in mind. In Volume 5 of this series, I used as an example of this two outcome studies by Kent and O'Leary (1976, 1977) on the treatment of conduct disorders in children (see Franks & Wilson, 1977, p. 245). The intervention was explicitly designed with the feasibility of its implementation by general practitioners in mind.

A pertinent example in the present context is the Klein *et al.* (1983) study described in the preceding section on evaluation of treatment outcome. As discussed there, the supportive psychotherapy in this study was almost certainly unrepresentative of what the average psychodynamic practitioner is able or willing to provide. As pointed out above, Klein *et al.* comment on how the provision of this therapy at a publicized clinic specializing in phobias resulted in specific expectations on the part of patients, which appear to have led them to actively attempt *in vivo* exposure practice between sessions. The therapists themselves may have been unwittingly encouraging of such "behavioral" intervention, especially as they also carried out the behavior therapy in this study. Removed from this teaching hospital setting, without the trappings of research, and without the osmotic influence on the therapists of applying behavior therapy as well as supportive psychotherapy, the supportive or psychodynamic psychotherapy practiced by the average therapist in routine clinical contexts is probably quite discriminable from the particular method that was implemented in the Klein *et al.* (1983) study.

The thrust of the foregoing observations argues for systematic research on the transferability of methods and results from controlled clinical outcome studies to actual clinical practice in different service delivery settings. This step has also been referred to as the dissemination of research findings. Little has been done in behavior therapy on this topic. It is for this reason that Kirk's (1983) paper on the behavioral treatment of obsessive–compulsive patients in routine clinical practice is instructive.

Kirk (1983) describes the treatment of 36 consecutive referrals to a National Health Service Clinic in England. In many ways this sample was similar to those treated in research studies (Rachman & Hodgson, 1980), although there were also differences. One such difference was the higher proportion of patients with pure obsessions than has been the case in controlled trials. The patients described by Kirk also had received less previous treatment. As for treatment, there was less time for therapist-assisted *in vivo* exposure. But there was a heavy emphasis on homework assignments, and patients were taught anxiety-coping skills more frequently than has been the case in controlled studies, which have focused mainly on exposure and response prevention methods. Of the 14 patients with obsessions who completed treatment, 11 were treated with thought stopping. Graded exposure was used in 7 cases, and relaxation training was used with 11 patients. All patients received support, encouragement, and reinforcement for homework assignments. In many cases the treatment was brief. Thus 19% had less than 5 sessions, and 58% received less than 10 sessions.

Outcome was reported in the form of global improvement ratings based on patients' self-recordings and therapists' judgments. Three-quarters of the sample were rated as moderately improved or better. Only 2 patients remained unchanged, and none became worse. Of the 16 patients with obsessions, 12 were rated as "goal achieved"; another was moderately improved. Kirk (1983) notes that this figure of 81% improved is far more favorable than outcomes in controlled studies (see Rachman & Hodgson, 1980). An examination of hospital files to see whether the patients sought subsequent psychiatric help, covering a period ranging from 1 to 5 years, indicated that in 81% of the cases there was no evidence of further contact. Five cases had been referred back for more behavioral treatment for obsessive–compulsive problems, and one had received antidepressant medication.

Taken on face value, these results are more encouraging. Not only do they suggest that the results of the controlled trials are a reflection of what is achieved in routine practice, but they even paint a brighter picture as far as obsessional patients are concerned. The success of thought stopping—Kirk describes it as successful in all patients with whom it was used—is surprising in view of previous evidence. The widespread use of relaxation training, a procedure that was used essentially as a placebo control condition in the studies of Rachman, Hodgson, and Marks at the London Institute of Psychiatry, is also surprising. Finally, the global outcome measure used requires caution in interpreting these results. Subsequent uncontrolled clinical series of this kind are called for in helping to uncover the generalizability of the methods and results of controlled clinical studies to actual practice. Their value would be still further increased if more reliable and specific measures were included, as suggested by Barlow (1980).

Analyses of Treatment Failures

Foa, Grayson, Steketee, Doppelt, Turner, and Latimer (1983a) have reported the results of a detailed analysis of predictors of success and failure in the treatment of obsessive–compulsive disorders. They examined the data from 50 patients who had been treated in their program. These patients had participated in different treatment outcome studies that had evaluated the effects of three main treatment methods alone or in combination: *in vivo* exposure, imaginal exposure, and response prevention. The details of these methods, as well as the various outcome measures, have been spelled out in previous publications by Foa and her colleagues. Suffice it to note here that the outcome measures were based on the ratings of 45-minute interviews by two independent assessors. The familiar 9-point rating scales were used.

Using a composite score of change in both obsessions and compulsions, 58% of the patients were classified at posttreatment as much improved (i.e., an improvement of at least 70%); 38% as improved (i.e., an improvement of 31%–69%); and 2% as failures. At follow-up the comparable figures were 59%, 17%, and 24%. Although Foa *et al.* (1983a) comment that patients who received both imaginal and *in vivo* exposure fared better than those who received only *in vivo* exposure, differences between groups did not reach statistical significance. A correlation of .49 was found between outcome at posttreatment and at follow-up. Patients rated as much improved maintained their improvement. Patients who were only moderately improved showed unstable patterns of functioning during follow-up.

These results are most encouraging, given the recalcitrance of obsessive–compulsive disorders to previous forms of therapy. One wonders, however, about combining the evaluation of obsessions and compulsions into a single score. In view of evidence that behavioral treatments have been less successful in modifying obsessions than compulsive rituals (Rachman & Hodgson, 1980), separate assessments of these two problems might have been informative.

Foa *et al.* (1983a) identified several variables that were related to outcome. The process variables of reactivity and habituation to feared stimuli within and between sessions were all negatively related to outcome. "Reactivity" in this context refers to the highest subjective anxiety level reported during the session in which patients were first exposed to their most feared stimulus. "Habituation within sessions" was defined as the percentage of change between the highest level of anxiety reported in response to the first presentation of the most feared stimulus to the lowest level reported during the same session. "Habituation between sessions" was defined as percentage change in self-reported anxiety from the highest level in response to the first presentation of the most feared stimulus in the fifth or sixth session to the highest level in response to the same stimulus in exposure session 10.

Pretreatment level of depression was also negatively related to treatment outcome. This finding is consistent with the results of other outcome studies (e.g., Rachman, Cobb, Grey, MacDonald, Mawson, Sartory, & Stern, 1979). By using path analysis, an innovative approach to identifying predictors of outcome, Foa *et al.* (1983a) concluded that depression exercised its negative effect via its positive association with reactivity, which, in turn, impairs habituation. Initial severity of obsessive–compulsive symptoms was not related to outcome. Foa *et al.* (1983a) plausibly attribute this surprising finding to the fact that they only included severely distressed patients in their treatment studies in the first place. This latter fact makes their results all the more promising.

Rachman (1983e) also addressed the question of failures in treating obsessions and compulsions. He begins by stating flatly, "The main obstacle to the successful treatment of obsessions is the absence of effective techniques. Fruitful contemplation of the causes of therapeutic failures can be undertaken only against a background of successes" (p. 35). This observation on therapeutic failures in general can be contrasted with other approaches that attempt to ferret out reasons for failure even in the absence of unambiguous evidence of efficacy. For example, Strupp and Hadley (1979) demonstrated that their psychoanalytically oriented psychotherapy was no more effective than a comparison "treatment" in which clients (students) met regularly with sensitive and caring professors without any therapeutic training. Nevertheless, the Vanderbilt group then proceeded to make a variety of internal analyses of these data in an effort to isolate reasons for success and failure. These post hoc analyses are, at best, simply suggestive of lines of future research. They cannot establish what it is about this form of psychodynamic therapy that accounts for success or failure in the absence of a demonstration that there is success to be explained.

Rachman's (1983e) discussion of clinical failures in the behavioral treatment of obsessive–compulsives covers some familiar ground. Thus he notes that inadequate assessment may result in failure. Robertson, Wendiggensen, and Kaplan (1983) emphasize the need for carrying out a complete behavioral analysis of presenting problems and for tailoring different methods to problems of the individual. Although this clinical wisdom cannot be disputed, it still remains unclear how much these individual analyses further treatment success. Among other problems discussed by Rachman (1983e), compliance (resistance) figures prominently. Some patients refuse behavioral treatment. Others accept treatment but adhere poorly or irregularly to the therapist's instructions, particularly with respect to between-sessions *in vivo* exposure. Therapists who inevitably have had to struggle with these difficulties will resonate to Rachman's description of "a planned treatment program [that] staggered from one watered-down compromise to the next until it came to a dismal and premature conclusion" (1983e, p. 38). Unfortunately, as Rachman adds, "there is nothing in our experience of treating obsessional patients that enables us to make a useful addition to the subject [of resistance] at this stage" (1983e, p. 38).

Other failures that currently defy adequate explanation include patients who make substantial improvement in some areas (e.g., compulsive rituals), but fail to improve in others (e.g., intrusive thoughts). Perhaps most puzzling of all is the sobering reality of patients who are cooperative and motivated for treatment, who participate fully in exposure and response prevention methods, but who still do not improve.

The foregoing examples underscore the fact that while behavioral methods have increased our effectiveness in treating obsessional patients, very large gaps remain in our understanding and in our ability to help the full range of clients who suffer from these disabling problems. Foa *et al.* (1983a) noted that a combination of all of the variables they found that were related to outcome accounted for only 40% of the variance, indicating the role of other unidentified factors. Improving our current capacity to treat obsessions and compulsions will require a better understanding of the problems themselves. In this connection, Sher, Frost, and Otto (1983) report research that has begun to demonstrate the existence of cognitive deficits in compulsive checkers. The implications of this line of inquiry are potentially far-ranging.

ACKNOWLEDGMENT

I am grateful to David Barlow for providing me with helpful suggestions in the preparation of this chapter.

COGNITIVE PROCESSES AND PROCEDURES IN BEHAVIOR THERAPY

PHILIP C. KENDALL

In just the past few years, the definition of cognitive–behavioral therapy, not unlike the changing constructions of behavior therapy, has undergone an evolutionary process. What is now considered part of cognitive–behavioral therapy seems more broad than the earlier accounts, and the associated theoretical systems seem to have undergone a more careful examination.

To some, cognitive–behavioral therapy represents a single-minded therapeutic approach. That such a perception is inaccurate and uninformed should be apparent to readers of the *Annual Review*. First, marked differences exist between cognitive–behavioral strategies applied with children and with adults. Child clients often experience cognitive–behavioral interventions where behavioral contingencies are encouraged and where training is geared toward teaching the use of reflective cognitive processing to solve interpersonal problems, whereas adults' problems are viewed as resulting from faulty thinking and the interventions are designed to correct mistaken cognitive processing.

Distinctions can also be made among the cognitive–behavioral approaches to working with adult clients. Stress inoculation, rational restructuring, cognitive therapy for depression, and rational–emotive therapy (RET) can be compared and constructed according to their theoretical orientation, the nature of the therapeutic relationship, the principal agent of cognitive change, source of evidence for reappraisals, and emphasis on self-control (Kendall & Kriss, 1983). For instance,

RET seeks a more philosophical change using didactic and confrontive experiences and rational re-evaluation, whereas cognitive therapy for depression seeks changes in cognition and behavior in a collaborative and empirical manner. Identifying the distinguishing features among the various cognitive–behavioral approaches will help to determine more precisely the elements of therapy that have the desired treatment effects. The recent literature, while not providing an empirically derived classification, has included several discussions of similarities across schools of therapy. Although not in agreement with all of the offerings, summaries and commentaries of the issues follow.

Parallels and divergences between and among cognitive–behavioral and other forms of therapy continue to appear. In a paper by Bohart (1982), humanistic therapies are argued to be similar to some of the cognitive therapies. For instance, Bohart (1982) sees the goals of both types of therapy as consistent—helping clients who are living in terms of rigid externalized schemata to adapt better to experiences. The work of Wexler and Rice (1974) is cited, and, based on this, the goals might be seen as consistent. However, Wexler and Rice are cognitively oriented humanists and not necessarily representative of all or even the majority of humanists. A second parallel described by Bohart concerns the cognitive therapist's efforts to eliminate dysfunctional thinking and the humanist's trying to get clients to live in the here and now (and stay in touch with their feeelings). Bohart appears correct in pointing out that cognitive therapists focusing on the verdicality of thoughts do, in fact, stress the present (e.g., "Don't assume that one event means the future is bleak"), but this does bypass the more distinctive feature of the cognitive (cognitive–behavioral) therapist, who employs "collaborative empiricism" to determine the veridicality of certain thoughts.

Bohart's (1982) analysis seeks to further the ecumenical search for commonalities across therapies and seems willing to assist open communication across approaches. These features are weakened, however, by the somewhat excessive reliance on small samples or excerpts from case transcripts as the basis for the arguments. A more theoretical examination, considering methodological, strategic, and epistomological features, would have furthered the author's position.

Integrationism continues with evidence of psychoanalysts adopting "action" into their otherwise "verbal" treatments. Weiner (1983), for instance, describes briefly a method he calls "ego activation," in which clients are challenged by tasks that require coping with the challenge and expressing feelings about the task. Encouraging the client to be more active and assertive, to accept self-responsibility, and to enhance self-mastery are features that Weiner sees as important. In this sense the integration is positive, for nonbehavioral therapists seem to have found wisdom in the demonstrated efficiencies of performance interventions.

Kuiper and MacDonald (1983) have examined the cognitive therapies with an eye toward the role of reason and emotion. These authors have included misattribution therapy along with Ellis's and Beck's cognitive approaches. While this is one of the first reviews to give such a placement to misattribution therapy and not to cover some more mainstream approaches, the authors' perspective on emotion is informative. After reviewing several theoretical and empirical works, Kuiper and MacDonald describe certain key features about emotions.

> First, no one behavior is considered a necessary and sufficient index to identify the occurrence of an emotion. Second, emotions might be thought of as complex organized response syndromes, which contain subjective and physiological components in addition to behavioral components. Furthermore, the judgment that an emotion has occurred very often requires an idiographic analysis of the individual's behavior in relation to his or her environment. (1983, p. 303)

As noted elsewhere, it is difficult to determine which comes first—cognition, emotion, physiological arousal, or whtever—since we can discover different prime movers, depending upon where we enter the chain of events. What is interesting, as pointed out by Kuiper and MacDonald (1983), is that the theories of the attribution therapists seem to be consistent with the idea that physiological arousal is perceived by the person as emotion. The cognitive therapists, Beck and Ellis, seem to persist in their conviction that cognitions precede emotions, and would seem to argue for a cognitive–physiological sequence of events. Kuiper and MacDonald later suggest that more attention be paid to the role of emotions in cognitive therapy. They suggest that emotions might be considered as a signaling system, where the experience of an emotion signals to the individual that a mismatch exists between the demands of the environment and the person's repertoire of behavior. This signaling function of emotion would suggest that clients be taught to become more aware of these emotions and to use them as cues for coping. Indeed, this has been described in Meichenbaum's (1977) stress inoculation approach. Consistent with the signaling role of emotion is that negative emotions might not always result from faulty cognitions.

Behaviorally oriented psychologists have assuaged the anxieties concerning their theoretical identities by reaffirming a solid point made by Bandura—that although the explanations of behavior change appear to be cognitive, the most effective means of producing the desired change is performance-based (behavioral). This weighty and timely comment placed self-efficacy theory within a reasoned behavioral framework and provided a guiding conceptual framework for further study. However, should we now begin to question the universality of the position? Could it be the case that for some problem behavior patterns, cognitive methods and changes may be essential and primary to engaging the client in the behavioral procedures? Could it be the case that cognitive processes are central to behavior change, that assessing these cognitive processes and bringing them into the client's awareness may require cognitive procedures, and that these strategies may supersede the behavioral practice component? It is not that the performance base could be eliminated, for I do not hold such a position; but it may be the case that not only are the processes of behavior change largely cognitive, but also that the most efficient and efficacious entry into these processes may be cognitive as well. This is not to suggest or encourage comparative outcome trials pitting solely cognitive against solely behavioral approaches. Rather, since interventions with documented records of successfully producing treatment gains have behavioral components and cognitive components, and since wise clinical practice involves both aspects as well, the studies that are needed must address the *sequencing* of methods to alter cognitive processes and behaviors and the likelihood that such sequencing will vary across types of disorders and be differentially interrelated with affective functioning. Theoretical and applied efforts to amalgamate the various systems have been discussed, but the less-than-perfect outcome justifies the more careful look at sequencing of techniques of change.

THE PROCESS OF CHANGE

Garfield (1983), in his candid account of the controversy in therapy outcome research, has pointed the field in the direction of variables that are active and therapeutic. That is, comparative studies may be passing, as a new emphasis is placed on the discovery of just what is therapeutic in the process of therapy. As in the more recent previous *Annual Reviews*, the need for investigations of the process of therapeutic change is duly underlined.

The process of change is addressed by Goldfried and Robins (1983) from the position of self-mastery. Taking cognitive perspectives such as self-efficacy theory and notions of schemata, Goldfried and Robins discuss the merits of self-mastery as a desired treatment goal and ways in which the clinician can shape and encourage the self-mastery process. For example, clinical guidelines are offered for the encouragement of new behaviors, for the distinguishing between past and present behaviors, for the recall of prior mastery experiences, and for the proper conduct of self-evaluation. "Process," in this instance, is the process of client achievement of self-mastery.

Does process predict outcome? If there is a relationship between process measures and positive gains, then the answer should also be likely to be yes in relation to negative change: Process measures should be predictive of the iatrogenic, negative effects of psychotherapy. Sachs (1983), working within the Vanderbilt Psychotherapy Research Project, developed the Vanderbilt Negative Indicators Scale (VNIS). The scale consists of 42 items comprising five subscales: Patient Qualities (e.g., passivity), Therapist Personal Qualities (e.g., exploitive tendencies), Errors in Technique (e.g., lack of structure or focus), Patient–Therapist Interaction (e.g., problems in the relationship), and Global Session Ratings (e.g, ineffectiveness of session). VNIS ratings represent clinical judgments based on the therapeutic interaction.

For Sachs's (1983) examination of the role of negative factors in therapy, 18 male college students with anxiety, depression, and un-satisfying interpersonal relationships served as subjects. Subjects were seen by one of seven experienced therapists (three psychoanalytic, four client-centered) for an average of 18 sessions. Measures of outcome included ratings by the patient, the therapist, and an independent clinician who conducted interviews. Interrater reliability on the VNIS was reported to be quite good (.94). Variation in the Errors in Technique scores were found to be associated with outcome—even when the effects of the other VNIS subscales were partialed out. Apparently the *lack of quality* was a major contributor to therapeutic ineffectiveness. This finding has special appeal, for I have elsewhere called for additional inquiry into the amount of outcome variability associated with therapy *quality* (Kendall & Hollon, 1983).

Sachs's conclusion, however, must be re-evaluated in light of the fact that process was examined without first providing convincing evidence of outcome. That is, while the 18 clients were rated for improvements, there were no control conditions to eliminate several of the rival hypotheses that might be credible explanations of the change. Process research is indeed an important area for current psychotherapy researchers, but process must be examined after the demonstration of successful outcome. It should be noted that this study examined psychodynamic and client-centered therapy and did not include behavioral and/or cognitive–behavioral therapies. Also, the relationships found between negative indicators and negative outcome were more highly associated within the psychodynamic treatments.

Further investigation of process relations were reported by O'Malley, Suh, and Strupp (1983). This report was also a part of the Vanderbilt

Psychotherapy Project. O'Malley *et al.* described the development of the Vanderbilt Psychotherapy Process Scale (VPPS) and reported its relationships to outcome. The VPPS was designed, for instance, to cover a broad range of theoretical orientations, to be descriptive rather than evaluative, and to require minimal inference. The VPPS was then employed on data from the first three treatment sessions. Thus, the authors sought to predict outcome from factors that would be evident early in the treatment process. Again, the clients were 38 unmarried males with anxiety, depression, and introversion problems.

The results of the O'Malley *et al.* study provide data that are consistent with several reports. First, O'Malley found, as did Braswell, Kendall, Braith, Carey, and Vye (in press), that the level of patient *involvement* was a predictor of outcome. Reports such as this are consistent and include another earlier study by the Vanderbilt group (e.g., Gomez-Schwartz, 1978). Although the outcome of treatment was not unequivocally demonstrated in the Vanderbilt project, the consistency across studies in uncovering "involvement" as a viable predictor of outcome merits further attention. As Braswell *et al.* suggest, involvement may be a factor that predicts outcome across schools of therapy and thereby reflects some portion of the common process across therapies.

One aspect of the process of psychotherapy that leaps forth for further thought is the extension of the uniformity myths (Kiesler, 1966) to include the process uniformity myth (Greenberg, 1983a). Process variables fluctuate over time (see Ford, 1978, for a look at behavior therapy), and it is therefore unacceptable to assume that process is the same across therapy tasks and contexts. Process has different meanings at different points in therapy, and, therefore, process must be studied specifically within the context in which it occurs. To quote Greenberg (1983a), "All process in psychotherapy is not the same, just as all clients, all treatments, and all therapies are not the same" (p. 172). Regarding this need for the study of process in its context, Greenberg sees merit in the study of the sequence and patterns of client performance. Indeed, Kiesler (1980) himself called for process measures for particular homogeneous groups of clients instead of continuing to proliferate mesures of "general" psychotherapy process reflecting untenable uniformity assumptions (p. 82).

In a summary statement regarding the existing process literature, Greenberg (1983a) notes that an active sense of participation by the client in therapy appears to be one of the factors consistently related to outcome. Strupp (1977) and others from nonbehavioral camps refer to this as a "working alliance." This notion, as described further by Greenberg, emphasizes the general relationship factors where a bond is formed through good personal contact and mutual affirmation. Lest our behavioral side be distressed by the lack of emphasis on technical factors, these are considered important, for they contribute to the alliance formation by engaging the client and convincing him or her that what is being done is relevant and helpful (Greenberg, 1983a). It may be that we can learn a great deal about how to facilitate nascent working alliances through the behavioral study of the contribution of various techniques to the establishment of an involved client.

Greenberg and Webster (1982) used information from the therapy process to categorize clients as either "resolvers" or "nonresolvers." These different clients were then examined in relation to the outcome produced by a treatment technique called the "two-chair dialogue." Of interest here, however, were the selected measures of process. For instance, the Experiencing Scale (Klein, Mathieu, Kiesler, & Gendlen, 1969), which taps client level of involvement, and the Structural Analysis of Social Behavior (Benjamin, 1979), which categorizes each statement into one of 36 categories, were used. Four mutually exclusive voice patterns were assessed using the Client Vocal Quality system (Rice, Koke, Greenberg, & Wagstaff, 1979). These measures are not without fault, and certain theoretical biases may detract from their merit for some researchers. Nevertheless, these are measures that were selected to assess process in at least one contemporary investigation (see also Greenberg, 1983b). Behavioral coding of tapes of the treatment sessions would provide another important vantage point. Research is needed to ascertain the degree of convergence across types of assessments of process. The emergence of "involvement" as a predictor suggests that we examine the various methods of assessing this concept and their relations to observed gains.

Interest in the process of cognitive–behavioral therapy for depression is very evident in several papers, including Fennell's (1983) paper on the mechanism of change. Her manuscript addresses the process question of "how" cognitive therapy works, dealing sequentially with immediate impact, change over the treatment course, maintenance, and relapse prevention. Fennell posits that an active program of thought modification can itself bring about an immediate impact, and she cites studies to support this view. Thus, cognitive change may enervate the change process. Regarding changes over the course of treatment, however, the role of behavioral change is underscored. Behaviors produce consequences that contradict negative thinking, and changing behavior produces the therapeutic change over the course of the treatment. Maintenance of gains and relapse prevention are seen as promoted by the therapeutic events, which have reduced the depressive schemata that were guiding behavior. By learning the skills taught in the cognitive treatment, the client can counter his or her own depressive thinking. While this seems plausible, some data suggest an equal relapse rate for different types of treatment. It should be noted, however, that cognitive therapy does seem to produce greater prevention of relapse than pharmacotherapies.

Fennell's (1983) analysis documents the growing interest in the process or mechanisms of change and points to the need to separate these stages of the change process: immediate effects, effects of the course of treatment, and persistent gains. It is interesting to speculate further that the cognitive processes of expectations and attributions, based upon the actual behavior of the therapist and client, may contribute differentially. That is, the process of change may require expectational features that promote initial change, whereas attributional changes may contribute to the eventual positive effects of low relapse rates.

A report by Simons, Garfield, and Murphy (1984) addresses the process of change in two treatments of depression: cognitive therapy and pharmacotherapy. Using the Beck Depression Inventory (BDI) and Hamilton ratings as indices of outcome, Simons *et al.* found that both treatments produced comparable gains. Using cognitive assessments (see also Chapter 2, this volume), the authors again reported comparable change. The relevance for the present consideration of the process of change is that both treatments had a positive and desired effect on cognition. Cognitive processes do change as a result of cognitive therapy, but they also change with pharmacotherapy. While this might suggest that distorted cognition represents a symptom of depression that is changed by medications, the data could also be viewed as suggesting that cognitive changes are a common change pathway. The process of change involves, across types of therapy, changes in cognition.

The cognitive treatment of test anxiety studied by Wise and Haynes (1983) involved a comparison of rational restructuring (identifying and modifying irrational beliefs), attentional training (reduce attention to task-relevant variables), and waiting-list controls. Subjects were undergraduate students with debilitating test anxiety (Achievement Anxiety test score of greater than 30). Subjects were assigned to treatments in randomized blocks, and treatment was provided in small groups. The outcome was assessed using self-report (a test anxiety scale, a state anxiety measure taken before an analogue task, and a social anxiety measure), and it was found that the cognitive treatments were effective in reducing unwanted anxiety. Subjects' performance on the analogue tasks also evidenced benefits derived from the two cognitive treatments. Positive gains were maintained at 8-month follow-up for those subjects who were available at that time. Regarding process, the authors explored the predictive validity of process assessments of anxiety reduction. Subjects' estimates of anxiety reduction during sessions was found to be a reliable addition to the prediction of gains on the outcome measures. This "look" at process is applauded, but the self-report to self-report prediction can be explained in ways other than a therapeutic effect (e.g., method variance).

Separate from the actual conduct of an outcome study, Monroe, Bellack, Hersen, and Himmelhoch (1983) examined life events and their association with the course of symptoms of depression in women. Findings indicated that events such as "making new friends," collectively referred to as entrances into the individual's social field, were consistently predictive of fewer symptoms at follow-up. Since these events seem related to the remission of depressive symptomatology, they may have important associations with implications for the therapeutic process.

AFFECT, COGNITION, AND THE BEHAVIORAL APPROACHES TO THERAPY

One cannot open the topic of affect and cognition without acknowledging that there will be some readers who will feel upset by what they read and others who will think that the material is less than desired. I have tried to illustrate in this opening sentence (although perhaps too subtlely) that I see affect and cognition as topics that produce variability among people: Some are affectively excessive (or overcontrolled), and others are overly cognitive (ruminative) or insufficiently cognitive (impulsive). It is, in my opinion, possible for there to be individual differences in the degree to which affect versus cognition contributes to the development and/or maintenance of certain types of maladjustment. Thus, any displeasure with this section may be perceived or experienced as upset by some and insight by others.

While I do not purport to cover all of the literature of the topics of affect and cognition, and while I certainly do not entertain the grandiose conviction that I can offer a resolution, the importance of affective functioning in behavioral and other psychological therapies mandates that space and time be devoted to at least a consideration of some of the pressing issues.

It is my opinion that a reasoned evaluation of the interface of cognition and emotion must include a perusal of the earlier works by Arnold (1960, 1970), Abelson (1963), and more recently, Zajonc (1980). True, there are other treatises that also deserve mention here, but space limitations and a reasoned expectation on my part dictate that I only bite off what I can presently chew. What follows are my nibbles at some fo the important conceptualizations.

Arnold's consideration of affect is notable for its distinguishing between appraisal and reappraisal processes. In the case of an immediate or intuitive reaction, physiological and experiential features are important components of the initial appraisal. The emotional appraisal is seen as independent of cognition: It is an emotional experience similar to a sense experience. Reappraisal, in contrast, involves cognitive processing. Reappraisal is the process during which the individual makes sense out of the initial experience. An individual who first recognizes a jittery stomach (appraisal) might then think, "I'm nervous." From this theoretical perspective, initial emotional reactions are noncognitive, yet secondary evaluations are cognitively influenced.

Abelson (1963), choosing more affectively laden terms, has described the relevance of distinguishing between "hot" and "cold" cognitions. Cognitive processes that are affect-free are cold; cognitive processes that are affective in nature are hot. It should be noted that this is not dissimilar to Mandler's (1982) analysis, which argues that "emotional experiences are the wholistic outcome of two separable but not necessarily independent processes and mechanisms. One is global autonomic (visceral) arousal; the other is cognitive evaluation" (p. 336).

Zajonc's (1980) treatise on "feeling and thinking" adds additional perspective to the affect–cognition discussion. Zajonc's position is that affect and cognition "are under the control of separate and partially independent systems" (p. 155). Thus, while Zajonc states that contemporary psychology regards affect as postcognitive, he argues that "feeling accompanies *all* cognitions, that it arises early in the process of registration and retrieval, albeit weakly and vaguely, and that it derives from a parallel, separate, and independent system in the organism" (p. 154). Zajonc also argues that "affect should not be treated as unalterably last and invariably postcognitive" (p. 172). Thus, affective reactions are not always accompanied by some form of cognitive representation.

Why do we find ourselves in the center of the feeling versus thinking debate? Of what practical value is the answer to this bemusing query? Are behavior therapists interested in affect? (Or in cognition?) To answer the last question first, the answer is yes. And, there are many reasons why the answer is yes. First, many of the problem behavior patterns that receive behavioral therapy are related to disorders of affect. Depression, the clearest example, makes the point alone. Behavioral procedures may be employed and the assessments may concern behavioral changes, but the target is a condition of affect. Second, affect may, in some cases, be an important moderating variable in determining the effectiveness of behavioral therapy procedures. For instance, consider behavioral couples therapy, where pinpointing of specific problems, rational problem solving, and communication skills training are provided—a reasonable treatment regimen. The couple may improve substantially on several measures, including the quantity and quality of problem solutions and the active listening and direct requesting aspects of communicating, but the gains may be temporarily washed out by an instance of excessive affective arousal. Colloquially, this is sometimes referred to as "seeing red." The client may report, "I did really well until I saw the guy my spouse had the affair with and then I saw red. I couldn't problem-solve, I was angry!" Some forms of recognition of the role of affective arousal and its potential moderating effects on skills training seems worthy of inquiry. Third, behavioral therapies have been, even if indirectly or unintentionally, concerned with at least one major aspect of affect: pleasure and aversion. The central feature of the effectiveness of reinforcement is that it is associated with an increase in the response that it follows. The reinforcement has a pleasurable effect. Noxious stimuli, and their unpleasurable effects, result in reductions in behavior. It is true that as behaviorists we have not typically measured affect in our studies, we have not focused on affect as a vehicle for changing behaviors, and we have not found the need to invoke affective principles in our theories about patterns of behavior, but affect has been there, even if only at an ancillary level.

When discussing self-talk, emotion, and behavior, I sometimes come to a conclusion that maybe we simply will not be able to determine the causal relationships between these most interesting aspects of human functioning. But then I come across an idea or an argument, even if microtheoretic, that seems persuasive—so much so that my optimism rises dramatically. Consider the following:

You are about to experience a situation for the first time. You have no history of behavior in this situation (that you are aware of), and you have no specific expectations. Assessments of your self-talk, perhaps reflecting general expectations based on related past experience, can be predictive of performance in the new situation. Correspondingly, some assessments of your affective reaction to the new situation might have predictive potency in determining the likelihood that you will again choose to be in the situation in the future. Simple positive versus negative affect distinctions may be sufficient to ascertain whether an individual will return for more. However, after several experiences in the situation, earlier performance is a better predictor of future performance than the earlier or the current affective reactions or self-directive verbalizations. Similarly, past failures or successes will be more predictive of future failures or successes than the feelings or cognitions, because one has had experience in the situation and the data are available. Without the prior data, current cognitive information and overall affective reactions can provide a sound springboard for predictions.

What this analysis suggests to me[1] is that cognitive self-talk, affect, and behavior can be predictive, but that the strength of the predictions varies according to the amount of experience in the actual situation. This notion is testable, and, therefore, gives rise to a renewed interest in trying to untie the affect–cognition–behavior knot.

Emotion and cognitions are interrelated, and such a statement typically receives support from diverse theoretical schools and often appears as a tenet of cognitive–behavioral therapy (e.g., Kendall & Bemis, 1983; Mahoney, 1977). However, not all experimental attempts (or correlational ones) provide unbending support, and few theoreticians or researches would pledge pure commitment to a one-way causal relationship. Whether or not cognition precedes emotions in all or even some circumstances is a "hot" topic.

Approaching the emotion–cognition connection from the point of view of appraisal and reappraisal (after Arnold, 1960, 1970), Safran and Greenberg (1982) describe the related processes and provide consideration of the clinical implications. According to Arnold, appraisal and reappraisal are distinct processes associated with emotionality. In the appraisal process, the individual experiences emotional reactions in a direct and immediate way. These emotional states are nonreflective "emotional perceptions" including phenomenology and physiology. The reappraisal process is an evaluation of the appraisal. The person recognizes a state of emotional arousal and, upon reflection, can either reduce or exacerbate the arousal. The example provided by Safran and Greenberg (1982), which I condense here, nicely illustrates the notions of appraisal and reappraisal. A student taking an exam reads the first test question. He or she experiences a jolt of fear, and his or her heart starts to pound. This is the appraisal process. Before panic sets in, the student reappraises, "I can handle this test." This coping-statement reaction to the experience of arousal resembles the self-talk that we teach clients to help them to manage and overcome fearful and/or stressful situations.

Safran and Greenberg (1982) speculate that it is therapeutically helpful to assist clients to disentangle the initial appraisal from the

---

1. Some of these ideas were generated by discussions that took place at the University of Houston and included Diane Chambless, John Foreyt, Don Meichenbaum, Ray Novaco, Lynn Rehm, Dennis Turk, and myself.

reappraisal process. This differentiation helps the client recognize how his or her cognitive activity contributes to the problem. Indeed, I would add that if initial appraisals do occur "prethought," then they can serve as cues for proper reappraisals. We cannot control the situations clients find themselves in, but we can teach effective reappraisals. Safran and Greenberg (1982) continue by illustrating how reappraisals can be particularly dysfunctional and speculating about how dysfunctional reappraisals can result in inaccurate attributional patterns.

Many therapists may be too sanctimonious and/or self-righteous to face the reality that their clients (subjects) need to enjoy themselves. In a sense, we, as therapists, are responsible for aiding others to experience some positive affect. Affect may not be the ideal target for therapy or the most efficacious vehicle for change, but the experience of positive affect is a most potent reinforcer, and behavioral therapists must recognize this fact. If we who are involved in aiding others to change behavior cannot make the process as interesting to a client as Christmas is to a child, then we have not made full use of the resources available to us. Successful behavior change is nothing if not exciting.

One great danger of the forthcoming "years of affect" is the rashness with which new topics are evaluated. Lesser clinicians will pop in and out of the affect arena, but many others will rise above sheer timeliness and document the virtue and strength of an incorporation of feelings into behaviors and cognitive–behavioral therapies. We must steer clear of lucky powders and snake oil, but we must also provide empirical evaluations.

TREATING DEPRESSION: RECENT REPORTS OF OUTCOME

Depression remains a topic of excitement for clinical researchers. Studies of basic psychopathological processes, symptomatology, and diagnostics, as well as advances in theory, grace the pages of a truly extensive list of professional journals. One of the central topics pertinent to the present review is the evaluation of Beck's cognitive-behavioral program for depression (e.g., Beck, Rush, Shaw, & Emery, 1979). Perhaps the central outcome issue facing those involved in this research arena is the relative efficacy of drugs and psychological treatment.

In a four-group comparison study, Murphy, Simons, Wetzel, and Lustman (1984) tested the relative effectiveness of 12 weeks of cognitive therapy, pharmacotherapy (nortriptyline), a combined cognitive and pharmacotherapy treatment, and cognitive therapy plus active placebo.

Unipolar primary affective-disordered patients (ages 18–60) with BDI scores greater than 20 and meeting appropriate diagnostic criteria were assigned to the treatments in a chance fashion. Patients in cognitive therapy received 20 50-minute sessions over 12 weeks, with the intervention following the program designed by Beck. Therapy sessions were audiotaped and reviewed to insure adherence to Beck's approach. Assessments included 13 clinical rating scales and self-report measures, though the authors focus solely on the results of the BDI and Hamilton ratings in their 1984 report.

Analyses of the target dependent measures created significant improvements over time. However, there were no significant differences across treatment modalities. When similar analyses were performed with the last recorded score for dropouts used as a termination score, the results were essentially unchanged. Using BDI scores of 9 or less as an indicator of patients' being no longer depressed, Murphy et al. (1984) reported that 63% of patients met this standard at the end of 12 weeks of treatment (13 patients were still moderately depressed; 8 patients continued to have BDI scores over 20). As Murphy et al. comment, "Nearly all patients in this study improved clinically. Neither mean improvement nor the proportion of patients who were considered not to be depressed at termination differed by type of treatment" (1984, p. 39).

The absence of differential treatment effects, along with the absence of a no-treatment control group, leaves open the question as to whether the observed changes were produced by treatment. Reported changes could be due to factors other than treatment. Murphy et al. (1984) counter the reasoning by pointing out that the medication has an established efficacy in treating depression, and that the effects produced by both medication and cognitive therapy are therefore likely to be treatment effects. The authors go on to summarize their study as having found cognitive therapy to be equally effective (but not superior to) medications. The combined treatment had no additive effect on reductions of depression.

The Murphy et al. study is an important one. It offers evidence to confirm the earlier findings of Rush, Beck, Kovacs, and Hollon (1977) and thereby to reaffirm the efficacy of cognitive–behavioral intervention in the remediation of depression. The major shortcoming that I wish to comment upon concerns the limited number and array of dependent variables that were analyzed and reported in the study. Readers should be aware that another paper by Simons and colleagues (1984) looks at several cognitive measures from a related study, but the criticism still pertains. Why were only two dependent variables (one self-report and one rating) given the burden of outcome responsibility? Multiple method assessments, such as use of two or more self-report scales, and inclusion of some behavioral data would have or could have buttressed the evidence. Follow-up data were lacking, though the authors noted that the data were collected and in the process of being examined statistically.

The absence of beneficial gains from the combination of drugs plus psychotherapy is consistent with earlier data (see Volume 9 of the *Annual Review*). As data along these lines accumulate, we must return to basics and question why one plus one equals one. Perhaps this statement is simplistic, but many persons might anticipate and even expect that one treatment would facilitate the effects of the other. I have heard it stated that medications act quickly and may therefore set the stage for a better learning experience provided by psychotherapy. The argument has been presented for children (e.g., drugs plus therapy for hyperactivity) as well as adults. Clinical lore is countered by the data, but what explanation is there for the fact that one plus one does not equal two? That one plus one does not even equal anything more than one? A more careful analysis is required, but it appears that a floor effect might hamper the degree of possible change. For instance, the BDI scores of those treated patients at posttreatment hovers around 8 to 10. Some researchers have used a cutoff score of 9 to describe cases that have improved. A change from a BDI of 30 to a score of 9 is a therapeutic change, but when 9 is viewed as a typical score for samples of non-depressed persons, can we justifiably expect mean scores to be as low as 2 or 3? Restriction in the amount of change that can be attained may result from conceptual and psychometric restrictions. Floor effects may prevent the identification of the additive effects of combinative treatments. Or treatment modalities as different as drugs and therapy may simply not be additive!

A brief intervention using cognitive therapy for depression was employed by Teasdale and Fennell (1982) to examine (1) whether or not reductions in the frequency and intensity of negative thoughts would alleviate depression in depressed patients and (2) whether one component of the cognitive-behavior therapy package would produce desired change. A within-subject design was used with each depressed patient (five female patients identified by the Research Diagnostic Criteria [RDC] and other criteria): 30 minutes of attempting to change depressive thought was compared to equal time exploring depressive thoughts. The comparison conditions were embedded within the general therapeutic content of cognitive–behavioral therapy, such that all subjects were a part of a treatment regimen with nonspecific factors and so on available to all. For all subjects, depressive thoughts were identified, and patients rated how strongly they believed the thoughts (e.g., "I will always be a cripple as a person"). In the thought change condition, the therapist encouraged the patient to reevaluate her thinking, to examine the full range of evidence, to consider alternatives, and to review other types of action. In the thought exploration condition, the therapist sought to identify more relevant information by questioning and providing reflective statements. Subjects rated their belief in the target thoughts and rated their level of depression. The researchers also timed the subjects' natural pace of counting from 1 to 10. The procedure was repeated, using the alternate experimental condition, at a later point in therapy.

An analysis of the tape-recorded treatment (manipulation check) documented that the two conditions were implemented as intended. Since only five patients were studied, the data analysis relied heavily on consistency across subjects and visual inspection. For instance, belief in the targeted thoughts changed in all patients as a result of the thought change condition, but changed only slightly in one patient after thought exploration. There was a significant reduction in depression following the thought change condition, but no differences on the measure of counting time (previously shown to correlate with self-ratings of depression). These findings suggest that changing thoughts, as embedded within cognitive–behavioral therapy for depression, produces greater change in the belief in the depressive thought and in reported depression than does further clarification of thoughts. While the authors further suggest that the data support "the specific effectiveness of 'cognitive' CBT techniques in producing immediate alleviation of depression" (Teasdale & Fennell, 1982, p. 349), they also recognize an important shortcoming in the study: The predicted effects were seen only on self-report measures. Some form of patient acquiescence (or demand effects) to the change efforts could account for the differences. A more compelling project would include a larger sample size, inferential statistical tests, and, if and when available, other measures of depression (besides self-report) that are less prone to critical commentary.

In a study conducted in Sydney, Australia, P. H. Wilson, Goldin, and Charbonneau-Powis (1983) compared cognitive and behavioral treatment strategies to a no-treatment (waiting-list) control with depressed subjects. Every effort was made, according to the authors, "to distinguish between the purely 'cognitive' components of treatment and the 'behavioral' components" (1983, p. 113). For example, the behavioral treatment (after Lewinsohn) aimed to increase the quality and range of social interactions and activities. Daily mood monitoring and social reinforcement for participating in activities were also employed. The cognitive treatment incorporated many of Beck's (1976) treatment procedures, "with the exception of behavioral task assignments" (P. H. Wilson et al., 1983, p. 117). Negative thoughts were examined and mood was monitored daily.

Twenty-five subjects were randomly assigned to the three conditions, with eight receiving behavioral therapy, eight receiving cognitive therapy, and nine placed on the waiting list. Dependent measures included the BDI, the Irrational Beliefs Test, mood ratings, the Hamilton Rating Scale, the Pleasant Events Schedule, and a Cognition Schedule. The Cognition Schedule was 137 items (69 positive thoughts and 68 negative thoughts) designed for the study. Subjects rated the frequency and impact of each thought on a 5-point scale.

P. H. Wilson et al. (1983) analyzed the data by making separate comparisons at pretreatment–midtreatment, pretreatment–posttreatment, and at follow-up. The midtreatment assessment was designed to evaluate whether the cognitive or the behavioral treatment had a more rapid effect. It was found that both treatments were equally effective in reducing the severity of depression in the first four sessions. At posttreatment, there were significant improvements, but the two treatment groups did not differ significantly. Similar results were reported at follow-up. Use of a mixed factorial design, with repeated measurements being the within-subjects factor and type of treatment the between-subjects factor, would have simplified the analyses. Moreover, interaction effects across assessment periods could have been examined.

The major conclusions of the P. H. Wilson et al. (1983) study were that the behavioral and cognitive treatments had comparable beneficial effects on depression, and that these effects were superior to no treatment. Although the actual cognitive and behavioral treatments in other studies (Taylor & Marshall, 1977; Zeiss, Lewinsohn, & Munoz, 1979; see earlier Annual Reviews) were different, there seems to be consistency in the finding of comparable effects. P. H. Wilson et al. added the midtreatment comparison and documented the comparable rapidity of therapeutic gains. Both active treatments resulted in "cognitive" changes (pretreatment–posttreatment) on the positive and negative Cognitions Schedule, with the cognitive treatment evidencing these gains earlier. The positive overall findings were seen on both self-report and clinician-rated measures of depression, and the no-treatment (waiting-list) control eliminated some rival hypotheses (effects due to passage of time and assessment reactivity), but the absence of an attention control condition does restrict the conclusiveness of the report.

Single-subject evaluations of the effects of cognitive–behavioral treatments of depression have also appeared. Hamilton and Waldman (1983), for example, reported on the successful treatment of a 20-year-old student who had a 4-year history of moderate to severe depression. Baseline frequency and intensity of negative thoughts were recorded throughout the treatments as well. The baseline lasted 18 days; a behavioral program lasted 14 days (a token program for reinforcing activities). During these two periods of the time series design, there were fluctuations in the frequencies and intensities of negative thoughts, but no apparent changes. The cognitive–behavioral intervention followed and produced notable reductions in the frequency and intensity of negative thoughts. The cognitive–behavioral program included self-modification of depressive ruminatory activity by rewarding the completion of tasks that had served to trigger negative thinking and by direct implementation of rational restructuring, covert modeling, and reinforcement. The positive gains seen during the 70-day cognitive–behavioral program were maintained at 6-month follow-up. There are, however, limitations to this study. As the authors themselves note, the single-subject strategy that was used was really an A-B design, and such a design does not rule out many of the potential threats to internal validity (Kazdin, 1982b; Kendall & Koehler, in press). One additional note: The cognitive–behavioral treatment produced more dramatic changes in intensity of negative thinking than in the frequency of negative thinking. Continued assessment of these two features of negative self-talk seems worthwhile in light of these findings and the potential for enhanced theoretical understandings.

Via descriptive case examples, Steuer and Hammen (1983) discuss the application of cognitive–behavioral groups to elderly depressed patients. Patients were 55–78 years of age and determined to be depressed using DSM-III criteria for major depressive (affective) disorder, the Hamilton Rating Scale, and the Zung Self-Ratings. Treatments were 1½ hours long, meeting twice weekly for 10 weeks and once a week for 26 weeks. Following four case descriptions, Steuer and Hammen examine how depression is different in older adults, with an emphasis on medical concerns and memory complaints, as well as on chronicity of the depression. The authors also discuss how the young-old (those aged 60–74) and old-old (those aged 75 and over) may differ, and note that the elderly in general differ from their more youthful counterparts in ways that affect the therapeutic process. Some of the elderly may not be able to articulate their negative thinking, and still others may hold the belief that they are too old to change now. Steuer and Hammen (1983) suggest that the behavioral features of treatment are more useful for the patients with difficulties in abstract thinking, whereas the cognitive features are helpful for those who can understand the relationship between thoughts and feelings. (Those interested in the treatment of geriatric depression could consult pp. 146–148 of Volume 9 of the *Annual Review*.)

As evidence in support of the cognitive–behavioral approach to the psychological treatment of depression continues to be reported (e.g., Murphy *et al.*, 1984), cautionary information has appeared as well. Should we expect all depressed persons to respond uniformly to any one treatment? The consensus answer is no; it is to be expected that qualifications to the population of choice for a specific therapy will help guide sound clinical practice. In one such report, Fennell and Teasdale (1982) selected five patients who had shown inadequate responses to antidepressants and fit the RDC criteria for major depressive disorder. The number of subjects was small, but Fennell and Teasdale point out that their patients' outcomes were inferior to those reported elsewhere. It is difficult to make sense of unsuccessful cases reported without methodological controls, comparison conditions, and the like. Perhaps what can be stated, however, is that we need additional methods of predicting "poor" cognitive therapy for depression candidates. Chronic, drug-resistant cases may be difficult for all clinical procedures.

RATIONAL–EMOTIVE THERAPY

Not wanting to be one who finds pleasure in saying (or at least not willing to admit it in print) "I told you so," it is with reluctance that I point out that a prediction that I made in Volume 9 of the *Annual Review* seems to hold true. My prediction, stated informally, was that RET, albeit a seminal and central theoretical and applied system, would receive more discussion than research evaluation. This year, as before, many of the papers, chapters, and texts dealing with RET have a "discussion" as opposed to "evaluation" focus. Many of the calls for research in recent years have been heard and responded to: We saw dismantling studies of systematic desensitization, a turn to clinical cases for the subjects of outcome trials, and comparisons of cognitive and behavioral approaches; also, more contemporary calls for process studies (Kendall, 1982b) have begun to receive attention (Braswell *et al.*, in press; O'Malley *et al.*, 1983; Sachs, 1983). The single most ignored call, in my opinion, is that which has asked for additional outcome evaluations of RET. To date, there are all too few studies (e.g., Lipsky, Kassinove, & Miller, 1980) where clinical cases are treated using RET methods (not RET-derived principles), and where outcome comparisons are made and reported. In contrast, RET discussions abound. For instance, in an edited book entitled *Rational–Emotive Approaches to the Problems of Childhood* (Ellis & Bernard, 1983), only a few of the 18 chapters can be described as subscribing to a research foundation, whereas many offer clinical insights and procedures. While I do not wish to detract from the merits of some of these discussions, I do intend to document my puzzlement and discouragement with the continued limited number of treatment outcome reports.

Procrastination is familiar to all of us. We may invent euphemisms, but it is procrastination nonetheless. Ellis and Knaus (1979) account for procrastination by invoking irrational beliefs related to the task to be accomplished. For instance, given the belief that you must do well, and that if you do not do well you are no good at all, it is better to procrastinate and do nothing. For RET, the task difficulty or the chance of failure serve as inhibitors of action. Rorer (1983) brings this topic to the attention of cognitive–behavioral researchers and therapists in his consideration of procrastination. Rorer does not take issue with the Ellis and Knaus analysis, but adds several cases and analytic points to further the applicability of irrationality in procrastination. But it is not just the possibility of failure that leads to procrastination, argues Rorer; features of success can have the same effects. If when one succeeds, for example, it brings the person closer to a condition where anxiety is greater or more likely, then procrastination may be mediated by irrationality associated with success.

A somewhat consistent impression in the lore surrounding RET is that there is a wealth of studies supporting the rational–emotive perspective. That there are also less supportive and equivocal findings as well receives less attention, while the supportive literature receives coverage. T. Smith (1983), in contrast, has underscored the need for a critical review of this literature. His critical examination covers the assessment of irrational beliefs, the role of irrational beliefs in causing emotional distress, and the role of irrational beliefs in the treatment of emotional distress.

Regarding the assessment of irrationality, T. Smith has noted that there is considerable confusion as to the nature of the concept of irrationality (see also Arnkoff & Glass, 1982) and that the most widely used measures of irrationality often have unstudied psychometric qualities. For example, Smith identifies as a major shortcoming the absence of any formal studies of the discriminant validity of tests of irrationality. The ability to assess beliefs independent of the concepts to which they are theoretically related (e.g., emotional distress) is obviously crucial to the empirical evaluation and development of the rational–emotive model (T. Smith, 1983). As Smith goes on to point out, some of the items on the R. G. Jones (1968) Irrational Beliefs Test (IBT) pull for affective judgments and are similar to items on widely used measures of social-evaluative anxiety (e.g., Watson & Friend, 1969). The item similarity detracts from the use of test intercorrelations as support for the RET model.

The lack of discriminant validity associated with the tests of irrationality has important implications for the consideration of the etiological role of irrationality in emotional distress. As D. Smith identifies, studies correlating paper-and-pencil measures of emotional distress and irrational beliefs have found positive relationships, and these correlations can be seen as consistent with the RET premise. However, as Smith continues, such an interpretation must be tempered by the caution that the same pattern of results are consistent with the problems of discriminant validity. That is, measures of irrationality may be measuring emotional distress. Correspondingly, Smith has found evidence that RET procedures produced therapeutic effects, but that there was limited evidence that changes in beliefs mediated the observed treatment effects. Not unlike many reviewers of the rational–emotive enterprise, Smith sees the challenge and the need for accumulating more convincing empirical support for the basic tenets of RET.

Readers interested in a critique of RET based on its lack of structure, confirmatory bias, and lack of sufficient concern for the influence of environmental factors on human behavior are referred to a paper by Eschenroeder (1982). Eschenroeder (1982) also questions the proposition that emotions are caused and maintained by self-talk, as well as the adequacy of the RET criteria for rationality. Like other writers who comment on Ellis's tendentious reviews (e.g., Kendall & Bemis, 1983), Eschenroeder notes that it is ironic that such a proponent of skepticism as Ellis would, in reviews of research, evidence such a lack of skepticism. The interested reader is referred to Ellis's (1982) reply to Eschenroeder.

Recent outcome studies of RET include its involvement as a comparison condition in an analogue study of anger reduction in college females (Conoley, Conoley, McConnell, & Kimzey, 1983) and its combination with self-instructional training. In the treatment of a 17-year-old girl's chronic hair pulling (Bernard, Kratochwill, & Keefauver, 1983), self-instructional training provided an enhancement to RET. The authors identified clients' maladaptive thought patterns associated with anxiety and provided sessions of RET (disputational training). The self-instructional training was introduced, since it was felt that hair pulling could be reduced further than was achieved by RET. The self-instructional training included problem definition, problem approach, focusing attention, coping statements, and self-reward. This series of self-instructions parallels that used in the treatment of impulse control problems, as the authors note. The introduction of the self-instructional training "led to a rapid cessation of hair pulling" (1983, p. 278). It should also be noted that Bernard *et al.* caution that it is impossible to determine whether the self-instructions would have been as effective had it not been preceded by RET. Thus, the design of the study leaves room for inconclusiveness.

Before closing, I would like to mention that the beliefs of RET practitioners would be of interest to me. That is, how rational are our best rational therapists? In my admittedly limited but not overly restricted experience, I have found RET practitioners to be rational— although I often find myself thinking that they have individually RET'ed themselves into rationality. Anecdotes and selective experience aside, it would be interesting to learn about therapist rationality. For instance, I hope no one believes that every patient he or she treats must be a success. This irrational expectation could itself benefit from RET.

COGNITIVE–BEHAVIORAL APPROACHES
WITH OTHER PROBLEM BEHAVIORS

Strategies for remediating difficulties associated with the Type A be-havior pattern and anger have continued to receive research attention, and contemporary reports are reviewed herein. In addition, there have been extensions of Beck's cognitive therapy to anorexia nervosa (Garner & Bemis, 1982), efforts to use cognitive–behavioral strategies to reduce delusional thinking (Hartman & Cashman, 1983), comparisons of skill training and cognitive training in treating outpatients who lack as-sertiveness (Hatzenbuehler & Schroeder, 1982), and evaluation of cogni-tive restructuring for empirically derived subtypes of speech-anxious subjects (Fremouw & Gross, 1983; Gross & Fremouw, 1982). In a case study, Collins and Carlin (1983) reported the use of a combination of relaxation training, cognitive restructuring, and behavioral rehearsal in the treatment of multiple-drug abusers. Interestingly, these authors emphasized the specific training of relapse prevention (Marlatt & Gordon, 1980). Relapse prevention via *in vivo* behavioral rehearsal was seen as a valuable factor in this successful case. Inquiries along these lines are encouraged, though more attention needs to be paid to the assessment of effects and the use of a research design to eliminate rival explanations of the outcome.

Type A

The Type A behavior pattern remains troublesome to those individuals so described. Increasing attention is being given to the modification of this behavior pattern, due to the evidence linking it with coronary heart disease and related physical problems.

Levenkron, Cohen, Mueller, and Fisher (1983) compared three strategies modifying the Type A pattern. What the authors called "comprehensive behavior therapy" (based on the description provided, it is aptly labeled a cognitive–behavioral program) was compared to group support and to a brief informational program (typical care). The comprehensive behavioral program is considered here as a cognitive–behavioral intervention because it included self-control training, relaxation training, changing internal self-talk, and viewing stressful situations (e.g., waiting in line, traffic) as cues to relax. Each of these treatment strategies is appropriate for Type A individuals and reflects the authors' integration of cognitive and behavioral perspectives. The group support treatment focused on achieving self-awareness of the Type A behaviors. Group discussions were used to promote motivation for behavior change. A major difference between the cognitive–behavioral and group support programs was that the group support condition did not include any explicit behavioral techniques for altering the Type A pattern.

The authors employed an impressive array of dependent measures, including measures of behavior seen as a part of the Type A pattern, such as the Jenkins Activity Schedule (JAS) (Jenkins, Zyzanski, & Rosenman, 1976), the Framingham Type A Scale (Haynes, Feinleib, & Kannel, 1980), and the Anger Inventory (Novaco, 1975). Additional self-report inventories, such as the State–Trait Anxiety Inventory and the Stress and Strain Questionnaire, were also administered. Physiological outcome measures included heart rate and blood pressure readings taken before and after a stressor task (catheter insertion), and two blood samples that were analyzed in several ways. Subjects also provided daily ratings of a number of aspects of the Type A behavior pattern.

Subjects, members of the business community, were randomly assigned to the treatments using a randomized block procedure. Fifty-six applicants were screened, and 48 were identified as Type A according to the JAS. Treatments were provided for 8 consecutive weeks, with 90-minute weekly meetings.

The results of this well-designed and well-executed research indicated that both group treatments, the cognitive–behavioral and the group support, led to desired gains on several characteristics associated with the Type A behavior pattern. Specifically, the cognitive–behavioral treatment reduced JAS scores, Framingham scores, and Anger Inventory scores. The group support treatment also produced gains on most of the measures used to assess Type A. Both the cognitive–behavioral and the group support treatments were superior to the brief informational intervention. As the authors note, this is important, since the brief intervention was modeled after typical clinical practice. That the cognitive–behavioral program surpassed the group support program in producing desired changes on the Anger Inventory suggests that the cognitive–behavioral program was more effective in reducing the anger reactivity feature of the Type A pattern.

Anger

Three programs for the control of anger were compared and reported by Moon and Eisler (1983). Cognitive stress inoculation, problem solving, and social skills training were compared to a minimal attention control. Subjects were 40 male undergraduates who scored above the mean on Novaco's (1975) Anger Inventory. The treatments were provided by male graduate students in clinical psychology. Training was provided in groups for five weekly sessions.

One strength of this study was its breadth of dependent variables. Measures of blood pressure, pulse, self-reported anger, and behavioral measures of assertion and aggression from role-play situations were obtained. In addition, the authors had subjects self-monitor their responses to real-life anger-provoking experiences.

Statistical analyses were performed, and the data were shown to support the effectiveness of the interventions. On the Anger Inventory, all treatment groups had greater gains than controls. Moreover, the cognitive stress inoculation group had significantly lower scores than the problem-solving and social skills groups, which did not differ from each other. On ratings of aggression from the role plays, all treatment groups again showed desired reductions; in this instance, the social skills group showed the greatest gains. On ratings of assertion, a similar pattern emerged; social skills and problem-solving training produced the greatest gains in this case. These findings suggest that the cognitive stress inoculation decreased anger-producing cognitions, but did not increase assertiveness. The problem-solving and social skills approaches reduced anger-provoking cognitions (though less than the cognitive treatment) and increased assertive behavior. Behavioral aggression was reduced in the cognitive stress inoculation group, but without the increase in assertiveness. The behavioral competence of assertiveness was most affected by social skills and problem-solving programs. Although it was not the intent of this study, and Moon and Eisler are therefore not culpable for failing to demonstrate it, it is interesting to speculate that the most effective treatment would be one that combined the cognitive and behavioral training. Such an investigation, employing clinical cases, would be a worthwhile next step.

Abusive parents are in need of psychological treatment, and it seems somewhat overdue that they are only now becoming a major focus of intervention researchers. In one program, Nomellini and Katz (1983) used a variant of the cognitive–behavioral program for anger control (Novaco, 1975). A multiple-baseline design across the three treated families was employed for purposes of evaluation. Three measures were taken: (1) in-home observations of positive and negative parent and child behaviors, (2) the Novaco (1975) Anger Inventory, and (3) self-monitoring of angry "urges." The anger control training program emphasized teaching parents the various components involved in anger arousal; ways in which to self-monitor, self-instruct, and relax, as well as self-reinforcement for control of anger; and opportunities to practice these skills. Training took place in the home, covering six to eight 90-minute sessions. As the authors noted, the anger control program evidenced decreases in angry urges and reductions in aversive behaviors. These changes were maintained at follow-up (2 to 6 months). Interestingly, while negative behaviors were reduced, positive behaviors did not increase unless special steps were taken, as was done in one of the three families.

COGNITIVE–BEHAVIORAL INTERVENTIONS WITH CHILDREN

Three recent books evidence the truly impressive growth and continuing interest in the applications of cognitive–behavioral strategies to children. Meyers and Craighead (1984) have edited an offering with 14 chapters, including historical, developmental, and family conceptualizations, and covering interventions for the range of child problems (e.g., learning disability, retardation, social isolation, stress, aggression). Reviews of research are interwoven with practical suggestions and helpful summaries.

Ellis and Bernard (1983), as noted earlier, have edited a volume entitled *Rational–Emotive Approaches to the Problems of Childhood*. As authors of their opening chapter, they offer an overview of RET with children, touching on historical background and current RET perspective. Other chapters include consideration of assessment (e.g., DiGiuseppe & Bernard, 1983), specific childhood problems (e.g., conduct disorders, underachievement, social isolation, obesity), and working with parents, families, groups, and educational settings. The book has an apparent RET stripe, with a heavy emphasis on beliefs and rationality, but a less than compelling data base.

The third book on this list takes a more detailed look at a single topic than is permitted in contributed texts. In this volume, entitled *Cognitive–Behavioral Therapy for Impulsive Children* (Kendall &

Braswell, 1984), the authors describe the types of children for whom the program is intended, assessments to employ for identifying appropriate cases, and the treatment strategies and how to implement them. A detailed literature review and a copy of the treatment manual (as an appendix) are also provided. Although the outcome data are not unequivocal or conclusive, a series of outcome evaluations have been conducted, and their results buttress the suggestions for clinical application.

Current descriptions of the work done with children are available in the above-mentioned texts, but there are several additional sources of note. Picking up from the end of the period reviewed and discussed by Pressley (1979), Pressley, Reynolds, Stark, and Gettinger (1983) have reviewed the work on cognitive–behavioral self-control treatments. This work includes discussion of Luria's (1982) contribution, delay of gratification, and the modification of impulsivity. K. R. Harris (1982) provides a consideration of the application of cognitive-behavior therapy to exceptional children, and Urbain (1983) describes a cognitive–behavioral group approach to the development of a positive self-image among adolescents. Within these cognitive–behavioral reports, and among behavior therapy more generally (e.g., S. L. Harris & Ferrari, 1983), there is an awareness of the need for additional attention to developmental factors (e.g., Cole & Kazdin, 1980; Kendall, 1977; Kendall & Braswell, 1984). In the following sections, recent studies pertinent to hyperactivity/impulsivity and aggression are reviewed, and a consideration of the future needs of cognitive-behavior therapy with children is described.

Hyperactivity/Impulsivity

Hyperactivity has been studied extensively. Numerous reports of prevalence rates (e.g., 3%–5% of school-aged children) and descriptive studies of what makes hyperactive children different from normals (see Ross & Ross, 1982) have appeared. Nevertheless, as Barkley (1982) points out, there has been a limited effort directed to understanding etiology and an absence of accepted criteria for diagnosing hyperactivity. While excessive motor behavior has been a central feature of diagnoses of hyperactivity, there is a movement away from motor behavior and toward an attention deficit as the key factor. Douglas (1972) and the DSM-III (American Psychiatric Association, 1980) place greater diagnostic emphasis on the inability of hyperactive children to sustain attention or to control impulsive responding. Indeed, the DSM-III criteria for attention deficit disorder specify (1) attention deficits and (2) impulsiveness. The appropriateness of cognitive–behavioral training (verbal self-instructions, response cost, modeling, role plays) may be enhanced by this diagnostic refinement.

I have elsewhere proposed that behavior problems of childhood may be differentiated, based on the role of types of cognitive problems (e.g., Kendall, 1981; Kendall & Braswell, 1984). The distinction is between cognitive deficiencies and cognitive distortions. To use other terms, deficiencies can be viewed as absences of thinking and distortions as errors of thinking. The impulsive problem-solving style of hyperactive, acting-out, non-self-controlled children seems to reflect a cognitive deficiency. When alternatives are simultaneously available, these children fail to evaluate the choices and do not think through the problem. Children with problems such as depression, isolation, and social withdrawal may not suffer from *not thinking*, but rather from distorted thinking. Using parents' ratings of 150 children aged 6–11 and assessments of the children's cognitive tempo, Fuhrman and Kendall (in press) reported that, as predicted, hyperactivity was associated with cognitive impulsivity, but that other behavior problems, such as depression, were not. This finding contrasts with that of Schwartz, Friedman, Lindsay, and Narrol (1982), who suggested that impulsivity was associated with depression. The use of verbal self-instructions to teach children strategies for problem solving seems to match the nature of the deficit seen in attention deficit/hyperactive disorders.

Response-cost contingencies have been encouraged and employed in the cognitive–behavioral therapy for impulsive children (Kendall & Braswell, 1984). A recent within-subject analysis of the relative effects of Ritalin and response cost (Rapport, Murphy, & Bailey, 1982) provided some valuable information. Two boys, 7 and 18 years of age and diagnosed as having an attentional deficit disorder, served as subjects. Using on-task behavior, problems completed, and problems completed correctly as dependent variables, the authors concluded that response cost was superior to Ritalin in raising levels of on-task behavior and in improving academic performance. Teacher ratings suggested that response cost was an effective intervention for improving the classroom behavior of hyperactive children. As the authors stated, although positive reinforcement is more desirable, its continuous application may actually distract a child from ongoing task demands (Firestone & Douglas, 1975).

Douglas and Parry (1983) compared the effects of several reward contingencies on the performance of hyperactive and normal control children's delayed reaction time. Continuous, partial, and noncontingent schedules of reward were contrasted. The reaction time of the control children improved under all reward conditions, whereas the hyperactives became less attentive under the noncontingent schedule. Douglas and Parry point to this as evidence that erratic or inconsistent reward can *impair* the performance of hyperactive children. Indeed, the authors go on to speculate that the impulsivity problems of hyperactive children probably make them unusually dependent upon the controlling effects of contingencies. These findings are consistent with the proposition that response cost prevents the spurious rewarding of fast guessing, which, when rewarded, tends to maintain impulse behavior (Kendall & Finch, 1979).

The generalization of the effects of training remains a question worthy of continued study. Regarding the present topic, it is possible that features of the disorder being treated contribute to difficulties in attaining generalization. For instance, conceptual tempo was found to be related to the transfer of strategy training. Reflective children trained to use an organization strategy performed better during transfer than impulsive children. Thus, impulsive children evidenced an inability to use strategies in new contexts (Borkowski, Peck, Reid, & Kurtz, 1983).

Generalization may require use of the context to which generalization is hoped as the context of training. In a recent paper, using multiple-baseline strategy, Bryant and Budd (1982) reported positive effects from self-instructional training on the classroom worksheets of their 4- and 5-year-old subjects. The authors draw conclusions similar to those of other researchers, stating that the generalization that took place was related to the type of training tasks. In this study, children were trained on naturalistic worksheets, and what might be called generalization was seen in class worksheets.

The clinical effectiveness of stimulant medications for hyperactivity is a documented finding. However, there are many reasons why pharmacotherapy may not be the treatment of choice, even if effective. Authors have called for greater emphasis on teaching children skills (and less on pills; O'Leary, 1980). Others have identified the possibility of negative psychological side effects of medications with children—an attribution of change to an external agent (Whalen & Henker, 1980). Perplexing as it may seem, little has been reported in the way of comparisons of the effects of medications and behavioral/cognitive–behavioral interventions. In one study conducted in Germany, Eisert, Eisert, and Schmidt (1982) examined a cognitive–behavioral treatment and methylphenidate. Twenty-three children, aged 8 years, were treated first with either the drugs or the cognitive–behavioral treatment, then were switched to the other treatment, and finally were given the combination of treatments. Observations of behavior in the classroom, teacher and parent ratings, and psychological tests were employed as indices of outcome. Although there were methodological shortcomings (which are not uncommon in clinical trials such as this), and although there were sequence effects (which also detract from definitive conclusions), the results supported the effectiveness of the combined treatment. Also, compared to an otherwise treated control group, the children receiving the combined treatment showed greater improvements.

Using a single-case design, Horn, Chatoor, and Connors (1983) evaluated the additive effects of psychostimulant medication and self-control training with a 9-year-old hyperactive boy. Results demonstrated that a combination of the medication and self-control training was more effective than either procedure alone. Some more specific effects for drugs and for the self-control program were also noted.

The use of cognitive–behavioral self-control training to assist hyperactive boys in anger control was studied in two studies reported by Hinshaw, Henker, and Whalen (1984). In their nicely designed and clinically sensitive program, comparisons were also made between pharmacotherapy (methylphenidate) and placebo.

In Hinshaw et al.'s first study, 24 hyperactive boys aged 8–13 who were receiving medications and who met the acceptance criteria were given the cognitive training in groups of three. Half the children were given medications and half placebos. The training curriculum involved self-instructions and problem solving and followed the paradigms of Douglas, Parry, Marton, and Garson (1976), Kendall (1977), Meichenbaum and Goodman (1971) and Spivack and Shure (1974), and was provided twice weekly for 2 hours for a 3-week period. To enhance the clinical meaningfulness and generalization of the training, Hinshaw et al. included a session where the trained subjects each took a turn coping with direct taunting and teasing from the other two children in each group. After the first round, the children discussed self-controlling strategies and practiced them with the therapist prior to the second round of provocation. The outcomes were derived from coding the videotapes of the provocations. Global ratings and time-sampled observations of verbal behaviors and motoric behaviors were recorded. As Hinshaw et al. (1984) reported, their results were encouraging, particularly with respect to globally rated and specifically rated self-control. The training resulted in the children's inhibition of aggressive action and deployment of alternative behaviors. Regarding medication status, there were no statistically significant interactions and a relatively isolated effect on the intensity of the children's behavior.

Given the absence of a control condition, Hinshaw et al. (1984) proceeded to implement a second study; again, 24 hyperactive boys participated. Training sessions covered a 3-week period, and each lasted 1 hour and 20 minutes. Training began with problem-solving, self-instructional, and attitudinal content. The second week focused on the application of self-instructional strategies to academic problems. The third week began the provocation assessments. The cognitive–behavioral program built on Novaco's (1975) ideas regarding anger inoculation. This training emphasized identifying the external threats that produce anger and the cognitive and visceral signs of impending anger; employing problem solving; and practicing self-control following provocation. The comparison condition focused on perspective taking, affective understanding, and empathy enhancement, but these children did not receive stress inoculation or specific strategy training or rehearsal. Regarding medications, 12 boys were receiving medication and 12 placebo capsules during the provocations and assessments.

The outcome on global ratings and time-sampled behaviors during the provocation included only one medication effect, which was on the specific category of intensity. In contrast, the cognitive–behavioral training (as compared to the alternate control training) evidenced meaningful improvements on self-control and gains on purposeful alternate activities. Also, following training, the children receiving cognitive–behavioral training demonstrated twice as many coping strategies as the controls. In brief, the cognitive–behavioral program enhanced general self-control and promoted the use of active coping strategies. Medications had little effect on dependent measures assessing aggression and use of coping strategies. While not providing an optimal comparison of cognitive–behavioral training and medication, the results nevertheless underscore the importance of training active strategies for self-control.

Two issues pertinent to the Hinshaw et al. (1984) results are discussed by the authors. First, it would have been of interest to have studied cognitive changes that may have been facilitated by the program and generalized changes to other contexts and situations. Lengthier treatment and follow-up assessment would also have been interesting to consider in evaluating the program's impact. The second concern, weighed cautiously by the authors, is that of the potential risks associated with direct fear provocation. One must exercise great caution to prevent the children from learning to be good provokers rather than good copers. It has been my experience that boys in this age range can be very effective provokers of affect, even without encouragement. What is especially needed is the devotion of time to ensure that the children realize that provocation is not being encouraged and that learning to cope is the goal. With such a caveat, I agree with Hinshaw et al. that the value of the ecologically valid situation outweighs the potential risk for iatrogenic effects. As a suggestion, one way to improve the ecological validity of the taunting experience would be to observe normal children in related situations. Athletic competition and the jousting that is given and taken by teammates might serve as prototype for normal acquisition and use of coping strategies within the context of an accepting social environment. Though I am not intending to be sexist, locker-room exchanges of the teaming variety may play a central role in children's development of patterns of coping with anger and aggression.

Aggression

The Hinshaw *et al.* (1984) study treated hyperactive boys in an effort to control aggression and serves as a bridge into the consideration of treatment of aggressive children. Results of research focusing on the cognitive–behavioral treatment of anger and aggression in children are often described as mixed. Kendall and Braswell (1984) point out, for instance, that impulsive behavior seems more amenable to treatment than aggressive behavior, using the programs now available. Similarly, Meyers and Cohen (1984) suggest that aggression seems less readily modified than impulsivity when treatment outcomes are examined.

In a recent report, Kettlewell and Kausch (1983) provided data on the generalization of a cognitive–behavioral program for aggressive children. Children were 7–12 years of age and participants in a day camp affiliated with a residential treatment center. In addition to consent to participate and an IQ of 80 or above, selected cases were reported to have enacted at least one physical or verbal aggressive behavior during each day of the pretrial period. A total of 40 children were assigned to either the treatment group or a no-treatment control. The 20 treated children met in one of four groups twice a week (90 minutes each) for 4 weeks, totaling eight sessions, and 1 individual hour per week. The treatment focused on coping skills to "keep cool" in tough situations. Treatment procedures included behavioral rehearsal and self-instructional training. While the authors mention that one-third of the time for each group session (at the end) was set aside for an ice cream treat, there were apparently no behavioral contingencies in operation. The ice cream was given for cooperation. It would have been preferable, in my opinion, to have tied the learning and performance in the treatment groups to the rewards given afterwards.

The assessment of outcome involved 12 measures grouped into five categories: two task performance ratings; self-report of anger; Means–Ends–Problem-Solving (MEPS) scores; and an index of aggressive behavior. The breadth of dependent measures is laudable, yet restraint on enthusiasm is called for; there were no behavioral observations, the

MEPS is a questionable index of outcome (see Kendall & Fischler, 1984), and some of the assessments are of unknown psychometric credibility. Analyses of these data indicated that the treatment group improved significantly from pretesting to posttesting, as compared to the control group. The most meaningful changes were seen on the MEPS and in a decrease in being disciplined for fighting. No changes were found in physical or verbal aggression and on peer ratings of aggression. Kettlewill and Kausch offer a balanced conclusion: "[O]utcome measures most similar to the treatment procedures reflected more change than measures representing a greater degree of generalization" (1983, p. 113). They also add that they see their data as providing support for cognitive–behavioral programs for aggressive youngsters, but they quickly point to the need for further investigation.

Angry children were targeted by Garrison and Stolberg (1983) for a program of affective imagery training. Thirty 8- to 11-year-olds who scored high on the Aggression scale of the Child Behavior Checklist (Achenbach & Edelbrock, 1979) were assigned to training, attention, or control conditions. Treatment lasted 30 to 40 minutes, for three sessions in one week. This seems, at best, brief—perhaps too brief to be able to provide any indication of the potency of the intervention program. Nevertheless, the intervention involved imagining affectively laden events, attending to the associated physiological responses, and labeling the emotional state. Each child imagined eight situations from his or her own experience. A Child Behavior Checklist and an affect questionnaire were examined at pretreatment, posttreatment and follow-up.

Garrison and Stolberg (1983) concluded that the children who underwent the affective imagery training "not only registered change in their perceptions and cognitions related to affective material, but also demonstrated reduced angry behavior in the classroom" (pp. 126–127). The reduction in angry behavior was recorded by classroom teachers. The findings are positive, though we would certainly want to see how the program would survive with a more disturbed sample and after more extended intervention.

Future Directions

When assessments identify a child as impulsive or non-self-controlled, there is a structured intervention program that, if implemented properly, can produce desired gains in the child's self-control (see Kendall & Braswell, 1984). However, even this rather circumscribed prescription would not receive unanimous endorsement; even if one does accept it, there are still other disorders, such as depression and/or social withdrawal, where there has not been a sufficient effort on the research front to propose an organized or prescriptive cognitive–behavioral intervention.

My reflections on the further needs of cognitive–behavioral therapy with children appear elsewhere (Kendall, 1984c). The present discussion both borrows excerpts from that report and adds to it.

SOCIAL ISOLATION AND DEPRESSION

If a treatment strategy designed for inhibiting thoughtless behavior is applied to the remediation of other disorders, are we not making a uniformity-myth error? If the treatment procedures are implemented without alteration, then the likelihood is that the outcome will be less than satisfactory. Take, for example, the use of self-instructions for the treatment of childhood social withdrawal. Standard self-instructional training would place an emphasis on caution and thoughtful behavior. Action is inhibited by the rehearsal of guiding self-talk. Will such an intervention strategy stimulate the socially isolated child to engage in social interactions? Even if the content of the self-instructions were changed so that the child practiced such self-statements as "Get out there and be involved," will the insertion of additional self-talk be encouraging action and interaction? I am curious, but I think not. It is not by chance that self-instructional procedures are linked with strategies to inhibit behavior. Rather, there are theoretical rationales and empirical supports for the matching of impulsive children with an intervention that inhibits action by inserting thoughtful reflection.

Should cognitive–behavioral procedures *not* be used with socially isolated children, then? No. There are procedures within the domain of cognitive–behavioral therapy that might be beneficial to withdrawn youngsters (e.g., modeling, coaching, modifying expectations; see Kendall & Morison, 1984). The outcome data are limited, and the interventions are in the initial stages of development, but the further development of such strategies is indeed worthwhile. Consider, for example, a child who is an isolate. The child engages in limited social interaction and is missing much of the experience with peers that contributes developmentally to adjustment. What makes the child isolated? One possibility is a lack of skills in social interactions, and a social skills training intervention might be the treatment of choice. However, isolates can have the skills in their repertoire but fail to display them. These children may be distorting and misperceiving the demands of the social situation. For example, a group of children are in the cafeteria, and the majority are involved in one of several small-group activities. Five children are working on a bulletin board, and four others are setting up tables and chairs. The target child, physically capable but socially avoidant, is alone. He or she glances at, occasionally watches, but does not focus on those setting up chairs. An aide takes an interest in the child and starts a conversation. "Come on, let's help out," states the aide, while moving toward the others and making an attempt to attract the child. The child turns away, not joining either group and no longer paying attention. What could it be that the child is saying to himself or herself? How is this child perceiving the demands of the environment? One possibility is that the child is seeing the other children as experts and viewing himself or herself as merely average. The child might be thinking, "They're good at moving furniture, I'm not so good." In this instance, we have an occasion to consider the problem as one that results from a cognitive *distortion* or *error*: The child is misperceiving the demands of the environment and engaging in undue self-deprecation. Isolated behavior patterns may be associated with a number of different cognitive processes, such as extensive self-criticism, inaccurate anticipation of rejection, and excessive internal standards for success. Here, as with the cognitive–behavioral strategies employed with adult clients, the therapist will have to pay specific attention to the identification and removal of the dysfunctional cognitive processing.

Childhood depression serves as another instance where new cognitive–behavioral approaches should be developed and/or existing programs for adults modified. Impulse control programs for children would be inappropriate as a sole treatment, and the strategies outlined so expertly in the Beck *et al.* (1979) book refer to adults and would require major modification prior to application with children. For instance, cognitive therapy for depression conceptualizes the client's depressed mood as the result of maladaptive negative thoughts, and negative views of the self, world, and future. "Collaborative empiricism," where the client and therapist serve as active collaborators (Hollon & Beck, 1979), is employed in the identification and modification of the client's faulty thinking. At what age or developmental period are children capable of the hypothesis-testing procedure that Beck *et al.* describe? One could be reasonably confident that the child would need to be at least at the Piagetian level of formal operations and to have accomplished some skill in perspective taking (cf. Selman, 1980). In the absence of perspective taking, the child would not be able to step outside himself or herself in order to evaluate the validity of his or her expectations or beliefs. Being able to take the position of an outside observer of oneself is a developmental skill that is probably not available to the majority of children under 10 or 11 years of age. When using a hypothesis-testing strategy with a young child, would a parent have to become involved in the hypothesis-testing process? The effects of involving a parent are to date unknown, and one can entertain speculations that the eventual outcome could be either beneficial or detrimental. Indeed, since some children are depressed because of the negative quality of their interaction with parents, parent involvement may detract from outcome unless the parents are treated also.

Mood monitoring comprises a hearty portion of the Beck *et al.* (1979) approach with adults. We are again in a position of having to question the capacity of children at various ages to accomplish this therapeutic task. At least, children will need to be taught to identify various moods, to examine variations in these moods, and to be able to develop the habit of recording these mood assessments outside of the treatment context. Some portions of the initial sessions would have to be set aside for the development of a "feelings dictionary" and an understanding of variability of mood.

Scheduling of pleasant events is rather straightforward for the autonomous adult. Scheduling a movie is easy; one simply plans to go on the chosen evening. With children, however, several adults (at least one) have to be involved. Pleasant events scheduling may require a sponsor to pay for the ticket, a contributor to provide a ride to the theater, and a friend or chaperone to attend the movie with the child. Indeed, it may be adult attention that is the pleasant event that has to be scheduled, and adult attention necessitates an interested and participatory adult. Pleasant events scheduling could best be accomplished when a family unit is cooperative, using the entire family. Viewing the task as scheduling pleasant family events may take some of the burden off the target child and secure a greater degree of cooperation among the family members.

The uniformity myths—the myths that patients, therapists, and outcome measures are uniform—were identified by Kiesler (1966). The resulting challenges for therapy researchers spurred important advances in the therapy outcome literature. There is another uniformity myth— one that I have described as involving the false belief that "children" are a homogeneous group (Kendall, 1984b). Children are not only different from adults, but also different among themselves. Another aspect of the myth is that children are stable. Quite the contrary is true, for children are in the most evanescent period of life, and the only thing that is truly stable is that they are changing. Therapeutic goals (changes) must be examined in light of a second set of change processes that are operative—a set we can label developmental processes. Developmental levels can inform us of interventions that may be more or less appropriate, and developmental predictions can inform us of a child's trajectory, so that we can provide preventive intervention (Kendall, Lerner, & Craighead, 1984). Developmental information offers a meaningful template for child-clinical interventions.

RAPID ENDORSEMENT AND RAPID DISILLUSIONMENT

As I have argued elsewhere (Kendall, 1984c), the true merits of an intervention should not be judged by the popularizing skills of its major proselytizer nor by the presence of absence of a wave of unbridled enthusiasm. Data-based evaluations are essential to the development of a clinical discipline that can be said to have a respect for the cumulation and synthesis of knowledge. As evident in D. Smith's (1982) survey, an impressive number of mental health practitioners are identified with cognitive–behavioral approaches (as many as psychoanalysis, and second only to eclecticism). The support is warmly received. Nevertheless, I am cautious of the unstinting application of cognitive–behavioral procedures until we have a better understanding of the disorders we are treating and some evidence that the treatment has the desired effects on the chosen disorder. There is a logical as well as an historical affinity between certain cognitive–behavioral procedures and their targeted behavior problems. These pairings are scarcely accidental, as they reflect the intentional design of the therapeutic modality. The trend toward an "expanded terrain," in which specific cognitive–behavioral strategies are being applied to virgin territory, must be guided by empirical information (Kendall & Bemis, 1983).

In contrast, but with equal if not greater vigor, I stress the need for empirical information to prevent premature dismissal of cognitive–behavioral approaches. I was most disheartened when I heard someone say, "Well, I tried it once with a delinquent who was impulsive and it didn't work." No assessments were conducted pre or post, and the therapy lasted 4 weeks, with a single 30-minute session each week. It would be difficult to find someone who would have believed that the gains, had they occurred, were due to such a cryptic treatment. Correspondingly, we should be careful not to dismiss the procedures on the basis of poor information.

The proper balance of enthusiasm and critical caution comes, I think, when we have adjusted our therapeutic expectations. If we expect that there is no way in hell that we can ever make Johnny a darling boy, then we are also creating expectations that will interfere with effective therapeutic programming. We must realize that experimental studies published in the literature tell us about variables that may be important in accounting for some of the variance observed in outcome. These same studies, however, are only a sample of the studies that were undertaken; some did not produce meaningful variations in the dependent measures. Expectations that we can facilitate adjustment, expectations that the strategy we have learned and are providing will help to produce gains, and expectations that not every case will be a cure nor every outcome study an exact success will best serve the researcher and practitioner as we enter this next decade of inquiry into the interfacing of thought and action in child psychotherapy.

ON THE "QUALITY OF THERAPY" IN OUTCOME STUDIES

I have, on at least two occasions, heard critics comment that treatment outcome research is too often conducted by PhD-bound dissertation writers who, prepared with a fresh literature review, enthusiasm, and a need to graduate, are nonetheless saddled with deadlines, inexperience, and some blind enthusiasm. How can we, the critics continue, base a science of therapeutic change on such nascent explorers? On one occasion, I was the critic. Presently, I argue that we stop the discourse and begin to assess quality.

Elsewhere (Kendall & Hollon, 1983), the idea of variations in the *quality* of therapy has been addressed as a future need. In this sense, I am not bemoaning the existing work, but promoting an emerging interest in research of variations in quality. It is proposed that the therapy provided as part of treatment-outcome research be taped and that these tapes be archived. Analysis of the tapes could focus on any of a multitude of topics, but the quality of treatment, as judged by trained raters, would certainly be a worthwhile focus. Quality would not have to be a single dimension, for various aspects of therapeutic quality across studies could be identified and examined.

Sachs (1983) reported that Errors in Technique, a subscale of the VNIS, was related to negative outcomes in therapy. Sachs cites other research to suggest that techniques have not been considered important because when comparisons of different types of therapy are undertaken, the various techniques yield similar results. However, in her report the *quality* of the therapy was examined, and indeed errors in technique, or low quality, were associated with negative outcomes. It seems only reasonable to speculate that higher quality would be associated with positive gains, though more empirical evaluations are required.

Schaffer (1983) also promotes the utility of measures of the skillfulness of therapeutic practice. Schaffer points to Kiesler's therapist uniformity myth (1966) and states that not all therapists are equally skillful! Tapes can be rated by independent judges, with an eye on how representative of the respective therapy the session actually was, and with an eye on how skillful the session was conducted. Schaffer argues for the use of a given theory of therapeutic technique to derive the definitions of skillfulness.

These concerns with the quality of treatment carry with them some important implications for the overall evaluation of treatment. For instance, if an outcome is unsuccessful, we cannot at present tell whether the treatment was inappropriate, impotent, or simply poorly provided.

PREDICTORS OF RESPONSE TO TREATMENT

There are rare times when I consider the massive and expanding literature on behavioral and other psychological therapies and conclude that we have not been as convincing in terms of documenting all of the positive effects as we might have been. True, there are strategies with demonstrated effectiveness, but it is equally true that there are cases where predictions regarding individual treatments are less than optimally accurate. My experience and reading of the literature suggest that one of the major problems is the weakness in predicting which clients will and will not benefit maximally from treatment and which will maintain the gains our interventions can produce.

Examination of differential outcome, following methodolgically sound evidence that the treatment was responsible for the observed change, requires a large sample size. In a report by Weissberg, Cowen, Lotyczewski, and Gesten (1983), the outcomes of a 7-year program of intervention were considered. Given the enlarged number of subjects available in such a cumulative report, the analysis of differential outcome would be especially powerful.

A direct look at prediction of treatment response was reported by Foa, Grayson, Steketee, Doppelt, Turner, and Latimer (1983a). These authors examined prediction of improvement with behavioral treatment for obsessive–compulsive disorder. For instance, Foa et al. (1983a) reported that pretreatment levels of depression and anxiety were related to outcome. In other words, patients high on depression and anxiety were able to obtain maximal overall relief. Also of interest, severity or duration of symptoms were not negative indicators in improvement.

Predictions of outcome in parent training were reported by Clark and Baker (1983). In this study, families that were found to be low in proficiency (limited knowledge, low scores on videotapes of technique, performance ratings during training) were from lower-socioeconomic-status backgrounds, had expected greater problems in teaching, and had less prior experience with behavior modification than highly proficient families.

Murphy *et al.* (1984) were most interested in medication versus cognitive treatment of depression, but they briefly discuss how learned resourcefulness, as measured by the Self-Control Schedule (SCS; Rosenbaum, 1980), may be helpful in matching patients to treatments. For example, patients who scored high on the SCS responded well in cognitive therapy, whereas low scorers on the SCS did well in pharmacotherapy.

Predictions of responsiveness to outcome go hand in hand with predictions of relapse. It was as part of my concern with the clinical significance of treatment outcomes that I began considering relapse rates as an outcome criterion. Briefly, published reports convey statistically significant changes produced by treatment (when proper controls are employed). The amount of change is said to be beyond that which could have occurred by chance alone. But the extent of the change, even if beyond chance levels, may not be significant to qualify as clinically meaningful change. One aspect of the search for clinical changes is relapse. If we can document significantly extended periods without relapse, we can make substantial impressions on those who query the effectiveness of behavioral therapy. Notice that I do not suggest a complete absence of relapse, but a period without relapse that is extended beyond what would have resulted without the intervention.

The fact that not all clients evidence total elimination of the targeted problem should not undermine our therapeutic enthusiasm. Rather, it can become the topic for direct investigation. Let us consider three topics of current interest and see how the prediction of relapse can be a source of exciting research.

The recent past has witnessed a series of studies comparing the effects of cognitive–behavioral therapy and pharmacotherapy for the treatment of depression. Some data suggest that there are comparable posttreatment gains, but that the cognitive–behavioral training has a superior record in terms of preventing relapse. This finding not only is of interest, but also gives rise to further questions: What features of clients differentiate those who relapsed from those who did not? Are there any pretreatment factors that are accurate and meaningful predictors of the rate of relapse?

Programs for weight loss have had a series of favorable outcomes suggesting that subjects can lose 15–18 pounds—but do they keep it off? Can they fool Mother Nature? It is evident that some do maintain weight loss, whereas others regain many of the pounds that have been taken off. What are the predictors of relapse? J. Foreyt (personal communication, January 29, 1984) suggests that one of the better predictors is the subject's pretreatment response to the question, "How confident are you that you are going to do well in this program?" Answers to this question, reflecting personal confidence, are sound predictors of drop-out and treatment success. If and when we have reasonable predictors of relapse, then we can select out those who do not respond well and can design alternate and superior programs. Although I do not want to get too far from the main point, let me reiterate that it is the study of the predictors—be they behavioral patterns, cognitive styles, or affective states—and of their accuracy in predicting differential outcome and relapse that is worthy of research attention.

When one reflects on some of the alcoholics who have kicked the drinking habit, one can see that there are often instances where the convert begins to proselytize others. Taking the role of the new savior, the recent convert, with an abundance of endowed self-righteousness, works to convince and convert others. Could it be the case that proselytizing is a maintenance strategy? In work with anorexic patients, K. Bemis (personal communication, 1984) has remarked that several of the most successful cases have gone out and tried to help other people not to be obsessed with thinness (or phobia of weight gain). For example, successful cases have become involved in going to schools to teach youngsters of the dangers of excessive thinness. Again, the effort to aid others that can follow the conversion experience serves as a powerful maintainer of behavior change. Studies could begin to investigate clients' natural choice or willingness to help others and its association with relapse prevention, and could later begin to assign or require such participation in an experimental manipulation study. The information that is produced would be rich in theoretical questions ripe for further study.

Consideration of the question "For whom does treatment work best?" returned me to an image of Kiesler's (1971) grid model for psychotherapy research. The model included the recommendation that individual differences among clients be considered as independent variables in outcome evaluation. Correspondingly, features of the therapists were also suggested as important sources of outcome variances. Moreover, the possible interactions of client features and therapist features could be identified.

I have since come to learn that while the model offers a powerful paradigm for researchers, clients often do not cooperate. Clients self-select the type of therapy they want to seek, and this self-selection can undermine the effort to find real matches between type of client and optimal treatment. Even when random assignment is employed, clients can and do refuse participation (e.g., 48 cases refused participation in the study by Murphy *et al.*, 1984). An anecdote illustrates my point. At a recent social gathering for a faculty colleague who was going on leave, I was engaged in conversation with two female associates from the Political Science Department. Both had been through psychoanalysis, and both argued that it was not possible to evaluate the effectiveness of therapy. For instance, one stated that while she was originally referred to a behavior therapist who immediately noted that her marriage was dead and that she needed to be more assertive both interpersonally and in terms of a career, she did not stay with the therapist because "it seemed too easy." Instead, she selected an analyst who, as she reported, identified her problem (some 4 years later) as passivity in an ineffective marital relationship. A divorce took place, and the woman returned to graduate school. She reported feeling great about the therapy but could not see how the outcome could be assessed—"I'm a different person now."

Not only does this anecdote give us an idea of the needs of some individuals to make therapy less of a science, but it also evidences how people self-select treatments. This woman's individual style was ruminative and philosophical. Her preference for extended debate and redirection was consistent with a lack of interest in practicality and pragmatism.

I am not arguing that psychoanalysis was effective or not for this client, nor am I arguing that the behaviorist could have solved her concerns years earlier (though I believe he could have), but I am suggesting that treatment outcome may be influenced by the degree to which the client holds beliefs that are consistent with the rationale of the treatment. An examination of the natural process of clients' selecting types of treatment might prove most informative.

CHAPTER

5

BEHAVIORAL MEDICINE

KELLY D. BROWNELL

INTRODUCTION

Behavioral medicine is a rapidly changing field. Since its birth in the middle and late 1970s, the field has acquired an image, several journals, annual meetings, professional organizations, and even experts! This is an impressive phenomenon, given the brief time that has elapsed.

I have watched my own impression of the field change as I have written on the topic in the last three volumes of the *Annual Review*. In the first of these volumes (Volume 8), I addressed the issue of whether behavioral medicine was a viable area. The definition of "behavioral medicine" was an important issue because it defined the scope and boundaries of the field. In the second volume (Volume 9), I questioned whether the field was established or still searching for an identity. It appeared at the time that the search was still in progress, and that there were several dangers faced by the field as it moved from birth through childhood and adolescence. In this volume, I show why I feel that behavioral medicine is here to stay. The evidence comes from many sources, scientific and otherwise.

The relevance of the field of public health to behavioral medicine is covered in this chapter. As psychologists in general and behavior therapists in particular move into the areas subsumed under the behavioral medicine banner, the field of public health becomes more and more important. We have much to learn from and much to contribute to the older and more established public health discipline (Singer & Krantz, 1982).

This chapter also covers several topics that, in my opinion, are central to the field of behavioral medicine. The first of these is training. The training that students receive all determine the character of the field in years to come, and there is growing attention to questions of which disciplines students should study, what degrees they should be granted, and so forth.

This discussion of training is followed by a section on cardio-vascular risk factors in children. There is tremendous excitement about the area of disease prevention and health promotion, and nowhere is the potential so great as in risk factor reduction in children. The shift from the treatment of disease in adults to the prevention of disease in children has turned the spotlight to several interesting issues, including the parent–child interactions that formulate life style habits, the degree to which specific behaviors relate to risk and then to disease endpoints, and the viability of prevention programs in the schools. This area of risk factor reduction provides a valuable opportunity for behavior therapists to become more involved in public health applications of behavior change programs.

THE STATUS AND CONDITION OF THE FIELD

Institutionalizing a Field

Behavioral medicine is now an established field (N. E. Miller, 1983a). The signs noted in earlier volumes of the *Annual Review* still exist, and more signs are occurring all the time. The most impressive sign is the institutionalization of the field. This has occurred in professional circles and has even been seen at the federal level, in the National Institutes of Health (NIH).

The professional commitment to behavioral medicine is still growing. The health psychology movement within the American Psychological Association (APA) was established very rapidly. Within only a few years, the APA formed Division 38 (Health Psychology), supported the publication of a journal (*Health Psychology*), and sponsored a major conference on education and training. The Society of Behavioral Medicine has increased in membership and serves a valuable service to scientists and other professionals with the publication of its two journals (*Behavioral Medicine Abstracts* and *Behavioral Medicine Update*) and with the sponsorship of its annual meeting. The *Journal of Behavioral Medicine* continues to publish articles that cover work in many areas of the field.

The issue of training, which is discussed in more detail below, is another example of the field's becoming more entrenched. Efforts have been made to establish training programs in behavioral medicine and to grant degrees in related areas such as health psychology. These efforts ensure a generation of professionals trained in the disciplines necessary to advance the field of behavioral medicine.

These are only examples of how professionals have grouped together to support the growth of behavioral medicine. The field is beginning to involve professionals in many disciplines, and its potential contributions to the health field are more widely recognized than ever. This is evident in the support of behavioral medicine at the federal level.

The National Heart, Lung and Blood Institute of the NIH was the first federal agency to establish a formal section devoted to behavioral medicine—the Behavioral Medicine Branch directed by Dr. Stephen M. Weiss (S. M. Weiss, 1982). Out of this effort was born the Behavioral Medicine Study Section, an NIH-wide group that reviews grant applications across the diverse areas covered by the different NIH institutes.

The National Cancer Institute, the largest of the institutes within NIH, also established a Behavioral Medicine Branch, whose name has now been changed to the Health Promotion Sciences Branch. The National Institute on Child Health and Human Development has a section on behavioral medicine, which in 1982 sponsored a special consultant conference on Behavioral Pediatrics. The National Institute of Mental Health is also establishing a behavioral medicine program.

These are powerful signs that the field will endure. It shows that the field has made a contribution to the health world and will continue to do so.

The Early Adulthood of the Field

The field of behavioral medicine has emerged from its childhood and adolescence and has reached young adulthood. Questions about its viability have been answered, and the struggle for identity has been addressed, if not answered. The field has now moved into a stage where what its members should and will do is the major issue.

The battles over definitions of behavioral medicine are over, at least for the time being. The emergence of health psychology as a specialty within the broader field of psychology has fueled the fire to some extent because of the need to distinguish it from behavioral medicine. In addition, Matarazzo (1980, 1982) feels that yet another term, "behavioral health," is necessary. However, the field has moved beyond these disputes to the interesting question of where it stands in relation to other fields and disciplines (N. E. Miller, 1983a).

The issue of *what* the researchers and practitioners of behavioral medicine should actually do is fascinating. Until recently, this was defined by whatever people in the field *were* doing, but the picture has changed. It is widely recognized that behavioral medicine could encompass nearly every aspect of the health care field. For example, in the area of coronary heart disease, behavioral medicine efforts could include genetic counseling to reduce risk for certain hyperlipidemias, school programs aimed at risk factor education, environmental engineering to reduce exposure to dangerous substances (e.g., cigarette smoke from others), political action to alter risk (e.g., changing the school lunch program to reduce fat in the diet), media programs to reach large audiences, compliance counseling to increase the effect of antihypertensive therapy, and more traditional behavioral programs of smoking cessation and weight reduction aimed at individuals.

There are more possibilities than this for behavioral medicine, even within the area of coronary heart disease. However, this range of possibilities raises some complex questions. Should professionals involved in any of these areas be considered members of the behavioral medicine field? Which of these areas should be the focus of training programs? Which areas should be granted space in journals and time at conventions?

I do not have the answers to these questions, and it will be several years before this degree of resolution will come to the field. In the meantime, I feel there are disciplines that are particularly relevant for the field of behavioral medicine. I discuss one of these, the field of public health, in the following section.

THE IMPORTANCE OF THE PUBLIC HEALTH FIELD

Public Health and Psychology

In Volume 8 of the *Annual Review*, I discussed the importance of the field of epidemiology to behavioral medicine. The basic principles of epidemiology were presented, along with concepts that had direct relevance to work in behavioral medicine. The field of public health is at least as important to our work.

An appreciation for the importance of public health to behavioral medicine can be obtained by examining the contents of several journals in that field. The two primary journals in public health are the *American Journal of Public Health,* published by the American Public Health Association, and *Public Health Reports*, published by the Office of Disease Prevention and Health Promotion of the U.S. Department of Health and Human Services. There are also related publications, such as the journal *Preventive Medicine*, which also deal with public health issues.

Some readers of this chapter will be familiar with these publications, but for those who are not, I recommend an examination of a few issues. The articles bring a perspective that is quite different than that of psychology, and I have found the information very useful in developing ideas about my own work and about the field of behavioral medicine.

In the August 1982 issue of *American Psychologist*, several articles were devoted to the potential of the interaction of public health and psychology (Michael, 1982; Singer & Krantz, 1982; Tanabe, 1982). Another paper on this topic was published recently by Runyan, DeVellis, DeVellis, and Hochbaum (1982). These papers show the conceptual foundations of the public health field and how collaboration between professionals in public health and psychology may produce impressive results.

The main distinguishing characteristic of public health is that the focus is on the community rather than the individual (Michael, 1982). Issues that deal with the health of large groups are relevant to public health. This might include methods for controlling epidemics, preventive measures such as fluoridation of water supplies, strategies for identifying high-risk groups, political issues involved in the dissemination of health information and health programs, and so forth.

Psychology and public health stand to complement each other in a very productive manner. Psychology focuses on the individual, and public health emphasizes larger groups. The interaction of these two bodies of knowledge may advance the field more rapidly than either area alone. This was the stance taken by Singer and Krantz (1982) in their discussion of the interface between psychology and public health:

> The major features of the public health approach include a focus on primary prevention, an orientation toward macro-level (e.g., community, nationwide, or societal) interventions, and public policy concerns. By contrast, psychology has traditionally been involved in secondary or tertiary aspects of health care delivery and has a distinct orientation toward the individual (cf. Sarason, 1981). Its concerns have included individual processes of learning; behavior theory and behavior change; intraindividual processes of persuasion and attitude change; and individual responses to research questionnaires, experiments, and surveys. Behavior theory is often emphasized even in the absence of available applications, public policy considerations are avoided as outside the domain of the scientist, and the larger group is examined primarily for its impact on individual behavior. (Singer & Krantz, 1982, p. 955)

The vast potential in this collaboration is made possible by the complex interactions between society and its individuals that determine patterns of health behavior. Public health can contribute to the relationship because of its emphasis on these group and societal factors, and psychology brings a knowledge of individual behavior. Each has more potential when considered in light of the other.

Some of the contributions of public health are quite interesting. Runyan *et al.* (1982) give an example of this with the case of cholera and its control in England. John Snow, in the mid-1800s, devoted years to mapping the distribution of cholera cases in London. He found that the patterns were associated with the use of water from a particular source, the Broad Street pump. In one of the first published health interventions, Snow prevented the spread of cholera: He removed the pump handle.

More sophisticated examples of public health applications have been involved in the control or elimination of such diseases as smallpox, polio, tuberculosis, pneumonia, and others. Sanitation was a major aspect of this work in public health, and the control of these infectious diseases was seen as the first health revolution (Michael, 1982). The second revolution has been the shift in attention to life style and environmental factors related to health—that is, the area of health promotion (Michael, 1982).

The Second Public Health Revolution

In 1979, the Surgeon General, Julius Richmond, released a landmark report entitled *Healthy People: The Surgeon General's Report on Health Promotion and Disease Prevention* (U.S. Department of Health, Education and Welfare, 1979a). The report was accompanied by a very detailed series of background papers on public health issues (U.S. Department of Health, Education and Welfare, 1979b).

One of the main issues addressed in the Surgeon General's report was that costs for health care have risen dramatically, to the point where health care reaches 10% of the gross national budget, yet there have been almost no changes in mortality and disability since the 1950s. Tremendous gains have been made in diagnosing and treating disease, yet overall death rates have not been declining. Whatever gains were made in the technology of medicine were counteracted by increasing rates of life-style-related diseases.

The fields of public health and behavioral medicine are relevant given this new approach to health care. The following statement from

Michael (1982) typifies widespread sentiment among many leaders in the health field:

> Today cardiovascular disease, including both heart disease and stroke, accounts for roughly half of all deaths. Cancer accounts for another 20%. Accidents exact a fearsome toll of death and disability. Clearly, the next health revolution must be aimed at these new killers and cripplers, and it clearly makes sense to emphasize strategies in that revolution for preventing these afflictions rather than to rely on treating them after they have already struck. (Michael, 1982, p. 936)

Time and time again, experts have noted the large contribution of life style to chronic illnesses such as coronary heart disease, cancer, diabetes, and so forth (Breslow, 1979; Haggerty, 1977; Hamburg, 1982; Levy & Moskowitz, 1982; Williams & Wynder, 1976). Using data from the Alameda County Study (Belloc & Breslow, 1972), Breslow (1979) estimates that a person who follows certain health habits, including not smoking, exercising regularly, maintaining normal weight, getting enough sleep, and so forth, may live an average of 11 years longer than a person who follows none of these habits.

Identifying the behavioral and social causes of disease is one thing, but changing the behaviors is another. The process of behavior change will require knowledge of both social and individual factors; hence the greatness of the potential for collaboration between psychology and public health.

The Implications for Behavioral Medicine

I agree that the potential for work between psychology and public health is enormous (Runyan et al., 1982; Singer & Krantz, 1982). This issue can be approached by examining what psychology can offer public health and vice versa.

Singer and Krantz (1982) have noted many of the areas in which these disciplines may aid each other. They feel that psychology can make a major contribution by examining the *mechanisms* linking behavior and health. They describe three main categories in which these mechanisms and processes might be studied:

1. *Health-impairing habits and life style.* These would include habits of life related to illness. Cigarette smoking, excessive eating, and physical inactivity are prime examples.
2. *Direct psychophysiological effects.* This category includes direct bodily effects caused by psychological and social stimuli. An example is stress and the Type A behavior pattern.

3. *Reactions to illness and the sick role.* This category involves such issues as a person's tendency to seek health care, compliance and self-cure.

These issues are typically not part of the training and background of professionals in public health, yet are crucial to developing and planning programs for large groups. Many public health programs, especially those targeting life style factors, require the active participation of the individual; in such programs, psychology can be instrumental.

Public health also has much to offer psychology. The perspective that public health professionals bring to health problems is novel and helpful to most psychology-trained people in behavioral medicine. Singer and Krantz (1982) list four areas in which the public health perspective is pertinent to behavioral medicine.

1. Some issues related to health are not under the control of the individual. Environmental conditions and pollutants are examples.

2. Health beliefs, attitudes, and behaviors occur in a social context and cannot be understood or altered without an appreciation of that context.

3. Our society is beginning to believe that there is a collective responsibility for health. Singer and Krantz note that the shift in terminology from "anxiety" to "stress" implies that the source of distress has moved from inside the individual to outside in the environment. Another example is that of passive smoking, where smokers are being made accountable for the health of others who inhale their smoke.

4. The public health field deals with issues of public policy. This began as a movement to control the spread of disease, but is now focusing also on life style issues.

It is easy to see how these issues are central to the area of behavioral medicine, yet they are not part of the training and background of persons in that field. This is certainly an opportune time for these two fields to come together.

There are signs that this interaction is beginning to occur. People with psychology and behavioral medicine backgrounds are taking part in some of the large-scale public health efforts at health promotion and disease prevention. Conversely, public health schools and professionals are seeking the advice and consultation of behavioral experts. Each group is beginning to publish in the literatures of the other group, and the collaborative efforts that have occurred thus far strengthen the proposition that training and working together will be fruitful.

THE CENTRAL ROLE OF TRAINING

The nature of training for persons entering the field of behavioral medicine may be the most important factor for the future of the field. The current leaders in the field were trained in a native discipline (e.g., psychology) long before "behavioral medicine" existed. It is the current generation of graduate students, postdoctoral fellows, interns, residents, and so forth who will determine the character of the field for years to come. There now exists the opportunity to focus their training to be consistent with some philosophical viewpoint.

There are many thorny issues involved here. Among the questions raised by discussions of training are these:

1. What departments or programs should sponsor such training? Departments of psychology, schools of medicine and public health, and programs in the allied health sciences are only some of the possibilities.
2. Should there be "behavioral medicine" programs at all? Will training programs destroy some of the richness of the field by homogenizing the backgrounds of those who practice?
3. What type of degree should be awarded?
4. Is behavioral medicine primarily "behavior" or "medicine"?
5. Is clinical experience an important aspect of the behavioral medicine background?
6. Should behavioral medicine specialists be licensed?
7. How important is third-party reimbursement?
8. What fields or disciplines or bodies of knowledge should be included in training?
9. Are there differences among behavioral medicine, health psychology, medical psychology, preventive medicine, health promotion, psychosomatic medicine, and the other related fields?

The Impetus from Health Psychology

The impetus for considering the issue of training has not come from the *field* of behavioral medicine, but from the *discipline* of health psychology. This is the case, despite the fact that behavioral medicine existed as an area before health psychology existed as a specialty within the broader field of psychology. This state of affairs prevails for several reasons and may have a major impact on the future of both research and clinical work.

Behavioral medicine arose as a field from the united efforts of persons in many disciplines, primarily psychology and psychiatry, but also of persons in specialty areas within either medicine or the behavioral sciences. Organizations like the Society of Behavioral Medicine and the Academy of Behavioral Medicine Research struggled to enlist involvement from professionals in different disciplines. As an example, the presidency of the Society of Behavioral Medicine alternates between persons with medical degrees and persons with behavioral science backgrounds.

It is unlikely that groups devoted to diversity in both background and training could agree on training programs for new professionals entering the field. This explains why there have been only sporadic attempts to define training issues from the groups typically identified with the field of behavioral medicine. These efforts have involved listings in journals and at conferences of opportunities for training at the postdoctoral or internship level. The issue may be best addressed by a single discipline; hence the lead has been taken by health psychology (Matarazzo, 1983; N. E. Miller, 1983b; Rodin, 1983; Stone, 1983).

The field of health psychology has evolved over the past 5–7 years. It differs from behavioral medicine in that it focuses on the special contribution that a particular discipline (psychology) can make to the understanding and promotion of health. I do not plan to discuss the virtues of approaching health from the behavioral medicine or health psychology perspective. Rather, I focus on the way the issue of training has been handled by health psychology. This group has made the most systematic and thorough effort to address the topic.

It is not surprising that the beginnings of consensus on training would come from professionals within a discipline. It is these professionals who share values, experiences, and ideas about professional training. The virtue in this approach is that some consensus is possible, but the potential hazard is that perspectives from other disciplines will not be considered. This question may be settled only by waiting to see whether health psychology will be more concerned with advancing knowledge in the health care area or with advancing the role of psycholgists in the health care system. This is a crucial conceptual difference that will be clarified only as the specialty matures.

The Conference on Education and Training in Health Psychology

In May 1983, a conference was held in Harriman, New York, on the issue of training. The conference was organized by members of Division 38 (Division of Health Psychology) of the APA. This meeting, the National Working Conference on Education and Training in Health

Psychology, produced the most detailed recommendations yet conceived in these areas. The proceedings and results of this conference were published in *Health Psychology*, 1983, *2*(5) (Supplement).

The impetus for the conference was described by Stephen Weiss, organizer of the meeting:

> These developments have stimulated a need for training resources at the graduate, postgraduate, and continuing education levels to adequately prepare psychologists to function in health settings related to basic and clinical research as well as applied care. Several academic programs have already been developed in health psychology in an effort to be responsive to this perceived need. Increasing numbers of academic institutions have expressed strong interest in developing such programs. It appeared timely for the Division of Health Psychology to review the accomplishments (and difficulties) experienced to date by the existing training programs, to assess requisite skills and knowledge required to function effectively in the various research, professional, and administrative health settings and to formulate guidelines and recommended standards for graduate, postgraduate, and continuing educational levels of training in health psychology. (S.M. Weiss, 1983, p. 19)

A main issue addressed at the conference was to define the boundaries and priorities of the field. The consensus was presented to the participants by Gary Schwartz:

> Health psychology is a generic field of psychology, with its own body of theory and knowledge, which is differentiated from other fields in psychology. Within health psychology a professional specialty is evolving. Health psychology has strong interdisciplinary ties of research and practice and it has clear professional implications that are developing and that relate to professional developments in the other applied specialties in psychology. The emergence of our specialty can help to facilitate the differentiation of what is core to all professional training in psychology and what is specialized. (Schwartz, 1983, p. 9)

The conference was attended by psychologists only. The philosophy behind this move was to get health psychology's "house in order" before interacting with other disciplines on the issue of training (S. M. Weiss, 1983). The participants were organized into task groups, which covered a broad array of topics; these included the relative importance of theory and practice, legal and ethical issues, and the possible career paths open to health psychologists.

The task groups presented their recommendations to the general conference, which then endorsed some ideas and not others. I list these recommendations not only because they are useful guidelines for directing the field, but because they show the breadth of issues to be considered. The highlights of the recommendations were presented by Stone (1983):

General recommendations
— Health psychology should offer two major training options: Scientist and professional.
— The professional path should be based on the scientist/practitioner model as enunciated at the Boulder Conference.
— Core training should fully meet the criteria set forth in the APA guidelines.
— Training programs should systematically review their performance at regular intervals to evaluate their achievement of stated goals and objectives and to assess the continuing appropriateness of such goals.
— Accreditation of programs should be under the aegis of the accreditation mechanisms of the APA's Education and Training Board.
— Institutions that engage in training must have sufficient breadth and depth of resources to ensure that students receive a comprehensive training that is not limited to one theoretical perspective or one methodology.

Training for students in both tracks should:
— Provide experience and course content stressing the role of diverse characteristics—cultural, ethnic, gender, lifestyle, age, and so on—in both providers' and consumers' participation in the health system.
— Provide an *integrated* mixture of theory and practice, including hands-on involvement in research under the direction of highly qualified mentors.
— Place strong emphasis on research methodology, including appropriate biostatistical methods in addition to the usual methods used by psychologists.
— Emphasize and provide the requisite skills for successful interdisciplinary collaboration.
— Engender an appreciation by trainees of the impact of the health psychologist on health care settings, patients, families, and so on.
— Provide instruction in ethical, legal, and professional issues.
— Provide instruction in health care organization and health care policy.
— Include appropriate training in assessment and intervention skills.
— Postdoctoral training is highly desirable for health psychologists preparing for both research and professional careers.

Training for health psychologists who will be providing direct health care services to individuals or groups will further require:
— An internship of at least a year's duration in an organized, interdisciplinary health service training program engaged in both psychological and physical health care.
— Internship experience should occur in settings in which a psychologist holds an appointment to the professional staff, or its equivalent.
— Internship mentors should predominantly include health psychologists who are themselves well qualified to practice professional health psychology, and effectively model the scientist/practitioner model.

— Respecialization in professional health psychology is not to be achieved through continuing education, but requires matriculation in an organized health psychology training program that is APA-accredited.

Regarding research careers in health psychology:
— Health psychology researchers and faculty should be strongly urged to become licensed.

Regarding appropriate actions for faculties and representatives of the field of health psychology:
— A Council of Training Programs should be established to designate programs that meet acceptable standards, to facilitate the knowledge of and development of employment opportunities for graduates, and the like.
— Awareness of existing funding sources should be developed and increasing funding, especially in the area of prevention, should be given a high priority.
— Prospective trainees should be clearly informed, before acceptance into a program, about the type of training offered, the skills provided, and the employment opportunities that exist for persons with such skills and knowledge.
— Programs should develop financial and other sources of support to assure equal availability of this program to persons from all strata and sets of circumstances who are willing and able to meet the academic requirements. (Stone, 1983, pp. 15–18)

One issue that arises from the dual goal of training scientists and professionals is that of quantity versus quality. This issue has been debated at length during the birth and development of professional schools of psychology. Since even the longest-established health psychology programs are in their infancy, this question is being debated.

N. E. Miller (1983b) and Brendan Maher (1983) addressed this issue at the conference described above. Both stated in strong terms that quality of training (N. E. Miller, 1983b) and of trainees (Maher, 1983) is of the utmost importance. I agree with this philosophy. The ability of psychology to contribute to the health care system will depend on the ability of psychologists to survive in a relatively new setting. It is only be producing consistently good professionals that health psychology will create a demand for its services.

Several factors are apparent from the preceding discussion. One factor is that psychology as a discipline is dominating the field of behavioral medicine, and that the organized effort in this direction is being made by the Division of Health Psychology of the APA. The result has been a constructive approach to the issue of education and training. If the principles stated above (Stone, 1983) are followed when programs are established, a generation of psychologists with a fresh and interdisciplinary view of health issues will soon emerge.

If such a generation of psychologists soon emerges, the interaction between its members and those of other disciplines will be interesting to observe. Also, the relationship between health psychology and the other organized behavioral medicine groups has yet to be worked out.

It is quite possible that health psychology will become a viable specialty within psychology (no different from clinical, social, etc.) that will prepare psychologists to enter the health care system and to deal effectively with other professionals. It is at this level that psychologists may interact in an organizational fashion with these other professionals. If this model is feasible, issues of training in these fields of behavioral medicine, health psychology, and so forth, may be best confronted by disciplines rather than fields.

CARDIOVASCULAR RISK REDUCTION IN CHILDREN

The area of cardiovascular risk reduction has received great attention in the literature, yet most of the attention and nearly all of the programs have focused on adults (Breslow, 1979; Levy & Moskowitz, 1982). Since prevention has received far less attention than treatment (U.S. Department of Health, Education and Welfare, 1979a), the emphasis on adults is not surprising.

This picture has been changing gradually, particularly since the middle and late 1970s. More information on the progression of cardiovascular disease has become available, leading some to believe that the problems have their roots in childhood (Kannel & Dawber, 1972; Williams & Wynder, 1976). Within the past several years, a number of reports have been published on the identification of risk factors in children, on the link between childhood risk factors and adult disease, and on programs aimed at altering the risk factors.

Two important books on cardiovascular risk in children appeared in 1980. One was a book by Berenson (1980) that provided a detailed description and evaluation of the Bogalusa Heart Study, a prospective epidemiological investigation of cardiovascular risk in school children in Louisiana. The second was an edited book by Lauer and Shekelle (1980), in which chapters from the leading authorities in the area were assembled. Both show the potential of programs aimed at identifying and modifying risk factors.

It is in this area of reduction of cardiovascular risk that behavioral scientists are able to make an important impact. Most prevention programs, other than those making environmental changes, require behavior changes in individuals. The principles, technology, and evaluation skills of behavior therapists are directly relevant.

Does Childhood Risk Predict Later Disease?

Studies that evaluate the association between childhood risk factors and disease in adulthood are, by their very nature, extremely difficult and costly to undertake. If continued long enough, some of the current epidemiology studies of childhood risk may provide some of these answers. There are only a few of these studies under way, the most notable of which are the Bogalusa Heart Study in Louisiana (Berenson, 1980) and the Muscatine Study in Iowa (Lauer & Clarke, 1980; Lauer, Conner, Leaverton, Reiter, & Clarke, 1975).

In the absence of direct studies of the link between childhood and adult disease, studies of risk factors at different ages are the next best approach. Here the data are suggestive, if not compelling. It does appear that children with cardiovascular risk factors in childhood tend to have the same risk factors later in childhood and perhaps in adult life.

There is evidence that at least four of the coronary risk factors in childhood persist into adulthood. These factors are blood pressure, serum lipid disorders, obesity, and cigarette smoking. The research in some areas (e.g., obesity, blood pressure) is more extensive than in others, but the results point in a consistent direction.

Blood pressures taken at different times in childhood tend to be highly correlated, so that Lauer and Clarke (1980) used data from the Muscatine study to show that "There is a high correlation of early measurements to later levels, and only extremes of the distributions show large changes in percentile ranks" (p. 288). The Bogalusa Heart Study showed similar results (Berenson, 1980; Voors, Foster, Frerichs, Webber, & Berenson, 1976). Thee is also some evidence, measured from family aggregation of blood pressure, that childhood levels will persist into adulthood (Zinner, Levy, & Kass, 1971).

Similar findings come from research on serum lipids and lipoproteins. Berenson, Srinivasan, and Webber (1980) found that children tended to remain in their respective ranks for at least 3 years with respect to lipoprotein levels. Evidence of this sort has led some to speculate that the atherogenic serum lipid disorders have their origins in childhood (Kannel & Dawber, 1972).

Obesity and smoking tend to follow patterns similar to those of blood pressure and serum lipids and lipoproteins, except that the relationship between childhood and adult patterns may be even stronger. Approximately 80% of overweight children become overweight adults (Abraham, Collins, & Nordsieck, 1971). Smoking in children also predicts smoking in adults (U.S. Department of Health, Education, and Welfare, 1979b), so it is important to address this most important risk factor before the adult years.

Prevalence of Cardiovascular Risk Factors in Children

The first step in establishing prevalence rates is to identify which health factors are *risk* factors. This is not an easy task in any case, but with children in whom disease must be diagnosed years later, the problem is particularly complex. For this reason, risk factors that have been associated with cardiovascular risk in adults have been of most interest in children.

The cardiovascular risk factors in adults have been established for some time, and now there is little dispute about their contribution to coronary heart disease (Levy & Moskowitz, 1982). The risk factors are generally categorized into first-order and second-order factors, depending on their relative contribution to overall risk. Three risk factors—cigarette smoking, elevated blood pressure, and elevated cholesterol levels—are the first-order factors, because their contribution to cardiovascular risk is both clear and very strong (Levy & Moskowitz, 1982; U.S. Department of Health, Education and Welfare, 1979b). These are the factors that have received the greatest attention in children, although smoking has been studied only in children in early adolescence.

The second-order risk factors identified by epidemiology studies are diabetes, obesity, physical inactivity, age, male sex, and coronary prone behavior (Type A personality). These are linked to risk for disease, but not as consistently and strongly as the first-order factors (Levy & Moskowitz, 1982). Of these factors, obesity is the one that has received most attention in children.

The prevalence of these cardiovascular risk factors is quite high in children. One of the early studies in this area was done by Wilmore and McNamara (1974). These authors studied a sample of 8- to 12-year-old boys in California. Fully 46% had one risk factor for coronary heart disease, and 14% had two or more risk factors. A number of studies, from a number of countries, have followed the Wilmore and McNamara study in noting the alarming prevalence of cardiovascular risk factors.

A large-scale screening and intervention program, sponsored by the American Health Foundation in New York City, has been going on since the mid-1970s. The program, known as the Know Your Body Program, has evaluated the risk factors for chronic disease (Williams, Arnold, & Wynder, 1977; Williams & Wynder, 1976). Data from the first sample of 3,000 school children aged 11–14 showed that 40% had one or more risk factors for coronary heart disease (overweight, elevated cholesterol, smoking, poor physical fitness, hypertension, or diabetes) (Williams & Wynder, 1976).

A similarly discouraging picture is obtained by viewing the risk factors separately. Many experts feel that cholesterol levels above 160 mg% in children are cause for concern (Kannel & Dawber, 1972), and the epidemiology studies show that at least 10% of children have levels over 200 mg% (Berenson, 1980; Williams *et al.*, 1977; Wilmore & McNamara, 1974). In some groups and some settings, levels are even higher. In the North Karelia project in Finland, the *mean* cholesterol level in 1,000 seventh-grade children was 197 mg% (Puska, Vartianen, Pallonen, Ruotsalainen, Tuomilheto, Koskela, Lahtinen, & Norppa, 1981). Since the prevalence of genetic hyperlidemia is only 2%, most of the elevated cholesterol appears to be diet-related (Berenson, 1980; Williams *et al.*, 1977).

The prevalence of obesity is also high in these studies of cardiovascular risk in children. The Know Your Body Program found prevalence rates of obesity (>20% overweight) to be 17% in a black and Hispanic population and 10% in a white, middle-class population (Williams *et al.*, 1977). Prevalence rates range in other studies from 5% to 25%, leading some to estimate that 15%–25% of all children are overweight (Forbes, 1975).

Associations between Behavior and Risk

Most programs aimed at altering cardiovascular risk in children focus on life style behaviors such as diet, smoking, exercise, and weight control. Few experts question the wisdom of altering these behaviors, yet there is only indirect evidence linking the behaviors to risk. One of the risk factors (smoking) *is* a behavior, so no link is needed, but in the other areas, the evidence is not so apparent.

It is widely assumed that a high-fat diet elevates serum cholesterol. The corollary of this is that a diet lower in fat will reduce cholesterol and that this lowers susceptibility to coronary heart disease. This issue spurred the famous "diet–heart debate," which still rages. The same type of debate ensues when one investigates the association between dietary sodium and blood pressure, between physical inactivity and obesity, and between caloric intake and obesity and hypertension.

One should conclude from this lack of certainty that studies have failed to show the associations between behavior and cardiovascular risk. The problem is that investigations in this area are extremely expensive, time-consuming, and open to practical and methodological problems. The answers, therefore, may never be provided according to strict scientific standards, so "waiting for the evidence," as some scientists are fond of doing, may be too conservative in view of the nature of the field. I discussed this in detail in Volume 8 of the *Annual Review*, in a review of information on dietary behavior and cholesterol.

These issues have been addressed in studies with adults. Many questions are unanswered, but the evidence from dozens of studies with both humans and animals points to a consistent conclusion. Individuals place themselves at greater risk for chronic disease by smoking, eating excessively, being overweight, following a high-fat diet, not exercising, having elevated blood pressure, and so forth (Breslow, 1979; Hamburg, 1982; Haggerty, 1977; Levy & Moskowitz, 1982; Stamler, 1980; Williams & Wynder, 1976).

The practical and methodological problems in these studies are even more serious in studies of children. Adults must be followed for 5–10 years or longer to find changes in rates of morbidity and mortality. Children would have to be followed for at least 40 years. Therefore, we must accept several notions on faith. The first is that children are similar to adults in that their behavior contributes to their risk factors. The second is that these risk factors predict adult status. The third is that the risk factors are actually related to disease endpoints. The degree to which each scientist or health policy professional supports prevention programs may depend on the degree of faith in these assumptions.

Some investigators feel this faith is warranted and that prevention programs are fully justified (Haggerty, 1977; Stamler, 1980; Williams & Wynder, 1976). I agree, and feel that the following statement captures what is known and what should be done.

> There seems little doubt that early stages of such chronic diseases as atherosclerosis begin in childhood. Risk factors for coronary heart disease, stroke, and tobacco- and nutrition-related cancers can not only be identified in this age group but are highly prevalent.
>   Since the majority of these risk factors are related to lifestyles that are acquired early in life, screening and health education must extend into pediatric practice. The schools provide the best opportunity for screening and education of the greatest numbers of children in a mass program of primary prevention. (Williams et al., 1977, p. 353)

Avenues for Intervention

As stated above by Williams et al. (1977), the schools are the most logical point of intervention for altering cardiovascular risk in children. This movement has its roots in the fields of public health and health education (Bartlett, 1981), and it has only been recently that psychologists have become involved. A discussion of existing programs is relevant for behavior therapists, because their knowledge and background could be valuable in designing and implementing comprehensive risk reduction programs.

All the programs mentioned below are school programs. Two types of programs are covered: those aimed at individual risk factors, and those aimed at multiple risk factors. Clinical programs have certainly been done with children, but these are better known to behavioral audiences. Because of my own bias, I discuss the broad-scale public health programs, because it is in these that the potential of behavior therapy is not realized.

Even though the schools have such great potential for health promotion, very few innovative and effective programs have been done (Bartlett, 1981). John Knowles (1977), one of the pioneers in the field of health promotion, dismissed existing school programs as "abysmal at best, confining themselves to preemptory sick calls and posters on brushing teeth and eating three meals a day" (p. 123). Fortunately, there are now school programs that promise more.

Individual Risk Factor Programs

Most common among the risk factor intervention programs are those addressing individual factors. The majority of programs have been done on smoking prevention with adolescents; next in frequency are weight reduction and nutrition education programs, followed by blood pressure education programs and a number of miscellaneous health education interventions.

Smoking prevention programs in the schools are becoming very popular. Programs are being funded by the National Heart, Lung and Blood Institute, the National Cancer Institute, and a variety of other federal and private agencies. The programs have been quite successful, and now most programs are very similar. Behavioral scientists have been the leaders in this movement (Evans, 1976; McAlister, Perry, & Maccoby, 1979; Perry, Killen, Telch, Slinkard, & Danaher, 1980).

This area was reviewed in Volume 9 of the *Annual Review*, so I do not repeat the details here. Most antismoking programs aim at children in the sixth or seventh grades and focus on specific methods for resisting social pressure to smoke. One widely used program, developed by Perry, McAlister, Pechacek, and colleagues at Stanford and the University of Minnesota, is called Counseling Leadership Against Smoking Pressure (CLASP). Some programs are administered by peers and others by teachers, but the results are consistently good.

The smoking programs in the recent literature show that the number of junior high school students who begin smoking can be halved by this educational and behavioral approach (Evans, 1979; Hurd, Johnson, Pechacek, Bast, Jacobs, & Luepker, 1980; McAlister, Perry, Killen, Slinkard, & Maccoby, 1980; McAlister et al., 1979; Perry et al., 1980). This is an impressive finding and has important public health implications, for every instance of smoking prevention in an individual is likely to return far more than the original cost.

Weight reduction programs have also been done in school settings (cf. Brownell, 1982). One of the first such programs was conducted by Seltzer and Mayer (1970). Children who received a program of nutrition education, physical activity, and psychological support showed small but significant reductions in their degree of obesity. The first controlled trial was by Botvin, Cantlon, Carter, and Williams (1979). Adolescents who participated in a 10-week program of behavior modification, nutrition counseling, and exercise lost more weight than a matched sample of children from a control school.

The largest losses in a school program were reported by Brownell and Kaye (1982). Children aged 5–12 received a program that emphasized behavior modification, nutrition education, exercise, and, most notably, social support. The social environment was emphasized by working with parents, peers, and school personnel such as the principal, teachers, and food service workers. Of the 63 children who participated in the 10-week program, 95% lost weight, with an average loss of 4.4 kg (9.7 lb).

The only controlled study with a follow-up was a recent report by Brownell, Foster, and Wadden (1984). A program similar to that of Brownell and Kaye (1982) was used, except that older peer "counselors" administered parts of the program, as is the case with many smoking prevention programs (Evans, 1979; Hurd et al., 1980; McAlister et al., 1979, 1980; Perry et al., 1980). The children showed a significant weight loss, but the losses were small. At an 18-week follow-up, the losses were only partially maintained.

One study in the diet modification area deserves mentioning here. Coates, Jeffery, and Slinkard (1981) devised a 12-session curriculum for fourth- and fifth-grade students in which a social learning approach was used to increase both "heart healthy" eating habits and physical activity. The program included feedback and incentives, behavioral commitment, and family involvement. The students who received the program showed significant increases in healthy foods in their lunches. This program targeted all children, not just high-risk (e.g., obese) children, and showed the feasibility of a general nutrition program administered within a behavioral framework.

In these school studies on smoking, weight, and nutrition, a single risk factor has been the focus. Much has been learned about behavior change in children and adolescents. It does appear that the schools may be an ideal setting for confronting the problems early. With the exception of one study (Brownell & Kaye, 1982), weight losses in school programs have been small. For children who are only slightly overweight, or not overweight at all, such a program might be very useful. For clinical cases of obesity, more intensive treatment may be necessary. Coates *et al.* (1981) showed positive results of a nutrition program aimed at the general school population, indicating that modest changes spread across large numbers can be meaningful. Smoking prevention is likely to be a more reasonable goal in school programs than is smoking cessation. Therefore, evidence from these programs does show the potential for primary prevention in the schools.

Multiple Risk Factor Programs

There are many multiple risk factor programs going on in the schools, and the next few years should bring the publication of results from many of these. Thus far, evaluative information is available for only two projects, and these have formed the basis for most current programs. These are the Know Your Body Program in New York City (Williams *et al.*, 1977; Williams & Wynder, 1976), and the North Karelia Youth Project in Finland (Puska *et al.*, 1981).

THE KNOW YOUR BODY PROGRAM

The first comprehensive and systematically evaluated program in the schools was the Know Your Body Program of the American Health Foundation (Williams *et al.*, 1977; Williams & Wynder, 1976). The program has three main components:

1. *Health screening.* The screening, done in the school, consists of height, weight, three resting blood pressures, plasma cholesterol, nonfasting glucose level, hematocrit, physical fitness (using a modified Harvard step test), a health knowledge questionnaire, and a health habits survey of cigarette smoking and alcohol use.
2. *Return of results.* The student and/or parents receive a Health Passport with the results of the tests. The Passport personalizes the results and is accompanied by educational material about each of the tests and risk factors.
3. *Health education.* The students receive an educational program aimed at alteration of the coronary risk factors, particularly smoking and elevated cholesterol levels.

The investigators who developed the Know Your Body Program believe firmly that the screening and feedback parts of the program are essential to its success:

> After screening, the results of the tests are returned to the child, his or her parents, and designated physicians. Explanations of desirable ranges for each test accompany the reports. Students record their results into a Health Passport, a small folding document attractively designed for children, during a classroom exercise supervised by a health education or science teacher. Possible stigmatization is avoided in three ways. First, the teaching emphasizes the positive value of awareness of risk factors during the early reversible phases of the natural course of the disease. Second, all results are returned in a medically confidential manner to preclude revelation of personal findings. In addition, program emphasis is on group behavior for healthy lifestyle rather than on individual deviations from an ideal. (Williams *et al.*, 1977, p. 348)

The health education aspect of the Know Your Body Program involves a number of activities for students, teachers, and parents. Questionnaires are given to families; workshops are conducted for teachers; and classroom activities are done with children. The program as first designed was mainly educational, not behavioral. The focus has been shifting gradually over the past several years.

The Know Your Body Program has been a real success from a public relations perspective. A number of school districts use the program, both in the United States and in other countries. In some cases, the program is being evaluated and in some cases not. It has great face validity, especially from an educational perspective, so it is not surprising that the program is popular. What are its effects?

Only preliminary data are available from the Know Your Body Program (Williams *et al.*, 1977; Williams & Wynder, 1976). The primary test of the program was undertaken in a massive controlled trial of thousands of school children from black and Hispanic neighborhoods in the Bronx and from middle-class and upper-middle-class white neighborhoods in Westchester County, New York. As of the date of this writing, the final results have not yet been reported.

The preliminary results from the Know Your Body Program were descriptive in nature (Williams *et al.*, 1977). The results of the screening phase were presented to show the prevalence of risk factors (discussed above) and to describe the number of students who participated, the return rate on the questionnaires, and so forth. The initial results were encouraging, but the final analysis must await the long-term results of the educational aspects of the program.

THE NORTH KARELIA YOUTH PROJECT

The second major school project is being undertaken in Finland (Puska
et al., 1981). The North Karelia Youth Project is part of the larger
North Karelia project, which is a coronary primary prevention trial
with adults in a region of eastern Finland. The need for such a program
there is great, as North Karelia has among the highest rates of coronary
disease in the world. The investigators noted the indication for early
intervention from cross-sectional data on rates of coronary disease at
different ages. The neonatal risk level in North Karelia is similar to
that in other parts of the world, but the relative risk rises rapidly, so
that the male population between ages 20 and 30 has the highest rate of
coronary disease in the world (Puska et al., 1981).

The North Karelia Youth Project is similar in design and implementation to the Know Your Body Program. In fact, it was developed
from the international version of the Know Your Body Program, which
has been used in several European centers. The program involves a
health screening, feedback of results via the Health Passport, and an
educational program aimed at specific risk reduction behaviors.

The North Karelia Youth Project is ongoing, and only preliminary
screening data are available (Puska et al., 1981). The results will provide
a replication of the Know Your Body Program with a different cultural
group and will assess the effects of the health education intervention
with a population with different risk factor patterns.

What makes the North Karelia Youth Project unique is that it is
being employed in the context of a community-wide coronary disease
prevention trial. The investigators wish to separate out the effects of
the general effort in the community from the specific effects of the
school program, so some schools in North Karelia are receiving the
program and others are not (Puska et al., 1981).

The design being used in the North Karelia Youth Project is
the natural one, given the intervention that is taking place among the
population in general. However, what may be most important is the
interaction of a community and a school program. It is not known how
the two programs may influence each other.

Possibilities for Behavior Therapy

The area of cardiovascular risk reduction in children is very exciting to
approach from a behavioral perspective. It is now widely acknowledged
that personal life style behaviors influence coronary risk in children
(Berenson, 1980; Lauer & Shekelle, 1980; Williams & Wynder, 1976).

These behaviors occur in a complex social and environmental context that requires investigation from a variety of perspectives. The behavioral perspective is one of these.

Some behavioral researchers are investigating family life style patterns that influence the earliest development of health behaviors. Interactions between children and parents regarding food, physical activity, and life style in general are not well understood and are perfectly suited for study with the assessment strategies developed by behavioral researchers.

The vast knowledge that behavioral scientists have in educational settings is also relevant to primary prevention programs. Classroom and parent management programs may be instrumental in creating the atmosphere in which health behaviors can be encouraged.

Perhaps the greatest contribution of behavioral scientists may be in the development and evaluation of programs and techniques aimed at altering behavior patterns in individuals. Social learning theory provides the most useful theoretical framework from which to develop interventions, and behavior therapists have the most experience in applying this framework to problems of social significance.

These are only some of the possible talents that behavior therapists can bring to the area of health promotion in children. As I have stated before, however, we have much to learn from our colleagues in different disciplines. Without this collaboration, we are unlikely to develop programs that are cost-effective, generalizable, or as effective as possible. The challenge to our field is to communicate our strengths to other disciplines and to allow them to communicate their strengths to us.

6

THE ADDICTIVE DISORDERS

KELLY D. BROWNELL

INTRODUCTION

Each year when I write portions of this series, I debate about whether to do an annual review of behavior therapy or an annual review for behavior therapists. The first signifies a review of a field, and the second signifies a review for the field. Thus far, I have chosen the second course because the journey is more interesting. My bias is the same this year.

Two issues presented in subsequent pages highlight this philosophy. In the "Obesity" section, I cover the topics of exercise and very-low-calorie diets. The discussions include information from physiology, metabolism, cardiology, internal medicine, nutrition, and, of course, behavior therapy. The information from behavior therapy alone would not yield such a comprehensive picture and would generate far fewer ideas for research and treatment.

The second example of this philosophy of coverage is in the section on smoking. Behavioral scientists are now considering public health issues such as the effect of smoke on nonsmokers, the influence of the antismoking campaign in the media, and the effectiveness of large-scale programs. To understand and to influence public health, we must consider information from many areas, including political science (Best, 1983).

This chapter covers some of the public health issues in the area of the addictive disorders. There are many opportunities for behavior therapists to take part in this effort. In many cases, assistance in behavioral matters is essential to the conduct of public health programs, a fact that is becoming more apparent to other professionals. It is my hope that this chapter will stimluate some thought about these issues. It is only through an interdisciplinary effort that behavior therapy will attain its potential.

OBESITY

It is almost obligatory for authors to state that many exciting developments have occurred in their field. To say that the field of obesity is changing rapidly may seem trite, but the evidence is all around us. Personally, I am gratified by this change, because it represents an important conceptual shift in the way obesity is viewed, both clinically and theoretically.

There existed a time, during the middle and late 1970s, in which advances in the obesity field were few and far between. This occurred partly because the initial burst of enthusiasm that greeted Stuart's (1971) clinical report wore off when the necessary experimentation showed more modest results. However, there was also a conceptual obstacle—namely, that the behavioral package of procedures was considered "effective" and only needed to be perfected by fine tuning.

This notion led to studies of self-reinforcement versus self-punishment, premeal versus postmeal monitoring, the presence or absence of such program components as assertion training and relaxation, and so forth. There were theoretical implications of this work, but our ability to help our patients improved very little. Wilson (1978) discussed this and noted that short-term studies with small weight losses were no longer fruitful. Yet, such work continued, and 4 years later, it seemed necessary to reiterate this idea (Brownell, 1982).

The most profound change has come from two concepts. The first is that disciplines outside behavioral psychology contain a wealth of information that could be used in understanding and treating obesity. The second is the recognition that factors other than the standard behavioral techniques may determine whether patients adhere to a dietary program.

There are several signs of this conceptual change, each one a positive advance in the field. The incorporation of information from other disciplines is one such sign. The increasing emphasis on exercise has shown an appreciation for the exercise physiology field (Brownell & Stunkard, 1980; Stern, 1984; Thompson, Jarvie, Lahey, & Cureton, 1982). The areas of clinical nutrition, internal medicine, and energy metabolism have also been considered in the experimentation with very-low-calorie diets (Wadden, Stunkard, & Brownell, 1983a).

Other signs are the focus on the social system as a method for improving adherence to the behavioral program and the attempt to use behavior therapy to maintain losses produced by other approaches. Research on the social system has involved studies of the family (e.g., Brownell, Heckerman, Westlake, Hayes, & Monti, 1978) and studies conducted at the work site (e.g., Abrams & Follick, 1983). An important study by Craighead, Stunkard, and O'Brien (1981) and a follow-up study by Brownell and Stunkard (1981) tested the combination of behavior therapy and pharmacotherapy, a trend which was signaled by an earlier paper by Öst and Götestam (1976).

These new directions promise major advances in the field. The particular avenues cited above are only the first examples of the new outlook in the field. If these do not bear fruit, other avenues generated by the broader conceptual approach may. It is this attitude I salute, as much as the specific topics now in vogue.

This year's section on obesity covers three areas. The first is the role of physical activity, an area with both physiological and psychological implications. The second is the use of very-low-calorie diets for the treatment of moderate obesity. The third is an innovative idea for maintenance, the waist cord used by Garrow (1981).

The Importance of Physical Activity

Most programs for weight reduction have given little attention to the topic of exercise. Of course, there is always the standard exhortation for patients to "exercise more," or perhaps even the provision of written instructions showing specific calisthenics, but this is usually buried among the rules of record keeping, putting the fork down between bites, and shopping on a full stomach. The picture is now changing.

The recent emphasis on exercise is attributable to several factors. A number of long-term studies have shown that level of physical activity is one of the few correlates on maintenance of weight loss (discussed below). In addition, the exercise physiology literature has shown benefits of exercise that far exceed the calories burned during the exercise itself.

THE PHYSIOLOGICAL BENEFITS OF EXERCISE

One may wonder why physiology is being discussed in this book on behavior therapy. The reason is simple: Part of our behavior therapy for obesity involves adherence to whatever techniques are prescribed.

Exercise is useful in this regard, not only because it is an important "technique" by itself, but because it may improve adherence to other parts of the behavioral program. In this respect, it is useful to describe to patients the benefits they can achieve through activity. It can be a powerful motivating factor. Detailed descriptions of this area are available elsewhere (Bray, 1976; Brownell & Stunkard, 1980; McArdle, Katch, & Katch, 1981; Stern, 1984; Thompson et al., 1982).

Energy Expenditure. When asked, "Why should an overweight person exercise?" most persons, professional or not, respond by saying that it "burns calories." It is true that exercise does burn calories, but the number is pitifully small when one considers what can be consumed in a short bout at the table. For instance, a jumbo hamburger from a fast-food restaurant, a small order of french fries, and a small cola drink add up to approximately 1,100 calories. To expend this energy in exercise would require 11 miles of jogging, and this compensates for only a portion of the day's eating.

This information distresses many dieters, and they may feel that exercise is fruitless. However, exercise may be more useful for its long-term effects on weight regulation, because of the metabolic factors discussed below. This is why life style activities, which may be subclinical from the standpoint of coronary conditioning, may be helpful in weight loss (Brownell, Stunkard, & Albaum, 1980; Epstein, Wing, Koeske, Ossip, & Beck, 1982b).

Appetite Regulation. Exercise has been cited by some as a means for overweight persons to control their appetites, presumably because mild bouts of exercise suppress intake (Brownell & Stunkard, 1980; Stern, 1984; Thompson et al., 1982). The issue is a very complex one. Animal studies may or may not show an appetite suppression effect, depending on the sex of animals, their body weight, and the nature of the exercise. Work with humans is even less clear.

Garrow (1978, 1981) conducted a scholarly review of the literature on this topic and concluded that exercise has no discernible effect on either intake or the rate of weight loss. This conclusion was fueled by two careful studies by Woo, Garrow, and Pi-Sunyer (1982a, 1982b). Obese women were studied in a metabolic ward. Food intake, weight, and other metabolic indices were measured during differing lengths and intensities of exercise. These authors found that the rate of weight loss and food intake did not change during the periods of exercise, leading them to conclude that the exercise has no particular benefit when the goal is weight loss. Woo et al. also noted, however, that energy balance *did* change when the subjects were exercising. The subjects increased energy expenditure by virtue of the exercise, but did not make a compensatory increase in intake. The negative balance was not sufficient to increase weight loss, but could be meaningful if extended chronically.

A similar study was undertaken by Durrant, Royston, and Wloch (1982), except that lean persons were included as controls. There were significant differences in intake patterns between obese and lean subjects when exercise was added. The lean subjects increased intake by 155 calories/day in response to the 100 calories/day of exercise, while the obese subjects ate 18 calories/day less during exercise periods.

The theoretical implication is that lean subjects are better at "defending" their body weight by compensating with increased intake if expenditure increases. The clinical implication is that overweight persons may not increase intake as expenditure increases, so energy balance moves in the negative direction. Whether this effect is meaningful is not yet clear. What is clear is that exercise certainly does not increase appetite in obese persons and may help with the overall energy balance equation.

Preservation of Lean Body Mass.   Weight loss in most persons is a combination of fat and lean body mass (muscle or protein). The loss of lean tissue may be undesirable, particularly if the tissue is lost from the vital organs. The loss of protein can be decreased, and in some cases minimized, by the addition of sufficient protein to the diet (Wadden *et al.*, 1983a). Exercise may also help prevent this loss because lean tissue is generally increased by certain types of activity.

Where this issue might be particularly important is in the cycle of losing and regaining weight that so may dieters experience. During weight gain, the body can build lean tissue at a fixed rate, so if the excess energy exceeds what the body can use to manufacture lean tissue, the excess is stored as fat. Many people regain weight rapidly when they relapse, so they may replace less lean tissue than they lost when dieting. An example can illustrate this.

A hypothetical patient may begin a program weighing 200 pounds. After losing 30 pounds, 25 of which are fat and 5 of which are lean tissue, the person regains back to 200. If the weight is regained rapidly, only 2 of the 5 pounds of lost muscle may be replaced; thus, even though the weight is the same 200 pounds before and after a diet, the body composition is not. Lean tissue is more metabolically active than fat, so this net loss of lean tissue decreases total energy expenditure, even at the same weight. Exercise during and after a diet may help prevent this shift in body composition.

Like the evidence supporting the argument for exercise and appetite, the evidence supporting the use of exercise to prevent lean tissue loss is preliminary. There is the possibility that this phenomenon occurs, but confirming evidence still needs to be collected. However, exercise does not have a negative effect on body composition, so the cautious approach is to include exercise in treatment.

Psychological Benefits. Folkins and Sime (1981) have done an extensive review of the psychological benefits of physical activity. Many of these benefits, particularly the effect of self-confidence and sense of well-being, are relevant for overweight persons. In my own clinical experience, which has not been documented experimentally, exercise serves as a cue to dieters that they are making progress and that self-improvement is occurring. This increases adherence to a diet and can offset some of the dysphoria that can weaken restraint and provoke eating.

Alteration of Metabolic Rate. Dieting and weight loss cause a reduction in basal metabolic rate (Bray, 1976). Since basal metabolic needs account for 60%–80% of total energy requirements (McArdle *et al.*, 1981), a drop in this rate can greatly reduce the energy the body expends on its normal functioning. The consequence is that dieting becomes more difficult as time goes on, and some patients do not lose weight even at very low calorie levels. Exercise can increase metabolic rate, although the duration and magnitude of the increase is being debated (McArdle *et al.*, 1981; Stern, 1984). There exists the possibility that physical activity can increase metabolic rate enough to offset the decline caused by dieting (Stern, 1984).

EXERCISE AS A PREDICTOR OF SUCCESS

Whether or not patients are exercising tends to be related to their long-term success at weight reduction. This is supported by both correlational and controlled studies. The correlational studies have been quite positive. People who are exercising at follow-up tend to be those with the greatest weight loss (Cohen, Gelfand, Dodd, Jensen, & Turner, 1980; Graham, Taylor, Hovell, & Siegel, 1983; Katahan, Pleas, Thackery, & Wallston, 1982; Stuart & Guire, 1978). These correlations do not show cause and effect, but it is noteworthy that exercise is one of the few predictors of success, despite countless attempts to correlate factors with weight loss (Brownell, in press; Wilson, 1980).

There have been only a few attempts to manipulate exercise as an experimental variable, but these results have been positive. Harris and Hallbauer (1973) had the first evidence that people who were prescribed exercise did better than people who were given the behavioral program without exercise.

More recent studies have provided well-controlled evaluations of exercise. Stalonas, Johnson, and Christ (1978) used a 2 × 2 design to evaluate contingency contracting and exercise. There was a positive effect (a trend) for both factors at a 1-year follow-up. The trend did not exist at an earlier follow-up, so exercise may exert its effect over the long term. Dahlkoetter, Callahan, and Linton (1979) also used exercise as an experimental variable and found that a combination of eating habit change and exercise was more effective than either alone. The Dahlkoetter et al. study also included fitness measures; exercise subjects showed the greatest improvement on these measures.

THE ADHERENCE CHALLENGE

Knowing that exercise is beneficial for overweight people is one thing; encouraging them to exercise is another. The patients themselves usually feel they should exercise more, and most have engaged in some sort of exercise program some time in the past. Few begin exercise with any hope of success, however, and fewer yet adopt exercise as a permanent part of the life style.

The inability to adhere to an exercise program is not specific to obese persons. Taylor, Buskirk, and Remington (1973) reported dropout rates of approximately 50% in men at high risk for heart disease. Carmody, Senner, Malinow, and Matarazzo (1980) tracked participation rates in an exercise program for men recovering from myocardial infarction and found that only 20% remained in a program after approximately 4 years. These are people in whom motivation should be high. Gwinup (1975) found similarly discouraging adherence rates in obese women in a program that required only walking.

Before designing strategies to improve adherence, it is helpful to understand that obese persons bring several distinct characteristics to a program. First, the excess weight creates a physical burden that can make even routine activities difficult. Second, the prolonged sedentary life style led by most obese persons makes it difficult for them to start a program, because they are capable only of very low levels of activity. Third, many overweight persons have negative associations with physical activity and sports. Many were teased as children, picked last for teams, and generally excluded from games. Fourth, a lifetime of inactivity does not foster the athletic ability needed to feel capable in a sport. For these reasons, negative attitudes must be overcome before many overweight people will become more active.

METHODS FOR IMPROVING ADHERENCE

Few studies have been done in this important area, so much of what is conveyed in the literature is based on clinical intuition. What follows has been distilled from scientific and clinical information.

Many behavioral principles that have been applied to other problems may also be useful for exercise. Martin and Dubbert (1982) reviewed the exercise literature and Epstein and Cluss (1982) reviewed the compliance literature in the special behavioral medicine issue of the *Journal of Consulting and Clinical Psychology*. Self-monitoring, stimulus control, contingency management, and cognitive factors seem to be particularly relevant.

One cognitive factor that impedes adherence is the "exercise threshold" that most members of the public embrace. This notion implies that a certain amount of exercise must be done for any benefit to occur. Patients ask me whether a bout of exercise is "enough to do any good." This idea is fostered by the exercise physiology equations that certain degrees of frequency, intensity, and duration of exercise are necessary for coronary conditioning to occur. There is such a threshold for this type of training, but this is not the only reason why overweight people should exercise. The patients need to learn that exercise in any amount is better than no exercise, and that they must start at low levels in order to progress to more vigorous activities.

This is consistent with the principle of shaping. In our program at the University of Pennsylvania, we prescribe low levels of exercise (walking) for patients in poor condition, and then gradually increase the time and intensity of the activity. This had its roots in the suggestion of Brownell and Stunkard (1980) and then of Thompson *et al.* (1982) that "routine" activities be the focus of initial treatment. These activities include day-to-day activities such as walking, using stairs, and so forth. Brownell *et al.* (1980) studied the use of stairs versus escalators in public places in such a context.

An impressive test of routine of "life style" activities was carried out by Epstein and colleagues at the University of Pittsburgh (Epstein *et al.*, 1982b). Overweight children received either a program of regular and programmed exercises (such as calisthenics) or an equicaloric regimen of life style activities (such as riding bikes, walking, and playing games). The programmed activities had a more positive effect (on physiological measure of fitness) early in treatment, but the long-term advantage fell to the life style activities. The better long-term results may have resulted from better adherence among the children in this group, as the other children were not able to continue the more structured activities.

SUMMARY

In summary, exercise has many benefits for the overweight person. It can be a useful clinical tool to discuss these benefits with the patients, because most do not realize the effects of activity on appetite, lean body mass, and basal metabolic rate. It is still very difficult to overcome the belief that exercise is just not enjoyable for most overweight persons. Behavioral principles, particularly those of shaping and cognitive restructuring, may be the most helpful.

The Use of Very-Low-Calorie Diets

A portion of the section on obesity in Volume 9 of the *Annual Review* was devoted to a description of "very-low-calorie diets," also known as "protein-sparing modified fasts." The use of these diets has become very popular within the past few years, especially within the past year, so an update is provided here.

Very-low-calorie diets are basically total fasts supplemented only with protein and, in some cases, a small amount of carbohydrate to prevent severe ketosis (Bistrian, 1978; Van Itallie, 1978; Wadden *et al.*, 1983a). The diets range from 400 to 800 calories per day. The theory behind the diets is that the most rapid weight loss is produced by fasting, but that total starvation has serious metabolic effects. The most notable of these effects is the tendency toward cardiac problems, particularly arrhythmias, created by mineral imbalance and/or protein depletion in the myocardium. Attempts have been made to minimize the loss of protein by supplementing such diets with protein from natural sources, and to prevent mineral imbalance with supplements of minerals, especially potassium, sodium, and magnesium.

Very careful metabolic work was being done on very-low-calorie diets when Robert Linn, an osteopath from a Philadelphia suburb, wrote *The Last Chance Diet* and popularized liquid protein (Linn, 1976). At least 60 deaths were attributed by the Food and Drug Administration and the Centers for Disease Control to the use of liquid protein. Many of these deaths could be directly tied to pre-existing coronary disease, absence of medical monitoring, protein of poor biological value, or mineral imbalance (Sours, Frattali, Brand, Feldman, Forbes, Swanson, & Paris, 1981). However, there were several unexplained deaths in dieters who seemingly were on good diets and were medically monitored.

The liquid protein scare of the 1970s (Van Itallie, 1978) took very-low-calorie diets out of the public domain once again. In the meantime, careful metabolic work was continuing in laboratories in Boston (Bistrian, Winterer, & Blackburn, 1977), Cleveland (Vertes, Genuth, & Hazelton, 1977), Paris (Apfelbaum, 1981), and Cambridge, England (Howard, Grant, Edwards, Littlewood, & McLean Baird, 1978). The results from these centers were very encouraging. Weight losses were large; there seemed to be few serious metabolic complications; and advances were being made in the nature of the diet and its administration.

In the early 1980s, the diet hit the public again, this time in many different forms. The most widespread, and controversial form the diet has taken has been the Cambridge Diet. The diet was formulated by Alan Howard at Cambridge (Howard *et al.*, 1978) and was marketed by the Feather family, which was most noted for earlier marketing of the Mark Eden Bust Developer. The diet is being marketed in an aggressive manner in a pyramid scheme and is available with no medical supervision. A person can become a Cambridge Diet Counselor (salesperson) with no special training. I recently encountered a Cambridge Diet Counselor—a man who repaired the fender of my car at the local body shop.

The Cambridge Diet has been used by millions of people, but the verdict is not yet in on whether it is a safe approach. A recent editorial in the *Journal of the American Medical Association* by Wadden, Stunkard, Brownell, and Van Itallie (1983b) noted that the diet violates a number of basic principles for the safe use of very-low-calorie diets. These include less protein than is usually recommended, no medical screening or monitoring, and the unsupervised use of the diet for longer than recommended periods. In addition to these safety concerns, the diet is administered without an accompanying program of behavior change, so the weight losses are likely to be transient.

Current very-low-calorie diets are also being used in a more professional manner. In addition to the university clinics where research is being conducted, several large companies, including highly respected medical–pharmaceutical firms, are opening clinics staffed by trained professionals in which very-low-calorie diets are used.

It appears, therefore, that very-low-calorie diets are here to stay, at least for the next few years. There is both danger and promise in the use of these diets, so the information that is available is presented here.

SAFETY

Very-low-calorie diets must be administered with several factors in mind, or else safety could be compromised. In clinics like those in Boston, Cleveland, and Paris mentioned above, thousands of patients have been treated with a most impressive safety record. The minimal safety precautions have been presented by Wadden *et al.* (1983a):

1. Patients should be given a careful medical examination before using such diets. This should include blood work, EKG, physi-

cal exam, and a medical history to check for coronary disease and the other problems that contraindicate use of these diets.

2. Patients should be medically monitored, by physicians expert in the use of these diets, throughout the use of the diets.

3. Protein of high biological value should be used in amounts equaling no less than 1.5 grams of protein per kilogram of ideal body weight.

4. The diets should be supplemented with vitamins and with specific minerals in specific amounts.

There are several other factors that are more controversial. The duration of such diets is one of these factors. No deaths have occurred on very-low-calorie diets used for 2 months or less, so a conservative approach would be to use them for no longer than this period. However, some centers have used such diets for up to a year in certain individuals and have had no obvious problems. Another point of controversy is whether carbohydrate should be included in the diets. The Boston group of Bistrian, Blackburn, and colleagues (Bistrian, 1978; Bistrian *et al.*, 1977) uses no carbohydrate, because these researchers note favorable metabolic effects from ketosis, and because they feel that the ketotic state aids the suppression of hunger. Others feel that carbohydrate is essential to the balance and safety of the diet (Yang & Van Itallie, 1976).

Very-low-calorie diets can be administered safely, but they must be used in a clinical or medical setting where the medical screening and monitoring is adequate. This is an area in which behavioral scientists and clinicians can collaborate with their medical colleagues.

EFFECTIVENESS

Data on the effectiveness of very-low-calorie diets have become available only recently, despite the fact that millions of people in the United States and other countries have been on different versions of the diet. One thing is clear: People lose a lot of weight, and they lose it rapidly. Figure 6-1, from Wadden *et al.* (1983a), shows the mean weight loss from studies in which the length of treatment has varied. There is a straightforward linear relationship between the length of time on the diet and weight loss. Average losses for very-low-calorie diets are in the range of 45–60 pounds; these losses are greater than those for any nonsurgical treatment for obesity.

People who have not been on such diets and professionals who have had no experience with the diets are surprised by how good compliance can be. There are, of course, compliance problems, but a

FIG. 6-1.

Relationship between weight loss and treatment duration in eight major studies (A–H) using very-low-calorie diets. Note the large weight losses and essentially linear trend for weight loss to increase as subjects use the diets for longer periods. (From "Very Low Calorie Diets: Their Efficacy, Safety, and Future" by T. A. Wadden, A. J. Stunkard, and K. D. Brownell, 1983, *Annals of Internal Medicine, 99,* 675–684. Copyright 1983, American College of Physicians. Reprinted by permission.)

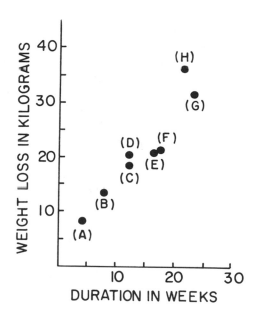

surprisingly large percentage of patients are pleased to be on the diets because of the rapid loss, and instead of feeling deprived because of the small amounts of food (which quickly become unpalatable), they are relieved to have no choices about what to eat. Many report cessation of hunger after a few days on such diets.

When the diets are used for periods averaging 12 weeks, weight losses are approximately 45 pounds (Wadden *et al.,* 1983a). The diets have very positive effects on the physiological complications of obesity, including hypertension, diabetes, and hypercholesterolemia (Bistrian, 1978; Wadden *et al.,* 1983a). The long-term results remain the most important unknown factor.

The first few reports on long-term maintenance show high rates of relapse. Genuth, Castro, and Vertes (1974) did a 22-month follow-up and found that more than half their patients had regained at least half the weight they had lost. Palgi, Bistrian, Greenburg, and Blackburn

(1982) followed patients from the Blackburn and Bistrian clinic in Boston for 2 to 7 years. The average posttreatment loss of 50 pounds had decreased to only 15 pounds at a follow-up that averaged 4.5 years. Lindner and Blackburn (1976) reported somewhat more encouraging results from a program that included a very-low-calorie diet plus behavior modification and exercise. A subgroup of their patients regained only 14 pounds of the average 46-pound loss during 18 to 24 months after treatment.

A recent quasi-controlled study showed very promising maintenance of weight losses (Wadden, Stunkard, Brownell, & Dey, 1984). A total of 17 subjects received a combination of a very-low-calorie diet and a comprehensive behavioral program (see Wadden *et al.*, 1984, for details). The subjects lost an average of 45 pounds during the initial treatment program, which lasted 16 weeks. At a 1-year follow-up, the average loss was still 41 pounds.

Wadden *et al.* (1984) plotted these figures in a graph showing the results of behavior therapy alone and behavior therapy plus pharmacotherapy from the study by Craighead *et al.* (1981) (see Figure 6-2). These are very encouraging results, considering the small losses produced by most treatments and the almost total relapse produced by others.

The short-term losses with the very-low-calorie diets are most impressive. Considering that many overweight persons have more to lose than the 10–20 pounds that can be achieved with behavior therapy, more aggressive approaches are warranted. Very-low-calorie diets provide one such approach. The real challenge may lie in developing treatments to maximize compliance to these diets and to help the patients sustain the losses once they finish the initial phases of the diets. This is where behavior therapy can make an important contribution.

The use of very-low-calorie diets is a fertile area for research and for clinical discoveries among behavioral experts. Many medical professionals using very-low-calorie diets recognize the need for behavioral input. This not only permits behavior therapists to influence and to learn from other professionals, but it furthers the conceptual notion that interdisciplinary efforts will be necessary for the field to advance.

An Innovative Approach to Maintenance

Many methods have been proposed for enhancing the maintenance of weight loss. These have been reviewed elsewhere (Brownell, 1982; Wilson, 1980). At the risk of supporting a procedure that is quite speculative, I now discuss an approach to the maintenance of weight loss that thus far has not come to the attention of behavioral researchers.

FIG. 6-2.

Weight loss at the end of 6 months of treatment and 1-year follow-up for subjects treated by behavior therapy plus a very-low-calorie diet, with comparison to results from Craighead, Stunkard, and O'Brien (1981) using behavior therapy alone and behavior therapy plus fenfluramine. (From "The Treatment of Moderate Obesity by Behavior Modification and Very-Low-Calorie Diets" by T. A. Wadden, A. J. Stunkard, K. D. Brownell, and S. C. Dey, 1984. *Journal of Consulting and Clinical Psychology.* Copyright American Psychological Association. Reprinted by permission.)

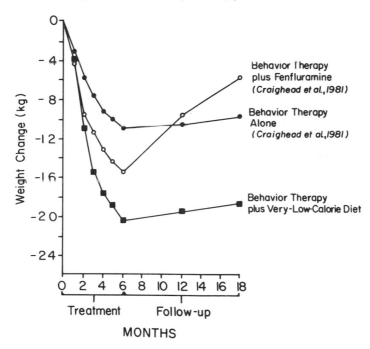

This innovative procedure was developed by John Garrow in England and involves the use of a waist cord after weight is lost (Garrow, 1978, 1981; Garrow & Gardiner, 1981). Garrow has used the waist cord to maintain weight lost from jaw wiring. With the wiring procedure, patients have their jaws wired by an oral surgeon and then consume 2 pints of whole cow's milk daily, vitamin and mineral supplements, and *ad libitum* noncaloric liquids. After 6 to 12 months, when the desired weight is achieved, the waist cord is used. The procedure is as follows:

> Initially cord 5 mm in diameter was used for the waist cord, but it was too bulky and showed through light clothing, so 2 mm cord was subsequently used. It was applied with the patient supine and fitted to a circumference of about 700 mm. The next day it was checked for tightness: ideally it had

to produce no indentation of the skin with the patient supine but make a white (not red) line on the skin when the patient was seated. The tension of the cord was adjusted until this tension was achieved, and then knot was then sealed by melting the end of the cord gently, taking care not to burn the patient. (Garrow & Gardiner, 1981, p. 858)

Garrow and Gardiner (1981) report the long-term progress of seven patients who used the cord and the results from nine patients who had been treated with jaw wiring previously, but without the cord. The subjects who did not use the waist cord regained an average of 39.2 pounds of the original loss of 66.7 pounds, while the waist cord subjects regained only 12.3 pounds of the original loss of 83.8 pounds (see Figure 6-3).

These data are subject to obvious criticisms. Only a small number of subjects were studied, and assignments to cord versus no-cord groups were not made randomly. Longer follow-ups are necessary (the waist

FIG. 6-3.

Weight changes in subjects who did and did not use Garrow's waist cord after an initial period of loss produced by jaw wiring. (From "Maintenance of Weight Loss in Obese Patients after Jaw Wiring" by J. S. Garrow and G. T. Gardiner, 1981, *British Medical Journal, 282,* 858–859. Copyright 1981, British Medical Association. Reprinted by permission.)

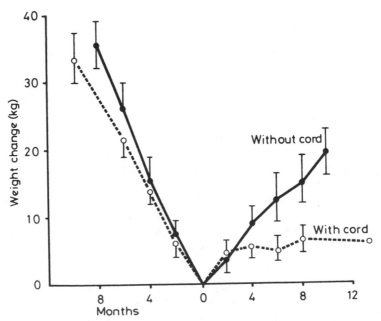

cord subjects were followed 4–14 months after the wires were removed). Whether the cord would be successful with patients losing weight by other means is also important. Finally, the therapeutic context in which the waist cord is used is undoubtedly important, and needs to be described in greater detail.

The use of the waist cord could be an important advance in the area of weight loss maintenance. It is a simple and cost-effective procedure that can be conceptualized in behavioral terms. The cord provides continuous and tactile feedback about weight status. Weight gain that would ordinarily produce only movement on the scale will produce negative sensory experiences because the cord becomes uncomfortable. This continuous and immediate feedback, followed by self-evaluation and then by self-reinforcement or self-punishment, provides short-term goals and rewards. The effectiveness of this approach may result from the fact that self-imposed proximal goals are more effective than distal goals in helping patients maintain weight loss (Bandura & Simon, 1977; Stuart & Guire, 1978).

This technique is perfectly suited for investigation in a controlled trial. It is a promising lead from the medical literature that might be perfected, extended, and generalized by careful behavioral research.

SMOKING

The coverage of smoking in Volume 9 of the *Annual Review* focused on public health issues. Specifically, the review covered the risk of cigarette smoke to nonsmokers (passive smoking), prevention of cigarette smoking in children and adolescents, and the effects of the anti-smoking campaign on the smoking habits of the nation.

My rationale for changing the focus from the usual individually oriented treatment to broad-scale public health matters included both clinical and cost-effectiveness reasons. The behavioral program for smoking cessation will undoubtedly be improved, particularly in the area of maintenance (Lichtenstein, 1982). However, the improvements are not occurring at a rapid rate, and the clinical treatment of individuals is not likely to have an important role in the overall cost of health care, morbidity and mortality rates, productivity for the nation's workforce, and so forth.

These public health issues are becoming more important for behavior therapists. This is a positive move in my opinion, because professionals with a knowledge of the principles of behavior change can make a significant impact in this area (Best, 1983). This impact is likely to come from large-scale collaborative efforts among professionals

in health education, psychology, communications, medicine, epidemiology, education, economics, and so forth.

This year's review of the smoking field focuses both on public
health issues and on several issues related to treatment. In the public
health arena, the review gives a brief update on the health consequences
of smoking, and then covers priorities for research, recent information
on passive smoking and media campaigns, and the implications for
large-scale programs. The review then moves to clinical issues and
covers controlled smoking, the relationship between smoking and
weight change, and a more speculative topic—the possible role of
exercise in smoking cessation and prevention.

Public Health Issues

AN UPDATE ON HEALTH RISKS

Almost everyone, including smokers, knows that smoking is related to
a variety of very serious diseases. However, the extent of the problem is
being shown more clearly each year. For instance, it is widely believed
that lung cancer is the most serious outcome of smoking. The most
recent Surgeon General's Report (U.S. Department of Health and
Human Services, 1983) shows that smoking causes more deaths from
heart disease than from all types of cancer combined, and that smoking
is a higher-order risk factor for heart disease than either hypertension
or hypercholesterolemia.

The following facts on the health risks of smoking have been
assembled from the Surgeon General's report and from information
from the Federal Trade Commission presented in *The Nation's Health*
(American Public Health Association, 1981):

1. On the average, cigarette smokers have a 70% greater rate of
   coronary heart disease than do nonsmokers. For persons who
   smoke two packs a day, the rate of heart disease is between two
   and three times that of nonsmokers. Heart disease accounts for
   nearly half the deaths in the United States.
2. Cigarette smoking causes 80% of the cases of lung canger in
   men, and lung cancer kills more people in the United States
   than any other malignant diseases. Of patients with lung
   cancer, 70% die within 1 year of diagnosis, and 90% die within
   5 years.
3. Cigarette smoking is the major cause of emphysema and
   chronic bronchitis.
4. In terms of overall mortality, a smoker is 70% more likely to die
   at a given age than is a comparable nonsmoker.

5. A smoker of two packs or more a day decreases life expectancy by more than 8 years. The decrease is 6 years for a smoker of one pack a day.
6. Between 70% and 80% of all emphysema and chronic bronchitis deaths are attributable to smoking.
7. Maternal smoking during pregnancy increases the risk of stillbirth or infant death by at least 20%, even in light smokers (less than one pack a day).
8. There is a synergistic relationship between smoking and alcohol use that greatly increases the risk of cancer of the larynx, oral cavity, and esophagus for those who smoke and drink heavily.
9. There is a synergistic relationship between smoking and exposure to some environmental carcinogens, particularly asbestos.
10. A woman who smokes and uses birth control pills is 20 times more likely to suffer stroke by cerebral hemorrhage than a woman who does neither.

These health matters are a serious concern because 32.6% of the population smokes regularly, thus making smoking the single most important preventable cause of death in the United States (U.S. Department of Health and Human Services, 1983). This is why the involvement of behavioral experts in public health interventions can have such an important influence on the smoking field.

AN UPDATE ON PASSIVE SMOKING

There has been great debate about whether it is harmful for nonsmokers or even for other smokers to be "passive smokers" (i.e., to breathe the air where others are smoking). The implications of this debate are enormous. If smokers place others at risk by their behavior, then legislative and other curbs on smoking may be justified. The topic of individual freedom arises repeatedly in this context.

The tobacco industry is waging a vigorous campaign to counter the claim of antismoking advocates that smoking is dangerous for people other than smokers. In a two-page advertisement in the November 8, 1982 issue of *Newsweek*, the Tobacco Institute—the public relations arm of the industry—addressed the impact of passive smoking:

WHAT HAPPENS TO SMOKE IN THE AIR?
The logical and obvious thing: cigarette smoke is immediately diluted by surrounding air.
And measurements of cigarette smoke in the air, taken under realistic conditions, show again and again that there is minimal tobacco smoke in the air we breathe.

In fact, based on one study, which measured nicotine in the air, it has been said that a nonsmoker would have to spend 100 hours in a smoke-filled room to consume the equivalent of a single filter-tipped cigarette. That's what we mean by minimal. . . .

In our view, smoking is an adult custom and the decision to smoke should be based on mature and informed individual freedom of choice. (Tobacco Institute, 1982, p. 52)

Viewing the scientific evidence suggests otherwise. Spengler and Sexton (1983) recently published a thorough review on indoor air pollution in *Science*. Among pollutants such as asbestos, formaldehyde, and carbon monoxide, passive smoking was listed as one of the most important pollutants. Repace and Lowery (1980) reported earlier that the levels of respirable particulates in smoke-filled environments greatly exceed those in smoke-free environments, outdoors, and even in vehicles on busy commuter highways.

In Volume 9 of the *Annual Review*, studies on this issue were reviewed; the evidence implicated passive smoking in a variety of illnesses, particularly in children of smokers. One study found that nonsmoking wives of heavy-smoking men had significantly increased risk of cancer (Hirayama, 1981). A study in the workplace by White and Froeb (1980) found that nonsmokers who were chronically exposed to cigarette smoke had pulmonary function levels similar to those of light smokers and worse than those of nonsmokers from a smoke-free environment.

Studies with children have had most distressing results. There is a relationship between parental smoking and acute respiratory illness in children (Bonham & Wilson, 1981). Dose–response relationships have been shown between bronchitis and pneumonia in children and smoking in their parents (Colley, Holland, & Corkhill, 1974). Gortmaker, Walker, Jacobs, and Ruch-Ross (1982) found a 50%–240% increase in risk for asthma and functionally impairing asthma in children of smokers in both urban and rural samples. Bonham and Wilson (1981) found similar effects for acute respiratory effects, restricted activity days, and disability days in children of smokers. There are also studies showing no differences in illness and medical care utilization of children from smoking and nonsmoking parents (Vogt, 1983). In addition, Friedman, Petitti, and Bawol (1983) note that many correlates of passive smoking must be considered in interpreting data on this subject.

There is evidence on both sides of this issue, but the weight of the evidence favors the conclusion that passive smoking is dangerous. This is the conclusion reached in the recent Surgeon General's Report (U.S. Department of Health and Human Services, 1983). The Committee on

Indoor Pollutants of the National Academy of Sciences went even further in recommending that the risk to nonsmokers be considered in public policy:

> The constituents of tobacco smoke are well-documented as hazardous, the prevalence of population exposure is very high, and there is an increased incidence of respiratory tract symptoms and functional decrements (decreases) in children residing in homes with smokers, compared with those homes without smokers. These considerations and recent evidence of increased lung cancer rates among nonsmoking women living with smoking husbands have led us to conclude that indoor exposure to tobacco smoke has adverse effects. Public policy should clearly articulate that involuntary exposure to tobacco smoke ought to [be] minimized or avoided where possible. (National Academy of Sciences, 1981, p. 103)

The cultural climate regarding smoking is changing, based partly on the feeling of nonsmokers that they are in jeopardy breathing the smoke of people who use cigarettes. The change has occurred recently and is visible in many ways.

THE PUBLIC SENTIMENT AGAINST SMOKERS

Smoking has changed in the public eye since the mid-1900s from an activity that signified individuality and social competence to an activity that is scorned by others, is thought to infringe on the rights of nonsmokers, and is illegal in some settings. An article on the subject in *Newsweek* ("Showdown on Smoking," 1983) mentioned a number of examples of this change in attitude:

- Antismoking groups like GASP (Group Against Smoking Pollution) exist in many states and are becoming more involved in legislative matters.
- In 1983, 36 states restrict smoking in some way, compared to 5 in 1971.
- Smoking is illegal in most public places in Berkeley, California, and no-smoking placards outnumber stop signs 10 to 1.
- In 1975, the Minnesota state legislature passed a Clean Indoor Air Act, which barred smoking in banks, stores, offices, and other public spaces, except where expressly permitted.
- The Non-Smokers Inn in Dallas adds a $100 fine to the bill of anyone caught smoking.
- Muse Airlines in Texas has only nonsmoking sections on their airplanes, and offers a "survival kit" of gum, candy, and plastic pacifiers for desperate smokers.

- At least 100 insurance companies give discounts to nonsmokers, and some advertise to attract the business of nonsmokers.
- The San Mateo County Fire Department in California will not hire anyone who smokes—on the job or off—citing savings in workers' compensation and decreases in job-related ailments. The firefighters' union is suing.
- The tobacco industry spents $6 million to help defeat a statewide referendum to restrict public smoking.

From a public health viewpoint, these are very positive developments. Social factors are thought to be at the root of smoking initiation in almost all cases (U.S. Department of Health, Education and Welfare, 1979c), so a change in the social climate will probably affect the likelihood of adolescents adopting the habit, if not the likelihood that current smokers will quit.

This knowledge that attitudes are changing may be useful information for planning large-scale studies or even individual treatment strategies. Most people are responsive to social factors, so the public sentiment against smoking may provide an additional incentive for some people to alter the habit.

THE POTENTIAL OF THE MEDIA

The use of the media presents great potential for the modification of smoking habits. This is a fertile area for behavioral scientists, as behavioral and social learning theories are the guiding principles for most of the large-scale public health efforts, many of which rely on the media as one major source of influence on their populations. These efforts, even with their appeal to large populations, eventually reduce to attempts to alter behavior in individuals. Behavior therapists can make valuable contributions in this capacity.

There are three major ways in which the media have been used for changes in the nation's smoking patterns. The first is the antismoking campaign, which is a combination of a ban on televised cigarette advertisements and the use of anticigarette public service announcements. The second is the use of the media to prevent smoking in adolescents. Specific skills, such as behavioral rehearsal and assertion training, are used in these programs. The third involves smoking cessation programs. These use many of the familiar techniques to aid smokers in quitting. It is easy to see the role for behavioral scientists in activities of this type; the first and third are discussed in detail here.

The Antismoking Campaign. One piece of evidence that the media may influence smoking rates is research by Warner and colleagues at the University of Michigan on the effects of the antismoking campaign that has been waged since the 1960s (Warner, 1977, 1981; Warner & Murt, 1983). These data show a clear decrease in smoking rates during the campaign, and the authors' sophisticated analysis suggests that much of the effect is due to the campaign. Warner and Murt (1983) have estimated that the antismoking movement has resulted in the prevention of more than 200,000 premature deaths between 1964 and 1978.

The view that the antismoking campaign has had a positive effect on public health is not shared universally (Danaher, Berkanovic, & Gerber, 1983). There is some suggestion that the ban on television advertising for cigarettes has been counterproductive for two reasons (Fritschler, 1975; Hamilton, 1972). First, the cigarette companies have been forced to focus on less expensive, and perhaps more effective, forms of advertising—namely, the print media and promotional events (distribution of free samples, hosting of sporting events, etc). Second, the ban on cigarette advertising was a serious blow to the antismoking advertisements because an estimated $75 million in free broadcast time from the Fairness Doctrine was lost (U.S. Department of Health, Education and Welfare, 1979c).

This dispute is difficult to resolve. The debate, however, revolves around the effects of a specific strategy—the antismoking campaign. Irrespective of this particular approach, the use of the media does appear to be one powerful avenue for influencing smoking behavior.

Televised Smoking Cessation Programs. Danaher *et al.* (1983), in a review of smoking programs on television, estimated that dozens of smoking cessation programs have been produced and broadcast. The large number of programs is testimony to their popularity, if not their effectiveness. The unfortunate fact is that evaluations have been done on only a small number of programs. The programs with some information on evaluation are discussed here. The information is adapted from the review by Danaher *et al.* (1983).

The first published report of a televised program was from Dubren (1977). A local news show in New York City offered stop-smoking material in 20 segments of 30–90 seconds each, delivered by the station's science editor. The material involved hints drawn from the smoking literature. Persons who desired materials sent in postcards (4,794 persons responded). A sample of 634 subjects was identified for study, and 49% of these were contacted by phone after the program; 46% were contacted 1 month later for follow-up. The percentages of smokers who were abstinent in the New York program were 9.3% after the program and 9.6% 1 month later. Men reported an abstinence rate of 15.2%, compared to 6.8% for women. The weaknesses in this study were the use of self-reports and a short follow-up period (Danaher *et al.*, 1983).

A sophisticated clinical program was offered in Bellingham, Washington, by Best (1980). Social learning theory was used to develop a program aired on six consecutive Saturday evenings. The program included role playing and the now-standard behavioral techniques, and used cartoons, graphs, and other innovative visual aids. Best (1980) estimated viewership at 20,000. Viewers were asked to register by phone or mail, and a sample of 1,103 was identified. Of this sample, 85% were contacted after the program. The percentage of subjects who reported quitting was 11.5% The percentages increased to 14.7% at a 3-month follow-up and 17.6% at a 6-month follow-up. Best estimated the cost per abstinent registrant at $48. Danaher *et al.* (1983) noted the varying rates on subjects contacted over the follow-up, along with the possibility of response bias.

A third important smoking program was done in Finland as part of the North Karelia heart disease prevention project (Tuomilheto, Koskela, Puska, Bjorkqvist, & Salonen, 1978). Seven 45-minute episodes were broadcast over 1 month. The episodes were largely unedited segments showing a group of 10 volunteers who participated in a studio-based clinic. The content was much the same as that of Best (1980), with two exceptions. The studio subjects went through the rapid smoking procedure, even though viewers were cautioned not to do so themselves. In addition, the program was done within the context of an intensive community organization effort. A total of 44% of the population of North Karelia saw at least one show, and 7% saw four to seven shows. The number of smokers declined from 45.7% to 44% in men and from 27.3% to 25.5% for women. Of the persons who viewed the program, 11% quit after the program, and 4.2% were still abstinent 1 year later (Tuomilehto *et al.*, 1978).

These studies show small but perhaps cost-effective changes in smoking in samples of subjects who viewed televised smoking cessation programs (Danaher *et al.*, 1983). As is the case with any innovative approach, these programs raise as many questions as they answer. Danaher *et al.* (1983) noted some of the prominent issues, including the frequency and number of shows, the time spent per broadcast, whether the moderator should be a health expert or a television personality, and whether the surveys done on these subjects were representative of the total population of viewers, which includes "silent" participations who do not identify themselves but who may profit from a program.

The advantage of televised programs is that "treatment" can be delivered at low cost to large numbers of people. Some authors feel that this provides a favorable cost-effectiveness ratio when compared to traditional smoking cessation clinics (Best, 1980). Danaher *et al.* (1983) felt that smoking clinics are not the appropriate reference group for a cost-effectiveness analysis of televised programs; televised programs should be compared to alternative approaches for persons who do *not* enroll in clinical programs.

PRIORITIES FOR RESEARCH AND PROGRAM DEVELOPMENT

The extent to which good research is done and the findings are applied to the general public depends on many factors. Most reviews of this nature focus on the quality of the science (i.e., whether the internal and external validity of studies is sufficient to have confidence in the findings). This is a matter of great importance, but the other issue— whether science is applied—is also important. This topic has been considered at length in the health education field and in the general area of applications research. In the field of behavior therapy, the issue is relatively new.

One priority in the smoking area is to integrate information from many disciplines. A few examples may illustrate this point. Anthropology brings a special perspective to the smoking problem. Eckert (1983) views smoking as a social symbol and claims that antismoking campaigns based on an inaccurate understanding of the social context of smoking can actually strengthen the desire to smoke. Economics is also a relevant discipline. Governmental supports to the tobacco industry, taxes on cigarettes, and the general economic climate influence the prevalence of smoking. These are only a few areas of information that need to be included in an integrated understanding of smoking.

Best (1983) has taken this concept an important step further by emphasizing the political factors that influence health programs. The political process influences smoking in numerous ways. Legislation influences the cost and availability of tobacco. Funding bodies such as the National Institutes of Health determine the focus of much of the research on any health topic. National, state, and local politics are key factors in determining whether health programs are supported and disseminated.

The recommendation made by Best (1983), which I endorse, is that social scientists (including political scientists) collaborate on health research. Since many of the important factors, such as political decision making, do not lend themselves to neat experimental designs, innovative and flexible approaches to research will be necessary. Best (1983), in a report to the World Conference on Smoking and Health, recommended that the following factors be considered by social scientists:

1. Factors that influence political decision making require much more attention from health researchers.
2. Survey and other epidemiological techniques are necessary to describe and analyze attitude and other characteristics of the population that influence political behavior. Since a politician will usually take action if he or she perceives acceptance or support, public support for health programs needs to be documented.
3. Research is necessary on how public attitudes can be communicated to politicians. Among the possible methods are the use of the media, letter writing, and other public displays.
4. Data are needed on the political factors that influence the actual implementation of health programs, once the need and willingness are identified.
5. Data are needed on the politicians themselves to determine the factors that motivate their own behavior, their beliefs about health, and how and why they make certain decisions.
6. Research is needed on the impact of information, and perhaps misinformation, disseminated to the public from a number of sources. (An example is the advertisement from the Tobacco Institute shown earlier in this section.)

These are only a few of the important priorities for smoking research, but these points do highlight the importance of interdisciplinary efforts and the ultimate importance of political factors in the ability of health programs to reach large populations.

Controlled Smoking

An innovative and relatively new approach to the treatment of cigarette smokers is controlled smoking, a concept introduced by Frederiksen and colleagues (Frederiksen, 1979; Frederiksen, Peterson, & Murphy, 1976; Frederiksen & Simon, 1978). The procedure involves changes in smoking substance, rate, and topography, but does not focus on cessation.

Controlled smoking was proposed as an alternative to abstinence for several reasons. The first is that many people wish to smoke less, but do not want to quit smoking. The second is that long-term success rates for smoking cessation programs are no more than 20% (Bernstein & Glasgow, 1979; Lichtenstein, 1982; Pechacek, 1979). It is possible that changes in the act of smoking will help reduce risk in people who are unwilling or unable to cease smoking.

The early studies on controlled smoking were positive. For example, Frederiksen and Simon (1978) produced changes in smokers that were maintained at a 1-year follow-up. Other groups have examined changes in one of the characteristics of smoking, such as brand fading (Foxx & Brown, 1979; Prue, Krapfl, & Martin, 1981); however, until recently, only Frederiksen's group had investigated changes in substance, rate, and topography.

Two recent studies by Glasgow and colleagues lend support to the controlled smoking approach. In the first study, 60 smokers were assigned to one of three conditions: controlled smoking, controlled smoking plus weekly carbon monoxide feedback, and delayed treatment (Glasgow, Klesges, Godding, & Gegelman, 1983a). The carbon monoxide feedback was included to determine whether physiological feedback would be motivational. The treatment lasted 5 weeks and focused in a sequential fashion on making 50% reductions in (1) nicotine content of the brand smoked; (2) number of cigarettes smoked per day; and (3) the percentage of each cigarette smoked.

Both treatment groups in this study showed significant changes in self-reports of smoking and in carbon monoxide levels, compared to the control group. There was no advantage to including carbon monoxide feedback. The changes in smoking behavior and carbon monoxide levels were maintained at 3-month and 6-month follow-ups. Interestingly, subjects were better able to make changes in the brand of cigarette smoked than in the number and percentage of cigarettes smoked.

A study then followed by Glasgow, Klesges, and Vasey (1983b), which was an extension and replication of the earlier work. Nine subjects were treated in a seven-session program using a multiple-baseline design across the three aspects of the controlled smoking program. Data from self-monitoring records indicated that subjects made reductions in each of the three areas and that the changes coincided with the application of treatment for the specific areas. Carbon monoxide levels were reduced, and these reductions were maintained at a 6-month follow-up. The authors attempted to increase reductions in number and percentage of cigarettes smoked from the first study by using more gradual reduction goals and by including feedback on daily nicotine intake. These procedures were not successful.

It does appear that subjects can be encouraged to make changes that are consistent with the goals of the controlled smoking program. Even more importantly, the changes seem to be maintained far better than is abstinence in traditional programs. The key question, of course, is whether controlled smoking actually reduces health risk.

Research on smoking topography is central to the potential utility of controlled smoking. If subjects change to a cigarette lower in tar and nicotine, but smoke more cigarettes or draw more heavily, the advantage may be lost. In the study of Glasgow *et al.* (1983a), the carbon monoxide reductions were not as great as would be expected, given the behavioral changes obtained by self-reports. These authors acknowledged that subjects made compensatory changes in topography, although it was clear that the subjects did not compensate completely for the factors they changed.

Carefully controlled studies on smoking topography have been appearing in the literature for the past several years. These studies have investigated puff volume as a key measure and have evaluated the complex interrelationships among aspects of topography (Epstein, Dickson, Ossip, Stiller, Russel, & Winter, 1982a; Gust, Pickens, & Pechacek, 1983; Ossip-Klein, Martin, Prue, & Davis, 1983). The picture on topography is becoming more clear, but much is yet to be learned. The next several years should bring the crucial information, and perhaps with it, a verdict on whether controlled smoking actually alters health risk.

Smoking and Weight Gain

There is an interesting and important relationship between smoking and body weight. It is clear that smokers weigh less than nonsmokers (Goldbourt & Medalie, 1977; Wack & Rodin, 1982). It is a widespread opinion that smokers gain weight when they quit, and this is one major reason cited by smokers for resisting cessation (U.S. Department of Health, Education and Welfare, 1979c). In fact, some who have given up smoking have been distressed by the weight gain and have resumed smoking (Wack & Rodin, 1982).

The change in body weight with change in smoking status has major implications for the treatment of smoking. If weight gain occurs with smoking cessation, this may trade one risk factor for another, although smoking is a much stronger risk factor than obesity for most diseases. The potential of weight gain may impede clinical efforts to aid smokers in quitting, and the weight gain after smoking cessation may increase the likelihood of relapse.

The common notion is that smoking cessation leads to weight gain. Is this true? The Surgeon General's Report on Smoking and Health (U.S. Department of Health, Education and Welfare, 1979c) stated that one-third of people gain weight after quitting, one-third stay the same, and one-third lose weight. This, however, does not seem to be the case.

The prevailing sentiment is that smokers gain weight when they quit. Gordon, Kannel, Dawber, and McGee (1975) found such a relationship in the Framingham Heart Study. Coates and Li (1983) reported weight gains in asbestos-exposed shipyard workers who quit smoking.

Grunberg (1982) claimed that weight gain in ex-smokers is an "unequivocal fact." Wack and Rodin (1982) did a thorough review of the literature on smoking and its effects on weight. They concluded that "smokers, who appear to maintain a constant weight below that of nonsmokers, go through a period of dynamic weight increase upon the cessation of smoking until, once again, a weight plateau is attained that is no different from that of people who have never smoked" (p. 367).

The mechanism of this change is important for both theoretical and practical reasons. One possible factor that has received attention is the preference for sweet foods (Grunberg, 1982; Wack & Rodin, 1982). Grunberg and colleagues carried out several detailed and carefully controlled studies with both humans and animals to evaluate this factor (Grunberg, 1982; Grunberg, Bowen, & Morse, in press). In these studies, nicotine administration (in animals) or cigarette smoking (in humans) was accompanied by decreased consumption of sweet-tasting high-calorie foods. Abstinence from smoking was related to increased preference for sweets and increased consumption of sweets. Intake of other foods did not change, although high-fat (high-energy-density) foods were not studied. Grunberg and Morse (in press) even found negative correlations between per capita consumption of cigarettes and sugar in the United States over many years.

Wack and Rodin (1982) agree that increased preference for sweet foods may explain the weight gain that follows smoking cessation, although they do note studies showing smokers who eat more than nonsmokers and who make unpredictable changes in intake when they quit. They note several other possible mediating factors. One is that smoking lowers the efficiency of calorie storage and/or metabolic rate and that the system recovers when smoking is terminated. It is clear that more physiological work is necessary to establish the factors that control this phenomenon.

Research in this area could lead to useful clinical information. The psychological resistance to smoking cessation may in some people be due to the fear of weight gain. A better understanding of the relationship between smoking and weight gain could suggest dietary methods to prevent the weight gain and to help ex-smokers resist the natural cravings that might occur.

A Possible Role for Exercise?

The relationship between physical activity and smoking has not been mentioned in the behavioral literature, and, for that matter, has received little attention from any discipline. A few recent studies suggest some interesting possibilities, so they are discussed here. This section is short because so little evidence exists and because the idea that exercise may aid in the prevention or cessation of smoking is very speculative.

Two recent studies from the medical literature have shown a relationship, albeit correlational, between exercise and smoking (Koplan, Powell, Sikes, Shirley, & Campbell, 1982; Oldridge, Donner, Buck, Jones, Andrew, Parker, Cunningham, Kavanaugh, Rechnitzer, & Sutton, 1983). The studies examined quite different populations, and each addressed the issue of smoking and weight in a different way, but the results lead in the same direction.

The study by Koplan *et al.* (1982), published in the *Journal of the American Medical Association*, evaluated the correlates of running in persons who ran in the Peachtree Road Race (a 10-km race in Atlanta). The authors, from the Centers for Disease Control, sent questionnaires 1 year after the race to 1,250 randomly selected males and the same number of females. The response rates were 55% and 58%, but the investigators did telephone interviews to determine differences between responders and nonresponders.

One striking finding of this study was that 81% of men and 75% of women who had smoked cigarettes when they started running had stopped smoking after beginning the running. In addition, giving up smoking was significantly more common among those who continued to run than among those who discontinued the running.

There are many competing explanations to the appealing one that the running caused people to quit, but the high percentages are quite impressive, and this topic deserves more attention. It is possible that smokers who would run in a competitive race would tend to be light smokers with some degree of athletic ability, so giving up the habit may come more easily to them than to the more difficult cases seen in clinical settings. The running may also have been part of an overall change in life style that included smoking cessation, so the running and quitting may not have been related in a cause-and-effect manner. Whatever the reason, this is an interesting relationship.

The second piece of evidence comes from the Ontario Exercise–Heart Collaborative Study (Oldridge *et al.*, 1983). In this study, 733 men recovering from myocardial infarction were followed for 3 years in an exercise rehabilitation program. Fully 46.5% of the subjects dropped out during the 3 years. The two most powerful predictors of dropout were smoking and blue-collar occupation. Again, a cause-and-effect relationship is not demonstrated by these correlations, but there exists the possibility that exercise and smoking are related in an important manner.

These two studies suggest the possibility that smoking makes it difficult for people to exercise, and, more importantly, that smokers who begin an exercise program are likely to quit smoking. This area is wide open for research, as, to my knowledge, there have been no studies that use exercise as a component of treatment or even as the sole treatment for smokers.

ALCOHOLISM

In Volume 8 of the *Annual Review*, I covered many aspects of the field of alcoholism, including assessment, process variables, and treatment outcome issues. In Volume 9, I covered only one topic, that of controlled drinking. This was an unusual stance for this series—to cover a single topic—but this topic was unusual. The debate over controlled drinking versus abstinence had implications for theories of alcoholism, treatment of the problem, the process of reviewing and publishing scientific information, and the role of the popular media in a scientific dispute.

This year, I cover two topics—controlled drinking and the prevention of alcoholism. The issue of prevention has received little attention in the field in general (Nathan, 1983), and this series has been no exception; the time has come to remedy this deficit. The issue of the utility of controlled drinking continues to be important to the field. I provide an update on the topic and focus on both the debate and the implications of the debate.

In giving so much attention to the controlled drinking versus abstinence issue, I risk disapproval from some colleagues. As Program Chair for the World Congress on Behavior Therapy, which was held in December 1983, I invited Dr. Alan Marlatt of the University of Washington to chair a symposium on the controlled drinking and abstinence approaches. Several colleagues complained that this issue did not represent the entire field of alcoholism and only contributed to the idea that all behavior therapists favor controlled drinking. I agree on both counts.

I accept this criticism and respond by stating my bias: No other issue in the field of alcoholism has captured the attention of so many persons, both professional and not. No other issue creates such strong feelings. No other issue touches on so many topics relating to the scientific and clinical enterprise. With that, let me begin discussion of the controversy.

The Controlled Drinking Controversy: An Update

The furor over controlled drinking and abstinence was raging furiously when I was writing my contributions to Volume 9 of the *Annual*

Review. The controversy continues, although the debate is almost forgotten by the popular media. The issue is now back where it belongs—in the scientific literature where some degree of objectivity can prevail.

It is not clear whether the field of alcoholism has profited from the heated debate that has now spanned the past several years. Actually, the debate has occurred at least since Davies published an opinion about controlled drinking in 1962. It reached its peak in the summer and fall of 1982 when an article by Pendery, Maltzman, and West (1982) criticizing work by Sobell and Sobell (1973a, 1973b) appeared in the journal *Science.*

The Pendery *et al.* (1982) paper was greeted by tremendous attention in the popular press. As journalists are inclined to do, most writers and producers focused on the most sensational aspect of the "story"—namely that Pendery *et al.* either stated or implied that data from the Sobells were fraudulent. It was only by implication that controlled drinking was condemned, but condemned it was.

Many new developments have occurred in the past year; these are reviewed here. It is useful to examine the reasons for the controversy and the ways in which scientific, editorial, investigative, and legislative bodies have responded to a very serious matter.

THE CONTROVERSY AND THE INVESTIGATIVE FINDINGS

The accusations of fraud that followed the critique of the Sobells' work by Pendery *et al.* (1982) were taken seriously in many quarters. In fact, the issue of whether the Sobells engaged in fraudulent practices garnered far more attention than the actual issue of controlled drinking versus abstinence. Several investigations by special committees began in 1982 and continued into 1983. These have been described by Marlatt (1983).

Mark and Linda Sobell, authors of the early investigation of controlled drinking (Sobell & Sobell, 1973a, 1973b), are employed by the Addiction Research Foundation in Toronto. The president of the Foundation launched an investigation of the Sobells' work by convening a blue-ribbon panel of independent scientists and scholars. The panel was chaired by Bernard Dickens, professor of law, criminology, and community health at the University of Toronto. The other committee members were Harold Warwick, professor emeritus of medicine at the University of Western Ontario; Anthony Doob, professor of psychology and director of the Centre of Criminology at the University of Toronto; and William Winegard, former president of the University of Guelph and past chair of the Ontario Council on University Affairs.

This panel released its report on November 5, 1982. The report was lengthy and contained detailed accounts of the methods with which the Sobells had collected data, the way in which Pendery *et al.* had evaluated the Sobells' work, and the issue of whether the Sobells were guilty of fraud. Pendery and her colleagues refused to cooperate with the panel, stating three reasons: The panel would be biased because it was convened by the Sobells' institution; the panel did not have the rights of cross-examination and subpoena needed to get valid information; and the panel members would not have the time to do a thorough examination of the data.

The report of this panel leaves no doubt as to the conclusions reached by these respected investigators:

> The Committee has reviewed all of the allegations made against the Sobells by Pendery et al. in their Draft manuscript, in their published *Science* article, and in various statements quoted in the public media. In response to these allegations, the Committee examined both the published papers authored by the Sobells as well as a great quantity of data which formed the basis of these published reports. After isolating each of the separate allegations, the Committee examined all available evidence. The Committee's conclusion is clear and unequivocal: The Committee finds there to be no reasonable cause to doubt the scientific or personal integrity of either Dr. Mark Sobell or Dr. Linda Sobell. (Dickens, Doob, Warwick, & Winegard, 1982, p. 109)

A second investigation was conducted by the Subcommittee on Investigations and Oversight, Committee on Science and Technology, House of Representatives, U.S. Congress. This inquiry began because some of the original work of the Sobells was supported by funds from the U.S. government.

The Congressional investigation reached essentially the same conclusion as the committee of the Addiction Research Foundation. In a letter to the Sobells by James E. Jensen, Investigator for the Subcommittee, the following statements were made:

> Based upon my review of the evidence, I have concluded that their is no evidence to support the allegation that your study was based upon fallacious, falsified or otherwise invented data.
>
> The correlation between your notes of contacts with patients, your phone logs and the tape recordings of those contacts have convinced me that your report of your study was made in good faith. With the exception of errors in calculating the number of collateral contacts, your representation of the study conducted is an accurate one, and there is no evidence of the willful manufacturing of data.
>
> My review of all available [evidence] supports the findings of the Commission convened by the Addiction Research Foundation (also known as the "Dickens Commission") and fully supports their conclusions. (Jensen, 1983)

These two independent investigative bodies, one composed of scientists and scholars and the other of legal professionals, reached the same conclusion—that the Sobells had accurately represented their data in their reports on controlled drinking (Sobell & Sobell, 1973a, 1973b, 1978). I have seen no response to these inquiries by Pendery and colleagues.

It seems clear that the Sobells reported their data as collected. Why, then, is there such disagreement from Pendery et al. (1982), when they presumably evaluated the same data? Also, why were the investigators in the Pendery group willing to accuse the Sobells of fraud when such action has serious ethical implications?

THE CONTROVERSY AND THE MEDIA

Nowhere has the issue of controlled drinking versus abstinence been debated than in the press. With the publication of the *Science* article by Pendery et al. (1982), there was tremendous coverage of the issue on television, in the newspapers, on the radio, and so forth. The press, for the most part, felt that fraud had occurred, and they made the point in very dramatic fashion.

Reports of the Pendery et al. (1982) study and the accompanying allegations or implications of fraud were carried on CBS News, in the *New York Times*, on the major wire services, and on several special television programs. Two examples from prominent sources show the attitude of the press.

The CBS television show *60 Minutes* covered the controversy on March 6, 1983. The show was quite critical of the Sobells' work and did not question the validity of the Pendery et al. (1982) findings. At one point, Harry Reasoner, the commentator, stood at the gravesite of one of the controlled drinking subjects from the Sobells' original work in California and proclaimed that this victim was not the only one who suffered from the controlled drinking treatment. Marlatt (1983, p. 1106) asked, "Why didn't Mr. Reasoner also visit the graves of patients in the control group who received the abstinence-oriented treatment?" This, in fact, is the key issue of the entire controversy, a fact discussed below.

The second example is a series of articles in the *New York Times* written by Philip M. Boffey. To Boffey's credit, his point of view in the articles changed as new evidence became available. This sequence is interesting.

After the initial fanfare and condemnation of the Sobells in the summer of 1982, Boffey and the *New York Times* began to cover the events that followed. This is somewhat unusual because the events that followed pointed away from fraud—the issue that captured the attention of most people in the media. In fact, the *Times* was one of the few publications to report the findings of the committee of the Addiction Research Foundation.

Beginning in November of 1982, the nature of the *Times* articles began to change. The first was still critical of the Sobells. It covered the development of the controversy and showed that the struggle pitted Pendery's group against the Sobells.

> There have been few holds barred. At every step of the way the Sobells have tried to block the investigation by Dr. Pendery and Dr. Maltzman and insure that any follow-up study remained in friendly hands. But each time, the pursuers have found a way around the practical and legal roadblocks. . . . But while the Sobells were blocking the Pendery investigation, they quickly arranged for a more friendly follow-up study. (Boffey, 1982a, p. C1).

One of the most serious issues to arise from the articles in the *Times* was a quote from Irving Maltzman, a psychologist at the University of California at Los Angeles, and coauthor on the Pendery *et al.* (1982) paper:

> Dr. Maltzman makes no bones about what the charges add up to. "Beyond any reasonable doubt," he says, "It's fraud." (Boffey, 1982a, p. C2)

These findings of the investigative committee of the Addictions Research Foundation were released a few days later. The *Times* did not give as much play to the information that cleared the Sobells as they did to the information that condemned them, but unlike most papers and television stations, they gave it some coverage.

> Two alcoholism researchers who had been accused of perpetrating a scientific fraud were exonerated by a prestigious review committee in a report released here today.
>
> The committee's findings appeared to be a repudiation of the most serious charges made against the Sobells by Mary Pendery. . . .
>
> In its report today, the committee dismissed most of the allegations made against the Sobells and minimized the importance of the few discrepancies that it found. (Boffey, 1982b, p. c3)

Approximately 1 year later, Boffey and the *New York Times* reported a quite objective view of controlled drinking after interviews with two alcohol researchers in Scotland (Heather & Robertson, 1981). The interview quoted not only these researchers, but other prominent workers in the field from Europe and the United States.

> Many problem drinkers and even some victims of severe alcoholism can learn to control their drinking without having to abandon it entirely, according to several leading experts in Europe.

That opinion is still in the minority on both sides of the Atlantic. The
National Institute of Alcohol Abuse and Alcoholism in this country has
consistently maintained that "abstinence is the appropriate goal of alcoholism treatment," and governmental health authorities in Europe have
given only limited endorsement to the concept of "controlled drinking."
Still, the idea that at least some alcoholics and problem drinkers can
successfully learn to limit their consumption rather than abstain altogether
appears to be gaining influence and recognition, especially in Great
Britain and Scandinavia. (Boffey, 1983, p. C1)

I was pleased to see this article in the *New York Times*. Its most
important virtue, in my mind, was that it separated the issue of controlled drinking versus abstinence from the issue of Pendery *et al.*
versus the Sobells. It acknowledged that other fine investigators had
been working in the area and that even these scientists and clinicians
recommended controlled drinking only under very specific circumstances. In other words, this journalist approached the topic in an
objective fashion. There are far too few examples of this in the media
because the issue of fraud remains in the limelight, and no matter what
is said about the integrity of the Sobells, controlled drinking is dis-
credited by implication.

THE CONTROVERSY AND EDITORIAL PRACTICES

The case of the Sobells and Pendery *et al.* raises some basic questions
about the way scientific information is screened and disseminated. The
publication of the Pendery *et al.* (1982) paper in *Science* drew attention
to the editorial practices of this prestigious journal and to judgments of
what should appear in print.

There are differences of opinion about how the editorial process
proceeded and how the Sobells and the staff of *Science* interacted
(Abelson, 1983; Barlow, Bellack, Buchwald, Garfield, Hartmann, Herman, Hersen, Miller, Rachman, & Wolpe, 1983a; Sobell & Sobell, 1984).
One volley in this dispute was fired by the editors of 10 psychology
journals in a letter to *Science*:

[W]e express concern about *Science's* editorial decision to publish a re-
interpretation of an original data set, or even some new data that contradict the original data set, *without simultaneous comment from the
investigators concerned.* We realize that this situation was an unusual one
that was complicated by possible legal actions. However, as Editors of
clinical-research-oriented journals, we believe that the course of action
followed, particularly when there are strong disagreements for whatever
reasons, can give a very biased, one-sided picture of this issue which makes
objective evaluation difficult. By following this course of action, science
has not been advanced. (Barlow *et al.*, 1983a, p. 555)

There was a simultaneous reply to the Barlow *et al.* (1983a) piece by the editor of *Science*, Philip H. Abelson:

> In the absence of criticism of experiments and replication of results, the integrity of science would be destroyed. The overwhelming majority of scientists understand this, and most cooperate with those who challenge their work. The behavior of the Sobells with respect to the research report by Pendery at al., was unprecedented in my experience of more than 20 years as editor.
>
> The Sobells, in writing, threatened us with legal action while we were in the initial phase of considering the paper. Shortly after, we received a letter from their attorney. Under such circumstances, prudence dictates that contact between principals cease and that one deal with the matter through attorneys.
>
> For years the Sobell paper of 1973 went virtually unchallenged. Their work received a large play in the media. Attempts by Mary Pendery to examine the basic data and to follow up on patients' subsequent histories were impeded by repeated legal action by the Sobells. The avenue of technical comment has been and remains open to the Sobells. They have not so far availed themselves of it. (Abelson, 1983, pp. 555–556)

The Sobells responded to their interaction with *Science* in a different way:

> *After* the publication of the Pendery et al. (1982) article, we were informed by *Science* that we could submit for review for publication, a technical comment on the issues raised in that article, but that our response would have to be limited to 2,000 words. In the context of all the events surrounding this controversy, it was our opinion that a more thorough examination of the issues was warranted and necessary. (Sobell & Sobell, 1984)

It is difficult to resolve these differences, but it is possible to comment on the editorial practices involved in the selection of a controversial article for publication. I see two major deficits in the editorial process by which *Science* saw fit to publish the Pendery *et al.* (1982) article. First, Pendery *et al.* mentioned not a single bit of evidence from the numerous studies on controlled drinking done by investigators other than the Sobells. The article implied that controlled drinking is dangerous and that abstinence is the only acceptable goal for alcoholics. This is precisely what the press seized upon and the notion that was carried to the public.

The inadequate literature review weakened the article considerably and diverted attention from the most important issue (i.e., whether controlled drinking is useful) to the debate about whether the Sobells' data were valid. This issue of the integrity of researchers is not one to be debated in the pages of one of science's most esteemed journals. It should be left to independent investigators, who, it now is shown, interpret the matter very differently than the *Science* article did. What does it matter to *Science* that the data from a handful of subjects were valid when a large literature can be summoned to evaluate the topic of controlled drinking?

The second failure in the editorial process of *Science* was not to demand that Pendery *et al.* (1982) collect and report data from the group of subjects who received the abstinence-oriented program. It is well known that alcoholic subjects are at very high risk for the tragic outcomes reported by Pendery *et al.* (e.g., see Vaillant, 1983). To expect the controlled drinking subjects to fare otherwise (as a group) is to demand that the controlled drinking treatment wipe away many years of physical and social disability in these subjects, who had been chronic alcoholics.

Even the supporters of the controlled drinking approach never claimed it was a cure-all for the problem or that it should be used in all cases (Sobell & Sobell, 1978). Therefore, the issue is a *comparative* one; that is, the virtues of the controlled drinking and abstinence approaches must be compared with one another. This basic scientific principle was lost when *Science* agreed to publish the Pendery *et al.* (1982) article. This point was addressed by the investigative committee of the Addiction Research Foundation:

> Pendery et al. do not, however, compare group outcomes. Without comparisons of any kind, we are left, for example, with tragic stories (played up by the mass media) of four CD-E (controlled drinking) subjects' deaths (relating at least in some cases to alcohol). Deaths are often tragic. As unpleasant as they might be, however, drawing inferences from them with respect to treatment effectiveness *demands* a comparison. Science, the activity, would have demanded such a comparison even though *Science*, the magazine, did not. (Dickens *et al.*, 1982, p. 16)

If one really examines what *Science* published in light of the demands of the scientific method, it appears that standards were loosened and that a mistake was made. The consequences were unfortunate.

THE CONTROVERSY: WHO WAS RIGHT?

"Who was right?" is the burning question in the minds of most observers, even though it has little to do with whether controlled drinking is viable. Marlatt (1983) did a scholarly review of this area and concluded that there are weaknesses both in the data collected by Sobell and Sobell (1973a, 1973b) and in those collected by Pendery *et al.* (1982), because of the reliance on self-report:

[I]t is very unlikely that the "truth" of what really happened will be uncovered by any further interrogation of subjects who participated in the original study. (Marlatt, 1983, p. 1099)

Sobell and Sobell (1984) have responded to the Pendery *et al.* (1982) paper in a very detailed way. The Sobells felt that the Pendery *et al.* paper raised three main issues: (1) that the two subject groups were not comparable when the study began; (2) that data collected by the Pendery group contradicted what the Sobells had reported for the first 2 years of follow-up; and (3) that the long-term outcome presented over an 11-year follow-up for the controlled drinking subjects was damaging.

The first issue has been covered adequately in the Dickens *et al.* (1982) report and the recent review by Marlatt (1983). Subjects were indeed assigned to groups randomly, and the treatment groups appeared to be comparable when the program began. The second issue has also been covered in great detail elsewhere (Dickens *et al.*, 1982; Marlatt 1983; Sobell & Sobell, 1984). The Sobells did make mistakes in reporting the number of contacts with subjects, but this was not important in considering how the subjects functioned after their treatment of controlled drinking. This leaves the third issue, which, in my mind, is central to the dispute.

It is true that the controlled drinking subjects did not do well in the long term. Four of them died, and there were cases of arrests, hospitalizations, and so forth. One could also examine patients with a chronic disease—say, coronary heart disease—and say that they do not fare well. Many die or have debilitating symptoms. Does this mean that their treatment is ineffective, or, worse yet, harmful? This question is impossible to answer without comparing subjects who received a treatment to subjects receiving no treatment or a comparison treatment. This logic is understood by almost everybody.

The biased view created by the Pendery *et al.* (1982) approach is illustrated by the mortality data. Four subjects from the controlled drinking group died. This is sad, but the number has no meaning without some perspective on how the subjects would have done otherwise. There are two ways to collect this information: to compare the mortality rate with that reported in the literature, or to compare the controlled drinking subjects with the abstinence-oriented subjects. Both lead to much different conclusions than those raised by Pendery *et al.* (1982).

Data in the alcoholism literature show that the subjects of Sobell and Sobell (1973a, 1973b) had no more than the expected rate of mortality (Schmidt, 1980). It is a fact that alcoholics tend to die prematurely, so the rate of 4 deaths in 20 subjects over such a long follow-up is certainly not surprising.

What is even more damaging to the Pendery *et al.* (1982) argument is that *six* of the subjects in the abstinence-oriented group died by 1981 (Sobell & Sobell, 1984). This is two *more* deaths than in the controlled drinking group, and is *higher* than the expected rate of mortality.

One can ponder the outcome if a group of researchers had done just what Pendery and colleagues had done, but focused only on the abstinence-oriented subjects rather than on the controlled drinking subjects. The *Science* article could probably be rewritten word for word, and simply be replacing "controlled drinking" with "abstinence treatment" and correcting the numbers (in a negative direction!), the conclusion would be the same, but the approach being condemned would change. Would Harry Reasoner then stand by the grave of an abstinence-oriented treatment subject and imply that abstinence kills?

THE FUTURE OF CONTROLLED DRINKING

Some writers feel that the controversy stirred by Pendery *et al.* (1982) has proven the death of the controlled drinking approach (Peele, 1983). It is true that research and clinical work on controlled drinking occurs in a climate of antagonism, and that supporters of the abstinence model react with religious fervor to the thought of alcoholics drinking alcohol. This does not make objective and scientific evaluations of alternative approaches any easier, but it has not and probably will not stop honest inquiry from occurring.

There are several reasons why work on controlled drinking will continue. The first is the recognition, even by professionals using the abstinence model, that some alcoholics manage to control their drinking. An example is the recent book by Vaillant (1983), *The Natural History of Alcoholism*. He reports on the long-term progress of 110 alcohol abusers, 71 of whom were "alcohol dependent." Fully 20% of this group was drinking moderately and 34% were abstaining. Even among the "abstainers," Vaillant (1983, p. 184) notes, "relatively few men with long periods of abstinence had never taken another drink." Reports of controlled drinking have been reported time and time again (Armor, Polich, & Stambul, 1978; Heather & Robertson, 1981; Marlatt, 1983; W. R. Miller, 1983a; W. R. Miller & Hester, 1980; Pattison, Sobell, & Sobell, 1977).

The second reason is that it is not altogether clear that abstinence-oriented treatment has proven its effectiveness. This is true despite widespread sentiment that it has been proven. A quote from a *New York Times* article described earlier highlights this:

Frank A. Seixas, former medical director of the National Council on Alcoholism, an abstinence-only group, said that abstinence is the only goal of the vast majority of alcoholism programs "because it has worked so well," whereas controlled drinking experiments "have not demonstrated positive effects to my satisfaction." (Boffey, 1983, p. C7)

It is puzzling to understand what data Frank A. Seixas is referring to in support of abstinence, or how he dismisses the data on controlled drinking. Vaillant (1983) reported the results of his traditional abstinence-oriented treatment in a Massachusetts hospital, and after including his results among other studies in the literature, he concluded, "Once again, our results were no better than the natural history of the disorder" (p. 285).

The third reason for the survival of the controlled drinking idea is the existence of data on its possible utility (Marlatt, 1983). If science advances the way it should, and if the public accepts what science reports, controlled drinking will remain at least a possibility among the options for treating alcoholism.

Treatment and Prevention: Disorded Priorities?

The argument may be as old as the problem of alcoholism itself: Is it better to prevent the problem or to treat it once it occurs? The answer that our society and its health establishment give to that question is rooted deeply in philosophy about social and individual responsibility, the way in which the legal system should deal with psychological and behavioral problems, the perceived expense and utility of prevention, and disagreement about how and where the problem should be confronted.

The bias in this area is clear—prevention programs receive far less attention and support than treatment programs (Nathan, 1983). The field of behavior therapy provides a good example of this trend. The literature is replete with studies on understanding factors related to problem drinking and studies on treatment of relatively small numbers of subjects. Studies dealing even remotely with prevention can be counted on one hand.

This issue is important for the field of behavior therapy. There are many important contributions to be made by behavior therapists in the area of prevention. These efforts may have a greater impact on the alcoholism problem than will treatment endeavors, although the work on treatment has obvious importance. It may be helpful for our field to examine its conceptual biases to determine how cultural, legal, moral, and individual factors guide our practices and our research.

THE SOCIAL RAMIFICATIONS OF ALCOHOLISM

Greater attention is being given to the prevention of alcohol problems, even though the effort (in terms of dollars expended) pales in comparison to other funds spent on the problem (Nathan, 1983). One reason for this gradual change is the recognition that alcoholism is a serious problem, not only for the person so afflicted, but for society in general. What is even more alarming to some is the impact of alcoholism on individuals who are victimized (victims of drunk driving accidents, families of alcoholics, and so forth).

To understand society's view of the problem, which will influence how alcoholism is studied and treated, we can examine the viewpoints of "opinion leaders." One such person is Dan Quayle, U.S. Senator from Indiana. Senator Quayle (1983) recently contributed an article on alcoholism and productivity to *American Psychologist*.

The Quayle (1983) article mentions the tremendous cost to society of the alcohol problem. While recognizing the devastating effects of alcoholism on individuals, this article focuses on worker productivity.

> Employees with a drinking or drug problem are absent 16 times more than the average employee, have an accident rate that it 4 times greater, use a third more sickness benefits, and have five times more compensation claims while on the job. Forty percent of industrial fatalities and 47% of industrial injuries can be traced to alcohol abuse. (Quayle, 1983, p. 455)

These business-related costs are only part of the social consequence of alcoholism. Premature death in alcoholics influences the person's social network. Intoxicated drivers who injure or kill others create enormous damage. When all these social and personal costs of alcoholism are summed up, it is clear that the problem deserves serious attention.

This sentiment prevails in the United States; hence the establishment of the National Institute on Alcohol Abuse and Alcoholism, the important role of Alcoholics Anonymous, and the existence of numerous citizens groups to deal with the problem. That something should be done is no longer debated. *What* should be done is still controversial.

THE WEAK PREVENTION EFFORT

Although most people agree in principle that prevention is better (and easier) than cure, surprisingly little support is given the prevention movement. Nathan (1983), in an article following Quayle's (1983) in *American Psychologist*, notes how troubling the problem really is:

> There is another story to be told that is even more discouraging than Senator Quayle's (1983) portrayal of our country's vain efforts to counter

the devastating effect of alcoholism and drug abuse on American productivity. The second story is of the nation's efforts, unsuccessful to this time, to prevent alcoholism *before* it lowers productivity, impairs quality of life, and destroys health. (Nathan, 1983, p. 459)

The lackluster prevention effort is a function both of unsuccessful programs and of the lack of support for research on new and innovative programs. Without this support, particularly from the federal government, the problem of alcoholism will continue to exact its terrible cost.

> Prevention has ranked lowest among all alcoholism and drug dependence funding priorities established by the U.S. Government. Prevention is an infrequent component of employee assistance programs in industry, despite its proven favorable cost-effectiveness ratio. Prevention activities directed to groups at risk for alcoholism—among them women, youth, minority groups, and the elderly—have increased in number but have failed to yield reductions in drinking rates by target groups. Although drunk driving and fetal alcohol syndrome are now recognized as major public health problems and have begun to be serious targets for prevention, debilitating disagreement interferes with efforts to prevent drunk driving and the incidence of fetal alcohol syndrome remains unconscionably high. In other words, Senator Quayle's lament that American industry is doing less than it should to treat alcoholic employees can be joined by an equally fervent plaint that the nation and its drug and alcohol establishment have done little that has been strongly effective to prevent alcoholism from developing in the first place. (Nathan, 1983, p. 459)

The U.S. government has been by far the biggest contributor to prevention efforts. In total, $24.4 million were allocated for prevention. This is 63% of all public funds spent for prevention, so compared to state, local, and private expenditures, the federal commitment seems large. However, the $24.4 million is only 4% of the total federal expenditure for alcohol problems (Nathan, 1983). This is a small effort for a big problem.

> [F]rom the perspective that just 4% ($24.4 million of $584.1 million) of federal funds and less than 3% ($38.4 million of $1,309.8 million) of all public funds for alcohol-related activities were spent on prevention activities, the level of federal support is scandalous, shortsighted, and cost-ineffective, given the clear potential of primary prevention to return its costs many times over. (Nathan, 1983, pp. 459–460)

THE IMPORTANCE OF PREVENTION

There are several possible approaches to prevention. As examples, educational programs aimed at children may prevent the onset of potential future drinkers, while legislative efforts to impose severe penalties on drunk drivers may discourage some social drinking in adults that can progress to problem drinking. Which approach is best?

So little is known about the effects of the few existing prevention programs that a comparison is not possible. Furthermore, the programs may have additive or synergistic effects. A given approach may be completely ineffective if it does not occur in the general social climate that supports a particular approach to alcoholism.

It is possible at this point only to categorize prevention efforts and to develop ideas about possible avenues for intervention. Each leads to different targets and methods for dealing with the problem. It is fully possible that some combination of approaches is necessary to influence behavior.

In his review on prevention, Nathan (1983) lists four categories of prevention efforts:

1. *Prevention of alcoholism in at-risk groups.* This would involve identification and targeting of groups at high risk for alcohol problems, including adolescents, the elderly, and members of minority groups.
2. *Prevention of the consequences of alcoholism in at-risk groups.* This would involve a focus on the special effects of alcoholism, such as drunk driving and fetal alcohol syndrome.
3. *Prevention by restricting the agent.* This would include legislative efforts to impose taxes on alcohol, thus increasing the price; establishing higher drinking ages; and so forth.
4. *Prevention in the environment.* This involves education of the general public, via campaigns in the workplace, through the media, etc.

Whether programs in these settings are accepted and implemented may ultimately depend on cost-effectiveness. Cost is difficult enough to determine; effectiveness is even more so. The next section discusses possible programs and some of the factors relevant for behavioral scientists.

METHODS FOR PREVENTION

Social and Legal Approaches. Social and legal approaches to combatting and preventing alcoholism have been rising to a yet-to-be defined peak in recent years, with the outcry against drunk drivers. Citizens groups like Mothers Against Drunk Driving (MADD) have formed and have been active in fund raising, lobbying, mobilizing the media, and influencing the decisions of lawmakers.

Social and legal efforts to curb alcoholism are not new. Prohibition is the most obvious example, but antidrinking groups have existed for a very long time. Some religions prohibit the use of alcohol among members, and there are still "dry" towns and counties in the United States where liquor cannot be purchased or served. How effective are these approaches?

There is some debate on this issue, and, of course, the answer depends on the nature of the approach being considered. It is widely assumed that reducing the availability of alcohol by legislative action will have the desired effect. It may not be true:

> Most policymakers worldwide take the position that reducing availability of alcoholic beverages, by increasing price, raising legal drinking age, or both: (a) reduces consumption, (b) reduces consumption by heavy drinkers, and (c) reduces the incidence of phenomena associated with consumption by heavy drinkers, including liver cirrhosis, drunk driving, and auto fatality and accident rates. Although modest empirical data provide some support for the first of these relationships, crucial design problems in pointing to this relationship militate against its uncritical acceptance. More important, no studies have linked decreased availability with decreased drinking by the heaviest segment of drinkers in any society and to concomitant decreases in the sequelae of heavy drinking. (Nathan, 1983, p. 464)

There are few professionals who think that the Prohibition era of the 1920s in the United States had the desired effect, so the only large-scale trial of banning alcohol was not successful. However, more focused efforts may have some effect.

Legislation against drunk driving has been greeted with mixed opinions from professionals, but with relative enthusiasm from the public. One thing is certain: Strict drunk driving laws are being passed in many states. It sometimes appears that states are proud to boast of the "toughest drunk driving laws in the country." Politicians feel that they create good will among their constituents by speaking out on this issue. This action is supported by most, who feel that they and their families are potential victims of another person's problem. Others condemn the idea because roadside checks by the police and mandatory breath tests are considered infringements on individual rights. The proponents are winning the battle, at least for now.

The drunk driving laws appear to have the intended effect, but perhaps only temporarily. Ross (1982) has done a scholarly analysis of the evidence in this area by using interrupted time series analyses. This method analyzes trends over time while accounting for factors such as price, seasonal effects, and the like. The data come from "natural experiments" because no controlled research could be done on legislative practices.

Ross (1982) has concluded that tougher drunk driving laws are associated with a significant decline in drunk driving and in alcohol-related traffic accidents and deaths. He attributes the decline to legal threat. The perceived risk of being incarcerated or fined increases when laws are enacted. The perception is widespread because this legislative process is typically given much attention in the media.

Unfortunately, Ross (1982) has found that the effects are not permanent. He notes that law enforcement activities may subside over time because the original effort cannot be sustained, but, more importantly, people *assume* that enforcement efforts get weaker with time. It is this perception, rather than actual enforcement, that controls the change in drunk driving.

This is an ideal opportunity for research by experts in the behavioral and communications sciences. If perception of enforcement has an effect, as Ross (1982) claims, studies could examine the utility of media, environmental, or educational campaigns aimed at sustaining the desired perception over time. This work could focus on awareness of media messages or on environmental changes (e.g., posting warning signs with the fines listed). Educational programs could also foster the sustained perception.

Another important area for research here is whether these social and legislative actions influence alcoholism itself or just the visible effects of the problem. It is possible that a reduction in drunk driving means that intoxicated persons are moving about in other ways, but that they still exist in the same numbers. To my knowledge, this has not been investigated.

The Cultural Context of Drinking. Culture plays an enormous role in controlling patterns of alcohol use. George Vaillant (1983) examined alcoholics in long-term prospective research and concluded that cultural and ethnic factors were important correlates of alcoholism. In a paper on the etiology of alcoholism, Vaillant and Milofsky (1982) found that ethnicity was the most powerful childhood predictor of alcoholism and that premorbid antisocial behavior was the most powerful predictor in adult life. These authors note that cultures that teach the restrained use of alcohol to children have lower rates of alcohol abuse.

One cross-cultural example given by Vaillant (1983) is the difference in alcohol patterns in France and Italy. There is a higher rate of alcoholism in France. Both cultures emphasize responsible drinking behavior, but France finds public drunkenness acceptable and Italy does not. The French teach their children to drink, but do not encourage moderation. In Italy, it is socially acceptable to refuse a drink, while in France, the same refusal signifies an antisocial or even a ridiculous behavior.

The cultural context of drinking in the United States is changing in a positive direction. However, it still is the case that drinking, even to the point of intoxication, is usually socially acceptable.

> At another level, drinking in particular has become a socially acceptable behavior, even to the point that manslaughter at the hands of a drunk driver is a socially acceptable form of homicide. The drunk driver in the United States today is likely to get off with a small fine or a slap on the wrist, free to perhaps kill and maim again. If the nation were confronted with an epidemic that left 26,000 people dead every year, there would be a groundswell of public outrage that would not end until a halt was put to the carnage. Drunk driving alone takes 26,000 lives a year, but no outcry is heard. (Quayle, 1983, p. 456)

I feel that the outcry *is* being heard. Campaigns urging people not to drive while drinking have begun in the media, using the public service announcement spots that have been so important to the anti-smoking campaign. Sports stars are doing some of these spots, and television and movie celebrities are also calling for more sensible drinking and driving habits. As mentioned above, citizens' groups are gaining influence, and legislators are responsive to the antialcohol sentiment.

In the long run, these cultural sanctions against alcohol abuse will probably be more effective than legislative actions in decreasing the alcoholism problem. Vaillant (1983) has stated that *"proscriptions* against alcohol use have rarely been as effective as social *prescriptions* for alcohol use" (p. 58). Since these social and cultural forces are so powerful, a shift toward making people more responsible for the control of their alcohol intake could have a major influence in overall rates of alcoholism. Legislative actions may simply be a reflection of the more general shift in cultural attitudes.

Educational Programs. There are a host of educational programs that focus on alcohol problems, or that at least include alcohol problems as part of the curriculum. The National Institute on Alcohol Abuse and Alcoholism (1982) funds programs aimed at educating children and adolescents about the dangers of alcoholism. The National Highway and Traffic Safety Administration has been active in this area for years with their driver education courses and with special education efforts focused on drunk driving. Far too few of these programs have been evaluated.

Several reviews have been done on the alcohol education efforts (Hochheimer, 1981; Nathan, 1983). These reviews note that most educational programs focus on knowledge and attitudes, even though behavior is the ultimate target of any program. Behavior is much more difficult to evaluate than knowledge and attitudes, so this bias in evaluation is not surprising. It does, however, have negative consequences. What is missing from these programs, according to Hochheimer (1981), is a focus on principles of communication and behavior change as derived from social learning theory.

The implication of these reviews of educational approaches (Hochheimer, 1981; Nathan, 1983) is that only a shift in emphasis toward behavior will allow a true test of interventions of this nature. Such a test has not been done and will require collaborative efforts of persons in education, communications, economics, and the behavioral sciences.

This is the opening for behavior therapy. If behavior change is to be the focus of educational programs, specific techniques for encouraging behavior change will be necessary. This requires a new type of research, which not only must identify the techniques, but must be sensitive to methods for disseminating the information to the public.

Institutional Programs. There are many institutional possibilities for alcohol prevention. Work-site programs have great potential, because a large percentage of the population could be reached this way (Nathan, 1983). Government employees and members of the military are prime possibilities for such an approach. This idea of institutional programs deals with channels for intervention. This issue must be addressed, even after effective interventions have been established.

One innovative program was reported recently by Mills, McCarty, Ward, Minuto, and Patzynski (1983). These authors coordinated the construction, administration, and evaluation of a tavern in two college dormitories. The program was initiated as part of a class on alcohol education at the University of North Carolina. Forty upperclass students enrolled in this three-semester hour course. These students planned the tavern and designed a quasi-control group of students in other dormitories.

The tavern activities involved both educational and social activities. There were weekly showings of films on drunk driving, a weekly nonalcoholic beverage hour, frequent Breathalyzer demonstrations, recipes for low-alcohol drinks, and the provision of nonalcoholic beverages at weekend social functions. Mills *et al.* (1983) intended the tavern as "a realistic and entertaining setting in which the students could practice new behaviors associated with moderate alcohol consumption (p. 106).

In the dormitories receiving the program, 93.1% of the students reported seeing posters and pamphlets provided by the program. Two-thirds of the students reported attending the residence hall parties sponsored by the program, and two-thirds of these students tried the nonalcoholic beverages. Only 15.5% participated in a prevention workshop, and 16.8% viewed and discussed the film.

The evaluation of drinking-related factors in the Mills *et al.* (1983) study yielded several interesting findings. Students in the program were significantly more likely to have friends who disapproved of heavy drinking and who expected moderate drinking while driving. There were no differences in alcohol consumption.

The absence of an effect on alcohol consumption is disappointing, but not surprising. The social forces that govern alcohol use in college students are complex, and reduction in alcohol use will probably require a more intensive effort. Nonetheless, Mills *et al.* (1983) were creative in identifying a high-risk situation (residence hall parties) and in establishing an alternative. The rate of usage of the tavern was impressive, so these authors have developed a method for reaching students (although these may not be the students with drinking problems).

The Mills *et al.* (1983) study represents a different approach from that of traditional educational or treatment programs. As much as their approach might be promising, the conceptual move into a new setting with new strategies for behavior change is most appealing.

CHAPTER

7

BEHAVIOR THERAPY WITH CHILDREN AND ADOLESCENTS

CYRIL M. FRANKS

INTRODUCTION

While no major text in the area of child behavior therapy has appeared during the past year, there are several new publications that warrant recognition. Despite the somewhat misleading nature of the book's title, Morris and Kratochwill's (1983) *The Practice of Child Therapy*, an edited text, contains a number of chapters that exemplify child behavior therapy at its best. Could it be that Morris and Kratochwill equate child therapy with child behavior therapy? Then there is an important new book by LeBow (1983), which deals with child obesity from the perspective of the behavior therapist. For obvious reasons, childhood obesity is a disorder that readily lends itself to new fads, brief procedures, and innovative techniques of questionable value, and there is a constant temptation for the unwary behavior therapist whose sights are set upon rapid cure to fall into one of these traps. Le Bow looks at childhood obesity from the vantage of the contemporary behavior therapist and manages to avoid almost all the political disaster areas.

While matters of assessment properly belong elsewhere (see Chapter 2), attention cannot help but be drawn to Ollendick and Hersen's (1984a) *Child Behavioral Assessment: Principles and Procedures*. Not so long ago, child behavioral assessment consisted largely of directly observable events examined from an exclusively operant perspective. Normal developmental processes and normative comparisons were ignored, as were data derived from other disciplines. Contemporary child behavioral assessment as presented by Ollendick and Hersen is

236

quite different. While the need for an empirical base remains paramount, established psychiatric principles are not automatically discarded, and the data source is expanded to reflect information and strategies culled from a wide cross-section of related bodies of knowledge. (See Kazdin, 1983, and Ollendick & Hersen, 1984b.)

With this "new look" in child behavior therapy goes the danger of this broadening process occurring at the expense of a valid data base. For example, Cautela, Cautela, and Esonis (1983) have compiled a collection of forms for behavioral analysis with children that seems, at first examination, to be eminently useful—a step in the direction of acquiring normative data before plunging into intervention. Unfortunately, while the intent is admirable, most of these forms are presented with no validating, reliability, or normative data whatsoever. The discerning reader is therefore better advised to regard such books as blueprints for future investigation rather than as manuals for immediate use.

Bellack, Hersen, and Kazdin's (1982) *International Handbook of Behavior Modification and Therapy* contains some 200 double-columned pages of child-focused material. The relevant chapters are discussed in the appropriate sections of this chapter. Also of interest this year is a timely survey of behavioral approaches to prevention and intervention with juvenile offenders by P. Feldman (1983). Emphasis seems to have shifted away from intervention after the event to prevention beforehand by reducing the opportunities for crime.

In Chapter 1, attention has been drawn to failures in behavior therapy and to the appearance of the first volume devoted exclusively to this neglected topic (Foa & Emmelkamp, 1983). One of the more significant contributions to this text is Graziano and Bythell's (1983) discussion of failures in child behavior therapy. In their brief but closely reasoned chapter, Graziano and Bythell document the many forms that such failures can take. Strategies are suggested for the reduction of untoward side effects as they occur; even more important, Graziano and Bythell weave the sad fact of failure into a better behavioral understanding of the overall therapeutic process.

In the first chapter, the changing role of the consumer is discussed in some detail. While many child behavior therapy investigations now include consumer satisfaction measures in their assessment battery, it is still the exception rather than the rule for the children themselves to be asked to evaluate treatment received. The primary respondent to whom these inquiries are addressed is usually a treatment mediator, such as a parent or teacher. Furthermore, even when these inquiries are addressed to the children, the measures employed tend to be psychometrically unsophisticated and lacking in validity.

It used to be that developmental psychologists and child behavior therapists pursued largely independent courses. While the same cannot be said about child behavior therapists, developmental psychologists have long since created a highly sophisticated methodology for the study of children. By ignoring such advances, child behavior therapists may be compelled to make mistakes that could be avoided. It is therefore particularly encouraging to note recent attempts to incorporate information gleaned from developmental research into the armamentarium of the practicing behavior therapist (Harris & Ferrari, 1983).

An apparently new thought in the world of child behavior therapy is that children can significantly affect the behavior and cognitions of the adults in their environment. Despite repeated reminders of the impact children can have on adults, until recently the clinical implications of these effects have continued to receive little research attention. Perhaps because it is adults who carry out the research, virtually all the effort has gone in the other direction. Children have been viewed as *tabulae rasae* and the adults in their lives as the exclusive independent variables. Fortunately, as Bob Dylan would put it, "the times they are a-changin'," and contemporary emphasis is now upon reciprocal and systemic influences, as well as upon the complex interaction effects that prevail between children and adults (Emery, Binkoff, Houts, & Carr, 1983).

This, of course, does not mean that adult-mediated treatments have outlived their utility. As Emery *et al.* caution, a reciprocal influence model may not always lead to the most appropriate intervention strategy. Parent-mediated change programs, for example, may continue to offer the most effective means of changing certain behaviors in children.

What these changing directions do give rise to are certain interesting and important ethical concerns that cannot be readily resolved. Who, for example, is the client? Children and adolescents are usually less than fully voluntary participants in treatment. Typically, they are brought to a mental health professional by a third party, such as a parent, a teacher, or another authority figure. It is this individual who helps shape treatment goals and assumes financial responsibility for the service. Should this situation prevail, and under what circumstances? Those who think in terms of reciprocal influences will also have to think through the implications of this changing impetus.

If children are to be given more active roles, measuring devices that take these influences into account have to be developed. A variety of instruments for the direct evaluation of the perceptions of the children themselves with respect to parental behaviors and other activities are now available (see Goldin's [1969] review of children's reports of parent behaviors). Hazzard, Christensen and Margolin's (1983) Parent Perception Inventory (PPI) is an easily administered 18-item scale that seems to function well as a measure of children's perceptions of parental behaviors and is probably one of the most effective measuring devices for this purpose available to date.

To sum up so far: Multimethod and multiperspective approaches are gradually becoming part of the child behavior therapy scene (see Christensen, Phillips, Glasgow, & Johnson, 1983). Unfortunately, while the technology for implementation of these changing notions is already available, general acceptance and usage presently lag behind (Fawcett, Seekins, & Braukmann, in press). The remaining portions of this chapter attempt to chronic recent developments in child behavior therapy from these perspectives. Since no "breakthrough" has occurred, the selected areas of significance and section headings remain essentially the same as in the corresponding chapter of Volume 9.

HOME AND FAMILY IN BEHAVIOR THERAPY

It would be gratifying to report some major advance in the application of behavior modification principles in the area of "home and family." Regrettably, the past year has seen no such development. The climate is more one of consolidation and broadening, and research in this area reflects these trends. In this respect, the most comprehensive review of behavior modification in the home to appear in recent years in chapter form is probably that of Sulzer-Azaroff and Pollack (1982), and the reader would be well advised to refer to this publication directly. It is too bad that these authors did not extend their survey into a whole book.

Despite the development of instruments that purport to address such issues, there are still no adequate answers to such questions as these: How does one decide whether a particular goal is reasonable for a particular child in a particular home setting? What is the "normal" range of distribution of any particular behavior among children? What are the relationships between parental characteristics and interactional dysfunction in families with child behavior problems?

One problem is that, as measuring instruments become more precise, they also become more complicated. T. J. McIntyre, Bornstein, Isaacs, Woody, Bornstein, Clucas, and Long (1983) analyzed 43 home-observation-based studies of conduct-disordered children culled from leading behaviorally oriented journals over the past decade. All included some type of objective system for recording behavior in their procedures, ranging from relatively simple measures to "gas-guzzling," multielement, complex behavioral codes (to use T. J. McIntyre *et al.*'s colorful terminology). The more recent the study, the more the latter trend predominated. As these observational codes were examined, certain characteristics began to emerge. Too many of the observed behaviors were infrequently coded, did not change as a result of treatment, or failed to differentiate conduct-disordered from normal children. It would seem that these complex, costly, and time-consuming instruments provided surprisingly little in return for effort expended.

Despite the changing times, investigators still fail to think in terms of clinical and social as well as experimental and statistical significance. A somewhat related concern pertains to the utilization of cost-effectiveness analysis as another method of evaluating treatment efficacy. Of the 43 articles reviewed by T. J. McIntyre *et al.* (1983), not one conducted cost-effectiveness analysis.

In their review of home and family variables, Sulzer-Azaroff and Pollack (1982) highlight a number of potentially significant trends and lacunae, such as the de-emphasis on highly contrived material reward systems in the home setting. Another trend noted by these authors seems to be toward the more prominent use of stimulus control procedures to modify children's behavior. Rules, self-instruction, visual cues, and physical guidance are being utilized more and more as antecedent conditions to be paired with reinforcing consequences.

Sulzer-Azaroff and Pollack conclude their review with some timely questions: What are the conditions that support long-term maintenance of behavior change in parents and their children? What are the circumstances that facilitate the transfer of parental behavior modification skills across different behaviors within the same child or across siblings or settings? What are the effects of diverse child management strategies with respect to behavior outside the home? Do certain strategies tend to promote positive spinoffs, whereas others generate disadvantages such as antisocial reactions?

At this stage, there are more questions than answers. For example, it is still not at all clear what specific childhood disorders, if any, are associated with specific family types of family disturbance (Mash, in press). While the cumulative weight of the by now considerable literature strongly suggests an association between child and family disturbance, there is still much controversy surrounding the nature of these relationships, how they are to be assessed, and how they are to be interpreted. It is such issues that Mash addresses in a forthcoming chapter for a volume dealing with families under stress. To a large extent, resolution will have to await the development of appropriate measuring instruments for the assessment of family functioning and reciprocal influences.

Sometimes the system is one step removed from the child, but its influence is nevertheless felt. For example, the work pattern of the parent can affect the entire family. Investigation of alternative work patterns is therefore in the interest of all family members and not just the employee directly involved. Studies of "flexitime" and its impact on the family offer a good example of this process. Under flexitime, employees are permitted to vary their times of arrival and departure from work, and this is supposed to lead to increased morale and productivity, and to a reduction in tardiness and unnecessary leave. Flexitime is also seen as a mechanism to facilitate the balance between work and home in terms of enhanced leisure pursuits and child care.

Winett, Neale, and Williams (1982b) carried out two quasi-experimental studies of parents employed in federal agencies to examine the effects of flexitime on the coordination of various home and work schedules. In Agency I, 32 parents were studied over a 5-month period; in Agency II, 65 parents were studied for 9 months. Participants, parents of at least one young child, were all dual-earner, single-earner, or single-parent families. In both agencies, flexitime workers spent more afternoon and evening time with their families and engaged constructively in a greater range of family-related activities.

It is important to note that, even though the permitted changes in work schedules were small, the modifications in family and environmental systems that occurred were substantive. For the future, as the authors point out, relevant ecological issues could be usefully explored by more sharply focused studies of work settings and schedules that incorporate appropriate controls and longitudinal examination into the overall research design.

Home and family research means more than the study of the family within the home. Parents interact with their children across a diversity of settings, and the various subsystems interact in ways that are documented rarely and inadequately understood at this time. Numerous advice packages have been developed for teaching parents a broad range of child management and parent–child interactional skills. Many involve diverse environments and settings, mostly outside the home. For example, Bauman, Reiss, Rogers, and Bailey (1983) have produced an advice package for parents confronted with the problem of inappropriate restaurant behavior in their small children. The design of this study is exemplary and the findings are encouraging. When used appropriately, the procedure leads to marked decreases in inappropriate restaurant behavior, which generalize readily to other restaurant situations. Whether such packages can be made attractive to parents who have not specifically requested help is another matter. As yet, no one seems to have explored this issue in any systematic fashion.

No matter how well-conceived and well-implemented it may be, the information generated by small-scale, single-situation, short-term studies is limited. Holden's (1983) look at mother–child interactions in the supermarket is a case in point. It leads to a plausible model of parental management for that particular setting but little more.

Finally, attention is drawn to the training of behavioral family therapists. Positive change in the targeted client population is one of the more convincing measures of success in any training program, and it is here that research is lacking. Precise and detailed descriptions of training procedures and the skills that are being trained are commonplace. What is more conspicuously lacking, as Isaacs, Embry, and Baer (1982) found in their critical appraisal of the pertinent literature, is an equally thorough documentation of significant positive changes in the target population. Most of the time, this crucial variable is not even mentioned.

Three behaviors emerged consistently as dependent measures in the Isaacs et al. (1982) survey. Parents are given instructions; they are informed about child development, child-rearing practices, and parent–child relationships; and they are praised for performance as good parents.

Isaacs et al. followed up their survey by examination of the effectiveness of a specific multicomponent training program for the training of family therapists and its impact upon both parents and children. The training program, designed to teach five trainees the skills of effective family therapy, consisted of a written manual, videotape modeling, behavior rehearsal, role playing, and performance feedback. The focus of the study was the manner in which therapists learned to use the three target behaviors of instructing, informing, and praising. Each therapist, paired with a parent and a preschool child, was trained in the clinic to use and show the parent how to use certain behavioral skills relevant to teaching child compliance. A multiple-baseline design across the therapist–parent–child triad was used to demonstrate increases in rates of instructing, praising, and informing the parents as consequences of the program. All the parents praised their children more, focusing on positive support for attention to compliant behavior rather than on criticism of behavior viewed as uncooperative. All the children likewise increased their rates of compliant behavior and decreased their noncompliant activities.

As the authors note, this investigation raises many questions for future research. What, for example, are the parameters involved in generalization to parents and trainers with different backgrounds and characteristics? In the Isaacs et al. (1982) study, trainees were chosen, in part, because of their diverse backgrounds and work experiences with families. Interestingly enough, these qualities made little if any difference in the trainees' abilities either to learn or to teach the relevant skills. However, larger samples, better designs, more adequate controls, and some form of follow-up are required before reliable conclusions can be drawn.

COMPLIANCE AND NONCOMPLIANCE IN CHILDREN AND THEIR PARENTS

Regardless of the terminology used—"compliance" or "adherence"— the basic issues involved in compliance remain much the same for children as for adults (see Stuart, 1982a). Children, however, present certain complications that make an already complex situation even more intricate. Because they are less free agents than adults, the compliance behavior of children is determined to a large part not only by developmental status, but by a variety of external circumstances that are mostly beyond their direct control.

Compliance is as compliance does, and the issues to be explored depend upon the definition adopted. "Compliance" is a more complex notion than hitherto supposed, and many unquestioned assumptions could benefit from professional challenge. For example, there is the belief that compliance to a therapeutic drug regimen is greater when the side effects are minimal, or the idea that a client's belief in the relevance of a particular treatment program increases the probability of compliance, or the belief that educating clients about the regimen is necessarily an advantage. As Stuart (1982b) sagely notes, such unresearched assumptions are, at best, applicable only under certain limited circumstances. Applied generally, they would probably lead to frustration and failure.

If compliance with simple instructions in the taking of specific medications on a long-term basis is poor, even when compliance is obviously to the client's advantage, then it should come as no surprise that the imposition of more complex requirements leads to even less conformity with expectations.

Ley's (1982a, 1982b) ongoing foray into the world of compliance continues to expose the disquieting gap between data and assumption. For example, contrary to hope and assumption, information given to patients by their physicians is rarely recalled with accuracy, and horrendous distortions sometimes occur. The circumstances surrounding recall and their relationships to such basic parameters as the nature and quality of the instructions and a host of personal characteristics within the patient are still little understood, despite over half a century of seemingly relevant research in applied psychology. Children would seem to be particularly vulnerable to information distortion, but here, too, there is more speculation than data.

Suedfeld (1982) examines compliance from the perspective of the social psychologist. Effective compliance rests upon persuasion and attitude change, in addition to behavioral modification. With relevance to the antismoking campaign, for example, "it does very little good to persuade a client that smoking is unhealthy if he also believes that nonsmokers are sissies, that good social interaction can occur only when you have a cigarette nearby, that nicotine withdrawal is extremely painful and that antismoking individuals are kooks" (1982, p. 135).

The decision to endorse compliance with any program, no matter how well-intentioned it may be, raises formidable ethical issues and a host of value judgments to be determined. Situations involving small children, adults, incarcerated individuals, those for whom the consequences of noncompliance are minor, and those for whom the consequences are major are all very different, and it is doubtful whether any general set of rules can be applied across the board (Ley, 1982b).

It cannot be assumed that health care professionals invariably serve as good role models. Would that this were so. As noted in Volume 9 of the *Annual Review*, levels of noncompliance with recommended standards and methods of care are running at an "alarmingly high level." Ley's (1981) review of the compliance records of psychologists, pharmacists, nurses, and physicians evokes three possible reasons for the often high levels of noncompliance. These include lack of appropriate knowledge, disagreement with the rule or principle involved, and social pressure leading to ignoring the rules. For example, even when the situation demands that this should be done, it is difficult for a nurse to resist a physician's orders. The campaign for reduction in noncompliance by health professionals is clearly in the interests of all concerned, and psychologists are best qualified to carry out the necessary studies of the issues involved (Ley, 1982a; Stuart, 1982b). In Rapoff and Christophersen's (1982) outline of directions for future research, one variable of special relevance to those who work with children pertains to the need for normative data across different situations and age levels. Rapoff and Christophersen review the diversity of compliance measures currently in vogue. Each has its advantages and disadvantages, and none is ideal. For example, drug assays may be objective, but they tend to be evasive and readily amenable to distortion, and patient reports are highly subjective to social desirability. Educational strategies are advantageous when the compliance is short-term, but less effective over the long haul. Social control by way of monitoring and feedback leads to equivocal results and seems to be less effective than token economies or written contracts. As yet, no consistent pattern has emerged. No wonder, then, that for the present, Butler (1983) recommends, a broad-spectrum compliance package involving as many procedures as possible, leaving the necessary dismantling research to the future.

Dunbar (1983) draws further attention to the additional complexities involved when working with a pediatric population. As noted, children are rarely free agents, and it is generally difficult if not impossible to unravel the "compliance motivation" of parent and child. A mother's perception of the seriousness of her child's illness may differ from that of the child. Parental perception or even misperception of lack of control over the possible recurrence of the child's illness may also be associated with noncompliance. And a mother overwhelmed by family responsibilities and the competing demands of other children may not be able to give the same time and attention to the needs of her sick child as her counterpart in a smaller family may.

There are numerous assessment devices for the prediction of compliance in situations involving children. None has had much success to date. For example, Becker and Maiman's (1975) Health Belief Model uses a vast number of demographic, attitudinal, and regimen measures stemming from social-psychological theory to arrive at a probability figure for individual compliance with a specific medical recommendation. Unfortunately, as its originators reluctantly conclude, its predictive value is minimal (Becker, Maiman, Kirscht, Haefner, Drachman, & Taylor, 1979; Rapoff & Christophersen, 1982).

The notion that compliance in either the children themselves or their parents is related to the health beliefs and perceptions of the parents may be mistaken. The available data suggest that improved compliance is directly related neither to change in health belief nor to parental perception. What seems more likely is that health beliefs and perceptions are related more to experience with specific regimens than to general attitudinal change (Taylor, 1979). It would also seem helpful to know something about the "normal" rates of compliance for children of various ages in different everyday situations.

Many other parameters of compliance have been investigated, none as yet in a completely satisfactory fashion: clinical versus non-clinical populations; number and type of verbal commands; consequence of noncompliance; other presenting problems; age, socioeconomic status, and sex (Sulzer-Azaroff & Pollack, 1982).

A major compliance problem to receive attention in recent years in the pediatric literature is that of parents' failure to keep appointments for their children. While a number of behavioral intervention programs to promote appointment keeping have been developed, systematic investigation remains limited. Kolko, Parrish, and Wilson (in press) report an investigation of 100 parents who failed to attend either an initial evaluation or a subsequent parent training session in an outpatient child behavior management clinic. Parents in both groups reported such obstacles as their own or their children's poor health status, difficulties in securing transportation, competing home and work responsibilities, and sudden crises as the major impediments to keeping appointments. Prompting strategies, such as telephone calls, home visits, postcards, or various combinations thereof, have all been shown to be relatively ineffective (e.g., Meyers, Thackwray, Johnson, & Schleser, 1983). Appointment-keeping failures brought about by basic living problems such as transportation difficulties, inadequate babysitters, or lost work hours are unlikely to be corrected by a postcard or a telephone call.

This year has seen many small-sample studies of specific compliance problems involving either children or their parents. For example, Gross (1982) reports a promising self-management training procedure for working with diabetic children; but his sample consisted of only four boys. Other investigators focus upon the relationships between noncompliance behavior and home problems (e.g., Brown, Cunningham, & Birkimer, 1983). And there have been many investigations into compliance in the classroom (e.g., Neef, Shafer, Egel, Cataldo, & Parrish, 1983; Snyder & Brown, 1983; Strain, Lambert, Kerr, Stagg, & Lenkner, 1983). But, with the exception of the Strain *et al.* (1983) study, none has been incorporated into a longitudinally based program of systematic research, and it is this that is needed most.

BEHAVIORAL PARENT TRAINING

In a recent article provocatively entitled "Behavioral Parent Training: There's So Much More to Do," Lutzker, McGimsey, McRae, and Campbell (1983) remind their readers of the disquieting fact that the sale of "behavioral" parent training guides has not come close to that of parent advice offerings such as *Parent Effectiveness Training* (Gordon, 1975) or trade books covering areas of parental concern not even mentioned by behavior therapists. It is true that behavior therapists are fortunately handicapped by a need for validation prior to publication, and that this places them at a disadvantage when it comes to the sales countdown. But there is more to it than this. What parents really want to know about are the more personal or "human" aspects of parent–child relationships. Behavior therapists have much to offer in this area, but do not do so as yet. According to Lutzker *et al.* (1983), and I have no reason to disagree with their conclusion, there is no popular behavioral manual that deals with the things that parents really worry about (e.g., how to talk to their children about sex, death, or religion). So far, behavior therapists do not seem to be meeting parental needs and expectations (O'Dell, 1982).

When Lutzker *et al.* (1983) surveyed a decade of behavioral parent training literature, they came up with some devastating findings. For example, in 25% of their studies, the behavioral parent training was carried out by graduate students, and in 56% it was unspecified who provided the training. In only 11% of the studies examined was the therapist known to hold a doctorate. Even then, it was not known how experienced in treating families these therapists actually were. No wonder, then, that Lutzker *et al.* plaintively ask: "From *whose* data and *whose* experience are we basing our conclusions about the effects on families of behavioral parental training?" (1983, p. 111).

Information about independent variables and other training criteria essential to replication is also generally lacking. Of the studies examined by Lutzker *et al.*, 94% fail to specify adequate details about the delivery of the independent variables, and 90% fail to specify performance criteria by which training could be measured. Finally, in 21% of their studies, some form of restriction was placed on the families in either the treatment or the observation session, and another 20% of the studies were laboratory-based. Thus, at least 40% are primarily analogue in nature.

However, all is not quite lost, and several of Lutzker *et al.*'s recommendations are already in evidence. The work of Sanders and Glynn (1981) in looking at training and programming for generalization across several natural settings is particularly encouraging. Along these lines, Sanders and Dadds (1982) examined the use of antecedent activities in addition to consequences in parent training. This may herald the beginning of an approach to parent training that satisfies the pratical needs of the parent and the methodological demands of the behavior therapist.

Some quarter of a century ago, the Russell Sage Foundation published a volume entitled *Education for Child Rearing* (Brim, 1959). At that time, it was the only comprehensive volume available in the area of parent education. The 1980 update of this volume by Harman and Brim, *Learning to Be Parents: Principles, Programs and Methods*, highlights the developments that have taken place across the intervening decades. The growth of educational programs aimed at instructing parents in child rearing is as phenomenal as the number of popular volumes directed specifically toward this end. There has been a parallel growth in the number of practitioners, and, most encouraging, parent and adult education have become "legitimate" areas of academic concern. The field is now respectable and open for scholarly exploration.

These developments notwithstanding, Harman and Brim still conclude that current research, especially in the area of outcome evaluation, is "woefully inadequate." For example, with all our knowledge, it is not possible to come to any definitive conclusion as to the superiority of one approach over another, or as to what type of instructor is more effective than another and under what circumstances. If behavior therapists do not attend to these matters, who will?

Parents are unique among the paraprofessional community in that they seek training neither to enhance their occupational skills or status nor to apply these skills to help individuals with whom they have had no prior or close personal commitment. They are directly and intimately involved in the care of their children, and, as such, may be presumed to be a well-motivated and readily available source of research data. But despite the potential fertility of the ground, Graziano and Katz (1982) are forced to conclude that as yet, remarkably little has been reaped.

Griest and Wells (1983) take issue with the behavioral parent training model on quite different grounds: namely, that its basic premise is at fault. They seriously question the assumption that it is exclusively a deficit in parental skills that brings about a child's problems. Other overlooked aspects of parental functioning—in particular, relationships with the community at large—may be of equal significance.

In the unidirectional world of most parent training, parent behavior leads directly to child behavior. The primary focus of parent training programs then becomes the teaching of new skills for managing positive and negative child behaviors. It is Griest and Wells's contention that using parents as vehicles for the treatment of the problems of their children is not always appropriate and rarely sufficient. Intervention is required in areas other than child management skills. As often as not, conduct disorders in children are related in sometimes intricate fashion to the adjustment of the parents across a variety of social and psychological areas. Failure to assess and treat all the variables that potentially contribute to the conduct disorder may be responsible for the failure to achieve clinically meaningful effects. To this end, Griest and Wells recommend expansion of the current child behavior therapy model to a "behavioral family therapy model," and, by implication, recommend that this strategy be incorporated into current and planned programs of behavioral parent training.

Schreibman (1983) presents the problem in a slightly different manner: What are the effects of parent training on the parents' adjustment and on the family life as a whole? Schreibman's interest, however, is more in the parental perceptions of the training program than in understanding the variables contributing to the conduct disorder per se. Schreibman's concern is that we not forget the *parent* in parent training. She makes the compelling point that, no matter how effective a parent training program is in bringing about behavior change in the targeted child, it will not be used if the parents perceive it to be ineffective, to require too much effort, or to have a negative impact on family life. In short, parents who do not like parent training will not use it. What can we do to help parents see that changes in the behavior of their children are related to their own efforts? How can we increase parental self-confidence in their skills, and thus the likelihood that they will use these skills? Is there some optimal combination of clinical treatment and parental training? In the absence of data, meaningful answers to these extremely relevant questions do not exist.

There is much that we do not know. Parent training has been virtually limited to mothers, and it is largely through serendipity that fathers become involved at all. Thus, when Reisinger (1982) trained mothers to be proficient in the application of behavior modification technology with their oppositional preschool children, the fathers benefited even though they had received no formal instruction. Unprogrammed learning occurred, and the fathers' constructive use of differential attention with their children increased. To shed light upon the role of the father or the circumstances surrounding the use of unprogrammed learning would necessitate intensive research. A similar argument applies to the largely unresearched roles of siblings in the training of their brothers and sisters (Furman & Buhrmester, 1982).

The circumstances determining the length of a particular program for particular problems and with particular types of parents likewise remain largely unexplored. Demonstrably effective brief parental training offers many advantages. When the problem is relatively straightforward, such as helping children with their homework, it is more appropriate to think in terms of minimal parent training rather than complicated programs (Anesko & O'Leary, 1982). Complex issues— and situations are rarely as straightforward as they seem at first glance— require much more planning and professional involvement.

Issues in Outcome Evaluation

Effective outcome evaluation rests upon a judicious combination of methodological sophistication, careful planning, and the availability of financial and time resources. For the busy professional working within a clinic or school setting, large caseloads leave little opportunity for evaluation and the unhurried selection of appropriate measuring instruments, which the complexity of the presenting problem usually demands. Understandably, clinician/researchers are forced to rely upon parent reports and pencil-and-paper measures to assess treatment outcome. Most investigators recognize the limitations of such tactics, but the exigencies of the situation restrict the range of alternatives available to them.

Numerous technologically sophisticated objective coding systems for recording parent–child interactions during direct observation sessions have been developed and applied in a variety of research-oriented parent training programs. The most comprehensive and well-designed observational instrument developed to date, according to Budd, Riner, and Brockman (1983), has 29 categories of child or parent behavior. This makes it an excellent measuring device for the research psychologist, but of limited value to the clinician. Although it imposes minimal restrictions on family activities, valid and reliable application requires much training prior to usage and extensive data analysis after the fact. Thus, while the technology for direct observation of families involved in parent training exists as a research tool, it has yet to evolve into a practical system that can be readily applied by the busy professional with limited resources.

A potentially more promising approach involves the use of standardized observation situations. Structuring the activities in which parent and child engage during the observation period may restrict spontaneity, but, as such pioneers as Hanf and Forehand have demonstrated (see Budd *et al.*, 1983), it does provide a more manageable number of pertinent responses for observation and recording.

The multipurpose direct observation system for the assessment of parental use of child management techniques within a broad-based clinical parent training program developed by Budd *et al.* (1983) is an outgrowth of these earlier projects noted above. Five standardized situations were devised, each oriented toward a specific set of child management skills. In so doing, the authors' goals were to develop a system that met three criteria: (1) applicability across a diversity of parents, children, and behavior problems; (2) the provision of pertinent data within a short period of time; and (3) amenability to reliable usage by observers with limited training.

The skills to be assessed included instruction giving, differential attending, use of a token system, teaching new skills, and use of time out. The subjects consisted of 14 parent–child pairs referred to an outpatient clinic for behavioral parent training. Observations were conducted in the home on at least six occasions during the training program, and parent training was introduced sequentially across individual skill areas in a multiple-baseline design. Their findings are encouraging. The system successfully met all three criteria; it was highly reliable and valid in its documentation of changes in performance for all child management skills involved in the training. Paper-and-pencil measures pertaining to knowledge of child management principles, collected before and after training, corroborated the parental observational data. As with any structured assessment device, Budd *et al.*'s system provides only part of the information needed in a fully comprehensive evaluation. This limitation is acknowledged in all their reports.

Dropout is always a problem in outcome evaluation. The fact that dropout rate in psychological treatment is generally high (see Baekeland & Laundwall, 1975, for a review) does not make the excessive rate of dropout encountered in behavioral parent training (e.g., Worland, Carney, Weinberg, & Milch, 1982) more acceptable. Forehand, Middlebrook, Rogers, and Steffe (1983a) critically examined parent training studies reported in the professional literature over the past decade. Of 45 such studies, only 22 even mentioned dropout; of those that did briefly report such data, few indicated precisely when the dropout occurred.

While the overall dropout rate of 28% for these 45 studies compares favorably with that of an earlier survey (Baekeland & Laundwall, 1975), Forehand *et al.* (1983a) find little room for complacency. By way of remediation, they raise three general issues that await resolution prior to detailed investigation of the problem of dropout and its eventual control. First, there is ambiguity with respect to the concept of dropout as an outcome measure in parent training. As Bornstein and Rychtarik (1983) note, provided that contamination by other factors such as relocation or excessive expense is limited, dropping out may perhaps most advantageously be viewed as a measure of consumer satisfaction. (See also the discussion of consumer satisfaction in Chapter 1.)

Second, there is the matter of the identification of the primary client. The child is supposed to be the target, but much, perhaps most, of the more immediate intervention is carried out with the parents. Therefore, the characteristics of the parent need to be considered at least as much as those of the child in any attempt to evaluate client motivation. Parents may choose to terminate therapy for reasons that are not related to behavior change in their children. The needs of the parent may therefore take precedence over those of the child in the identification of dropout determinants.

According to Forehand *et al.* (1983a), parents who are depressed or come from a low-socioeconomic-status group are prone to drop out.

But to look at this variable in isolation is to oversimplify it. Information about the relationships of other potentially pertinent client variables to dropout rate is essential if the problem is to be given full
contextual appraisal. Seemingly prosaic items, such as fees charged or
the availability of parking and other clinic facilities, may be contributing variables of major significance. And, finally, there are the
characteristics of the therapist—but to venture here is indeed to open
up a Pandora's box!

There is ample evidence with respect to the effectiveness of behavioral parent training while the program is still going on and
immediately following its termination. There is much less evidence
with respect to the endurance of this training over the months and
years that follow. The three long-term evaluations reviewed by Forehand, Steffe, Furey, and Walley (1983b) all fail to make use of direct
behavioral observation in arriving at their conclusions. While acknowledging this need for behavioral observation, Forehand et al. (1983b) also
draw attention to two other key measures in the evaluation of long-term
effects: parental perceptions of child behavior and adjustment; and
parental satisfaction with the treatment program and its general consequences.

In 1981, Baum and Forehand reported a high level of declared
satisfaction with treatment up to 4½ years following termination. In this
latest investigation, a follow-up of their earlier study, Forehand et al.
(1983b) examined long-term effects for a parent training program
carried out with 68 mother–child pairs. Mothers who had completed
treatment some 3.6 years earlier were asked to respond to questions
dealing with parental perceptions of child adjustment and general
satisfaction with treatment received. 50% of the 68 mothers returned
adequately completed questionnaires. The comparisons of pretreatment, posttreatment, and follow-up child adjustment scores unequivocally indicate that, as a group, mothers perceived their children as
significantly better adjusted after treatment, and that this effect was
maintained at follow-up. Generally favorable responses were also reported by mothers in response to a consumer satisfaction questionnaire.

In a somewhat related vein, Griest, Forehand, and Wells (1981)
investigated pretreatment factors predictive of parent–child pairs likely
to cooperate in follow-up after termination of training. Sixteen parents
and their behavior problem children took part in a study of pretreatment, treatment, and posttreatment variables considered potentially
relevant to willingness to participate in follow-up assessment 8 months
later. Participation involved four 40-minute home observation sessions
conducted by independent observers. The parents were also expected to
complete various adjustment questionnaires pertaining to themselves
and their children. Of the 16 parents, 10 agreed to participate. Once

again, maternal depression emerged as a significant variable in the determination of susceptibility to dropout some 10 months later. Studies such as these point to the need to include parental adjustment measures in future investigations of this sort.

Wahler's approach (see previous volumes in this series) is another example of the sophisticated investigation of treatment outcome variables in parent training. It rests upon the concept of the "insular" mother. "Insularity" pertains both to the quantity and quality of extrafamily contacts and is defined by Wahler as "a specific pattern of social contacts within the community that is characterized by a high level of negatively perceived coercive interchanges with kinfolk and/or helping agency representatives" (Dumas & Wahler, 1983, p. 302). According to Dumas and Wahler, insular mothers generally report most of their contacts to consist of unsolicited, coercive, and otherwise negatively valenced approaches by extended family members and social service agents. By contrast, noninsular mothers report the majority of their contacts to be solicited and to involve positive interchanges with friends.

In a study of insularity as related to training outcome by Wahler and Afton (1980), low-income mothers who reported frequent adult coercion in their lives failed to maintain adequate parent training benefits at a 4-month follow-up. In sharp contrast, a group of middle-income mothers with few self-reports of adult coercive experiences and many social contacts maintained their gains during this same period. It seems likely that, as Dumas and Wahler suggest, socioeconomic disadvantages and insularity are positively correlated, and that both are predictive of parent training outcome.

As part of this ongoing attempt to evaluate a parent training program for families with oppositional children, Dumas and Wahler (1983) report two studies, a replication and an extension involving 49 and 18 mothers, respectively. In sharp contrast to most investigations in this area, parent training effectiveness was assessed through direct home observations of mother–child interactions during training and at a 1-year follow-up. Discriminant analyses generated two predictor variables: an index of socioeconomic disadvantage and an index of insularity. Together, these two indices account for some 49% of the variance in treatment outcome and the correct classification of 80% of the participants. It would seem that, at least in this study, socioeconomic disadvantage and insularity are significant predictors of parent training outcome: Mothers who experience high levels of social and personal coercion are likely to fare poorly in parent training programs designed to improve relationships between themselves and their children.

Dumas and Wahler carefully itemize the implications of their data. First, there is the importance of measuring, analyzing, and reporting social-interactional and demographic variables in research and clinical programs involving mothers of oppositional children. Second, the lack of treatment success reported by more than half of their sample casts "serious doubt" on the effectiveness of parent training as a single therapy for the majority of insular and/or disadvantaged families. Finally, they pinpoint the dangers of ignoring ecological variables in studies of mother–child behavior change because they are indirect and seemingly less relevant than the more usual parameters included in such investigations. Overlooking such contextual factors in high-risk families could conceivably turn the therapeutic experience into one of failure. Accordingly, Dumas and Wahler caution the behavioral clinician not to become just another partner in the cycle of coercion, one more aversive figure to be coped with by dropping out of therapy or by "lip service" compliance bereft of serious intent to follow through.

Program Evaluation

Family and school tend to remain distinct and separate systems. Each is based upon its own reinforcement and control schedules, and each keeps appropriate distance from the other. School-organized parent training programs is one possible way of bridging this gap, and many schools are now beginning to develop classes geared toward structured parent training. Programs emphasizing behavioral technology, effective communications, or self-concept enhancement are all examples of such efforts. But no single modality of parent education is likely to be appropriate for all parents. Some parents may be resistant to a program that emphasizes behavioral management, while others will find such a system ideally suited to their personal values and needs (Beutler & Oró-Beutler, 1982).

Beutler and Oró-Beutler compared two basic, readily differentiated approaches. Over a 2-year period, 14 groups were initiated, 150 parents began the training, and 100 completed the series. Three of the six participating counselors selected a behaviorally oriented training program as the approach of choice, and three developed a program known as Systematic Training for Effective Parenting (STEP), which combined Parent Effectiveness Training and Drikurs's concepts of misbehavior. The behaviorally oriented treatment program involved training in the basic principles and methodology of behavioral observation and intervention through such well-established procedures as token systems and homework assignments to help parents utilize the various strategies. In contrast, the STEP program focused upon communication, the understanding of subconscious goals, and the learning of problem ownership by the parents in confronting relationships with their children.

Direct communication of feeling was the primary focus whereby these issues of ownership were understood and resolved.

Training in both programs involved didactic instruction and various home assignments. Follow-up took place from 6 months to a year after termination of the training programs.

There were no major differences in benefits obtained. In both groups, changes in the parents' sense of competency and self-control were produced. Parents were uniformly pleased with the results, and it was not possible to isolate specific indicators or contraindicators for either treatment. Parents who valued interpersonal control tended to experience more benefit from behaviorally oriented training programs, whereas those who valued emotional expression may have been more likely to benefit from the STEP program. But most of these differences are small and point to the need for further investigation more than anything else.

Zangwill (1983) was likewise interested in contrasting these "feeling" and "behavioral" models, to use his terminology. While most programs emphasize one or the other approach, the Hanf and Kling model of parent training cited by Zangwill appears to be a synthesis of both. The various programs developed over the years by Forehand and his associates at the University of Georgia reflect a similar tradition. In the main, as documented throughout the years in this series, the findings are quite positive.

Zangwill's (1983) project, carried out at the University of Oregon, had four major purposes: first, to establish an independent replication; second, to focus upon clinical as well as statistical significance; third, to develop additional comparison control groups; and fourth, to assess the degree to which skills learned in the clinic generalized to the home.

Fifteen families with conduct problem children were assessed and assigned to either an immediate or a delayed treatment group. One professor and nine graduate students served as therapists. Training took place exclusively at the Psychological Clinic of the University of Oregon; assessments were carried out in the clinic and in the homes.

"Qualified support" for the validity of this program emerged. The impact was strongest with respect to the behavior of parents and their attitudes toward their children. Less consistent improvements were noted in the behavior of the children. Though compliance increased, there was no significant decrease in deviant behavior. Regrettably, the limited follow-up was too informal to permit more than tentative conclusions. It seemed as if the gains were maintained as long as there was no major stress in the family, but, for the reason stated, little reliance can be placed on this impression.

Sanders (1982), an often-cited and seasoned investigator, reports the latest study in his program of research in self-management training, utilizing a multiple-baseline approach across families. Two families were sequentially introduced to either instructions plus feedback or self-management training. Instructions plus feedback provided home-based training both in stimulus control techniques and in the use of consequences. Self-management training taught parents to manage their own behaviors in specific parenting situations. Training involved self-monitoring, goal setting, and the acquisition of specific parental skills. There was a 4-month follow-up. Self-management training increased the accuracy with which parents were able to implement treatment procedures, both at home and in new settings within the community. Instructions plus feedback were adequate in showing parents how to reduce problem behaviors within the home; they were far less effective in teaching parents how to implement these procedures in other settings.

It would seem from these data that it is the addition of self-management training that provides the necessary increase in effectiveness. However, as Sanders cautions, the durable changes in parent behavior that occurred could have resulted from either the prior self-management training and/or from posttraining contingencies occurring "naturally" within the family milieu (e.g., spouse support, improved child behavior). Furthermore, the Sanders study was carried out with well-motivated middle-class volunteers. Further research is required to unravel the critical controlling variables.

Finally, attention is drawn to an early intervention program of Reisinger and Lavigne (1980) for parents with problem children. Organized into units that focus both on the specific needs of the child and on more general parent–child interactions, the program emphasizes parent training and skill development through the application of behavioral and social learning principles. As families progress through the different units, the parents themselves become increasingly qualified to serve in various training capacities, and the training programs were set up by Reisinger and Lavigne with this expectation in mind. Thus, as the number of families served increased and more parent trainers became available, the cost per family decreased. Additional advantages of the program include the intangible benefits associated with the realization by the parents that they are not alone with their problems and the positive feelings that are generated from helping others.

Working with Special Groups

A closely reasoned chapter by Turnbull (1983) highlights a special predicament that can confront parents of handicapped children. The scenario goes something like this: The social climate surrounding these parents is usually one of veiled blame, with diagnosis followed rapidly by encouragement to place the handicapped child in an institution. The implicit message is that rearing such a child requires special coping skills and attitudes the parents cannot and will not possess. When eductional programs are made available, they are usually insufficiently thought through and do more harm than good. The hapless parents, overwhelmed with extra responsibilities thrust precipitously upon them by judgmental and demanding professionals, end up being viewed as unresponsive and uncaring by those in charge of the program.

Most attempts to establish positive interactions among professionals and parents are doomed to probable failure from the start. Some failures relate to unwillingness to listen and respond appropriately to concerns and problems. Parents wondering where the next meal is coming from are not likely to be interested in home visits to explain positive reinforcement.

While her sympathies are clearly with the parent rather than the professional, Turnbull tries to be relatively objective in her attempt at resolution of the dilemma. Negative interactions result from lack of awareness and sensitivity on the part of both groups, and Turnbull's carefully reasoned plea is for a program geared toward the needs of both parties, with a view to improved parent–professional interactions based upon mutual respect, open communication, and sensitivity to each other's roles and responsibilities.

Special problems involved in the training of parents of developmentally disabled children are reviewed in detail by Altman and Mira (1983). Training needs for these children are likely to be long-term and to require more general environmental programming that the specific settings involved in parent training with normal children. Recent legislative changes, as well as the expanding role of parents of developmentally disabled children as advocates, decision makers, and enlightened consumers of child care services, mandate increasing sophistication with respect to training methods. While Turnbull's (1983) thesis is well taken, the fact remains that parents of developmentally disabled children *can* assume more active, varied, and complex roles in the training of their children. No longer need they be viewed as passive and sometimes resistant recipients of services.

The training of those parents presents problems and challenges common to the field, plus those noted above. There is the need to maximize the active and concerned participation of individuals other than the mother, the necessity for building appropriate generalization and maintenance procedures, and more. Altman and Mira (1983) propose a specific strategy for the development of an ideal parent training program. First, short- and long-term effectiveness is documented under tightly controlled circumstances involving the use of multiple measures. Next, the program is applied in more natural situations, but still on a limited basis. Then comes the systematic evaluation of a package program on a larger scale, and an analysis of the circumstances surrounding its effectiveness. Supplementary and branching programs are then developed for those individuals whose additional needs are not met by the standard treatment package. Finally, a components analysis is to be conducted to determine essential elements and their relative contributions. The package is then ready to be refined for consumer use.

In his review of training programs for parents of the mentally retarded, Tymchuk (1983) draws attention to a much-neglected research group—parents who, for one reason or another, refuse or are unable to participate in a training program. There are virtually no studies in this area.

For cooperative parents of mentally retarded, autistic, or organically damaged children, and those who wish to work with them, Harris (1983) has produced a most readable text. She makes the seemingly obvious but often overlooked point that, effective as behavioral techniques are in parental training, they work only when the family as a whole is receptive to their use. Angry, depressed, or otherwise disturbed parents are not likely to be effective students or sources of leadership for their children. It is therefore important that clinicians go beyond their more usual didactic roles and help parents come to terms both with their children's handicaps per se and with their roles as parents in the training process.

Behaviorally oriented training programs have been developed for many other special groups. For example, W. S. Feldman and her associates focus their attention upon spina bifida children, who have perhaps the most common congenital nervous system defect in the United States (W. S. Feldman, Manella, Apodaca, & Varni, 1982; W. S. Feldman & Varni, 1983). Another area of concern for Feldman and her associates is the provision of behavioral training programs for single mothers of physically handicapped children (W. S. Feldman, Manella & Varni, 1983). The single parent is likely to experience a variety of unique problems. More than most two-person parental units, single parents are likely to feel helpless in controlling either their own behavior or that of their children. The many situational pressures placed upon them, together with the need to make decisions for themselves, seem to engender pervasive feelings of helplessness and withdrawal. Adequately researched behavioral training programs for the single parent do not as yet exist.

At the other end of the training spectrum for parents of special groups, the literature on hyperactivity (HA) continues to flourish. Dubey, O'Leary, and Kaufman's (1983) comparative outcome study of training for parents of HA children in the principles of child management is an example of recent research in this area at its behavioral best. Parents of 44 HA children were assigned to a behavior modification group, a communications group involving Parent Effectiveness Training/Communications, or a delayed-treatment control group. Parents and children were assessed before and after a 9-week training workshop with various measures of HA, a daily checklist of problem occurrence, parental attitude scales, and direct observation in a laboratory setting.

Both treatments were more effective than a no-treatment control condition in the reduction of problem severity ratings and the actual occurrence of daily problems. Parents receiving behavior modification training rated their children as more improved than those in the Parent Effectiveness Training/Communications group. Furthermore, they were more willing to recommend the program to others and less inclined to drop out. Assessments at the 9-month follow-up indicated that treatment parents continued to view their children's behavior more positively than did the control group.

It should be noted that, in both groups, instruction and implementation of behavior change was entirely in the hands of the parents. There was no individual personal contact, no home observation, no telephone call, and no time allotted during sessions to instructor or group resolution of individual problems. In short, a strictly *educational* approach to parent training was apparently effective in improving overall competence in dealing with the problems of child management. It may be that different circumstances make different parents more amenable to some program than to others—a possibility already referred to in this chapter. What is important here, however, is that the Dubey *et al.* (1983) study is one of the few, possibly the first, to document systematically the long-term effectiveness of nonpharmacological management procedures designed for home application entirely by the parents.

CHILD ABUSE AND NEGLECT

The child abuse literature is mainly pragmatic, and theory seems to be consistently downplayed. Newberger, Newberger, and Hampton (1983) go so far as to suggest that an insufficient theory base may be contributing more to program failure than a lack of intervention resources may be.

Explanatory theories of child abuse are classified by Newberger *et al.* (1983) into two groups: unitary and interactive. Psychoanalytic, social learning, environmental, cognitive, developmental, and labeling theories are all unitary approaches. Each explains child abuse from a single perspective, and each is limited by an inability to account for enough of the data to guide intervention effectively. This, so Newberger *et al.*'s argument goes, has led to critical clinical and research evaluation and eventual incorporation of the more helpful components into the variety of interactive, multicausal models of child abuse that constitute their second category. These models characterize child abuse from multiple individual, family, and societal perspectives, and stress the use of any strategy that, regardless of origins, has been demonstrated to "work."

Time and time again, I have had occasion to draw attention to the theoretical and practical hazards of technical eclecticism and its off-shoots. For further elaboration of this point, the reader is referred to a recent chapter of mine in another book (Franks, 1984b), which documents in detail the reasons why this position is thought to be untenable. Perhaps the major advantage of this "new look" in child abuse is the impetus given to researcher clinicians looking for uncharted regions to explore. But, so far, there is more speculation than hard data, and the pragmatics of eclecticism remain equivocal.

Recent reviews of child abuse from the viewpoint of contemporary behavior therapy are either very general and elementary (e.g., Hutchings, 1982) or geared toward the practitioner (e.g., Kelly, 1983). Walker's (1979) conceptualization of the "battered woman" syndrome applies learning theory—in this instance, learned helplessness—to a situation that has elements in common with that of child abuse. But, here too, as Giles-Sims (1983) makes clear, to appreciate fully how the wife-battering process occurs, it may be necessary to take a multicausational look at forces within the larger social system. In this event, the quest for common determinants among child abuse, the battered woman, and related phenomena might yet be productive.

Wolfe's (1983) developmental model embodies many elements of this search for communality. Empirical findings are combined with theoretical assumptions derived from developmental and clinical psychology, pediatrics, and sociology within a broad-based learning theory framework that stresses the importance of antecedent events in triggering acts of abuse, as well as the short-term reinforcing consequences of the abusive act (Friedman, Sandler, Hernandez, & Wolfe, 1981). Because parents with very young children seem to be more willing to accept direction than parents of older children, whose interactional patterns have had many years to solidify, Wolfe's target population for application of these principles consists of young parents, usually single females in their late teens or early 20s with less than 5 years of child-rearing experience. Their children, usually infants or toddlers, often show some developmental decrement, such as limited or defective language, social interaction, or motor control.

To assert their initial level of current child management skills, parents entering Wolfe's program are subjected to an array of structured parent–child interaction procedures and parent attitude measures. Personal adjustment, expectancies, and reported child-rearing problems are all systematically explored. The physical, cognitive, and behavioral development of each child is assessed by the medical and psychological staff.

Parents receive individualized training in the principles and practice of positive reinforcement, ignoring, the giving of appropriate commands, and punishment. In addition, therapists train parents to engage in daily activities geared toward the strengthening of deficiency areas and the promotion of adaptive functioning. These activities include modeling, rehearsal, and social interaction training. A criterion-based assessment and tracking system is used to provide a framework and guidance for training. Once initial gains are established, therapist contact is reduced from twice a week to a fortnightly basis, with subsequent bimonthly follow-up evaluations.

Preliminary results are encouraging: Parents have shown measurable improvements in critical child-rearing skills and evidence fewer child-rearing concerns and annoyances after an average training period of only 2 months. What remains to be established is the effectiveness of the program as the children grow up.

It has been suggested that physiological responsiveness could be an important variable in the generation of child abuse behavior. Several investigators have demonstrated the role of infant behavior and facial expression as aversive stimuli for adults. For example, Frodi, Lamb, Leavitt, and Donovan (1978) found that normal adults tended to report pleasant reactions to infant smiles and unpleasant reactions to video-taped presentations of crying infants. Similarly, Donovan, Leavitt, and Balling (1978) found that differential responses as measured by physiological changes were related to maternal perception of infant temperament. Mothers who rated their infants as more difficult tended to be physiologically less sensitive to changes in infant expression. Extending this approach to abusive parents, Frodi and Lamb (1980) found that abusive mothers reported more aversion to infant cries than nonabusers.

While the relative significance of cognitive, physiological, and behavioral deviations cannot be relatively ascertained from any of these studies, the findings—especially those of Frodi and Lamb (1980)—do suggest that cognitive and physiological mediators of parent aggression require consideration in the assessment and treatment of abusive parents. To compare the physiological responses of abusive and non-abusive parents, Wolfe, Fairbank, Kelly, and Bradlyn (1983) showed videotaped scenes involving stressful and nonstressful behaviors in children to seven abusive and seven matched nonabusive control mothers. To assess maternal arousal, skin conductance response magnitude, heart rate, and respiration were monitored before, during, and after each scene presentation. Comparison of the two groups revealed significant group × scene interactions for skin conductance and respiration measures. Skin conductance response magnitudes indicated greater emotional arousal for the abusive group during the stressful scenes. The respiration data show that the abusers remained more aroused than the controls during both stressful and nonstressful scenes.

Unfortunately, this study must be considered as suggestive rather than definitive. As readily admitted, the methodology used by these investigators makes it impossible to determine why it was that abusive parents showed increased arousal to cues of child misbehavior. Abusive individuals may demonstrate increased arousal to numerous life problems, only some of which may happen to involve their children.

These limitations notwithstanding, Wolfe et al. (1983) extract several useful suggestions from their data. First, parents who appear to experience anger and rage toward their children should be assessed in terms of apparent degree of stress-related physiological arousal and its relationship to specific aversive child behaviors. Second, for those parents who do manifest patterns of increased arousal, specific training to help decrease emotional overreactivity could be an important component of the therapeutic program. Third, since abusive parents may conceivably be mislabeling the type and severity of their arousal, the cognitive components of this increased arousal may also require appropriate modification.

In terms of cognitive control, the work of Nomellini and Katz (1983) may be relevant. It could be that parents who experience arousal and immediately attribute their feelings to "anger" are more likely to manifest aggressive behavior than individuals who do not respond to physiological stimuli in this manner. Although it is still in an exploratory stage, cognitive restructuring with a view to anger control could be an important component of the child abuse treatment package. Most behaviorally oriented child abuse programs focus exclusively on the improvement of parental child management skills, rather than on the modification of cognitive–affective states.

To demonstrate the potential utility of this approach, Nomellini and Katz (1983) worked with three families referred from community agencies dealing with child abuse problems. Family 1 was an intact, low-middle-class family; the other two were single-parent, mother-only families of lower-class backgrounds. In all three families, the parents had beaten their children, had berated them verbally, or were in fear of hurting their children in angry rage.

Anger control training was instituted in a multiple-baseline design across families. The training consisted of three interrelated components: teaching parents about the functions, determinants, and physiological cues of anger arousal; teaching them the use of various self-monitoring and self-training techniques, such as deep breathing, relaxation, and self-reinforcement, to control angry feelings generated in anger-producing situations; and providing them with opportunities to practice these responses under real and simulated conditions. The entire training program was completed in the home in six to eight 90-minute sessions, and children were not involved in the training. Follow-up data were collected for 6 months with the first two families and for 2 months with the third. Because the third family showed less improvement after anger control training than the other two families, treatment of the mother was supplemented with child management skills training.

During and after anger control training, parents in all three families showed significant reductions in aversive behavior, together with decreases in anger urges and overall proneness to provocation. These results were maintained throughout the follow-up periods. Although the children were not included in the anger control study, they also showed reductions in aversive behavior, together with modest increases in positive behavior. The design of the study does not make it possible to determine which of the three training components was most responsible for changes in parental attitudes and behavior. Furthermore, generalizations based on a sample of three are not very meaningful. It should also be noted that the three mothers were relatively intact psychologically. These strategies may not be directly transferable to situations involving psychosis, alcoholism, or otherwise seriously inappropriate child management skills. But, on the positive side, the procedures required less than 10 hours of therapist time and $4.00 for materials per family; as the authors note, these are small prices to pay for what seem to be fairly significant benefits.

Numerous investigators have reported a strong and positive association between stressful life events and child abuse. Abusive parents have also been frequently characterized as socially isolated (Gaudin & Pollane, 1983). According to Garbarino (1977), isolation from environmental support systems is one of the necessary conditions for child maltreatment. Polansky, Chalmers, Buttenwieser, and Williams (1979) have similarly concluded that it is the social isolation of such families from supporting networks, together with certain parental personality characteristics, that sometimes contributes to child neglect among poor families. Garbarino (1977) further proposes that it is the unmanageability of stress that is the most important factor in the development of abuse, the argument being that this unmanageability is caused by the mismatch between level of stress experience and the strength of the informal social network of the child's caregiver.

In a primarily correlational study of the relationships between situational stress, strength of informal social networks and maternal child abuse, Gaudin and Pollane (1983) interviewed 41 abusive mothers and 59 nonabusive mothers. On average, the abusive mothers reported significantly weaker and less supportive informal social networks than the nonabusing mothers. Both situational stress and strength of social network were significant predictors of abuse. Unfortunately, as the authors point out, the presence of causal relationships between mothers' perceived strength of the social network and maternal child abuse cannot be determined from correlational data.

Social networks are but one facet of what is coming to be known as the ecobehavioral or larger-environment approach to the problem of child abuse (Driessen & Demetral, 1983; Sgroi, 1982). The ecobehavioral investigator analyzes all behaviors, including those of possibly pertinent adults, within the context of the larger environment (Scott, 1980). Particular emphasis is given to the role of setting events (Wahler & Fox, 1981). Wahler and Graves (1983) define a "setting event" as an environmental stimulus or S-R interaction that influences the function of later S-R interactions.

In Project 12-Ways, Lutzker (1984) demonstrates the successful application of an ecobehavioral model, including the utilization of setting theory, to the treatment of families where child abuse has occurred. The ecobehavioral approach to child abuse treats the overt behavior problem directly within the context of the immediate environment. This allows the behavior therapist to assess and manipulate the various antecedent and consequent events that affect the child's behavior more accurately, and thereby to develop appropriate behaviorally oriented intervention procedures (Driessen & Demetral, 1983).

Finally, attention is drawn to an unpublished child abuse survey by Garbarino (1981). The following discouraging conclusions emerged from Garbarino's survey; they speak for themselves.

1. Incidence estimates continue to be confused by lack of precision with respect to definitions used in research, policy making, law, or therapeutic practice.
2. The prediction of risk for maltreatment remains statistically

unreliable, thereby frustrating attempts at early intervention and prevention.

3. Treatment of child abuse remains inadequate, and successful treatment is imperfectly understood at best.

4. Nearly all treatment efforts focus on parents. The developmental and health needs of children tend to be ignored, and sometimes these hapless individuals are actually harmed by interventions involving foster home or institutional care settings.

5. Preventive initiatives remain largely unexplored.

6. The medium- and long-term consequences of physical and sexual abuse are poorly understood. Few longitudinal studies have been instituted, and, sad to report, these are likely to end soon because of nationwide constraints on research funding.

AUTISM AND BEHAVIOR THERAPY

Autism remains a devastating, fascinating, and little-understood syndrome. Research articles, theories of etiology, overviews, and practical manuals abound. However, little more is known now than when I wrote my contributions to Volume 9 of the *Annual Review*. What emerges is a picture of consolidation and small inroads here and there, rather than any spectacular advance.

The same very respectable names—such as Schreibman, Koegel, Egel, and Harris—appear repeatedly in reviews and guidelines, and it is understandable that there is more repetition than innovation (e.g., Schreibman, Koegel, Charlop & Egel, 1982). Nevertheless, some intriguing new possibilities are beginning to emerge, chiefly in the form of plausible ideas awaiting development. Schreibman *et al.* (1982), for example, raise the possibility of meaningful interaction between some form of neural plasticity and behavioral intervention. Their tentative conclusion from the limited data available to them points to a primary or secondary cortical dysfunction in the language-dominant hemisphere of certain autistic children.

Schreibman *et al.* (1982) point out limitations as well as strengths in the behavior therapy of autism. The strength is obvious and much touted: a research- and data-based approach that stresses a methodology based upon operational definition and empirical validation. The limitations are equally obvious but often overlooked, and Schreibman *et al.* perform a needed service in drawing attention to them in their review. When Schreibman and her group searched for a single behavior, or group of behaviors, which when altered would lead to profound "personality" change, their efforts met with repeated failures. To date, behavioral approaches to autism are characterized by limited successes in circumscribed areas rather than by across-the-board change. That this situation prevails throughout the field of autism, regardless of researchers' orientations, is small comfort. A technology for programming stimulus and response generalization is beginning to emerge, but as yet this has not been translated into practical terms leading to large-scale changes.

Schreibman *et al.*'s (1982) second criticism of the behavioral model is that, despite mounting evidence that autistic children can learn in group situations (see Volume 9 of the *Annual Review*), treatment still relies heavily on a one-to-one therapist–child ratio. Finally, they criticize behavior therapists for their continued reliance on primary (food) reinforcers to develop appropriate behaviors, despite the identification of other types of functional rewards (e.g., the combination of techniques developed over the years by Lovaas and his associates for conditioning social stimuli).

The three behavioral reviews of significance to appear this year are all much of a muchness in their delineations of high points, general conclusions, and notes of caution (Lovaas, Ackerman, & Taubman, 1983; Schreibman *et al.*, 1982; Schreibman & Mills, 1983). All recognize the disquieting fact that nothing about autism is simple and that, at best, systematic research has led to a variety of encouraging advances in certain circumscribed areas: for example, the development of group procedures for classroom instruction; the advent of the teaching-home model for working with autistic children; the emphasis upon social validation; the need to take into consideration the feelings of parents; and last, but far from least, the impact (not always for the better) of recent legislation mandating classrooms for all autistic children in the United States.

Two relatively specialized behavioral reviews of significance have appeared recently (Egel, Koegel, & Schreibman, 1980; Murphy, 1982). Murphy (1982) reviews sensory reinforcement in mentally handicapped and autistic children. Across a variety of approaches and different samples of handicapped children, the findings are relatively consistent: With certain key differences, sensory stimuli can serve as reinforcers for these populations in much the same way that they do for normal children. For normal children, even noncontingent general stimulation is sufficient to contribute to the many skills of everyday living. In sharp contrast, a growing number of handicapped children living at home in apparently stimulating environments show behaviors similar to those of similarly handicapped children who live in institutions. Thus, for handicapped children wherever they are, general stimulation does not seem to be the answer to their problems. For these children, it is contingent stimulation, and in particular contingent sensory stimulation (referred to by Murphy as "sensory reinforcers"), that seems to offer promise to researchers and clinicians alike. Sensory reinforcement studies may yet provide some of the more promising leads in the understanding and modification of stereotyped behavior in autistic and handicapped children to date.

The other review, by Egel *et al.* (1980), is rather specialized and focuses exclusively upon educational treatment procedures for autistic children. It offers little that is different from the many other rather closely related publications of this group of investigators, but it does offer a useful description of current, replicable educational strategies based upon empirical data.

In addition to those texts noted in Volume 9 of the *Annual Review*, there are four relatively recent books that warrant mention. Harris's (1983) guide to behavioral intervention with the families of autistic children has already been discussed. Then there is a workmanlike manual by Hinerman (1983), which offers a step-by-step process for teaching communication to the uncommunicative child. This little book is technically sound and meets its stated goals very well, even though it offers nothing that is new or very different. Also falling into this category is a little manual by Romanczyk and Lockshin (1981), which manages to pack a remarkable amount of practical yet readily comprehensive detail into its 46 pages. But perhaps the most important new text in this area is an edited volume by Koegel, Rincover, and Egel (1982), dealing with the education and understanding of autistic children. The 20 or so highly qualified contributors include a more than representative sampling of the work of the editors and their collaborators—a situation that offers both advantages and disadvantages. Even if the terms of enquiry were to be restricted entirely to the behavioral literature, those who seek a comprehensive overview of recent developments would be unwise to rely exclusively upon this volume. However, the way the various chapters dovetail neatly together to offer an integrated overview of experimentally validated "program" research is a distinct plus.

Ever seeking new avenues for the behavioral training of autistic children, Schreibman and her associates have now turned to the siblings (Schreibman, O'Neill, & Koegel, 1983). Most research in this area has concentrated on training parents to serve as therapists or cotherapists. But there is increasing evidence to suggest that, for certain autistic children, interactions with normal peers outside the family can have beneficial effects (e.g., Strain, Kerr, & Ragland, 1979). This led Schreibman *et al.* (1983) to speculate that normal children could be trained to participate in training programs for their impaired siblings. To investigate the effectiveness of such a program, three sibling pairs were trained to teach their autistic brother or sister a variety of learning tasks. A multiple-baseline study was used to generate answers to three questions: (1) Could siblings of autistic children be taught to conduct correct behavior modification procedures at a high level of proficiency? (2) If so, would implementation also generalize to other, nonexperimental environments? (3) Would this implementation produce measurable improvements in the actual behavior of the autistic children? All experimental sessions, other than the generalization probes, were conducted in the children's homes over eight training sessions.

Overall, while these data lack the advantages of any follow-up, and replication with larger and different groups is needed, the results are encouraging and provide reasonably positive answers to the questions posed above. Furthermore, parents reported a decrease in negative statements about their autistic siblings by the normal children in the family. There are also certain obvious implications (noted by Schreibman *et al.*, 1983) for those who plan to work with such families, such as the need for careful monitoring by appropriately trained parents to make sure that no abuse or exploitation of the autistic siblings by the normal children occurs.

Social validation is now the order of the day, and it is virtually obligatory for all investigators to ask the parents concerned what they think about what is going on, but little systematic or controlled research exists with respect to these parental perceptions. What do parents really think about this approach? Do they feel more successful in handling their children and dealing with new problems as a consequence of the program? Do parents have similar views to the professionals with respect to the treatment, its aims, and its results? How well do parents really understand and feel able to implement the techniques suggested?

An opportunity to make a preliminary investigation of these and related issues arose in a follow-up study of a University of London Institute of Psychiatry (Maudsley Hospital) home-based study, in which parents of autistic children were enlisted as cotherapists (Holmes, Hemsley, Rickett, & Likierman, 1982). Some 16 autistic boys and their families, together with a matched control group, took part in this 18-month project. In general, parents viewed the treatment more favorably than a comparison group of parents receiving more usual forms of treatment. Most had an accurate impression of the treatment, although approximately half of them found the suggested method difficult to use. Most of the parents in the experimental group welcomed the visits by psychologists to their homes, did not find them intrusive, and, in many instances, struck up positive relationships with the psychologists concerned.

In retrospect, while encouraged by the general success of the study —a testimony to the care with which the project had been designed and carried out—Holmes *et al.* (1982) felt that parents should have been taught general coping strategies rather than techniques for dealing with individual problems. This might have helped them feel more able to manage new problems as they arose. It also became increasingly apparent as the data accumulated that, to maintain gains made during treatment, some form of follow-up or booster sessions would be advisable.

Numerous programs for autistic children within the school system have been established, but few give attention to the school setting as an ecological totality in which social behavior as well as material reinforcers need to be prominently featured. According to Gaylord-Ross and Pitts-Conway (1983), social behavior is the key to the future ability of autistic children to succeed in more normalized school settings. In this context, they point to three potential impediments to the successful integration of autistic students into the regular high school. First, there is the large developmental–intellectual disparity that exists between these students and their nonhandicapped peers. Second, because of their very visible deviant behaviors, secondary-level autistic students could become targets for exclusion and abuse by nonhandicapped students. Third, there is the presumed threat of disorderly behavior by the autistic students themselves.

Gaylord-Ross and Pitts-Conway suggest that these obstacles can be overcome by systematic efforts to promote social interaction, and that this can be accomplished with a minimum of specialized resources. Most current projects still focus on the preschool children of at least middle-class parents in university settings who have more than their share of financial and personal resources. The more broad-based technology that is gradually being developed for increasing rates of social interactions in a diversity of settings is usually disregarded.

The program described in detail by Gaylord-Ross and Pitts-Conway (1983) is an outstanding example of an integrated secondary school "autistic program" that takes into account the aforementioned considerations. The program, part of the regular activities of San Rafael High School in Marin County, California, has a number of components. An operant instructional methodology is used to structure the content of learning into a discriminative S-R framework. For students with limited stimulus control, a continuous reinforcement schedule using primary, edible reinforcers is used. As students display more appropriate and regulated behavior, they move to a token reinforcement system utilizing such activities as listening to records or playing table games as backup reinforcers. As the students progress, verbal praise becomes an increasingly larger part of the reinforcement schedule used to structure the learning activities. Most important, instruction occurs in multiple settings, such as the gymnasium and pool, various school functions, and the school cafeteria. To generalize settings yet further, students are trained to visit local stores and restaurants and to engage in a variety of near and distant off-campus activities. On- and off-campus vocational training is provided for those who can benefit from this experience.

Gaylord-Ross and Pitts-Conway expect a lot from their teachers, and they offer a formidable list of characteristics that the ideal teacher should possess. First and foremost, special education teachers must view themselves as integral parts of the school faculty; they must become active in the community in order to increase awareness of the presence of both the program and their pupils; they must engage in active relationships with parents in order to gain and maintain support; in school, they must approach teachers of normal children who have classes that could mainstream their autistic charges.

Gaylord-Ross and Pitts-Conway make a final, telling point with respect to the very different preschool and high school worlds with which autistic children seeking integration might have to contend. The preschool world is generally controlled and influenced by adults. The teenage culture, at least in the great American society, is separate from the mainstream culture, and it possesses a style of its own. When discussing integration into the "mainstream," it is important, therefore, not only to examine the types of intervention that facilitate socialization, but also the characteristics of the subculture in which this integration is expected to occur.

On a less ambitious scale, several investigators have examined specific classroom parameters as they pertain to autistic children. For example, Egel, Richman, and Koegel (1981) have explored the possibilities of utilizing nonhandicapped peers in the classroom as role models for appropriate behavior. Within the context of a multiple-baseline design, four autistic children were trained to work on five discrimination tasks that their teachers had reported were posing difficulties for them. Throughout the baseline condition, all four children manifested very low levels of correct responding on five tasks. In the subsequent treatment condition, during which normal peers modeled the correct responses, the autistic children's rates of correct responding increased dramatically. In each case, peer modeling produced a rapid achievement of the acquisition criterion, which was maintained even after the peer models were removed. For whatever reasons, the data suggest that autistic children, at least those with moderate impairments such as those who were the subjects of the reported investigation, can benefit from the opportunity to observe normal peers in the classroom setting. But, as Egel *et al.* (1981) wisely caution, it may be that the ability to learn from observation alone is not sufficient to account for successful classroom integration. Other factors, such as language ability, a child's effects on normal peers, the child's overall functioning, and the level of the classroom teacher's sophistication in the use of behavioral techniques may all be important areas for future research.

A constant problem when working with autistic children in any structured setting, particularly the classroom, is that of motivation. According to Egel (1981), autistic children make significantly more and faster responses when the reinforcements are varied. Because most studies have only a laboratory setting, Egel conducted a controlled-reversal investigation of the differential effects of constant versus varied reinforcers on the behavior of autistic children within the classroom. Declining trends in both correct responding and on-task behavior occurred when the reinforcers were consistently presented. Varying the reinforcers produced statistically significant improved and more stable levels of responding. The simple edible reinforcers used in this study are readily amenable to satiation, and this restricts the complexity and range of possible investigations. Different kinds of reinforcers, perhaps less amenable to satiation, might be more appropriate for the follow-up research that is needed. Nevertheless, this study is of importance because it provides further documentation of the special need to provide classroom variation when working with autistic children.

Another important variable is the setting in which the intervention is carried out. Typically, treatment carried out with severely disabled children fails to generalize to other environments when the training has not been carried out in a variety of settings in the first instance. The identification of those variables responsible for generalization of treatment gains to other environments within the home and school is essential for meaningful programming. Handleman and Harris (1983b) report a study of training in one classroom as opposed to a variety of instructional settings. Five autistic boys were taught answers to common questions, either in their own classrooms or in two different rooms. All five youngsters were then tested on six sets of five questions, first in the two classrooms and then at the day care center. While the responses taught in school did not generalize automatically to the day care center, four of the five boys involved in the study demonstrated encouragingly high rates of responding in the various settings. For the most part, generalization was clearly greater when the training occurred in more than one classroom.

Finally, attention is drawn to a related study by the same authors, comparing individual and couplet instruction with autistic children (Handleman & Harris, 1983a). If couplet training could be demonstrated to be as effective as one-to-one instruction, it would have obvious advantages. Handleman and Harris worked with only four children, making it difficult to form any clear impression from their limited data. Couplet training seemed to have disruptive effects for two of their four children and clear benefits for the others. Handleman and Harris raise the possibility that, for certain children, couplet teaching needs to be preceded by one-to-one training. What seems to be of primary importance, therefore, is not the superiority of couplet or individual training, but the circumstances surrounding this superiority and the degree of readiness of a given child for one form of instruction over another. The worn cliché that further research is needed would seem as apposite in regard to this particular problem as it is to the field of autism at large.

HYPERACTIVITY: BEHAVIORAL APPROACHES

Hyperactivity (HA) is considered by many to be the most prevalent of the childhood behavior disorders, and much has been written about its recognition, etiology, and correction. Despite this flurry of activity, the area remains characterized by heterogeneity rather than consensus, as much this year as in the past. One of the generalities that seems reasonably well established, however, is that as far as treatment is concerned, pharmacotherapy is rarely sufficient in itself, while necessary upon occasion (Whalen, 1983). Recognition of this impasse may, in part, account for the current resurgence of interest in the design and evaluation of behavioral and cognitive interventions, either as adjuncts to or as replacements for medication. Another promising trend noted by Whalen in her review of HA is the identification of subgroups that are more or less homogeneous with respect to certain core characteristics and therefore possibly more likely to respond consistently to specific treatment modalities.

There is a general movement in behavior therapy toward an ecological perspective, and this has now reached the domain of child behavior therapy. Inevitably, this trend is just beginning to percolate through to the HA literature. The first edition of Ross and Ross's (1976) text was somewhat ahead of its time in this respect. The second edition (Ross & Ross, 1982), updated and expanded, is once again perhaps the most important single contribution to the field in recent years; it is one of the few works to examine HA in comprehensive fashion—and within a behavioral context, to boot. Like Whalen, Ross and Ross (1982) welcome the fundamental and long overdue shift from the conceptualization of HA as primarily a medical problem to HA as a multifaceted behavioral disorder. However, as they point out, the accurate matching of intervention and problem constellations rests upon a multifactorial research program that has yet to be carried out.

By the time most HA children reach the referral stage, the problem has become so complicated and exacerbated by a variety of social and nonsocial factors that it can only be meaningfully approached within the framework of the entire social organization of the child. Consequently, at this time, HA cannot be easily modified by any one therapeutic approach, and Ross and Ross (1982) recommend multiple intervention strategies. To make their point, Ross and Ross cite a multidimensional 3-year study by Satterfield, Satterfield, and Cantwell (1981). Children were accepted for a multimodality treatment program individually tailored to each child and family, with the explicit stipulation that the parents concerned agree to becoming actively involved in the treatment process. Children who remained in the program for 3 years fared well in terms of both HA behavior and academic progress. Those who participated for only 1 to 2 years did not do as well.

Contrary to popular and even occasional professional belief, a child does not "grow out" of HA without adequate intervention. As Hechtman and Weiss (1983) report in their outcome review, the social, emotional, and impulse problems persist into young adulthood and beyond for the majority of these children. While few HA children become grossly disturbed or chronic legal offenders, the majority continue as young adults to exhibit various symptoms related to the HA syndrome. The problem then becomes one of identifying those children destined to have the poorest outcome. In this respect, the multifaceted approach advocated by Ross and Ross (1982) seems promising.

Whalen's (1982) review of HA and the newly titled "attention deficit disorder" (ADD) is thorough and informative. For the American Psychiatric Association, the problem of definition is resolved by the recognition of two forms of ADD—with and without hyperactivity—in DSM-III (American Psychiatric Association, 1980). But, as Whalen notes, DSM-III is still to be tested, and there is as yet limited evidence with respect to its utility.

Barkley (1982) has probably thought more about the problems of definition and classification in HA than any individual to date. In logical sequence, he examines the various attempts to develop definitional criteria to date and finds them all wanting in one aspect or another. One might presume that researchers working in the area are the "best bet" for coming up with an adequate operational definition. Unfortunately, when Barkley and an associate reviewed a cross-section of scientific papers dealing with HA—some 210 studies representing much of the research over the past two decades—they were disappointed. More than 64% used nothing more than the opinions of the investigators to define HA. Generally, no criterion whatsoever was used in making these decisions, or at least none was reported. If these 210 studies are representative of research in this area, and there is every reason to think that they are, then it is little wonder that conflicting findings across studies occur, or that it is sometimes concluded that HA as a distinct disorder of childhood does not exist (e.g., Carey & McDevitt, 1980).

If the scientists are of little help, can clinicians be expected to do any better? Barkley (1982) poses this question, reviews the pertinent literature, and comes to the conclusion that the answer is negative. Then, asks Barkley, if empirical scientists do not seem to know which children should be identified as HA and if clinicians do not fare much better, is it not possible that theorists who have written more speculatively about the nature of HA might have come up with some valid operational criteria? To shed light on this possibility, Barkley once again reviews the pertinent literature; once again, his findings are not very encouraging. According to Barkley, no single definition to date "provides even a modicum of operationally defined diagnostic parameters that could aid a clinician or scientist in trying to decide whether or not a child is hyperactive (1982, p. 149). As Barkley plaintively comments, how one could expect to render a credible, reliable, and potentially useful diagnosis based on either current research or clinical practice is difficult to comprehend.

As a prerequisite to the formulation of a much-needed set of guidelines, Barkley has established the following working definition of HA:

> Hyperactivity, or attention deficit disorder, is a significant deficiency in age-appropriate attention, impulse control, and rule governed behavior (compliance, self-control and problem solving) that arises by infancy or early childhood, is significantly pervasive in nature, and is not the direct result of general intellectual retardation, severe language delay or emotional disturbance, or gross sensory or motor impairment. (1982, p. 153)

Fortified by this definition, Barkley offers the following diagnostic criteria for HA or ADD:

1) Parental/teacher complaints of inattention, impulsivity, restlessness and poor compliance and self-control;
2) A score on a standardized rating scale of hyperactive behavior of at least two standard deviations above the mean for normal children;
3) Reported age of onset of problematic behavior of 5 years 11 months or earlier;
4) Duration of symptoms of at least 12 months;
5) Pervasiveness of symptoms across at least 50% of the situations on the

Home Situations Questionnaire (For a description and discussion of the Home Situations Questionnaire (HSQ) see Barkley, 1981);
6) An I.Q. estimate of at least seventy;
7) Exclusion of autism, psychosis, severe language delay, blindness, deafness or gross neurological disease. (1982, p. 134f)

Justification is provided by Barkley (1982) for each diagnostic criterion. Evidence is presented to show that HA is quite distinct from learning disabilities, and most likely distinct from aggression or other conduct problems. But as Barkley points out, these three types of disorders are not necessarily mutually exclusive. A determination of their precise interrelationships must await further research. In the interim, Barkley's guidelines establish a set of objective and data-based criteria for research and clinical intervention.

The changing role of the educator and the expanding boundaries of the school's responsibilities are still matters of dispute, with marked polarization between those who enthusiastically press for expansion of the school's role and those who angrily denounce such trends. This polarization is particularly acute with respect to the education of the HA child. Drug intervention, teachers usurping the physician's role by dispensing stimulant medication on their own initiative, the possibility of school-induced HA, the alternative of changing the school to fit the child rather than vice versa, and more are discussed in detail by Ross and Ross (1982).

The gains maintained during the investigator-present stage of a study frequently diminish sharply once the investigator leaves the classroom and the teacher is on his or her own. The tendency then is to attribute the sharp decrease in target behavior performance either to inadequacies in the program per se or to the child's becoming habituated to the reinforcers. But as Ross and Ross (1982) suggest, the evidence points to the far more likely explanation that the failure to maintain initial gains simply reflects the fact that the teacher has discontinued the program out of lack of interest. Disappointing long-term data then become little more than measures of a back-to-baseline condition.

Ross and Ross (1982) raise another telling point with respect to the implementation of Public Law 94-142, a law that they aptly describe as "long on idealism and short on practicality." The goal of regular class placement is commendable, but difficult to implement without concrete advice about the practical mechanics of classroom integration. It is here that behavior therapists could come into their own if only they could learn to apply the knowledge and technology that are currently available. In this respect, the demonstration by Whalen and Henker (1980) that varying certain ecological classroom parameters is at least as effective as medication in modifying some HA behaviors is impressive.

This, of course, is not to imply that ecology is the total solution. Functional relationships between the ecology of the classroom and sociobehavioral outcome are but one facet of the HA network. There is more to the problems of most HA or ADD children than behavioral abnormalities; a variety of sociobehavioral, psychological, and educational components must be considered (Keogh & Barkett, 1980).

The attitudes toward HA of those adults who are meaningfully involved in the care of these young people is of obvious importance. What is surprising is how little relevant research has been carried out. When Stevens and Gardner (1983) made a Q-sort analysis of the attitudes of elementary school teachers toward HA children, they arrived at three distinct conceptual frameworks. There were those teachers who conceived of HA as stemming from indulgent and overpermissive parenting; there were those who stressed a biological basis; and there were those who placed greater faith in some form of learning excess or deficiency. As Stevens and Gardner point out, these distinctions are of more than academic concern. The beliefs that a teacher holds about HA are likely to determine the intervention strategy that he or she will recommend. Those with a biological orientation may be more likely to refer their charges to a physician, whereas a parent conference or referral to a mental health professional may be the strategy of choice for others.

Mash and Johnston (1983a) compared perceptions with respect to child behavior, self-esteem, and mothers' reported stress in parents of younger and older HA and normal children. The complexity of their findings makes clear that there is no simple answer; multidimensional assessments, tapping a wide range of child problems and parental views, are more likely to yield meaningful data than is any single measure. This study, it might be noted, is part of an ongoing series of investigations into the nature of parent–child interactions in HA children (Mash & Johnston, 1982, 1983b, 1983c).

On balance, judicially applied behavioral intervention, perhaps in combination with other procedures, seems to be the treatment of choice for HA children at this time. The most common alternatives to behavioral treatment are drug and diet therapies. The shortcomings of drug therapies used alone have been pointed out repeatedly in this series, and most recent reviewers have come to a similar conclusion. Apart from adverse side effects, the short-term gains achieved with drugs do not last, and, as Barkley (1981) notes, appropriately directed behavioral interventions are more likely to produce and sustain academic gains than is the use of drugs alone.

As far as diet therapy is concerned, bringing about dietary changes within a family milieu requires heroic endeavors and is only to be advocated when the evidence in favor of such a strategy is compelling. Unfortunately, although some successes have been reported, recent literature reviews are less than encouraging. Only a small percentage of HA children undergoing diet therapy improve (Brunner, Vorhees, & Butcher, 1981). At one time or another, numerous foods and food additives have been put on trial for their allegedly harmful behavioral and cognitive effects. For example, Prinz, Roberts, and Hantman (1980) generate data to suggest that excessive sugar consumption is the culprit with respect to the deviant behavior of certain HA children. But this study is completely correlational, and there is no reason to infer causality from their findings. It is probably more appropriate at this stage to conclude, with Friman and Christophersen (1983) that unless a child clearly responds adversely to specific foods or food additives, the effort necessary for diet therapy is probably better invested in behavior therapy.

BEHAVIOR MODIFICATION AND THE SCHOOL SYSTEM

Had this section been written a decade earlier, the title would have been "Behavior Modification in the School" or some simple variation thereof. It is no accident that the section heading for the 1980s includes the word "system." Ten years ago, most school behavior modification consisted either of traditional one-to-one procedures carried out in the classroom or psychologist's office, or some form of straightforward classroom or school-wide token economy.

Traditionalists still review this far from extinct literature. For example, Sharpley and Sharpley (1981) focus on the controversy surrounding contingent versus noncontingent classroom rewards and manage to incorporate their entire review into four pages. Whether this reflects implicit recognition of the passé nature of this type of investigation, consummate reviewing skill, or, more simply, lack of thoroughness is of little consequence.

A review by Albion (1983) of 26 self-control investigations carried out in classroom settings is more impressive. The procedures reviewed include self-instruction, self-determination of contingencies, self-evaluation, self-setting of goals, and the self-determination and administration of external reinforcement. The studies are carefully compared and described in terms of subjects and settings, dependent and independent variables, measurement systems, and design.

Albion's review raises a number of interesting research questions —for example, whether self-control frees the teacher to work with more dependent children, or whether the monitoring of such a self-directed system requires even more of the teacher's time than conventional classroom management. What is totally overlooked, and this is important in view of current developments in child behavior therapy, is the relationship of these procedures to the classroom and the school as a system. Similarly, Ruggles and LeBlanc (1982) make a sophisticated appraisal of behavior analysis procedures in the classroom and come up with a number of forward-looking suggestions for developing a behavioral technology of how to teach. But once again, the question of how this fits into the school as a system—one of the many systems with which children and adults have to contend—is overlooked.

To return to this section's introduction, "Behavior Modification and the School System" would seem to be a more appropriate heading for the 1980s than "Behavior Modification in the School." As behavioral strategies become increasingly sophisticated, it becomes virtually impossible to think in terms of one-to-one direct S-R relationships. A recent study by Mayer, Butterworth, Nafpaktitis, and Sulzer-Azaroff (1983) is a case in point, even though the word "system" is never used in their report. The problem facing Mayer et al. was one of vandalism. It was argued that a positive environment could displace previous events that might have set the occasion for vandalism, and that it was possible to design and implement an appropriate training and consultation package geared toward this end. Eighteen elementary and junior high schools were involved in a 3-year study. Following an appropriate baseline period, a delayed-treatment design was utilized. During treatment, teams of school personnel attended training workshops in the use of specified behavioral strategies for reducing vandalism and disruption in the school. Programs were implemented on a school-wide basis. Vandalism costs decreased significantly more in the treatment schools than in the controls. Off-task behavior (e.g., hitting, yelling, throwing objects, not doing assigned work) evidenced an equally dramatic decrease.

While the leads for future research are important (e.g., unraveling the relative impacts of the various ingredients in the intervention package), it is the implicit recognition by Mayer et al. (1983) of the need to think in terms of total school climate rather than discrete variables that is of primary significance here.

This trend toward systemic thinking is beginning to percolate through the behavior therapy literature. Its full effect probably has to await the emergence of a behaviorally compatible, clearly articulated systems theory. In the meantime working within a behavioral perspective, investigators are beginning to incorporate a systems framework into their thinking. For example, Piersel and Gutkin (1983) discuss the various forms of resistance on the part of school personnel encountered by consulting school psychologists. To cope with this phenomenon, they advocate a cognitive–behavioral strategy that makes use of standard intervention techniques. In so doing, they stress the need to work at both systems and individual levels, and this is all to the good. But unfortunately, they fail to specify precisely how intervention at the systems level is to be incorporated into or combined with a behavioral framework, and, except for a few vague generalities, the reader is left in the dark.

Similarly, Hannafin and Witt (1983) draw attention to the need for school psychologists to intervene at both individual and systems levels if meaningful change is to be effected. For these authors, "systems-level intervention" implies a consideration of direct and in-service needs within a school setting, together with the influence of the school system in contributing to both problems and solutions. They stress the need to acquire a basic understanding of the structure and mechanics of systems; however, once again, this is as far as they go, and we are not told precisely how this is to be accomplished or exactly what it means.

Fine and Holt (1983) have carried this process a step further in their examination of traditional models used by school-based professionals and their limitations. For example, a child's aggressive behavior might be viewed psychodynamically, as a reflection of poor impulse control coupled with hostility towards the female teacher. From a behavioral stance, the child's behavior could be understood as being caused and maintained by reinforcing consequent events. And from a phenomenological position, a child might be thought of as having a poor self-concept, perceiving others as threatening, and believing that an aggressive response is required for self-protection. The nature of the intervention would then depend upon the perspective of the therapist. For example, the behavior therapist might think in terms of home contingencies and parent training. The psychodynamic therapist might look to underlying parent–child issues, and the phenomenologist might concentrate on the building of self-esteem and the positive experiencing of success.

As Fine and Holt (1983) point out, each of these positions could be regarded as logical and internally consistent within the therapist's frame of reference. But from a systems viewpoint, each would miss understanding the child's behavior in the most potentially helpful way—that is, as a member of two key systems, home and school. It is necessary to think in terms of interacting systems that reciprocally influence each other according to a complex pattern. Presumably, the goal of a systemic approach then becomes that of helping members of the respective systems—in this instance, home and school—to disengage themselves emotionally so that they can collaborate constructively on behalf of the child. Once again, precise details about how this is to be accomplished are not forthcoming. Indeed, as Fine and Holt concede, there is an absence of data-based research pertaining either to the model itself or to its efficacy. In sum, little is known as yet about the application of systems approaches within the school or about their relationships to child behavior therapy.

In the meantime, behavior therapists are thinking more and more in terms of procedures for dealing with complex situations that go beyond the traditional one-to-one intervention framework. For example, there are the problems involved in the transition from one stage of the school program to another. For many children, entering a new school system is a critical developmental transition. To meet this problem, Sloan, Jason, and Bogat (in press) have developed a program for students ranging in age from 6 to 14 years who are faced with the problem of learning to cope with a new school. Their study attempted to determine which components of a school orientation program would be most helpful in facilitating the adjustment of new students to a temporarily alien setting: the transmission of basic school information, or a peer-led supportive discussion group. Supportive discussion turned out to be more effective in significantly reducing anxiety than information alone.

Another potentially anxiety-provoking time is the period between graduation from high school and the "unknown" that looms ahead. This is a period of great potential stress. Adolescents are confronted with the problems of possible separation from parents, siblings, and close friends; they are forced into greater autonomy in making important decisions; and they have to deal with a variety of new situations and challenges. As long ago as 1962, Cummings and Cummings suggested the use of graded crisis experience exercises to train students in coping strategies, which they might then be able to apply in real-life situations. Caplan (1965) also advocated such training programs to foster acquisition of protective responses by introducing limited stress under control conditions.

Jason and Burrows (1983) review several studies that have attempted to develop specific interventions for particular transitions at various stages in a child's life. Most involve some form of stress inoculation coupled with one or more problem-solving strategies. While varying degrees of success have been reported, none has been geared toward skills of general rather than specific applicability. To remedy this deficit, Jason and Burrows developed a graded experience preventive program for adolescents preparing to graduate from high school. Three types of coping strategies were compared: relaxation, cognitive restructuring, and problem solving. Participants who completed the 6-week program showed significantly higher scores on tests of cognitive restructuring, self-efficacy, and rational beliefs than did the control subjects. Many of these improvements were still in evidence at a 1-year follow-up (see also Bogat, Jones, & Jason, 1980).

Preventive transition training could well be effective in increasing feelings of self-efficacy and strengthening the necessary coping mechanisms needed for entering into adult life. But little is known about the long-term efficacy of these programs or the relative contributions of the various components (in the study by Jason and Burrows, for example, role playing, group discussion, and instruction were all included in the same intervention program), and it is not known how generally applicable any specific program might be.

Working with an entire school population does not in itself guarantee a systemic approach. For example, Holland and McLaughlin (1982) successfully demonstrated the utilization of response cost and public posting as a group contingency procedure in reducing the number of inappropriate behaviors of an entire elementary school population. This is traditional, nonsystemic, large-scale behavior therapy, and it is important not to confuse the two.

The expanding role of the school psychologist brings with it new dilemmas. In 1977, when behavior modification was still primarily individually based, Gast and Nelson (1977) noted the legal and ethnical problems that could arise when school psychologists used time out in special education settings. In 1984, with the development of more sophisticated procedures, public concerns about the application of behavior modification practices in school settings are voiced even more strongly. Because therapeutic processes and outcomes are clearly specifiable, behavior therapists are more accountable than most. The prevailing climate of advocacy for the constitutional rights of all individuals serves to precipitate the gathering legal storm. The stage is being set for an increase in judicial proceedings against the use of behavior modification in educational settings. As Wherry (1983) cautions, school psychologists would do well to consider the legal as well as the ethical implications of what they practice. Behavior therapists seeking to intervene at a systems level involving both school and community invite a host of subtle new issues. For example, a system transcends the individual, and this could raise problems of pressuring and responsibility for individuals other than oneself as the primary target.

BEHAVIOR MODIFICATION IN THE EDUCATION OF
THE ATYPICAL CHILD

There is a strong movement, rapidly becoming the consensus in service delivery, to place all severely handicapped children in public schools together with similar-age nonhandicapped peers. This creates a multitude of new and old problems; by virtue of their specialized training, it is behavior therapists who are best equipped to resolve these problems as they arise. Can educators and psychologists design interventions geared toward the needs of these children within the public school system? What are the circumstances surrounding acceptance or rejection of handicapped children by their peers, and what can be done about them? Is it really true that no one is ineducable if only the right methods can be found? Is it possible that, under certain circumstances, some handicapped children would fare better if taught outside the regular educational system? These are the challenges for educators in general and for behavior therapists in particular, since it is they who are committed to the determination of a data base as the necessary prelude to behavior change.

The passing of the Education of All Handicapped Children Act in 1975 by the U.S. Congress brings with it a set of obligations on the part of all states in this country to meet the needs of these children and, on the part of all professionals, particularly behavior therapists, to develop appropriate strategies for implementation. The definition of handicapped children includes the mentally retarded, the learning-disabled, the emotionally disturbed, and the physically handicapped. The "special education and related services" referred to specifically in the Act include classroom instruction, home instruction, physical education, transport, psychological services, physical services, counseling, medical services, and more.

However, as with many sweeping innovations, it is easier to say than to do. Mainstreaming—the placement of a child in the least restrictive setting compatible with the individual's needs—is a case in point. It cannot always be assumed, whatever our emotional feelings in this respect, that placing or not placing the handicapped child in the mainstream is necessarily advantageous. If it is bad to deny handicapped children their rights to education, if placement in an all-handicapped setting stigmatizes them unfairly, then they might conceivably be disadvantaged in other ways by premature or ill-planned integration into settings in which appropriate facilities are not available or the environment is hostile in one way or another.

The task of the behavior therapist becomes one of determining the complexities of the many parameters involved, assisting in the decisions that must be made, and developing appropriate procedures for facilitating the transfer to the mainstream setting if this is the strategy of choice. The heart of the 1975 Act rests upon more than the involvement of educational and clinical personnel in establishing appropriate plans for the handicapped child. There is also the right of parents to disagree with the conclusions of the evaluation, the proposed placement, or any action affecting the child's entitlement to special education. Understandably, few parents are aware of this provision, and even fewer parents take advantage of the detailed procedures established by the Act for formal consideration of these disagreements (Herr, Arons, & Wallace, 1983).

Fortunately or otherwise, the passing of laws is rarely contingent upon the acquisition of data; the fact that, regardless of severity of handicap, all children now have a legal right to attend appropriate educational programs in neighborhood public schools is very much a case in point. This may not be altogether bad if it forces educators and psychologists to attend to their business, which, in this case, is the resolution of the questions raised above. Unfortunately, while profes sionals are expected to take on increasingly complex consultant or advocate roles involving many multidisciplinary decisions, there is no general system or set of clear guidelines to show them how to go about this task (Voeltz, Evans, Derer, & Hanashiro, 1983).

Existing criteria for goal selection are usually applicable more to a skill or behavior in isolation than to the child's total response repertoire within a more general environmental context. For example, Heads (1978) offers a five-point checklist against which to evaluate behaviors as potential goals, but the checklist does not aid in the selection of one goal over another of equivalent concern. In the absence of any comprehensive system for selecting and evaluating priorities, parents, teachers, consultants, and others are forced to rely on idiosyncratic perceptions of the advantages and disadvantages of targeting particular behaviors.

Recognizing this deficit, Voeltz *et al.* (1983) offer a heuristic decision model for the identification of priority goals, objectives, and appropriate interventions on behalf of children with severe skill deficits and multiple excess behaviors. Their model presents a logical, sequential guide for making decisions as to when it is appropriate to include the modification of an excess behavior, rather than the acquisition of a new skill, as a priority goal. It takes into account differences in severity of behavior, potential child outcomes, recommendations, and procedures to implement, together with the relevant professional, legal, and ethical criteria that might apply to the selection process.

Most important, Voeltz *et al.*'s model is not intended as a prescriptive device for making specific decisions. Rather, its primary purposes are to clarify and organize the procedures that clinicians, teachers, and other service providers currently use in an intuitive rather than systematic fashion. While awaiting the necessary research that the authors hope their model will generate, clinicians will still need to exercise their best professional judgments in making decision with respect to any particular situation. But in so doing, with this model they now have a procedure for clarifying and systematizing their thinking and providing a minimal basis for making the necessary judgments. How useful this model is either in terms of practice or the generation of data is a matter that only the future can decide.

In making special education classification and placement decisions, traditional measures such as IQ and academic achievement are still weighed most heavily. Far less attention is focused upon behavioral assets in making mainstream program decisions. Gresham (1983) argues persuasively for the inclusion of social skills and other behavioral measures in the decision-making process.

One way to measure the success of a special education program is by the extent to which the academic and behavioral improvements brought about in the special classroom transfer to regular classroom settings. According to Rhode, Morgan, and Young (1983), when handicapped students are removed from their regular classrooms for treatment in special educational settings, they exhibit marked academic and behavioral improvements in this special education environment. But, unfortunately, these improvements are not maintained upon return to the regular classroom.

Among the many ways of bringing about the generalization and maintenance of treatment gains, the use of self-management training has received particular attention. Regrettably, despite clinical acceptance of this procedure, studies of self-management training with behaviorally handicapped children in naturalistic settings are lacking. Rhode et al. (1983) have carried out one of the few controlled studies of self-evaluation procedures with behaviorally handicapped elementary school students. Unlike most previous investigations, their study utilized procedures that were designed to promote generalization and maintenance of treatment gains and were deliberately programmed for use in the regular classroom. Once acceptable levels of appropriate behaviors were maintained with only minimal external reinforcement, and the students had been trained to evaluate their own work and behavior accurately, generalization and maintenance of behavior gains were sought by introducing a reduced form of the self-evaluation procedures in the students' regular classrooms. A multiple-baseline design across pairs of subjects was used to examine the behavior of the individual students. The students transferred and maintained high levels of appropriate behavior in their regular classrooms once self-evaluation procedures were extended into these settings.

While the small sample size, six students, limits the generalizability of Rhode *et al.*'s (1983) conclusions, the findings are encouraging. Handicapped students as young as 6 years old are able to evaluate themselves in a meaningful fashion. It is of interest that the student whose behavior throughout the study was the least satisfactory was also the student whose prior history and level of performance at the onset of the study were the most deviant. As Rhode *et al.* note, this points to the need for more careful examination of self-evaluation in terms of severity of the presenting behavior problem.

How the handicapped child fares in the regular classroom is also dependent upon the attitudes of the teachers and children with whom he or she comes in contact. As Martin (1974) observes, unless educators develop strategies for creating attitudes of acceptance within the regular classroom, "we will be painfully naive, and I fear we will subject many children to a painful and frustrating educational experience in the name of progress" (cited by Newman & Simpson, 1983, p. 103). To address this concern, Newman and Simpson (1983) designed a study to investigate the effects of providing children in regular classrooms information about and experiences with severely emotionally disturbed pupils. A direct observation procedure was employed to compare the social-interactional effects of providing nonhandicapped pupils information alone or information and experiences designed to create more favorable impressions toward handicapped individuals. The regular-class students consisted of approximately 34 normal children at each grade level, first through sixth. The handicapped population consisted of 10 severely emotionally disturbed males from two self-contained classrooms in the same school. Each class was composed of five pupils grouped according to age. One class was designed for pupils between the ages of 6 and 10, and the other for pupils aged 12 to 18. The handicapped pupils had all been diagnosed as schizophrenic, autistic, or autistic-like prior to the age of 3 by mental health professionals.

Unfortunately, administrative policy prevented the use of control groups or the gathering of pretreatment interaction data, and this limits the conclusions that can be drawn from the Newman and Simpson (1983) study. Nevertheless, their data serve to clarify the manner in which curricula and experiences can be used to create more favorable impressions among regular-class students toward their handicapped peers. Although tentative, their findings suggest that subjects provided information alone responded most positively to the seriously disturbed. In addition, younger students and females appeared to respond more favorably to the handicapped population than older students or males.

A factor analysis by Voeltz (1980) of attitude survey responses from 2,392 children revealed four underlying attitudes toward handicapped peers: "social-contact willingness" (a willingness to interact socially with children who might be referred to by such labels as "handicapped," "mentally retarded," or "special education students"); "deviance consequation" (disagreement with statements that imply stereotyping or exclusion from school and community on the basis of specific characteristics or specific types of behaviors); and two "actual contact" dimensions (related to actual contact with children labeled "mentally retarded" or with children in wheelchairs, respectively). Upper-elementary-age children, girls, and children in schools with most contact with severely handicapped peers expressed the most accepting attitudes.

Later, Voeltz (1982) studied the effects of intensive contacts between severely handicapped children and regular-education children in grades 4 through 6 who participated jointly in various structured social interaction learning situations. Results over two semesters revealed significantly higher acceptance of individual differences on three of the above-described attitudinal dimensions by children in the experimental school ($n = 241$), as compared with children from schools where no severely handicapped children were enrolled ($n = 288$) and schools with severely handicapped children enrolled, but without the interaction program ($n = 288$). These findings provide additional support for the use of structured social interactions between regular-education children and their severely handicapped peers as a means of facilitating social acceptance of handicapped children in integrated school settings.

Lest it be thought that the thrust is exclusively toward the development of strategies for the integration of handicapped children into the mainstream, it is appropriate at this point to draw attention to several recent studies of significance whose focus is the handicapped child within the special classroom. For example, noting that teacher approval in special classrooms tends to be low, Gross and Ekstrand (1983) developed a technique for increasing the rates of praise by teachers working within a classroom for children with handicaps such as mental retardation, blindness, deafness, or cerebral palsy. To investigate the effects of public posting of feedback on praising behavior, an A-B-A-B-C-A design was employed. Following baseline, the daily rate of teacher praise was posted on a graph in the classroom. To reduce the reactive effects of monitoring, observations of teacher behavior were made by use of random audiotape recordings.

To facilitate maintenance, public posting feedback was gradually faded. The procedure yielded an increase in teacher praise to a rate nearly twice that observed during baseline. Most important, this behavior was maintained for at least 2 months following termination of the experimental condition. As Gross and Ekstrand (1983) point out, the major contribution to the success of their strategy might have been the fact that, unlike many interventions, the experimental procedures were gradually rather than abruptly removed from the classroom.

Procedures that are effective with normal children cannot be assumed to be equally applicable to the special classroom without adequate demonstration that (appropriately modified if need be) this is indeed so. Nevertheless, as a working strategy, it would seem appropriate to begin with procedures that have been shown to be effective in the normal classroom rather than to start off from scratch, so to speak. The example of correspondence training and the relationship between what people say and what they do is very much a case in point. The assumption is that a correspondence exists between verbal and nonverbal behavior, and that it may be possible in clinical situations to control nonverbal behavior by modifying verbal behavior. As Whitman, Scibak, Butler, Richter, and Johnson (1982) point out, the appeal of this training procedure may be related to the ready accessibility of a person's verbal behavior to the trainer and to the fact that, with this training, nonverbal behavior may be readily maintained without any direct monitoring or reinforcing.

Most studies in correspondence training have used normal preschoolers with relatively well-developed language skills. Furthermore, most previous research investigations in this area are primarily analogue in nature. By contrast, Whitman et al. (1982) used low-IQ and mentally retarded students in situations that focused upon real classroom problems. Furthermore, unlike most previous correspondence training studies, this investigation attempted to establish whether treatment effects could be maintained over time, whether they could be generalized over situations, and whether experimental control could be transferred to the classroom teacher without a decrease in effectiveness.

The specific behaviors targeted for change included out-of-seat behavior, sitting posture, and on-task behavior. Three separate single-subject study designs were used, and all provided strong evidence that correspondence training could be effectively used with educationally handicapped children. Once again, such studies are suggestive rather than definitive, and point the way to the much-needed research that will almost certainly be carried out in the coming years. For example, the authors themselves draw attention to the need to investigate correspondence training with subjects who are deaf or who have other learning disabilities. Comparison studies also need to investigate the relative effects of correspondence training and traditional procedures involving the reinforcement of only nonverbal behavior. Finally, extensive process and component analyses are needed to sift out the key components involved in correspondence training.

A much-neglected variable in the education of the handicapped child is the total environment of the classroom—what Forness, Guthrie, and MacMillan (1982) refer to as the "ecology of the classroom." Investigators are beginning to explore the environment of the classroom and its effects on observable behavior. Understandably, most studies focus on teacher behavior or on the behavior of specific pupils. For Forness et al., it is the total environment of the classroom that is important. To this end, they have developed a Classroom Environment Scale, a 90-item forced-choice instrument that measures teachers' perceptions of the emphasis placed on each of nine classroom dimensions. Preliminary data suggest that different classroom environments generate recognizable patterns of behavior and that certain environmental dimensions may be more important than others in classes for the educable mentally retarded. (See also Forness et al., 1982, p. 275f.)

Organizational behavior management (OBM) is one of the liveliest areas in behavior therapy, and it should come as a surprise to no one that its strategies have now been extended to the special classroom. It is perhaps understandable that a low incidence of systematic instruction is often the rule rather than the exception in many classes for handicapped children. Teacher burnout, low motivation, and lack of adequate staff training have all been cited as factors leading to reduced productivity of teaching staff. As Day, Lindeman, Havelka, Tucker, and Hasson (1983) point out, regardless of the cause of this low productivity, there is a need to examine methods for improving educational programs, and it is here that OBM comes into its own. These authors describe, in unfortunately minimal detail, one special education system's attempt to probe its educational program through the direct application of the principles of OBM. As yet, the necessary objective data seem to be lacking, and, as the authors are well aware, it is by this criterion that the effectiveness of these changes must be investigated. In this respect, the work of Maher (1981, 1982) is exemplary. Maher is a pioneer in the development of sophisticated designs for evaluating special education services on a systematic basis, and it is appropriate to conclude on this encouraging note. All in all, it is in the area of special education that behavior therapists are beginning to make maximum use of their unique combination of professional and methodological skills.

CONCLUSIONS

Consistent with the trend in behavior therapy at large, child behavior therapy is moving apace away from the traditional one-to-one, simple, S-R focus of the 1970s into the more sophisticated, community- and systems-oriented, multidimensional framework of the 1980s. Most encouraging, this is being accomplished with due regard for the methodological rigor and need for data base that is still the bastion of behavior therapy (Kazdin, 1983).

The increase in sophistication is evident at all levels. There would now seem to be general consensus among behavioral clinicians and researchers alike that intervention is much more complicated and time-consuming than had originally been envisioned (see O'Leary & Carr, 1982). Intervention is no longer directed exclusively at changing the child's immediate response repertoire. Thinking is more in terms of systems and integration with a diversity of disciplines and objective data gleaned from different conceptual modalities. The range of issues and topics reviewed in the present chapter is a far cry from the domain of behavior therapy as it might have been characterized as recently as a decade ago. The flavor of contemporary child behavior therapy is well captured by the titles of such recent articles as "Intervention Strategies and Research with Socially Isolated Children: An Ecological-Systems Perspective" (Ladd & Keeney, 1983) or "Toward More Behavioral Early Intervention Programs: A Rationale" (Kirschenbaum, 1983).

These developments are not taking place in isolation. Knowledge is accruing at an ever-increasing rate, and techological advances are intimately bound up with societal and cultural forces that are frequently beyond our control (Talbott, 1983). With the passing of laws such as the 1975 Education of All Handicapped Children Act, the "rights" of children are no longer only an ethical concern; they are a matter of legal mandate. This creates a set of obligations and issues with which all behavior therapists would do well to familiarize themselves.

The ethical guidelines offered by various professional associations are all predicated upon the assumption that the law of the land is paramount (Sametz, McLoughlin, & Streib, 1983). Professional guidelines are subordinate to Supreme Court decisions, and it would be as well to be aware of this fact and its implications. When McLoughlin and Sametz (1983) systematically surveyed school psychologists to assess their knowledge and understanding of these new developments with respect to the legal rights of children, a deplorable lack of knowledge, coupled with much misinformation, was uncovered. There is a need for formal training in the intricacies of legal developments as they affect the practice of psychology, rather than reliance, as at present, upon fortuitous gleanings.

Despite steady advances, there is still a need for advocacy on behalf of children. Children are politically disenfranchised; they are economically disadvantaged; they have only a passive legal status; they are in a sense chattels of their biological families; and, due to their lack of experience, they are particularly vulnerable to abuse and exploitation by our adult-governed culture (Vardin & Brody, 1979). But at the same time, the interests of parents in protecting family autonomy from state interference and preserving of personal and cultural family values have to be balanced against the interests of the state in protecting the child, providing an adequate system of mental health care, and ensuring that the child becomes an autonomous individual with adequate rights and privileges (Herr et al., 1983). The extent to which children can be permitted to enter into the decision-making process in their lives and futures is still a matter for debate, and it is possible that behavioral researchers can shed data-based light on this complex issue, rather than contributing to the speculation and emotional biases that currently predominate. Gaylin (1982) makes a start in attempting to define the criteria by which general guidelines might be established to help in deciding when and under what circumstances children ought to be allowed to enter into important decision-making processes in their lives. Whether such guidelines are feasible and whether behavior therapists can make meaningful contributions by virtue of their special skills are matters for the future to decide. For the present, the steady but disciplined expansion chronicled in these pages is encouraging.

8

CLINICAL ISSUES AND STRATEGIES IN THE PRACTICE OF BEHAVIOR THERAPY

G. TERENCE WILSON

THE INFLUENCE OF BEHAVIOR THERAPY ON THE TRAINING OF THERAPISTS AND CLINICAL PRACTICE

In the parallel chapter to this in Volume 9 of this series, I summarized D. Smith's (1982) survey of the theoretical orientations of members and fellows of Divisions 12 and 17 of the American Psychological Association (APA). After eclecticism, by far the most frequently held position, a cognitive–behavioral approach appeared to be the most dominant single theoretical orientation. Related surveys of other groups of professionals indicate that D. Smith's was not an isolated finding. Tuma and Pratt's (1982) survey of clinical child psychologists showed that their two major orientations were behavioral and psychodynamic. A similar survey of pediatric psychologists indicated a stronger influence of behavior therapy: 59% indicated that behavioral psychology was their primary orientation, with 39% expressing a preference for psychodynamic therapy (Tuma & Cohen, 1981). And in a sample of practitioners from the National Health Register, a behavioral approach proved to be one of the three most common theoretical orientations (Tyron, 1983). In assessing the prevalence of a behavioral or cognitive–behavioral orientation among clinicians, O'Leary (1983) concluded,

> [W]ith children, a behavioral orientation seems to be a clearly dominant trend with approximately half of all child clinicians identifying with this orientation. With adults, no single theoretical orientation is ascribed to by

most professionals; eclecticism is the most popular identification and a
wide variety of orientations are mentioned. However, a behavioral orientation is clearly emerging as one of the top three ranked orientations. (p. 5)

In Volume 9, I noted that D. Smith's (1982) survey did not cover an
important development in clinical psychology—namely, the rapid
growth of professional schools offering degrees based on a practitioner
model of clinical training. (Given the recency of these programs, it is
unlikely that the other surveys mentioned above did justice to their
graduates' orientations, either.) There are at least two reasons for being
concerned about the impact of behavior therapy on practitioners graduated from the new schools of professional psychology.

The first is the sheer number of practitioners that these schools are
beginning to produce. In his overview of the practitioner-model programs in the United States, Caddy (1982) was able to conclude,

[T]here has been a veritable explosion in the development of [these]
programs over the past decade. Whereas in 1968 there were only four
practitioner-model psychology training programs, today there are over 30
with another seven or so in the final stages of development. . . . Cum-
ming's prediction that practitioner model programs soon will be producing 95 percent of the graduates in professional psychology . . . may
well be coming true. (p. 10)

The second reason is that it must be asked is how the changes inherent
in the new practitioner-model training programs will affect the theoretical orientations or professional activities of their graduates. For
example, although some variability exists, most of these schools de-
emphasize or completely eliminate research training. Can behavior
therapists be trained under such intellectual conditions?

I believe that the answer to this last question of the majority of
behavior therapists would be a resounding "no." Behavior therapy
bases itself largely, although by no means exclusively, on the principles
and procedures of experimental psychology (Wilson & Franks, 1982). It
self-consciously emphasizes links to basic and applied research to a
greater extent than any other psychotherapeutic approach. Within a
behavioral framework, Barlow (1980) has advocated the idea of the
"empirical clinician" in an attempt to close the much discussed gap
between research and practice in clinical psychology. At the heart of
this notion is the assumption that practitioners can conduct clinically
relevant research, provided that they acquire knowledge in single-case
experimental designs (Hayes, 1981). It is hard to imagine practitioners
developing these skills without explicit training in this type of research.
As a consequence, the practitioner model would seem to be incompatible with Barlow's (1980) concept of the empirical clinician. Even

those who take the view that it is neither necessary nor desirable for practitioners to engage in research (e.g., Agras, Kazdin, & Wilson, 1979; Wilson, 1982a) argue strongly for systematically exposing practitioners in training to applied research programs to ensure the needed interaction between the science of psychology and the practice of therapy.

In an attempt to obtain information on the views of graduates of practitioner-model training programs, I (Wilson, 1984c) sent D. Smith's (1982) questionnaire to the graduates of the Rutgers School of Applied and Professional Psychology and randomly selected graduates of other responding schools of professional psychology. The total of 335 questionnaires yielded a response rate of 51%. The Rutgers sample all held the Doctor of Psychology (PsyD) degree, whereas the sample from other Schools of Professional Psychology held either PsyD or PhD degrees. Since there were no appreciable differences between the two samples, or within the PsyD and PhD degree holders in the latter sample, the results are combined here.

The professional school graduates were younger and included more women than D. Smith's (1982) respondents, although the majority of subjects were still men. Eclectic, psychoanalytic, and cognitive–behavioral orientations were the most preferred, in that order. While this pattern is consistent with D. Smith's findings, professional school graduates expressed less preference for eclecticism and more for specific theoretical approaches than their more traditionally trained counterparts. "Multimodalism" was the term most often chosen to describe the current trend in psychotherapy.

The responses of individuals who expressed a preference for one of the three major theoretical orientations (psychoanalytic, cognitive–behavioral, and eclectic) indicated that these three groups did not differ from one another in terms of age, number of years of psychological work, or primary job. These three groups concurred in their appraisal of the current status of exclusive schools of psychotherapy. Of the graduates of schools of professional psychology other than Rutgers, 89% of respondents in the cognitive–behavioral group, 90% in the psychoanalytic group, and 76% in the eclectic group rated this item on the questionnaire between 3 and 4. As for their personal evaluation of eclectic psychotherapy, 74% of the cognitive–behavioral group, 39% of the psychoanalytic group, and 90% of the eclectic group rated this item as 4 or more. That the eclectic group would endorse eclecticism is axiomatic. Somewhat surprising, however, is the high percentage of respondents with a cognitive–behavioral bias who evaluated eclecticism so favorably.

Of course, the limitations of this survey must be taken into account in interpreting these data. Of the 27 existing schools of professional psychology, other than that of Rutgers University, only 14 responded to the survey. There is no way of knowing how representative the present findings are of the graduates of the missing institutions. Although the return rates of the questionnaire from the two samples of 56% and 45%, respectively, are not unreasonable for this type of survey, they obviously are not necessarily representative of all the graduates of the institutions sampled. The latter reservation is especially pertinent to the Rutgers sample, where the relatively large percentage reporting a behavioral orientation is probably due to disproportionate responding by those graduates who were sympathetic to the behavioral approach.

To the extent that these results are generalizable, the relative popularity of a cognitive–behavioral orientation among graduates of the new professional schools is noteworthy and inconsistent with the analysis I presented last year (Wilson, 1984a). The expression of a cognitive–behavioral orientation among students who have neither completed original research nor received explicit graduate instruction in experimental research and its evaluation will come as a puzzle to those who insist that behavior therapy cannot be understood or effectively implemented in the absence of such training. The reality is, however, that full-time behavioral practitioners are being graduated from programs in which, at least in some instances, clinical training is divorced from research training.

Another way to assess the impact of behavior therapy is by analyzing the declared theoretical emphases of clinical training programs. In this vein, a survey of directors of scientist/practitioner clinical training programs in the United States revealed that a cognitive–behavioral orientation was the one most frequently emphasized (Newsletter, Section III, Division 12 of American Psychological Association, Winter 1983). The limitation of this index is that students do not necessarily adopt orientations emphasized by their graduate training programs.

In his recent presidential address to the Association for Advancement of Behavior Therapy (AABT), O'Leary (1983) sought to index the impact of behavior therapy on the helping professions not only by reference to the type of survey described above, but also in terms of an analysis of the contents of the 1983 journals of the three major mental health organizations in the United States. The journals were *Archives of General Psychiatry*, published by the American Medical Association; the *Journal of Consulting and Clinical Psychology* (*JCCP*), published by the American Psychological Association; and *Social Work*, published by the National Association of Social Workers. Specifically, O'Leary examined the treatment outcome research in these journals. The results showed that of the nonpharmacological treatment studies in *Archives* and *JCCP*, most involved behavioral methods. (There were no outcome studies in *Social Work*.)

These findings demonstrate that contemporary outcome research on psychological treatment is dominated by behavioral investigators. O'Leary's further analysis of the makeup of the editorial board of *JCCP*, and of the treatment research that is funded by the National Institute of Mental Health, underscores this conclusion. This dominance in the research arena might be impressive, but it does not necessarily translate into influence on the professions in the broader sense. The notoriously limited impact of research findings on the practice of psychotherapy is a well-advertised fact (e.g., Barlow, 1980).

THE PUBLIC IMAGE OF BEHAVIOR THERAPY

O'Leary (1983) scoured the *New York Times* from 1965 to 1983 to find references to behavior therapy. References to behavior therapy, behavior modification, or behaviorism were rated on a 7-point scale from "conveyed very negative view of behavior therapy" to "conveyed very positive view of behavior therapy." No references were made to behavior therapy from 1965 to 1967, but 35 articles appeared between 1968 and 1983. The mean rating of articles published in the decade between 1968 and 1978 was slightly negative (3.8), with most references to Skinner's social concerns and the use of "behavior modification" in prisons. Since 1978, however, references to behavior therapy were rated more positively ($M = 5.0$). Descriptions of behavior therapy in the treatment of fears and depression were particularly favorable.

An important measure of public satisfaction is the evaluation of behavior therapists and their methods by consumers of treatment services. As O'Leary points out (see also Parloff's [1983] cogent comments), consumer assessments of satisfaction with therapy cannot be used as a substitute for controlled empirical evaluations of treatment outcome. They provide different but nonetheless valuable information about therapists and treatments. In general, behavior therapy has been rated positively in existing consumer evaluations. For example, in evaluations of group, family-style homes for delinquents, both by teachers and by the youths themselves, the behavioral approach was perceived more favorably than comparison facilities (Kirigin, Braukmann, Atwater, & Wolf, 1982). Other positive evaluations of behavior therapy for aggressive and retarded children, respectively, by teachers and parents, have been reported (Hampson & Tavormina, 1980; Kent & O'Leary, 1976).

The scanty data that exist on behavior therapy for adults are consistent with this positive picture. In behavioral marital therapy, using a 7-point scale with higher scores indicating favorable responses, Turkewitz and O'Leary (1981) found that wives' ratings averaged 6.83 and the husbands' mean score was 6.71 across the four personal characteristics of empathy, concern, likeableness, and competence. Some 90% of the clients indicated that they would recommend the treatment to a friend. In West Germany, Hahlweg, Revenstorf, and Schindler (1982) found that clients highly valued both communication training and behavioral marital therapy. Approximately 93% of the clients saw the therapy as a "worthwhile experience," and 94% would recommend the treatment to a friend. These findings are consistent with the social validity study of behavioral treatment for agoraphobia by Norton, Allen, and Hilton (1983) (see Chapter 3 in the present volume).

In their comprehensive review of consumer satisfaction with adult behavior therapy, Bornstein and Rychtarik (1983) conclude, "The fact that (positive findings) continue to occur across measures, methods employed, and samples surveyed attests to the fact that the majority of consumers do appear substantially satisfied with services rendered" (p. 196). They hasten to caution, however, that "while these continuing findings may reflect actual levels of satisfaction, methodologically they also may result from sampling bias, distorted response sets, reactivity, social desirability, and a myriad of other unnamed (and uncontrolled) influences" (p. 198).

THE BEHAVIOR THERAPIST IN CLINICAL PRACTICE

In a recent piece in *The Behavior Therapist*, Goldfried (1983) voiced an opinion that I have frequently heard from clinical practitioners: "[T]he behavior therapy literature does not accurately depict what really goes on in clinical practice" (p. 45). This perception demands careful analysis, and, to the extent that it is valid, requires explicit steps to remedy the situation.

What is it about clinical practice that is not reflected in the literature? Goldfried (1983) provides several examples. The first is a failure of the literature to indicate that there is more to behavior therapy than applying the appropriate technique. Goldfried notes:

> Quite often, the rules for selecting the technique that is "appropriate" are poorly spelled out. In order to make such difficult clinical decisions, one needs to depend on the sensitivity of the therapist to pick upon subtle cues within the clinical interaction, the understanding of how various behavior patterns and life styles interrelate, and a keen appreciation of the environmental forces and contingencies that direct people's lives. Much of this

knowledge and the rules that follow from it are not readily found in the literature, but instead come from clinicians' earlier social learning experiences, their personal experiences as human beings, and the accumulation of actual clinical experience. (p. 45)

I concur completely with this emphasis on the therapist's personal skills in clinical practice, as I assume most behavior therapists would. However, while this has not always been emphasized in the research literature, it is not as if these issues have not been addressed. There have been repeated assertions that behavior therapy cannot be reduced to a collection of techniques, that it is a general approach that needs to be tailored to the individual case by a suitably trained clinician (e.g., Bandura, 1969; Franks & Wilson, 1973–1979; Kanfer & Phillips, 1970; O'Leary & Wilson, 1975; Wolpe, 1973). In this process, much of which is the art rather than the science of behavior therapy, the personal contributions of the therapist will inevitably prove to be an important factor. In 1968, Wilson, Hannon, and Evans, borrowing a term from Kanfer and Saslow (1969), referred to the key role of the therapist as a "menschenkenner."

A second omission in the behavior therapy literature, according to Goldfried (1983), concerns the problems therapists encounter with resistance to their behavioral interventions. Goldfried is surely correct in noting that doing therapy rarely seems to be as straightforward as the literature suggests. It is only recently, for example, that resistance, or noncompliance, has begun to receive systematic attention in the behavioral literature (e.g., Lazarus & Fay, 1982; Meichenbaum & Gilmore, 1982).

What is puzzling, however, is Goldfried's assertion that solutions are available to the therapist's dilemmas with clients who do not carry out their homework assignments and present other challenges familiar to all therapists. The source? Other practicing therapists via the "therapeutic underground," an informal body of knowledge "consisting of what practicing clinicians know to be so on the basis of their personal experiences" (p. 46).

Seasoned therapists obviously acquire useful knowledge that does not appear in textbooks. But one has to be careful not to accept this knowledge born of experience too uncritically. Oscar Wilde, of course, defined experience as "the name every one gives to their mistakes." In Volume 8 of this series, I indicated how Goldfried's notion of simple consensus by clinicians does not necessarily ensure that their shared views are valid (Wilson, 1982a). Similarly, as discussed below, Rachman (1983a) draws on modern cognitive psychology in analyzing how clinicians' reasoning is subject to systematic bias (error). Unlike Goldfried,

I am not convinced that the answers to problems of resistance are to be had by consulting with experienced therapists from other theoretical persuasions. The ample evidence demonstrating the extremely modest success of these other approaches hardly requires belaboring here. Rather, I believe that these issues have been inadequately addressed by previous nonbehavioral approaches as well as by current behavioral ones, and that "resistance" remains resistant to the best therapists' ministrations. We need fresh ideas about how to improve upon this unsatisfactory state of affairs, whatever the source of such innovation.

Clinical Reasoning

Debate about the merits of clinical inference versus statistical prediction has a long history in clinical psychology (Meehl, 1954). Rachman (1983a) has recently revived this discussion, framing the issues within the context of modern cognitive psychology and technological advances. Although his purpose is to discuss behavioral medicine, and thereby to consider the physician's clinical reasoning and judgment, Rachman's ideas clearly apply also to psychological therapies.

The practitioner, particularly someone working independently, is subject to what Rachman and Philips (1975) describe as an "erratic and unbalanced flow of information coming back from his patients" (p. 31). Patients drop out of therapy or seek treatment elsewhere in ways that make it difficult for the therapist to assess his or her influence. Even treatment successes do not always provide unambiguous feedback to the therapist about his or her efforts. Given this uneven and perhaps inaccurate feedback about therapeutic outcome, the argument that therapists with enough clinical experience are "shaped" into using what "really works," irrespective of their initial theoretical orientations, becomes difficult to sustain. Indeed, Rachman probably does not overstate his case in commenting that a physician (read "therapist") forced to rely solely upon his or her own clinical experience would be making judgments on the basis of "systematic chaos." Fortunately, practitioners have other sources of information, including consultations with colleagues (easier for some than for others), the literature (including audiotapes and videotapes), conferences, and specialized workshops and continuing education offerings.

Reviewing past arguments, Rachman (1983a) notes that it "is difficult to show that clinical experience improves the accuracy of one's clinical predictions; nor is it necessarily the case that trained clinicians predict more accurately than novices. As for the much admired masters of clinical intuition, one begins to suspect that some reputations were supported by theatricality rather than by accuracy" (p. 324). He recalls Sarbin, Taft, and Bailey's (1960) argument that clinical inference is a subclass of inferential processes in general. Thus to the degree that human inference is subject to error and systematic bias, so clinical reasoning would be similarly subject. We are now in a better position to assess human inference in general and clinical inference in particular, thanks to the ground-breaking investigations of Tversky and Kahneman (1974, 1981). (See Nisbett & Ross, 1980, for an informative discussion of these concepts.)

The considerable potential of applying Tversky and Kahneman's analyses of errors in reasoning (or "judgmental heuristics," as they call them) to understanding the cognitive schemata that are involved in different clinical disorders and that limit the effectiveness of some of our treatment methods has begun to be explored in the behavior therapy literature (e.g., Goldfried & Robins, 1983; Rachman, 1983c). But as the research in question shows, therapists and trained scientists are as susceptible to these cognitive biases as our patients. The clinical reasoning of therapists can then be usefully examined in the light of these concepts from cognitive psychology. This will help us to understand the previously documented problems with clinical inference, and may allow steps to be taken that might correct some of these cognitive errors.

Three types of judgmental heuristics that often serve us well and efficiently can also lead to systematic cognitive biases—namely, representativeness, availability, and anchoring (Tversky & Kahneman, 1974). The net effect of these heuristics is that we tend to neglect prior probabilities and may erroneously be influenced by vivid, salient, and easily available information, rather than by more abstract yet probative information. In Volume 9 in this series (Wilson, 1984a), I indicated how these concepts explain therapists' traditional reliance on the uncontrolled clinical case study, often in preference to more probative statistical data. Rachman (1983a) makes a similar point:

> It is highly probable that most diagnostic and prognostic decisions are more strongly influenced by the clinician's experience of a vivid case thought to be similar to the presenting case, and that insufficient weight is given to prior probabilities and normative data. Clinical reasoning probably is saturated by the presentativeness heuristic. (p. 326)

Before reaching for some appropriate antidepressant agent in the face of our many documented cognitive fallabilities, it is well to remember that therapists have access to other sorts of information than their own personal experience—information that can mitigate the biasing effects of judgmental heuristics. Regular consultation with colleagues would seem to be especially indicated as a means of counter-acting our cognitive biases; this would appear particularly important for practitioners who work in isolated contexts. Nisbett and Ross (1980) concluded that "the potential for collective inferential improvement may far outstrip the potential for individual improvement. We are likely to be better able to see the motes in our brothers' eyes than to see the beams in our own" (p. 291). Rachman (1983a) suggests that the microprocessing revolution may provide the electronic technology that will enable practitioners to access statistical information to improve diagnosis and assessment.

Can therapists be trained to recognize and avoid these cognitive errors? Rachman (1983a) cites Einhorn and Hogarth's (1978) proposal that there be a greater emphasis on formal training in experimental design, logic, and statistics. Ironically, these are the subjects that are rapidly being de-emphasized in practitioner-model training programs in schools of professional psychology. Critics can easily charge that the presence of these courses in traditional PhD programs in clinical psychology has done little to improve clinical judgments, although the final word on this is not yet in. Rachman (1983a) counters with the plausible view that "it is not *general* training and experience that is required, but highly specific instruction and selected experiences" (p. 327). In other words, the training would be different from the typical experimental design and logic course in doctoral training programs and would have somewhat different goals—namely, to make students aware of the inevitable influence of our judgmental heuristics.

Nisbett and Ross (1980), like Rachman (1983a), propose that education may be useful in improving human inference. But they observe that such educational or preventive benefits are likely to be modest at best. A consistent finding that has emerged is that it is those judgments and inferences that are of greatest personal significance that will be least influenced by education in normative considerations: "This is true to such an extent that people may have different standards of rationality, indeed even different standards of sanity, for inferences that touch deeply on the self than for those that pertain to other matters" (Nisbett & Ross, 1980, p. 288). At the very least, these findings indicate that it is most important for therapists to be as aware as possible of their own personal biases and agendas in interacting with patients.

TREATMENT FAILURES IN BEHAVIOR THERAPY

One of Goldfried's (1983) suggestions for making the behavior therapy literature more relevant to practitioners' immediate clinical concerns is for researchers to focus on treatment failures as well as successes. This is precisely what Foa and Emmelkamp (1983) have done in their edited volume, *Failures in Behavior Therapy.*

Any serious attempt to analyze treatment failure in behavioral weight control programs must be based upon the operational specification of treatment outcome criteria and acceptable definitions of therapeutic success and failure. In the Foa and Emmelkamp volume, Dubbert and Wilson (1983) propose a comprehensive five-fold classification of treatment failure:

1. Meeting of predetermined criteria for admission into treatment.
2. Completion of the treatment program.
3. Adherence to the requirements of the treatment program.
4. Loss of weight and/or registering of other related forms of improvement (e.g., enhanced cardiovascular functioning).
5. Maintenance of treatment-produced improvement over time (i.e., relapse).

The first stage in this classificatory system addresses the question of external validity, since different selection criteria at this crucial entry point into treatment might affect outcome and determine the extent to which findings may be generalized. A particularly common complaint of practitioners is that the subjects of controlled outcome studies are different from the clients they see in therapy (i.e., more amenable to treatment). Indeed, research studies almost always screen subjects in ways that eliminate some of the more difficult problems.

It would be unwise, however, to uncritically view the subjects treated in various outcome studies as inevitably "easier to treat" than the clients who seek out practitioners. At least in some instances, the argument could be reversed and the point made that some self-referred clients may be easier to treat by virtue of their greater motivation (see Kazdin & Wilson, 1978, for details). Then there is the admittedly limited evidence indicating that the results achieved in controlled treatment outcome studies might be realistic reflections of what is obtained in actual clinical practice. In Chapter 3 of the present volume, I discuss Kirk's (1983) clinical findings with obsessive–compulsive patients in routine clinical practice, which closely approximate the results obtained in research studies. Moreover, at least in this one instance, the patients treated by Kirk were probably less chronic and hence arguably had less severe problems than those that had been included in treatment outcome studies. Data on this sort discredit simplistic laments about the inevitable lack of external validity in treatment studies in the service of methodological rigor.

What is needed is a greater awareness of the issue of external validity of outcome studies on the part of researchers, coupled with detailed information on the number of individuals who apply for treatment programs, the number screened out, and the specific selection criteria. This easily available information may then allow consumers of this research to evaluate more accurately the extent to which the study's data bear directly on specific clients they might treat.

A related problem is the still fashionable criticism of some outcome studies because they include so-called "volunteer" subjects as opposed to "real" patients. A recent example of this line of reasoning is Poppen's (1983) defense of practitioners' continued use of biofeedback in the face of numerous studies showing that alternative, less expensive methods are as effective. Although it is claimed that individuals who are recruited for studies through advertising their availability (so-called "volunteers") are not "real patients" and present fewer therapeutic difficulties than clients who initiate contact with therapists themselves (e.g., Gurman, 1978; Marks, 1978; Poppen, 1983), contrasting "volunteers" with "real patients" is a false dichotomy that obscures evaluation of treatment efficacy (see Kazdin & Wilson, 1978, and Rachman & Wilson, 1980; for a critical re-analysis of this argument). The important issues that determine outcome are the type, severity, duration, and complexity of the individual's problem, rather than his or her arbitrarily defined status as a "volunteer." In the treatment of obesity, for example, Foreyt, Goodrick, and Gotto (1981) compared studies that included patients referred by health professionals to those that recruited subjects through advertising the program. They concluded; "There appears to be no relationship between mode of referral and either treatment success or percent lost to follow-up" (p. 159).

The arbitrary and unsubstantiated discounting of the value of patients recruited for specific research trials has implications that extend beyond discussions of behavior therapy research. It applies to any treatment research that recruits patients, and, if taken to its logical conclusion, would undermine the entire research process. Emmelkamp (1983), for example, a behavior therapist, unreasonably criticizes the Klein, Zitrin, Woerner, and Ross (1983) study of the efficacy of imipramine in the treatment phobic disorders (see Chapter 3 of the present volume) because the New York group recruited patients for the study.

Detailed discussion of the other four stages of the classification of treatment failures put forward by Dubbert and Wilson (1983) is beyond the scope of the present chapter. Suffice it to mention a few pertinent points. The literature to which Goldfried (1983) and others object would be made more informative to the practitioner if publication of research studies would include details of dropouts, together with analyses of adherence to therapeutic instructions. The latter is especially important in behavior therapy, given our emphasis on assigning homework tasks. (This matter is discussed in greater detail in Volume 9 of this series; see Wilson, 1984a.)

Then there is the often complicated issue of what constitutes treatment success and failure. Obviously, different therapeutic approaches may disagree about how outcome should be gauged. Several authors in the Foa and Emmelkamp (1983) anthology discuss how therapists and their patients might also disagree about definitions of success and failure (e.g., Dubbert & Wilson, 1983; Emmelkamp & Foa, 1983; Everaerd, 1983; Marzillier & Winter, 1983).

Why Do We Fail?

Analyses of reasons for failure and identification of predictors of outcome in the treatment of anxiety disorders are summarized in Chapter 3 of the present volume. Not surprisingly, the factors identified as responsible for therapeutic failures in treating anxiety disorders are also implicated in treatment failures by the many different contributors to the Foa and Emmelkamp (1983) book, using different techniques across a wide range of clinical disorders.

Commonly cited reasons for failure have a familiar ring. They include the necessity of making the correct diagnosis; the need to carry out searching behavioral analyses of individuals' particular problems; clients with problems of motivation for participation in therapy and change (the issues of resistance and lack of adherence to therapeutic instructions); the quality of the therapist–patient relationship; and forces within patients' social networks that undermine treatment effects. There is little here that has not long been noted in the literature. And as some of the contributors observe, beyond reaffirming the problems posed by these various factors, not much is added to the therapist's existing armamentarium for overcoming such obstacles to progress.

The frequency with which treatment failures are attributed to patients' presumed lack of motivation for change is worthy of comment. Gone are the days when it was believed that lack of motivation to change could be readily overcome by the use of bigger and better external reinforcements. Behavior therapists today clearly see these issues in more complex terms and are conducting increasingly sophisticated analyses of reasons for motivational problems (e.g., Lazarus & Fay, 1982). While they are aware of the self-serving and stultifying consequences of blaming all treatment failures on patients' lack of motivation for change (a not uncommon tendency among some traditional psychoanalytic approaches), behavior therapists appear to be increasingly willing to acknowledge their limitations in helping some patients. Noting that "lack of motivation" for treatment can be an excuse for poor therapeutic methods, Zeiss and Jones (1983) nonetheless declare,

[I]n our clinical experience there are clients who are simply unmotivated for change. Although not totally endorsing a rationalistic model for client cognitive processes, we might hypothesize that all clients conduct some form of a cost–benefit analysis of coming into treatment. If the aversive consequences of remaining ["sick"] do not out-weigh the uncertainties and aversive elements of going through behavioral treatment, the client will not stay in therapy. (p. 214)

In a similar vein, Dubbert and Wilson (1983), discussing why it is that some obese clients finally make progress despite previous therapeutic failures, comment,

[I]t is our admittedly unsupported view that, for whatever reasons, some clients finally become more motivated to succeed and make whatever program they are in work. We customarily ask new clients what they feel will be different this time. Why do they think they might succeed this time? Aside from comments about promising sounding elements of our treatment program, clients' answers also often include statements about being "more motivated" this time, or that the decision to seek therapy is really their own, whereas in the past they had felt pressured into seeking treatment by family or friends. Of course, these assertions of motivation and commitment do not always translate into therapeutic success, but they warrant more systematic exploration in future research. (pp. 283–284)

The foregoing comments do not mean that behavior therapists do not have effective methods for overcoming problems of motivation. Rush and Shaw (1983) address this issue in a discussion of treatment failures with depressed patients—patients who by definition are un-motivated at the outset of therapy. They maintain that the two major obstacles to engaging the depressed patient in therapy are a lack of trust and pervasive negative anticipation of the future. They advise therapists to address these problems early in treatment. Issues of trust are reframed in cognitive terms. Rush and Shaw (1983) offer the following example:

[T]he patient may believe, "If I really tell you [the therapist] how I think, you won't like me." There is often an anticipation of rejection or disappointment underlying the patient's reluctance to engage as a full collaborator with the therapist. Such patients will often begin to work in treatment and then back off, reduce compliance, and voice more hopeless and helpless notions. These notions are atypically also involve denigration of the therapist or the therapy process. Such behaviors and views may serve to protect the patient from developing an emotional personal relationship (a therapeutic alliance) and, consequently, avoid the presumed rejection and disappointment as the treatment is terminated. Again, these fears are identified, framed cognitively into "if . . . , then . . ." statements (e.g., "If I put my hopes into this treatment or the therapist and don't get better, then I'll be shattered or it means I'm incurable, etc."), and discussed logically. (p. 219)

Overcoming resistance or lack of motivation is also the focus of a paper by W. R. Miller (1983b). He tackles another disorder that is characteristically associated with "lack of motivation" for change— namely, alcoholism. Miller criticizes traditional views of alcoholics that attribute almost all motivational properties to the personality of the person. In terms of this familiar thinking, the alcoholic must "bottom out" until he or she is really "ready" to take therapy seriously. Treatment failures are chalked up to the alcoholic's "denial" or "resistance." Yet therapeutic successes are usually ascribed to the nature of the treatment program. As Miller observes, "Successes in Alcoholics Anonymous, for example, are often said to be due to the quality of 'the program,' whereas lack of success is attributed to 'failure to use the program'" (1983b, p. 148).

To counteract this traditional approach to alcoholics, which essentially holds the afflicted individual responsible for his or her lack of motivation and progress, W. R. Miller (1983b) provides a detailed outline of what he calls "motivational interviewing." The approach is based on social-psychological principles of attitude change and is predicated on the assumption that the therapist not only can overcome the patient's so-called "lack of motivation," but may also contribute directly to treatment failures.

W. R. Miller disputes the notion that alcoholics are characterized by "denial," pointing out the overwhelming evidence that has failed to identify this or any other distinctive personality trait of alcoholics. Instead, he argues that "denial is not inherent in the alcoholic in- dividual, but rather is the product of the way in which counselors have chosen to interact with problem drinkers" (1983b, p. 150). Briefly, the argument goes that by directly confronting the alcoholic, by insisting that he or she is "an alcoholic" and that total abstinence is the only alternative to continuing deterioration, the therapist elicits resistance or denial from the patient. Miller calls for a more subtle, indirect approach, in which the alcoholic's conflicting desires both to stop drinking and to continue drinking are recognized, and the former is gradually encouraged while the latter is undermined. Although Miller invokes broadly applicable social-psychological principles in explain- ing his motivational interviewing, it must be emphasized that he is selecting and emphasizing particular aspects of alcoholics' problems in therapy. He himself comments that his approach may be optimally suited to individuals who are not severe alcoholics.

W. R. Miller argues that there are four key principles for motivating alcoholic patients: (1) De-emphasize labels such as "I am an alcoholic"; (2) stress the patient's own responsibility for choosing treatment goals and for change; (3) emphasize internal attribution of change—namely, the patient's ability to make choices about his or her drinking; and (4) induce cognitive dissonance with a view to producing changes in behavior.

Among the actual strategies that are dictated by these principles are the development of an empathic relationship with the alcoholic patient, the selective and directive use of reflection, and eliciting and shaping self-motivational statements in the alcoholics themselves. W. R. Miller claims that too many counselors and therapists do not display accurate empathy with alcoholic patients. He also cites the findings of his own research, indicating that there is a strong association between successful treatment outcome and the degree to which therapists show accurate empathy (e.g., W. R. Miller & Baca, 1983). Contrary to the Rogerian approach, reflection is not used "nondirectively," but is deliberately employed to strengthen the patient's awareness of his or her problem drinking and the negative consequences it entails.

Even a cursory reading of W. R. Miller's principles and procedures will indicate how different this approach is from traditional treatments, such as Alcoholics Anonymous. The latter is built on the public and repeated admission by the person that he or she is "an alcoholic" who is powerless over alcohol—someone for whom any control over or choice about drinking is illusory. Here, again, it would be well to caution that different approaches might be necessary with different alcoholics. Clinical experience would suggest that some (typically severely dependent) alcoholics respond well to the "all-or-nothing" rationale of traditional treatment programs. Others find the rigid insistence on fundamental assumptions of these programs alien and offensive. W. R. Miller's approach, which is largely consistent with the social learning conceptualization of alcohol use and abuse, would provide a promising alternative for the latter type of drinker.

CLINICAL RESEARCH AND PRACTICE: RECIPROCAL RESPONSIBILITIES

It is easy to call for better communication and cooperation between clinical researchers and practitioners. It is another matter to spell out ways in which this laudable objective may be achieved. As discussed above, outcome research in behavior therapy must increasingly address issues that concern the practitioner directly. Careful description of patient samples, complete reporting of information on selection criteria for inclusion in the study, and details of adherence and dropouts will all improve the value of published research and enable more accurate judgments to be made about the generalizability of research findings to the clinic. In addition, more research is needed on how the results of controlled research hold up when the procedures that are evaluated are applied under the conditions of routine clinical practice. Studies can be designed to test this transferability of controlled clinical studies to the less optimal conditions of most service delivery settings. This is a priority for applied researchers. But there is also an important role for practitioners in this process.

Practitioners must assume some responsibility in making the behavior therapy literature more clinically relevant in the sense that Goldfried (1983) and others have indicated. It is not good enough for practitioners simply to object to the real limitations of clinical research and demand that researchers somehow deal with the practitioners' immediate concerns. If there is the "therapeutic underground" of experienced and effective therapists to which Goldfried (1983) and Wachtel (1982b) refer, they should go public and publish. Observations that "are often not clearly articulated, may be unsystematic or at times idiosyncratic, and are typically kept informal" should be articulated and made more systematic. Without this step, there is little hope of systematically upgrading clinical training or practice.

Consider another example. Poppen (1983), in discussing the relationship between clinical practice and research on biofeedback, has asked the question, "Are the data really necessary?" He describes a state of affairs that has been noted previously in this series and elsewhere— namely, that biofeedback in clinical practice continues to flourish, despite the unremitting series of well-controlled research studies showing that for most problems, biofeedback, with its expensive gadgetry, is no more effective than good old relaxation training. The reason? According to Poppen, "Until researchers address the questions which could improve or enhance current practices, however, the clinician is likely to regard the data as irrelevant to what he/she does" (1983, p. 147). In other words, the alleged inadequacies of biofeedback research are what is wrong. Nothing is required of clinicians. They are apparently to conduct business as usual until researchers come up to vaguely stated ecological standards. (In some ways, this line of reasoning resembles Fuller's [1978], which was discussed in Volume 7 of this series; see Franks & Wilson, 1979, pp. 376–377.)

Pertinent to the present discussion are not the specific pros and cons of biofeedback, but the general principle of the influence of research on clinical practice. The case Poppen summarizes is often used to rationalize clinicians' disregard of research studies. Why, it must be asked, are the research data "irrelevant" to the clinical practice of biofeedback? Poppen first asserts that the recruited subjects of research are different from "real" clients: "One suspects the latter of

being more highly motivated for treatment, with perhaps more severe
or complex disorders, and a longer history of treatment" (1983, p. 146).
The shortcomings of this general argument are summarized above. Of
course, it may well be that research subjects suffer less severe problems,
and so on. But this would have to be established via careful critiques of
the studies in question. To "suspect" is not enough. Why not "suspect"
just the opposite? Remember that Kirk's (1983) experience (see Chapter 3
of the present volume) contradicts Poppen's assertion. To repeat: The
range of severity, chronicity, and so forth, of participants in clinical
research studies will vary from study to study, and judgments of external validity will need to be adjusted accordingly. Similarly, the patients
seen in routine clinical practice will also vary along these dimensions.
It is untenable to assume *a priori* that there are qualitative differences
among the two groups of individuals, and to compound this first false
assumption by using it to dismiss what might be the uncomfortable
implications of controlled clinical research.

Poppen's (1983) second point is that research procedures may not
realistically reflect the therapist's expert, unconstrained use of the same
method. As he points out, this is an empirical question. Yet there are
problems with Poppen's particular defense of biofeedback. First, it is
not as though research studies do not produce positive clinical outcomes. They do. Second, whatever limitations research protocols place
on biofeedback in these comparative outcome studies, the same limitations apply to relaxation training. It is far-fetched to assume that these
considerations would apply only to biofeedback. In short, while additional empirical evidence would be welcome, Poppen's point fails to
justify the disregard of existing research evidence showing that biofeedback procedures usually do not appear to be superior to alternative
methods.

The practitioner can—indeed, must—play an important role in
taking us beyond the less than happy state of affairs summarized above.
He or she cannot afford to sit back and wait for the clinical researchers.
In the ultimate analysis, of course, all clinical research, no matter how
attuned to issues of external validity, is necessarily limited in the extent
to which it can be generalized. Practitioners can enrich the literature
and provide researchers with the clinical observations that should be
guiding their studies by reporting the results of their treatment. They
are not required to complete controlled research (Wilson, 1982a), but to
report well-defined treatment methods applied to carefully described
patient populations. This is the approach proposed by Barlow (1980)
and more recently developed in Barlow, Hayes, and Nelson's (1983b)
informative book on how practitioners can contribute their unique

observations and findings to the development of more effective treatment methods.

Is it feasible to require that primarily full-time clinical practitioners contribute to the treatment literature as proposed above? There are certainly precedents; one has only to think of Wolpe's (1958) and Lazarus's (1963) reports of their treatment of series of patients. These clinical series helped to lay the foundation for the clinical practice of behavior therapy with adults and to trigger subsequent research.

It is often objected that behavioral journals are not receptive to publishing case studies or information from the sort of uncontrolled clinical trials described above. The facts suggest otherwise. The Kirk (1983) paper, described in Chapter 3, is only one example. Barlow, the new editor of *Behavior Therapy*, has announced an explicit editorial policy encouraging the material discussed here. Similarly, Stockwell (1982), in an editorial in *Behavioural Psychotherapy*, the journal of the British Association of Behavioural Psychotherapy, has explicitly encouraged the submission of clinical reports to complement research studies. For example, Stockwell, in suggesting what features make clinical reports worthwhile, states that "Therapeutic procedures should be presented fully not just the aims of these. It is unusual for practical problems faced in applying a therapeutic principle to get written up. Knowledge of these annoying snags and their resolution may be more valuable to the reader than any other aspect of the report" (1982, p. 216). Other journals are just as eager to publish appropriate material.

What becomes important are the clearcut criteria that both Barlow and Stockwell spell out about what constitutes an informative clinical report or case study. Clear descriptions of procedures and patients, coupled with reasonable measures of treatment outcome and information on follow-up, are essential. In short, consistent with the seminal philosophical underpinnings of behavior therapy, procedures must be described in a manner that would allow other investigators or practitioners to replicate them.

THE THERAPIST–PATIENT RELATIONSHIP

In his introduction to a collection of chapters on psychotherapy and patient relationships, Lambert (1983) states that "behavioral theories . . . have mentioned the therapist–patient relationship only in passing and only as a part of the administrative functions of the therapist, not as an integrated facet of a theory of change" (p. 4). Relationship issues have received far less attention in the literature than the development and evaluation of particular assessment and intervention strategies. Nonetheless, the analyses of the therapeutic relationship by Beck, Rush, Shaw, and Emery (1979), Brady (1980), Goldfried and Davison (1976), Lazarus 1971), Wilson (1982a), Wilson and Evans (1976), and Wilson et al. (1968), among others, cannot be characterized as merely passing comments. Rather, the attempt has been to interpret the inter-personal processes that occur between therapist and patient within a social learning framework and as an integral part of behavior therapy. This analysis has a long way to go, and it is encouraging to note that an increasing number of researchers and therapists are addressing relationship issues in behavior therapy.

Behaviorally oriented practitioners report that relationship en-hancement methods are the most frequently used treatment strategies (Swan & MacDonald, 1978). Ratings of behavior therapists in practice reveal that they are more flexible with and supportive of their clients than Gestalt or psychoanalytic therapists (Brunink & Schroeder, 1979) and that they show more warmth and empathy than psychoanalytically oriented psychotherapists (Sloane, Staples, Cristol, Yorkston, & Whipple, 1975). Patients themselves rate the personal qualities of their behavior therapists at least as highly as those of therapists from other theoretical persuasions (O'Leary & Wilson, in press; Sloane et al., 1975). All of this adds up to demonstrating that the therapeutic relationship is most important, that behavioral practitioners know it, and that they are effective in developing helping relationships.

The Therapeutic Relationship and Treatment Failures

Many of the contributors to Foa and Emmelkamp's (1983) volume on treatment failures in behavior therapy address the role of the thera-peutic relationship. Foa, Steketee, Grayson, and Doppelt (1983b) ob-serve that "the personal qualities of the therapist, which appear to be central to outcome of psychotherapy, have less impact on the more precisely formulated techniques of behavioral therapy. It is likely that the more powerful the therapeutic procedure employed, the less potent will be the effect of the therapist" (p. 15). This sort of statement is not uncommon in the behavior therapy literature (e.g., Telch, 1981). How-ever, it is misleading and suggests a greater simplicity to behavior therapy than is the case—the point Goldfried (1983) makes.

Foa et al. (1983b) themselves hasten to add that in the assessment stage of therapy, the interaction between therapist and client might make the difference between obtaining the necessary information or not. Establishing a good working relationship, characterized by trust and credibility, is vital to the assessment process and throughout therapy, no matter how highly specified or potent the technique(s) in question may be. To take only one example, overcoming ("working through") clients' resistance or lack of compliance with emotionally demanding and threatening activities (e.g., asking a bulimic to participate in exposure and response prevention treatment during the therapy session; see Wilson, in press-a) or even routine homework assignments (e.g., an agoraphobic doing *in vivo* exposure) is crucially dependent on an effective therapeutic alliance between therapist and client.

Beyond the preceding observation, it is clear that behavior therapists do not always have potent techniques with which to treat the full range of problems they encounter. The reality is that they are often struggling on a trial-and-error basis informed largely by the clinical lore that has developed within the field. When one adds to this the issues of deciding whether the presenting problem is the real problem, or working with the client to identify what the problems, it is inescapably the case that the therapeutic relationship will play an important role in determining treatment success or failure. A good working relationship is always necessary, even though it is rarely sufficient.

Emmelkamp and van der Hout (1983) tried to assess the role of the therapeutic relationship in the behavioral treatment of agoraphobics. Of 23 patients asked to participate in the study, only 13 cooperated. (This high refusal rate might in itself provide telling evidence of these patients' experience of their treatment.) All patients had participated in standardized group *in vivo* exposure. The correlation between outcome and 13 patients' scores on a Dutch version of the Barrett-Lennard Relationship Scale (Barrett-Lennard, 1973, cited in Emmelkamp & van der Hout, 1983) indicated that there was a significant positive relationship between success and such therapist characteristics as empathy and positive regard.

Emmelkamp and van der Hout are aware of the limitations of this analysis. They prudently observe,

> [T]he patients' rating of outcome and therapist may be reflections of the patient's overall satisfaction with the treatment. If the latter is the case, one may not conclude that the therapists' characteristics were causal in effecting the favorable outcome inasmuch as the favorable outcome of therapy might have influenced the patient's recall of their therapists' characteristics. (1983, p. 72)

This latter question of interpreting correlational findings obtained at the completion of treatment has been raised time and again in the literature. Sloane *et al.* (1975) found that successful patients in both their behaviorally and their psychoanalytically oriented therapies attributed their success mainly to relationship variables, such as empathy and active involvement by the therapist. Mathews, Johnston, Lancashire, Munby, Shaw, and Gelder (1976; reprinted in Volume 5 of this series) asked their patients to rank eight features of their treatments in the order of the perceived value. The results showed that "all patients attributed important effects to the therapists' encouragement and sympathy, and to a slightly lesser extent the practice component and learning to cope with panic" (p. 369). Lazarus (1971) and Ryan and Gizynski (1971) reported similar post hoc findings. The overarching methodological problem remains, however: As Lambert (1983) also acknowledges, patients may not know how they were helped.

Patients' attributions of success to their therapists' personalities can easily be understood in terms of the availability heuristic. According to this concept, judgments are strongly influenced by evidence or events that are readily available, and are insufficiently affected by evidence that might be important but is not easily accessible. Availability is also influenced by other less obvious factors, as Rachman (1983c) points out, including biases caused by prior cognitive sets, biases introduced by imaginability, and biases caused by what Chapman and Chapman (1967) called "illusory correlations." It would not be far-fetched to view patients' attributions of success as reflecting a prior set that it is the therapist's personality that will help, and to see in this an illusory correlation. Particularly as we are dealing with issues that are of considerable personal and emotional significance, it follows from the Nisbett and Ross (1980) analysis described earlier in this chapter that patients would not have access to the reasons for their improvement.

Marzillier and Winter (1983) declare that without the development of a good therapeutic relationship, "it is unlikely that a therapist will have much impact on a patient's social anxieties" (p. 117). Ellis (1983) offers a number of reasons for treatment outcome using rational-emotive therapy (RET). Aside from technical errors in using RET (e.g., too simplistic an assessment of clients' symptoms and the irrational thoughts behind them), and various client characteristics that make work against successful outcome (e.g., low frustration tolerance), many of the factors Ellis highlights involve the therapist's style or judgment. Failure is likely when "[t]herapists have significant degrees of low frustration tolerance, and do not strongly persist in using RET with clients but instead discourage themselves with difficult clients, give up too easily, and act impatiently" and when "RET therapists are not too bright or not too good at disputing irrational beliefs themselves and, therefore, are not too helpful to clients in showing them how to do RET disputation" (p. 168). Success is enhanced, given the "[c]onviction by the therapist that the scientific method is not only good for under-standing human processes and for research into psychotherapy, but that it also has immense usefulness when specifically applied to the personal problems of disturbed individuals" (p. 169). Put in broader terms, this suggestion of Ellis's that the effective therapist should be intelligent, able to withstand frustration and frustrating clients, and firmly committed to the assumptions of his or her preferred approach probably holds true for most forms of psychological therapy.

Specific Relationship Factors in Cognitive–Behavioral Therapy

In a detailed analysis of the therapeutic relationship in cognitive–behavioral therapy, Arnkoff (1983) differentiates between those aspects of the relationship that are common to other psychological approaches and those that are distinctive. Psychodynamic therapy is largely defined by its emphasis on the transference relationship, which centers on the "reliving and modification of historically meaningful patterns [of behavior]" (Strupp, 1977, p. 17). Arnkoff summarizes the ways in which cognitive–behavioral treatment differs from this view of trans-ference:

1. There is far less emphasis on past history. The more immediate causes of present functioning are the focus of attention.
2. The content of the therapeutic process differs: Dysfunctional cognitions and behavioral deficits and excesses are stressed, as opposed to psychosexual conflicts and other putative motiva-tional states.
3. Transference issues are "far more central to psychodynamic therapy than to cognitive therapy. In cognitive therapy, client distortions toward the therapist are addressed like any other distortions" (1983, p. 111).
4. Even if analysis and modification of the in-session relationship between therapist and client are viewed as part of cognitive–behavioral treatment, the goal is to have these changes generalize to relationships in the client's natural environment. The social learning conceptualization of personality and behavior change makes it clear that generalization of this sort cannot be auto-matically expected and must be explicitly fostered through appropriate homework assignments.

In terms of a social learning analysis, the extent to which a focus on in-session interactions between therapist and client can directly produce behavior change will vary, according to the client's specific

problems and goals. In general, the more interpersonal issues are of
concern, the more likely it is that focus on in-session interactions carry
direct therapeutic potential. But this will also depend on other factors,
such as the person's particular social learning history and current
social relationships. As a rule, behavior therapists see working on their
interactions with the client directly as much more limited as a means of
change than many of their psychotherapeutic counterparts do. The
hard-line version of this was expressed by Bandura (1969), who stated,
"Most likely, the relatively artificial relationship provides substitute
gratifications for those lacking in the clients' natural relationships
instead of serving as a major vehicle for personality change" (p. 58).
Taking a more positive view that is probably more typical of practitioners, Arnkoff (1983) suggests three ways in which a focus on in-
session therapeutic interactions are useful.

The first is that therapeutic interactions provide the therapist with
first-hand observations about the client's current functioning. Second,

> dealing with current behavior in the session rivets the attention of both
> therapist and client, especially because of the emotional arousal that
> comes from discussing the current situation. Third, a focus on in-therapy
> behavior allows the client to try out new behavior with the therapist. . . .
> To the extent that . . . therapy accurately recreates the client's problem
> and corresponding emotions, the client can make discoveries and try out
> new behavior that will be generalizable outside therapy. (1983, pp. 108–109)

Here again, it must be emphasized that different views of what the
client's "problem" is will result in different evaluations of the value of
this in-session exploration of the interaction. To take an example, this
type of interaction will be of little use in helping an agoraphobic
overcome his or her problems. The situation and emotions that must
be worked through in this and other similar cases can only be elicited
through exposure to the critical environmental triggers outside of
therapy.

Sources of Clinical Inferences

Wachtel (1977) has argued that behavior therapy and psychodynamic
therapy have much to learn from each other. In a recent paper, Wachtel
(1982b) suggests how a psychodynamic perspective can remedy an
ostensible deficit in behavioral treatment. Wachtel states that behavior
therapy is based on theories that "are essentially content-free, theories

concerned with basic processes, with how but not particularly with what is learned or thought or found reinforcing. Consequently, since these theories do not guide them in this respect, behavior therapists have tended to base their content assumptions on general cultural assumptions" (1982b, p. 597). Psychoanalysts, on the contrary, as Wachtel points out, are very concerned with content and with inferences about people's motives. He grants that psychoanalysts are often too "creative" in the inferences they draw about patients' motivation, but he faults behavior therapists for not drawing sufficient inferences. In short, he expresses the frequently heard psychodynamic view that behavior therapists naively take too much at face value in accordance with cultural norms.

Wachtel (1982b) illustrates his argument with reference to the use of praise as a reinforcer. In terms of cultural norms, he asserts, praise is invariably viewed as positive. The corollary of this, allegedly, is the view that the more one has of it the better—one cannot have too much of a good thing. Since they are guided by these normative assumptions, behavior therapists are said to be "often too effusive in their praise" (1982b, p. 599). Negative therapeutic consequences may follow from this position, says Wachtel. Praise may lose its value or the therapist may be regarded as insincere. Furthermore, "if the therapist's criteria for praise are not reasonably close to the client's, praise can be noxious. To be told you have done something worthwhile when you regard it as a meager step can lead to feeling that the therapist is insulting or doesn't understand you" (1982b, p. 599). Psychoanalysts, it is said, since they are grounded in the study of non-normative, unconscious motives, would be less likely to make these errors.

Since Wachtel's (1982b) analysis reflects a much broader body of clinical thinking on these issues, it warrants careful scrutiny. Perhaps the first point that must be made is a prosaic one. Were Wachtel correct, behavior therapists undoubtedly would be experienced as insincere, noxious, or simply naive. One would be bound to predict a greater rate of dropouts from therapy and less efficacy than that obtained by their more clinically savvy psychodynamic counterparts. Fortunately, none of these nasty implications is true. First, as pointed out earlier in this chapter and elsewhere (O'Leary & Wilson, in press), behavior therapists are viewed as favorably as psychodynamic practitioners by clients—if not more so. Second, although the data are sketchy, the case can be made that behavior therapy has fewer dropouts from treatment than other treatment approaches have. And third, behavior therapy has certainly not been shown to be inferior to other psychological treatments in outcome efficacy. Rather, it is demonstrably superior in the treatment of several child and adult disorders (Rachman & Wilson, 1980).

Moving to a different level of analysis, one can easily contest Wachtel's (1982b) appraisal of normative cultural assumptions. I for one would very much doubt that the average person, without the benefits of formal psychotherapeutic training, would not realize that praise is not always praise, so to speak. Wachtel paints too simplistic a picture of the perspicacious layperson's general interpersonal know-how.

An extremely important point is at issue here. It is true that behavior therapists tend to take of their clients' self-reports at face value, just as our perspicacious layperson would be inclined to do. But obviously, they are keenly aware that these self-reports are not always veridical, that they may mask hidden agendas, or that they may provide distorted views for one or another reason. They are aware that a client's presenting problem is not always the "real problem." Behavior therapists in clinical practice have always been informed by this knowledge (e.g., Goldfried & Davison, 1976; Lazarus, 1971; Wolpe & Lazarus, 1966). Again, how else could they possibly have achieved their clinical successes? More recently, with the influence of recent research in cognitive psychology and social cognition on human inference—the work of Tversky and Kahneman and others, as described above—behavior therapists have good theoretical reasons for being cautious about their own and their clients' verbal reports of their motives and intentions.

On what basis do behavior therapists look beyond their clients' self-reports in making inferences about their real motives and intentions? They make use of essentially the same cues that other therapists would. They would be alert to patterns of functioning, inconsistencies between verbal report and action, contradictions in accounts of events, unacknowledged emotional reactions to significant life events (desynchrony among response systems?), nonverbal cues, and other signs that things do not quite fit together. Quoting Kelly (1955), Mahoney (1980) emphasizes the value of listening with the "third ear," noting the general theme as well as the specific content of what the clients says. The former may be more revealing than the latter. As in other therapeutic approaches, and as in other walks of life, some behavior therapists will be better than others in making insightful observations and analyses, and it is likely that they will achieve superior overall success. Where do behavior therapists acquire these skills? Obviously not from textbooks on experimental psychology. But no one ever suggested that they might. They learn develop these personal qualities through their own social learning histories and life experiences, as Goldfried (1983) indicates, and through clinical training. Clinical supervision in behavior therapy is far less discussed than psychoanalytic supervision, but it clearly focuses on what has been called the nonspecifics of therapy.

Wachtel (1982b) maintains that psychodynamicists enjoy an advantage over behavior therapists in this regard by virtue of specific training in the content of one theoretical system's view of the meaning of behavior and the motives of people. This is what he says is missing in behavior therapy, and this is why he thinks that behavior therapists have much to learn from their psychodynamic counterparts. But Wachtel is implicitly assuming that this psychodynamic training produces more effective assessment and treatment. There is simply no convincing empirical evidence to support such an assertion. While stressing the value of psychodynamic inferences (illustrated by one of his own insightful analyses of a thorny therapeutic issue), Wachtel does not consider the well-known dangers of this approach.

A study by Langer and Abelson (1974; reprinted in Volume 3 of this series) showed that psychoanalytically oriented therapists produced dramatically different assessments of the same interview of the same person as a function of labeling the person a "patient" or a "job interviewee." There is no need to belabor the negative implications of this inferential bias for treatment. The behavior therapists in the Langer and Abelson study correctly assessed the person similarly, regardless of label, suggesting that they were guided more by the person's actual behavior than by a pre-existing subjective set. Of course, as Wilson and Evans (1976) have mentioned, demonstrating the bias inherent in psychoanalytic therapists does not mean that behavior therapists might not be shown to have their own biases. As often suggested, this might entail too much attention to overt behavior and less awareness of the more subtle themes in therapy. All we can safely conclude at the present time is that this is a possibility. And behavior therapists would do well to be aware that their own conceptual commitments necessarily bias their observations in certain directions. We need more information on this theoretically and clinically important matter. Still, the fact remains that it cannot be concluded that psychodynamic therapists as a class, are more insightful or arrive at more valid inferences about clients' problems than behavior therapists.

I believe that Wachtel (1982b) is wrong in suggesting that behavior therapists make significantly fewer inferences than psychodynamic therapists. It would be more accurate to state that behavior therapists make different inferences, at least in part, which often emanate from different theoretical assumptions and serve different purposes. Behavior therapists do take clients' self-report of their behavior more seriously than psychodynamic therapists. And for good reason. Mischel (1968, 1982) has shown that self-report is often the most accurate means of personality assessment, providing more accurate information than experienced clinicians' predictions. Naturally, it is subject to limitations and distortions, but so is every method of assessment.

As Mischel (1982) has discussed, psychoanalytically oriented therapists have tended to assume "that what a person says about himself or herself in response to direct questions is likely to be either superficial or defensively distorted and misleading. Consequently, seemingly irrelevant behaviors (casual comments, jokes, slips of the tongue) were often taken as important clues of the individual's 'underlying' dispositions, while the client's own reports of concerns, beliefs, interests, and personality attributes were treated with suspicion" (p. xx). Wachtel's (1982b) thesis is consistent with this position—and suffers from the same difficulties. More recently, Nisbett and Wilson's (1977) heavily cited article about the limits of introspective accuracy has brought the value of self-report into question again. While Nisbett and Wilson's thesis illustrates the limits of inferences we make about our own behavior, it does not vitiate the unique value of clients' verbal reports about their thinking or behavior for the purposes of clinical assessment (see Mischel, 1982). Ironically, radical behaviorism has shared with psychoanalysis an eschewal of self-report. For Skinner, for example, verbal report is simply an epiphenomenon that is correlated with the environmental contingencies that determine behavior. From necessity, if not from commitment to the mediational model of social learning theory, behavior therapists in clinical practice have never subscribed to this radical philosophy.

Wachtel (1982b) pursues his argument that behavior therapists pay insufficient attention to the complexities of motivation with the following statement:

> Not only may praise have idiosyncratic meanings for the client but so, too, can such things as the therapist's tone of voice, silence, questions, or way of phrasing comments. For one client, gentle, carefully measured statements may be reinforcing; for another the same kind of therapist behavior may be aversive (a sign the client must be treated with kid gloves; a sign the therapist is not clear about what should be done, etc.). (pp. 602–603)

But here Wachtel is preaching to the converted. The obvious clinical necessity of being alert to different and unpredictable impacts on different clients of particular therapeutic styles has long been recognized by behavior therapists, not only in actual practice (again, how else could they possibly have achieved their results?), but also in the literature (e.g., see Lazarus, 1971). Volume 8 of this series contains quotes from Brady (1980) and Beck et al. (1979) explicitly making this point (see Wilson, 1982a, pp. 339–341). Consider the following comments from Beck *et al.* (characteristic of clinical behavior therapy as a whole):

> If the therapist is too active in demonstrating a warm, caring concern (or more importantly, if the patient thinks the warm attitude is too intense), the patient may react negatively. For example, the patient may think, "I am undeserving of such caring," or "I am deceiving the therapist because he appears to like me and I know I am worthless." Or the patient may misconstrue the therapist's motives: "He's insincere," or "How can he like a worthless person like me?" . . . In essence, the therapist must strike an appropriate balance in displaying warmth. The patient may construe minimal warmth as rejection, while too hearty a display of caring may be misinterpreted in either a negative or overly positive way. Thus, the therapist must carefully attend to signs that suggest that his attitudes are counterproductive. (1979, pp. 46–47)

Quite clearly, Beck *et al.* are expressing the same clinical sagacity as Wachtel. Continuing misrepresentations of behavior therapy serve no constructive purpose.

Notice that in the foregoing quote from Beck *et al.* (1979), the therapist is cautioned about discriminately displaying warmth toward his or her client. Although behavior therapists as a rule are warm, supportive, disclosing, and advice-giving, the need to be flexible with different clients is a given. (Both Arnkoff, 1983, and Morris & Magrath, 1983, provide detailed, recent analyses of the role of the specificity factor in therapeutic relationships in cognitive–behavioral therapy.) At least in principle, this emphasis on flexibility would appear to distinguish behavior therapists from some other therapists who assume predetermined therapeutic postures (e.g., psychoanalysts, who are explicitly against an open, supportive, and disclosing relationship). If behavior therapists operated only on the basis of some naive normative cultural assumption, as Wachtel (1982b) suggests, it is likely that they would always try to be warm and would surmise that "the warmer the better." This brings to mind the very basis of Rogerian psychotherapy and the accumulated evidence showing that warmth and empathy are simply not enough (Rachman & Wilson, 1980).

As Wachtel (1982b) emphasizes, psychodynamic therapy is predicated upon specific assumptions about the content of clients' motives. These assumptions can be criticized on several grounds, including lack of empirical support. Recently, Guidano and Liotti (1983) have offered another set of assumptions about content to guide the therapeutic relationship in what they call "structural cognitive therapy." Although many of their strategies overlap directly with the more familiar cognitive–behavioral approach of Beck, for example, their theory and its implications for the therapeutic relationship are distinctive by virtue of their putative ontological perspective. Guidano and Liotti maintain that an understanding of the distinctive cognitive organization underlying each clinical syndrome is necessary if the therapist is to develop a helpful relationship—and possibly to avoid a harmful one. Suffice it to note here that Guidano and Liotti have only their clinical speculations and reference to Bowlby's (1977) theory of emotional development to offer by way of support for their ambitious assumptions. If one prunes their practical recommendations to the therapist of these highly questionable syndromic assumptions, then their views about a collaborative relationship closely resemble the standard fare of cognitive–behavioral therapy.

REFERENCES

Abelson, P. II. (1983). [Editorial reply to letter to the editor by Barlow, Bellack, Buchwald, Garfield, Hartmann, Herman, Hersen, Miller, Rachman, & Wolpe]. *Science, 200,* 555-556.

Abelson, R. P. (1963). Computer simulation of "hot cognitions." In S. Tomkins & S. Messick (Eds.), *Computer simulations of personality* (pp. 277-298). New York: Wiley.

Abraham, S., Collins, G., & Nordsieck, M. (1971). Relationship of childhood weight status to morbidity in adults. *Public Health Reports, 86,* 273-284.

Abrams, D. B., Elder, J. P., Carleton, R. A., & Artz, L. M. (1983). *Organizational health promotion: An integrated approach.* Paper presented at the annual meeting of the Society for Behavioral Medicine, Baltimore.

Abrams, D. B., & Follick, M. J. (1983). Behavioral weight loss intervention at the work-place: Feasibility and maintenance. *Journal of Consulting and Clinical Psychology, 51,* 226-233.

Achenbach, T. M., & Edelbrock, C. S. (1979). The Child Behavior Profile. II. Boys aged 6-11 and Girls aged 6-11 and 12-16. *Journal of Consulting and Clinical Psychology, 47,* 223-233.

Agras, W. S., Kazdin, A. E., & Wilson, G. T. (1979). *Behavior therapy: Towards an applied clinical science.* San Francisco: W. H. Freeman.

Albion, F. M. (1983). A methodological analysis of self-control in applied settings. *Behavioral Disorders, 8,* 87-102.

Alford, G. S., Wedding, D., & Jones, S. (1983). Faking "turns-ons" and "turn-offs": The effects of competitory covert imagery on penile tumescence responses to diverse extrinsic sexual stimulus materials. *Behavior Modification, 7,* 112-125.

Alloy, L. B., & Abramson, L. Y. (1979). Judgment of contingency in depressed and nondepressed students: Sadder but wiser? *Journal of Experimental Psychology: General, 108,* 441-485.

Altman, K., & Mira, M. (1983). Training parents of developmentally disabled children. In J. L. Matson & F. Andrasik (Eds.), *Treatment issues and innovations in mental retardation* (pp. 303-321). New York: Plenum.

American Psychiatric Association (1980). *Diagnostic and statistical manual of mental disorders* (3rd ed.). Washington, DC: Author.

American Psychological Association. (1983, Winter). *Newsletter,* Section III, Division 12, 7-12.

American Public Health Association. (1981, July). Some little known facts on smoking. *The Nation's Health,* p. 8.

Andrasik, F., & Holroyd, K. A. (1983). Specific and nonspecific effects in the biofeedback treatment of tension headache: 3-year follow-up. *Journal of Consulting and Clinical Psychology, 51,* 634–636.

Andrews, G. (1982). A treatment outline for agoraphobia. *Australian and New Zealand Journal of Psychiatry, 16,* 25–33.

Andrews, G., Moran, C., & Hall, W. (1983). *Agoraphobia: A meta-analysis of treatment outcome studies.* Unpublished manuscript, University of New South Wales Medical School, Australia.

Anesko, K. M., & O'Leary, S. G. (1982). The effectiveness of brief parent training for the management of children's homework problems. *Child and Family Behavior Therapy, 4,* 113–126.

Apfelbaum, M. (1981). Effects of very restrictive high-protein diets with special reference to nitrogen balance. *International Journal of Obesity, 5,* 209–214.

Armor, D. J., Polich, J. M., & Stambul, H. D. (1978). *Alcoholism and treatment.* New York: Wiley.

Arnkoff, D. B. (1983). Common and specific factors in cognitive therapy. In M. J. Lambert (Ed.), *Psychotherapy and patient relationships* (pp. 85–125). Homewood, IL: Dorsey.

Arnkoff, D. B., & Glass, C. R. (1982). Clinical cognitive constructs: Examination, evaluation, and elaboration. In P. C. Kendall (Ed.), *Advances in cognitive-behavioral research and therapy* (Vol. 1, pp. 1–34). New York: Academic.

Arnold, M. B. (1960). *Emotion and personality.* New York: Columbia University Press.

Arnold, M. B. (1970). *Feelings and emotions: The Loyola Symposium.* New York: Academic, 1970.

Ascher, L. M., & Edwards, N. B. (1972). Assessment of behavior therapy institutes. *Journal of Behavior Therapy and Experimental Psychology, 3,* 69–71.

Atchley, R. C. (1977). *The social forces in later life: An introduction to social gerontology.* Belmont, CA: Wadsworth.

Auerbach, A. H., & Luborsky, L. (1968). Accuracy of judgments of the "good hour." In J. M. Shlien (Ed.), *Research in psychotherapy* (Vol. 3, pp. 127–146). Washington, DC: American Psychological Association.

Augustine, A., & Cipani, E. (1982). Treating self-injurious behavior: Initial effects, maintenance and acceptability of treatment. *Child and Family Behavior Therapy, 4*(4), 53–69.

Axelrod, S., & Apsche, J. (Eds.). (1983). *The effects of punishment on human behavior.* New York: Academic.

Baekeland, F., & Laundwall, L. (1975). Dropping out of treatment: A critical review. *Psychological Bulletin, 82,* 738–783.

Balsam, P. D., & Bondy, A. S. (1983). The negative side effects of reward. *Journal of Applied Behavior Analysis, 16,* 283–296.

Baltes, P. B., Reese, H. W., & Nesselroade, J. R. (1977). *Life-span developmental psychology: Introduction to research methods.* Monterey, CA: Brooks/Cole.

Bandura, A. (1969). *Principles of behavior modification.* New York: Holt, Rinehart & Winston.

Bandura, A. (1977). Self-efficacy: Toward a unifying theory of behavioral change. *Psychological Review, 84,* 191–215.

Bandura, A. (1981). Self-referent thought: A developmental analysis of self efficacy. In J. H. Flavell & L. Ross (Eds.), *Social cognitive development: Frontiers and possible futures* (pp. 200–239). New York: Cambridge University Press.

Bandura, A., Adams, N., Hardy, A., & Howells, G. (1980). Tests of the generality of self-efficacy theory. *Cognitive Therapy and Research, 4,* 39–66.

Bandura, A., & Cervone, D. (1983). Self-evaluative and self-efficacy mechanisms governing the motivational effects of goal systems. *Journal of Personality and Social Psychology, 45,* 1017–1028.

Bandura, A., Reese, L., & Adams, N. (1982). Microanalysis of action and fear arousal as a function of differential levels of perceived self-efficacy. *Journal of Personality and Social Psychology, 43,* 5–21.

Bandura, A., & Simon, K. M. (1977). The role of proximal intentions in self-regulation of refractory behavior. *Cognitive Therapy and Research, 1,* 177–193.

Barkley, R. A. (1981). *Hyperactive children: A handbook for diagnosis and treatment.* New York: Guilford.

Barkley, R. A. (1982). Guidelines for defining hyperactivity in children: Attention deficit disorder with hyperactivity. In B. B. Lahey & A. E. Kazdin (Eds.), *Advances in clinical child psychology,* (Vol. 5, pp. 137–180). New York: Plenum.

Barling, J., & Abel, M. (1983). Self-efficacy beliefs and tennis performance. *Cognitive Therapy and Research, 7,* 265–272.

Barling, J., & Beattie, R. (1983). Self-efficacy beliefs and sales performance. *Journal of Organizational Behavior Management, 5,* 41–51.

Barlow, D. H. (1980). Behavior therapy: The next decade. *Behavior Therapy, 11,* 315–328.

Barlow, D. H., Bellack, A. S., Buchwald, A. M., Garfield, S. L., Hartmann, D. P., Herman, C. P., Hersen, M., Miller, P. M., Rachman, S., & Wolpe, J. (1983a). Alcoholism studies [Letter to the editor]. *Science, 220,* 555.

Barlow, D. H., Hayes, G., & Nelson, R. (1983b). *The empirical clinician.* New York: Pergamon.

Barlow, D. H., O'Brien, G. T., Last, C. G., & Holden, A. E. (1983c). Couples treatment of agoraphobia: Initial outcome. In K. D. Craig & R. J. McMahon (Eds.), *Advances in clinical behavior therapy* (pp. 99–126). New York: Brunner/Mazel.

Barlow, D. H., & Wolfe, B. (1981). Behavioral approaches to anxiety disorders: A report on the NIMH-SUNY, Albany Research Conference. *Journal of Consulting and Clinical Psychology, 49,* 448–454.

Barrios, B. A. (1983). The role of cognitive mediators in heterosocial anxiety: A test of self-efficacy theory. *Cognitive Therapy and Research, 7,* 543–554.

Bartlett, E. E. (1981). The contribution of school health education to community health promotion: What can we reasonably expect? *American Journal of Public Health, 71,* 1384–1391.

Baum, C. G., & Forehand, R. (1981). Long-term follow-up assessment of parent training by use of multiple outcome measures. *Behavior Therapy, 12,* 643–652.

Bauman, K. E., Reiss, M. L., Rogers, R. W., & Bailey, J. S. (1983). Dining out with children: Effectiveness of a parent advice package on pre-meal unappropriate behavior. *Journal of Applied Behavior Analysis, 16,* 55–68.

Beck, A. T. (1976). *Cognitive therapy and the emotional disorders.* New York: International Universities Press.

Beck, A. T., Rush, A. J., Shaw, B. F., & Emery, G. (1979). *Cognitive therapy of depression.* New York: Guilford.

Beck, A. T., Weissman, A., Lester, D., & Trexler, L. (1974). The measurement of pessimism: The Hopelessness Scale. *Journal of Consulting and Clinical Psychology, 42,* 861–865.

Beck, S., Forehand, R., Neeper, R., & Baskin, C. H. (1982). A comparison of two analogue strategies for assessing children's social skills. *Journal of Consulting and Clinical Psychology, 50,* 596–597.

Becker, M. H., & Maiman, L. A. (1975). Sociobehavioral determinants of compliance with health and medical care recommendations. *Medical Care, 13,* 10–24.

Becker, M. H., Maiman, L. A., Kirscht, J. P., Haefner, D. P., Drachman, R. H., & Tay-
    lor, D. W. (1979). Patient perceptions and compliance: Recent studies of the health
    belief model. In R. B. Harnes, D. W. Taylor, & D. L. Sackett (Eds.), *Compli-
    ance in health care* (pp. 78–109). Baltimore: Johns Hopkins University Press.
Bellack, A. S., Hersen, M., & Kazdin, A. E. (Eds.). (1982). *International handbook of
    behavior modification and therapy.* New York: Plenum.
Belloc, N. B., & Breslow, L. (1972). Relationship of health status and health practices.
    Preventive Medicine, 1, 409–421.
Benjamin, L. S. (1979). Use of structural analysis of social behavior (SASB) and Markov
    chains to study dyadic interactions. *Journal of Abnormal Psychology, 88*, 303–319.
Berenson, G. S. (1980). *Cardiovascular risk factors in children: The early natural history of
    atherosclerosis and essential hypertension.* New York: Oxford University Press.
Berenson, G. S., Srinivasan, S. R., & Webber, L. S. (1980). Prognostic significance of
    lipid profiles in children. In R. M. Lauer & R. B. Shekelle (Eds.), *Childhood
    prevention of atherosclerosis and hypertension* (pp. 75–86). New York: Raven.
Bernard, M. E., Kratochwill, T. R., & Keefauver, L. W. (1983). The effects of rational–
    emotive therapy and self-instructional training on chronic hair pulling. *Cognitive
    Therapy and Research, 7*, 273–280.
Berndt, D. J., Schwartz, S., & Kaiser, C. F. (1983). Readability of self-report depression
    inventories. *Journal of Consulting and Clinical Psychology, 51*, 627–628.
Bernstein, D. A., & Glasgow, R. E. (1979). Smoking. In O. F. Pomerleau & J. P. Brady (Eds.),
    Behavioral medicine: Theory and practice. Baltimore: Williams & Wilkins.
Bernstein, G. S. (in press). Training of behavior change agents. In M. Hersen, P. M.
    Eisler, & P. M. Miller (Eds.), *Progress in behavior modification* (vol. 16). New
    York: Academic.
Bernstein, G. S., & Ziarnik, J. P. (1982). Proactive identification of staff development needs:
    A model and methodology. *The Association for the Severely Handicapped, 8*,
    97–104.
Best, J. A. (1980). Mass media, self-management, and smoking modification, In P. O.
    Davidson & S. M. Davidson (Eds.), *Behavioral medicine: Changing health lifestyles*
    (pp. 371–390). New York: Brunner/Mazel.
Best, J. A. (1983). *Priorities for social science research on smoking* (Report of the Fifth
    World Conference Working Group on Social Science and Program Related Re-
    search, University of Waterloo, Toronto, Canada).
Beutler, L. E., & Oró-Beutler, M. E. (1982). Management of behaviorally disruptive and
    emotionally disturbed children: A school based family program. In R. W. Greene &
    T. D. Yawkey (Eds.), *Early and middle childhood: Growth, abuse and delinquency*
    (pp. 215–228). Westport, CT: Technomic.
Bijou, S. W. (1963). Theory and research in mental (developmental) retardation. *Psycho-
    logical Record, 13*, 95–110.
Birren, J. E. (1983). Aging in America: Roles for psychology. *American Psychologist, 38*,
    298–299.
Bistrian, B. R. (1978). Clinical use of a protein-sparing modified fast. *Journal of the
    American Medical Association, 21*, 2299–2302.
Bistrian, B. R., Winterer, J., & Blackburn, G. L. (1977). Effect of a protein-sparing diet
    and brief fast on nitrogen metabolism in mildly obese subjects. *Journal of Labora-
    tory and Clinical Medicine, 89*, 1030–1035.
Bitgood, S. C., Crowe, M. J., Suarez, Y., & Peters, R. D. (1980). Immobilization: Effects and
    side effects on steroetyped behavior in children. *Behavior Modification, 4*, 187–208.
Blechman, E. A. (1981). Toward comprehensive behavioral family intervention: An
    algorithm for matching families and interventions. *Behavior Modification, 5*,
    221–236.

Boffey, P. M. (1982a, November 2). Showdown near in feud over alcohol studies. *New York Times*, pp. C1–C2.

Boffey, P. M. (1982b, November 5). Panel clears 2 accused of scientific fraud in alcoholism study. *New York Times*, p. C3.

Boffey, P. M. (1983, November 22). Controlled drinking gains as a treatment in Europe. *New York Times*, pp. C1, C7.

Bogat, G. A., Jones, J. W., & Jason, L. A. (1980). School transitions: Preventive intervention following an elementary school closing. *Journal of Community Psychology, 8*, 343–352.

Boice, R. (1983). Observational skills. *Psychological Bulletin, 93*, 3–29.

Bonham, G. S., & Wilson, R. W. (1981). Children's health in families with cigarette smokers. *American Journal of Public Health, 71*, 290–293.

Borck, L. E., Fawcett, S. B., & Lichtenberg, J. W. (1982). Training, counseling and problem-solving skills with university students. *American Journal of Community Psychology, 10*, 225–237.

Borkovec, T., & Rachman, S. (1979). The utility of analogue research. *Behaviour Research and Therapy, 17*, 253–262.

Borkowski, J. G., Peck, V. A., Reid, M. K., & Kurtz, B. E. (1983). Impulsivity and strategy transfer: Metamemory as mediator. *Child Development, 54*, 459–473.

Bornstein, P. H., & Rychtarik, R. G. (1983). Consumer satisfaction in adult behavior therapy: Procedures, problems, and future perspectives. *Behavior Therapy, 14*, 191–208.

Botvin, G. J., Cantlon, A., Carter, B. J., & Williams, C. L. (1979). Reducing adolescent obesity through a school health program. *Journal of Pediatrics, 95*, 1060–1062.

Boulougouris, J. C. (Ed.). (1982). *Learning theory approaches to psychiatry*. Chicester, England: Wiley.

Bourdon, R. (1982). Measuring and tracking management performances for accountability. *Journal of Organizational Behavior Management, 4*, 101–112.

Bower, G. H. (1981). Mood and memory. *American Psychologist, 36*, 129–148.

Bowlby, J. (1977). The making and breaking of affectional bonds: Etiology and psychopathology in the light of attachment theory. *British Journal of Psychiatry, 130*, 201–210.

Boyd, R. L., & Levis, D. J. (1983). Exposure is a necessary condition for fear reduction: A reply to deSilva and Rachman. *Behaviour Research and Therapy, 21*, 143–149.

Brady, J. B. (1980). Some views on effective principles of psychotherapy [Special issue]. *Cognitive Therapy and Research, 4*, 271–306.

Braswell, L., Kendall, P. C., Braith, J., Carey, M. P., & Vye, C. S. (in press). "Involvement" in cognitive–behavioral therapy with children: Process and its relationship to outcome. *Cognitive Therapy and Research*.

Bray, G. A. (1976). *The obese patient*. Philadelphia: W. B. Saunders.

Breslow, L. (1979). A positive strategy for the nation's health. *Journal of the American Medical Association, 242*, 2093–2094.

Brim, O. G. (1959). *Education for child rearing*. New York: Russell Sage Foundation.

Brophy, J. (1981). Teacher praise: A functional analysis. *Review of Educational Research, 51*, 5–32.

Brown, J. H., Cunningham, G., & Birkimer, J. C. (1983). A telephone home survey to identify parent–child problems and maintaining conditions. *Child and Family Behavior Therapy, 5*(1), 85–92.

Brown, P. H. (1982). *Managing behavior on the job*. New York: Wiley.

Brownell, K. D. (1982). Obesity: Understanding and treating a serious, prevalent, and refractory disorder. *Journal of Consulting and Clinical Psychology, 50*, 820–840.

Brownell, K. D. (in press). Behavioral, psychological, and environmental predictors of obesity and success at weight reduction. *International Journal of Obesity.*

Brownell, K. D., Foster, G. D., & Wadden, T. A. (1984). *A peer-led program for the treatment of obesity in the schools: Short-term and long-term changes in weight, self-concept, and food selection.* Manuscript submitted for publication.

Brownell, K. D., Heckerman, C. L., Westlake, R. J., Hayes, S. C., & Monti, P. M. (1978). The effect of couples training and partner cooperativeness in the behavioral treatment of obesity. *Behaviour Research and Therapy, 16,* 323-333.

Brownell, K. D., & Kaye, F. S. (1982). A school-based behavior modification, nutrition education, and physical activity program for obese children. *American Journal of Clinical Nutrition, 35,* 277-283.

Brownell, K. D., & Stunkard, A. J. (1980). Exercise in the development and control of obesity. In A. J. Stunkard (Ed.), *Obesity* (pp. 300-324). Philadelphia: W. B. Saunders.

Brownell, K. D., & Stundard, A. J. (1981). Couples training, pharmacotherapy, and behavior therapy in the treatment of obesity. *Archives of General Psychiatry, 38,* 1224-1229.

Brownell, K. D., Stunkard, A. J., & Albaum, J. M. (1980). Evaluation and modification of exercise patterns in the natural environment. *American Journal of Psychiatry, 137,* 1540-1545.

Brunink, S., & Schroeder, H. Verbal therapeutic behavior of expert psychoanalytically oriented, Gestalt, and behavior therapists. *Journal of Consulting and Clinical Psychology,* 1979, *47,* 567-574.

Brunner, R. L., Vorhees, C. V., & Butcher, R. E. (1981). Food colors and behavior. *Science, 212,* 578-585.

Bryant, L. E., & Budd, K. S. (1982). Self-instructional training to increase independent work performance in preschoolers. *Journal of Applied Behavior, 15,* 259-271.

Budd, K. S., Riner, L. S., & Brockman, M. P. (1983). A structured observation system for clinical evaluation of parent training. *Behavioral Assessment, 5,* 373-393.

Burchard, J. D., & Lane, T. W. (1982). Crime and delinquency. In A. S. Bellack, M. Hersen & A. E. Kazdin (Eds.), *International handbook of behavior modification and therapy* (pp. 613-652). New York: Plenum.

Burgio, L. D., Whitman, T. L., & Reid, D. H. (1983). A participative management approach for improving direct-care staff performance in an institutional setting. *Journal of Applied Behavior Analysis, 6,* 37-53.

Burns, L. E., Thorpe, G. L., & Cavallaro, L. A. (1983, December). *Agoraphobia eight years after behavioral treatment: A follow-up study with interview, questionnaire, and behavioral data.* Paper presented at the annual meeting of the Association for Advancement of Behavior Therapy, Washington, DC.

Butler, G., & Mathews, A. (1983). Cognitive processes in anxiety. *Advances in Behaviour Research and Therapy, 5,* 51-62.

Butler, J. F. (1983). Compliance enhancement procedures in clinical practice. *Behavioral Engineering, 8(2),* 49-57.

Caddy, G. R. (1982). The emergence of professional psychology: Background to the Virginia Beach conference and beyond. In G. R. Caddy, D. C. Rimm, N. Watson, & J. H. Johnson (Eds.), *Educating professional psychologists* (pp. 000-000). New Brunswick, NJ: Transaction.

Campbell, D. T., & Stanley, J. C. (1963). *Experimental and quasi-experimental designs for research.* Chicago: Rand McNally.

Caplan, G. (1965). Opportunities for school psychologists in the primary prevention of mental disorders in children. In N. M. Lambert (Ed.), *The protection and promotion of mental health in schools* (DHEW Publ. No. (PHS) 1226) Washington, DC: U.S. Government Printing Office.

Carey, K. B., Carey, M. P., & Turkat, I. D. (1983). Behavior modification in the media: A five-year follow-up. *American Psychologist, 38,* 498–500.

Carey, W. B., & McDevitt, S. C. (1980). Minimal brain dysfunction and hyperkinesis: A clinical viewpoint. *American Journal of Diseases of Children, 134,* 926–929.

Carmody, T. P., Senner, J. W., Malinow, M. R., & Matarazzo, J. D. (1980). Physical exercise rehabilitation: Long-term dropout rate in cardiac patients. *Journal of Behavioral Medicine, 3,* 163–168.

Carver, C. S., & Scheier, M. F. (1981). *Attention and self-regultion: A control theory approach to human behavior.* New York: Springer.

Cautela, J. R., Cautela, J., & Esonis, S. (1983). *Forms for behavior analysis with children.* Champaign, IL: Research Press.

Chambless, D., & Goldstein, A. (Eds.). (1982). *Agoraphobia.* New York: Wiley.

Chambless, D. L., Hunter, K., & Jackson, A. (1982). Social anxiety and assertiveness: A comparison of the conditions in phobic and college student samples. *Behavior Research and Therapy, 20,* 403–404.

Chapman, L. J., & Chapman, J. P. (1967). Genesis of popular but erroneous diagnostic observations. *Journal of Abnormal Psychology, 72,* 193–204.

Cheek, F. E., & Miller, M. D. (1980). *Intensive ½ and 1-day programs in stress and the role and image of the correctional officer: Avoiding the burn-out syndrome.* Unpublished manuscript.

Chiauzri, E., & Heimberg, R. G. (1982). *The effects of subjects' level of assertiveness, sex and legitimacy of request on assertion-relevant cognitions: An analysis by post performance videotape reconstruction.* Unpublished manuscript, State University of New York at Albany.

Christensen, A., Phillips, S., Glasgow, R. E., & Johnson, S. M. (1983). Parental characteristics and interactional dysfunction in families with child behavior problems: A preliminary investigation. *Journal of Abnormal Child Psychology, 11,* 153–166.

Christian, W. P. (1983a). Managing the performance of the human service consultant. *The Behavior Therapist, 6,* 47–49.

Christian, W. P. (1983b). Professional peer review: Recommended strategies for reviewer and reviewee. *The Behavior Therapist, 6,* 86–89.

Christiansen, B. A., & Goldman, M. S. (1983). Alcohol-related expectancies versus demographic/background variables in the prediction of adolescent drinking. *Journal of Consulting and Clinical Psychology, 51,* 249–257.

Cianni-Surridge, M., & Horan, J. J. (1983). On the wisdom of assertive job-seeking behavior. *Journal of Counseling Psychology, 30,* 209–214.

Clark, D. B., & Baker, B. L. (1983). Predicting outcome in parent training. *Journal of Consulting and Clinical Psychology, 51,* 309–311.

Coates, T. J., Jeffrey, R. W., & Slinkard, L. A. (1981). Heart healthy eating and exercise: Introducing and maintaining changes in health behaviors. *American Journal of Public Health, 71,* 15–23.

Coates, T. J., & Li, V. C. (1983). Does smoking cessation lead to weight gain?: The experience of asbestos-exposed shipyard workers. *American Journal of Public Health, 11,* 1303–1304.

Cohen, E. A., Gelfand, D. M., Dodd, D. K., Jensen, J., & Turner, C. (1980). Self-control practices associated with weight loss maintenance in children and adolescents. *Behavior Therapy, 11,* 26–37.

Cole, P. M., & Kazdin, A. E. (1980). Critical issues in self-instructional training with children. *Child Behavior Therapy, 2,* 1–23.

Colley, J. R. T., Holland, W. W., & Corkhill, R. T. (1974). Influence of passive smoking and parental phlegm on penumonia and bronchitis in early childhood. *Lancet, i,* 1031–1034.

Collins, R. L., & Carlin, A. S. (1983). Case study: The cognitive–behavioral treatment of a multiple-drug abuser. *Psychotherapy: Theory, Research and Practice, 20,* 101–106.

Compas, B. E., Adelman, H. S., Freundl, P. C., Nelson, P., & Taylor, L. (1982). Parent and child causal attributions during clinical interviews. *Journal of Abnormal Child Psychology, 10,* 77–84.

Condiotte, M. M., & Lichtenstein, E. (1981). Self-efficacy and relapse in smoking cessation programs. *Journal of Consulting and Clinical Psychology, 49,* 648–658.

Conoley, C. W., Conoley, J. C., McConnell, J. A., & Kimzey, C. E. (1983). The effect of the ABCs of rational emotive therapy and the empty chair technique of Gestalt therapy on anger reduction. *Psychotherapy: Theory, Research and Practice, 20,* 112–117.

Craighead, L. W., Stunkard, A. J., & O'Brien, R. (1981). Behavior therapy and pharmacotherapy for obesity. *Archives of General Psychiatry, 38,* 763–768.

Crandell, C. J., & Chambless, D. L. (1981). *The validation of an inventory for measuring depressive thoughts: The Crandell Cognitions Inventory.* Paper presented at the annual meeting of the Association for Advancement of Behavior Therapy, Toronto.

Crawford, D. A. (1983). Fagan—A suitable case for treatment? *Bulletin of the British Psychological Society, 36,* 153–155.

Crowell, C. R., & Anderson, D. C. (1982). The scientific and methodological basis of a systematic approach to human behavior management. *Journal of Organizational Behavior Management, 4,* 1–31.

Cullen, C. (1982). Questioning the foundations of cognitive behavior modification. In C. J. Main & W. R. Lindsay (Eds.), *Clinical psychology and medicine: A behavioral perspective* (pp. 69–83). New York: Plenum.

Cullen, C., Burton, M., Watts, S., & Thomas, M. (1983). A preliminary report on the nature of interactions in a mental handicap institution. *Behaviour Research and Therapy, 21,* 579–583.

Cullington, A., Butler, G., Hibbert, G., & Gelder, M. (in press). Problem solving: Not a treatment for agoraphobia. *Behavior Therapy.*

Cummings, J., & Cummings, E. (1962). *Ego and milieu: Theory and practice of environmental therapy.* New York: Atherton.

Curo, A. J., Leaf, R. B., & Borakove, L. S. (1978). Teaching janitorial skills to the mentally retarded: Acquisition, generalization, and maintenance. *Journal of Applied Behavior Analysis, 11,* 345–355.

Dahlkoetter, J., Callahan, E. J., & Linton, J. (1979). Obesity and the unbalanced energy equation: Exercise versus eating habit change. *Journal of Consulting and Clinical Psychology, 47,* 898–905.

Danaher, B. G., Berkanovic, E., & Gerber, B. (1983). Smoking and television: Review of the extant literature. *Addictive Behaviors, 8,* 173–182.

Davies, D. L. (1962). Normal drinking in recovered alcoholic addicts. *Quarterly Journal of Studies on Alcohol, 23,* 94–104.

Davison, G. C., Robins, C., & Johnson, M. K. (1983). Articulated thoughts during simulated situations: A paradigm for studying cognition in emotion and behavior. *Cognitive Therapy and Research, 7,* 17–40.

Day, R. M., Lindeman, D. P., Havelka, S. S., Tucker, D. J., & Hasson, D. C. (1983). The application of organizational behavior management to a special education program. *Mental Health and Mental Retardation Quarterly Digest, 2*(2).

Dentch, G. E., O'Farrell, T. J., & Cutter, H. S. G. (1980). Readability of marital assessment measures used by behavioral marriage therapists. *Journal of Consulting and Clinical Psychology, 48,* 790–792.

Depue, R. A., Slater, J. F., Wolfstetter-Kausch, H., Klein, D., Goplerud, E., & Farr, D. (1981). A behavioral paradigm for identifying persons at risk for bipolar depressive disorder: A conceptual framework and five validation studies. *Journal of Abnormal Psychology, 90,* 381–437.

de Silva, P., & Rachman, S. (1981). Is exposure a necessary condition for fear-reduction? *Behaviour Research and Therapy, 19,* 227–232.

de Silva, P., & Rachman, S. (1983). Exposure and fear-reduction. *Behaviour Research and Therapy, 21,* 151–152.

Dickens, B. M., Doob, A. N., Warwick, O. H., & Winegard, W. C. (1982). *Report of the Committee of Inquiry into Allegations Concerning Drs. Linda and Mark Sobell.* Toronto: Addictions Research Foundation.

DiClemente, C. C. (1981). Self-efficacy and smoking cessation maintenance. *Cognitive Therapy and Research, 5,* 175–187.

DiGiuseppe, R., & Bernard, M. (1983). Principles of assessment and methods of treatment with children: Special considerations. In A. Ellis & M. Bernard (Eds.), *Rational-emotive approaches to the problems of childhood* (pp. 45–88). New York: Plenum.

Dobson, K. S., & Breiter, H. J. (1983). Cognitive assessment of depression: Reliability and validity of three measures. *Journal of Abnormal Psychology, 92,* 107–109.

Donovan, W. L., Leavitt, L. A., & Balling, J. D. (1978). Material physiological response to infant signals. *Psychophysiology, 15,* 68–70.

Douglas, V. I. (1972). Stop, look, and listen: The problem of sustained attention and impulse control in hyperactive and normal children. *Canadian Journal of Behavioural Science, 4,* 259–282.

Douglas, V. I., & Parry, P. A. (1983). Effects of reward on a delayed reaction time task performance of hyperactive children. *Journal of Abnormal Child Psychology, 11,* 313–326.

Douglas, V. I., Parry, P., Marton, P., & Garson, C. (1976). Assessment of a cognitive training program for hyperactive children. *Journal of Abnormal Child Psychology, 4,* 389–410.

Driessen, J. R., & Demetral, G. D. (1983). A note on the ecobehavioral approach to the treatment of child sexual abuse. *The Behavior Therapist, 6,* 141–142.

Dubbert, P. M., & Wilson, G. T. (1983). Treatment failures in behavior therapy for obesity: Causes, correlates, and consequences. In E. Foa & P. M. G. Emmelkamp (Eds.), *Failures in behavior therapy* (pp. 263–288). New York: Wiley.

Dubey, D. R., O'Leary, S. G., & Kaufman, K. F. (1983). Training parents of hyperactive children in child management: A comparative outcome study. *Journal of Abnormal Child Psychology, 11,* 229–246.

Dubren, R., (1977). Evaluation of a televised stop-smoking clinic. *Public Health Reports, 92,* 81–84.

Dumas, J. E., & Wahler, R. G. (1983). Predictors of treatment outcome in parent training: Mother insularity and socioeconomic disadvantage. *Behavioral Assessment, 5,* 301–313.

Dunbar, J. (1983). Compliance in pediatric populations: A review. In P. J. McGrath & P. Firestone (Eds.), *Pediatric and adolescent behavioral medicine: Issues in treatment* (pp. 210–230). New York: Springer.

Durand, V. M. (1983). Behavioral ecology of a staff incentive program: Effects on absenteeism and resident disruptive behavior. *Behavior Modification, 7,* 165–181.

Durrant, M. L., Royston, J. P., & Wloch, R. T. (1982). Effect of exercise on energy intake and eating patterns in lean and obese humans. *Physiology and Behavior, 29,* 449–454.

Dush, D. M., Hirt, M. L., & Schroeder, H. E. (1983). *A meta-analysis of the effectiveness of self-statement modification with childhood disorders.* Manuscript submitted for publication.

Eckert, P. (1983). Beyond the statistics of adolescent smoking. *American Journal of Public Health, 73,* 439–441.

Egel, A. L. (1981). Reinforcer variation: Implication for motivating developmentally disabled children. *Journal of Applied Behavior Analysis, 14,* 345–350.

Egel, A. L., Koegel, R. L., & Schreibman, L. (1980). Review of educational-treatment procedures for autistic children. In L. Man & D. A. Sabatino (Eds.), *The fourth review of special education* (pp. 109–149). New York: Grune & Stratton.

Egel, A. L., Richman, G. S., & Koegel, R. L. (1981). Normal peer models and autistic children's learning. *Journal of Applied Behavior Analysis, 14,* 3–12.

Eidelson, R. J., & Epstein, N. (1982). Cognition and relationship maladjustment: Development of a measure of dysfunctional relationship beliefs. *Journal of Consulting and Clinical Psychology, 50,* 715–720.

Einhorn, H. J., & Hogarth, R. M. (1978). Confidence in judgment: Persistence of the illusion of validity. *Psychological Review, 85,* 39⁵,416.

Eisert, H. G., Eisert, M., & Schmidt, M. H. (1982). Stimulantientherapie und kognitive verhaltensmodifikation bei hyperaktiven kindern. *Zeitschrift für Kinderund Jugendpsychchiatrie, 10,* 193–215.

Ellis, A. (1982). A reappraisal of rational–emotive therapy's theoretical foundations and therapeutic methods: A reply to Eschenroeder. *Cognitive Therapy and Research, 6,* 393–398.

Ellis, A. (1983). Failures in rational–emotive therapy. In E. Foa & P. M. G. Emmelkamp (Eds.), *Failures in behavior therapy* (pp. 159–171). New York: Wiley.

Ellis, A., & Bernard, M. (Eds.). (1983). *Rational–emotive approaches to the problems of childhood.* New York: Plenum.

Ellis, A., & Knaus, W. (1979). *Overcoming procrastination.* New York: New American Library.

Elwood, R. W., & Jacobson, N. S. (1982). Spouses' agreement in reporting their behavioral interactions: A clinical replication. *Journal of Consulting and Clinical Psychology, 50,* 783–784.

Emery, R. E., Binkoff, J. A., Houts, A. C., & Carr, E. G. (1983). Children as independent variables: Some clinical implications of child-effects. *Behavior Therapy, 14,* 388–412.

Emmelkamp, P. M. G. (1982). *Phobic and obsessive-compulsive disorders.* New York: Plenum.

Emmelkamp, P. M. G., & Foa, E. (1983). Failures are a challenge. In E. Foa & P. M. G. Emmelkamp (Eds.), *Failures in behavior therapy.* New York: Wiley.

Emmelkamp, P. M. G., & Mersch, P. P. (1982). Cognition and exposure in vivo in the treatment of agoraphobia: Short term and delayed effects. *Cognitive Therapy and Research, 6,* 77–90.

Emmelkamp, P. M. G., & van der Hout, A. (1983). Failure in treating agoraphobia: In E. Foa & P. M. G. Emmelkamp (Eds.), *Failures in behavior therapy* (pp. 58–81). New York: Wiley.

Emmelkamp, P. M. G., van der Hout, A., & de Vries, K. (1983). Assertive training for agoraphobics. *Behaviour Research and Therapy, 21,* 63–68.

Epstein, L. H., & Cluss, P. A. (1982). A behavioral medicine perspective on adherence to long-term medical regimens. *Journal of Consulting and Clinical Psychology, 50,* 950–971.

Epstein, L. H., Dickson, B. E., Ossip, D. J., Stiller, R., Russel, P. O., & Winter, K. (1982a).

Relationships among measures of smoking topography. *Addictive Behaviors, 7,* 307-310.

Epstein, L. H., Wing, R. R., Koeske, R., Ossip, D., & Beck, S. (1982b). A comparison of lifestyle change and programmed aerobic exercise on weight and fitness changes in obese children. *Behavior Therapy, 13,* 638-650.

Erwin, E. (1978). *Behavior therapy: Scientific, philosophical and moral foundations.* New York: Cambridge University Press.

Erwin, E. (1984). Establishing caused connections: Meta-analysis and psychotherapy. *Midwest Studies in Philosophy, 9,* 1-29.

Eschenroeder, C. (1982). How rational is rational-emotive therapy?: A critical appraisal of its theoretical foundations and therapeutic methods. *Cognitive Therapy and Research, 6,* 381-392.

Evans, R. I. (1976). Smoking in children: Developing a social psychological strategy of deterrence. *Preventive Medicine, 5,* 122-127.

Evans, R. I. (1979). Smoking in children and adolescents: Psychological determinants and prevention strategies. In *Smoking and health: Report of the Surgeon General* (DHEW Publ. No. (PHS) 79-50066) (284-292). Washington, DC: U. S. Government Printing Office.

Everaerd, W. (1983). Failure in treating sexual dysfunctions. In E. Foa & P.M.G. Emmelkamp (Eds.), *Failures in behavior therapy* (pp. 392-405). New York: Wiley.

Eysenck, H. J. (1983a). The benefits of psychotherapy. *Behaviour Research and Therapy, 21,* 315-320.

Eysenck, H. J. (1983b). The social application of Pavlovian theories. *Pavlovian Journal of Biological Science, 18,* 117-125.

Fawcett, S. B., Mathews, R. M., & Fletcher, R. K. (1980). Behavioral technology for community application: Some promising directions. *Journal of Applied Behavior Analysis, 13,* 505-518.

Fawcett, S. B., Seekins, T., & Braukmann, C. J. (in press). Developing and transferring behavioral technologies for children and youth. *Children and Youth Services Review.*

Feinman, S., & Coon, R. H. (1983). The effect of status on the evaluation of behavior: Elderly, adults, and children aged 5-65. *Research on Aging, 5,* 119-135.

Feldman, M. P. (1983). Juvenile offending: Behavioral approach to preventive and interventive. *Child and Family Behavior Therapy, 5*(1), 37-50.

Feldman, M. P., & Peay, J. (1982). Ethical and legal issues. In A. S. Bellack, M. Hersen, & A. E. Kazdin (Eds.), *International handbook of behavior modification and therapy* (pp. 231-261). New York: Plenum.

Feldman, W. S., Manella, K. J., Apodaca, L., & Varni, J. W. (1982). Behavioral group parent training in spina bifida. *Journal of Clinical Child Psychology, 11,* 141-150.

Feldman, W. S., Manella, K. J., & Varni, J. W. (1983). A behavioural parent training programme for single mothers of physically handicapped children. *Child: Care, Health and Development, 9,* 157-168.

Feldman, W. S., & Varni, J. W. (1983). A parent training program for the child with spina bifida. *Spina Bifida Therapy, 4,* 77-89.

Fennell, M.J.V. (1983). Cognitive therapy of depression: The mechanism of change. *Behavioral Psychotherapy, 11,* 97-108.

Fennell, M. J. V., & Teasdale, J. D. (1982). Cognitive therapy with chronic, drug-refractory depressed outpatients: A note of caution. *Cognitive Therapy and Research, 6,* 455-460.

Fernandez, J. (1983). The token economy and beyond. *Irish Journal of Psychotherapy, 2,* 21-41.

Ferretti, R. P., & Cavalier, A. R. (1983). A critical assessment of overcorrection procedures mentally retarded persons. In J. L. Matson & F. Andrasik (Eds.), *Treatment issues and innovations in mental retardation* (pp. 261–301). New York: Plenum.

Fine, M. J., & Holt, R. (1983). Intervening with school problems: A family systems perspective. *Psychology in the Schools, 20,* 59–66.

Finkel, C. B., Glass, C. R., & Merluzzi, T. V. (1982). Differential discrimination of self-referent statements by depressives and nondepressives. *Cognitive Therapy, 6,* 173–184

Fiore, J., Becker, J., & Coppel, D. B. (1983). Social network interactions: A buffer or a stress. *American Journal of Community Psychology, 11,* 423–439.

Firestone, P., & Douglas, V. I. (1975). The effects of reward and punishment on reaction times and autonomic activity in hyperactive and normal children. *Journal of Abnormal Child Psychology, 3,* 201–216.

Fisher, L. M., & Wilson, G. T. (in press). A study of the psychology of agoraphobia. *Behaviour Research and Therapy.*

Fishman, D. B. (1981). *A cost-effectiveness methodology for community mental health centers: Development and pilot test* (CNIMH Series FN No. 3, DHHS Publ. No. (ADM) 81-767). Washington, DC: U.S. Government Printing Office.

Foa, E., & Emmelkamp, P. M. G. (1983). (Eds.). *Failures in behavior therapy.* New York: Wiley.

Foa, E., Grayson, J. B., Steketee, G. S., Doppelt, H. G., Turner, R. M., & Latimer, P. R. (1983a). Success and failure in the behavioral treatment of obsessive–compulsives. *Journal of Consulting and Clinical Psychology, 51,* 287–297.

Foa, E., Steketee, G., Grayson, J., & Doppelt, H. (1983b). Treatment of obsessive–compulsives: When do we fail? In E. Foa & P. M. G. Emmelkamp (Eds.), *Failures in behavior therapy* (pp. 10–34). New York: Wiley.

Folkins, C. H., & Sime, W. E. (1981). Physical fitness training and mental health. *American Psychologist, 36,* 373–389.

Forbes, G. B. (1975). Prevalence of obesity in childhood. In G. A. Bray (Ed.), *Obesity in perspective* (DHEW Publ. No. (NIH) 75-708) (Vol. 2, pp. 205–208). Washington, DC: U.S. Government Printing Office.

Ford, J. D. (1978). Therapeutic relationship in behavior therapy: An empirical analysis. *Journal of Consulting and Clinical Psychology, 46,* 1302–1314.

Forehand, R., Middlebrook, J., Rogers, T., & Steffe, M. (1983a). Dropping out of parent training. *Behaviour Research and Therapy, 21,* 663–668.

Forehand, R., Steffe, M. A., Furey, W. M., & Walley, P. B. (1983b). Mothers' evaluation of a parent training program completed three and one-half years earlier. *Journal of Behavior Therapy and Experimental Psychiatry, 14,* 339–342.

Foreyt, J. P., Goodrick, G. K., & Gotto, A. M. (1981). Limitations of behavioral treatment of obesity: Review and analysis. *Journal of Behavioral Medicine, 4,* 159–174.

Forness, S. R., Guthrie, D., & MacMillan, D. L. (1982). Classroom environments as they relate to mentally retarded children's observable behavior. *American Journal of Mental Deficiency, 87,* 259–265.

Foxworthy, R., Ellis, W., & McLeod, C. (1982). A management team system. *Journal of Organizational Behavior Management, 3*(4), 19–32.

Foxx, R. M., & Brown, R. A. (1979). Nicotine fading and self-monitoring for cigarette abstinence or controlled smoking. *Journal of Applied Behavior Analysis, 12,* 111–125.

Frank, P. J., Klein, S., & Jacobs, J. (1982). Cost–benefit analysis of a behavioral program for geriatric inpatients. *Hospital and Community Psychiatry, 33,* 374–377.

Franks, C. M. (1984a). Foreward. In J. L. Matson & T. M. DiLorenzo, *Punishment and its alternatives: A new perspective for behavior modification* (pp. ix–xiv). New York: Springer.

Franks, C. M. (1984b). On conceptual and technical integrity in psychoanalysis and behavior therapy, two fundamentally incompatible systems. In H. Arkowitz & S. Messer (Eds.), *Psychoanalysis and behavior therapy: Are they compatible?* (pp. 223–247). New York: Plenum.

Franks, C. M., & Rosenbaum, M. (1983). Behavior therapy: Overview and personal reflections. In M. Rosenbaum, C. M. Franks, & Y. Jaffe (Eds.), *Perspectives on behavior therapy in the eighties* (pp. 3–14). New York: Springer.

Franks, C. M., & Wilson, G. T. (Eds.). (1973). *Annual review of behavior therapy: Theory and practice* (Vol. 1). New York: Brunner/Mazel.

Franks, C. M., & Wilson, G. T. (Eds.). (1974). *Annual review of behavior therapy: Theory and practice* (Vol. 2). New York: Brunner/Mazel.

Franks, C. M., & Wilson, G. T. (Eds.). (1975). *Annual review of behavior therapy: Theory and practice* (Vol. 3). New York: Brunner/Mazel.

Franks, C. M., & Wilson, G. T. (Eds.). (1976). *Annual review of behavior therapy: Theory and practice* (Vol. 4). New York: Brunner/Mazel.

Franks, C. M., & Wilson, G. T. (Eds.). (1977). *Annual review of behavior therapy: Theory and practice* (Vol. 5). New York: Brunner/Mazel.

Franks, C. M., & Wilson, G. T. (Eds.). (1978). *Annual review of behavior therapy: Theory and practice* (Vol. 6). New York: Brunner/Mazel.

Franks, C. M., & Wilson, G. T. (Eds.). (1979). *Annual review of behavior therapy: Theory and practice* (Vol. 7). New York: Brunner/Mazel.

Frcka, G., Beyts, J., Levey, A. B., & Martin, I. (1983). The role of awareness in human conditioning. *Pavlovian Journal of Biological Science, 18*, 69–76.

Frederiksen, L. W. (1979). Controlled smoking. In N. A. Krasnegor (Ed.), *Behavioral analysis and treatment of substance abuse* (National Institute on Drug Abuse Research Monograph 25, DHEW Publ. No. (ADM) 79-839). (pp. 128–139). Washington, DC: U.S. Government Printing Office.

Frederiksen, L. W. (Ed.). (1982). *Handbook of organizational behavior management*. New York: Wiley.

Frederiksen, L. W., Peterson, G. L., & Murphy, W. D. (1976). Controlled smoking: Development and maintenance. *Addictive Behaviors, 1*, 193–196.

Frederiksen, L. W., Richter, W. T., Johnson, R. P., & Solomon, L. J. (1982). Specificity of performance feedback in a professional service delivery setting. *Journal of Organizational Behavior Management, 3*(4), 41–52.

Frederiksen, L. W., & Simon, S. J. (1978). Modification of smoking topography: A preliminary analysis. *Behavior Therapy, 9*, 946–949.

Fremouw, W. J., & Gross, R. (1983). Issues in cognitive–behavioral treatment of performance anxiety. In P. C. Kendall (Ed.), *Advances in cognitive–behavioral research and therapy* (Vol. 2, pp. 280–306). New York: Academic.

Friedman, G. D., Petitti, D. B., & Bawol, R. D. (1983). Prevalence and correlates of passive smoking. *American Journal of Public Health, 73*, 401–405.

Friedman, R. M., Sandler, J., Hernandez, M., & Wolfe, D. A. (1981). Child abuse. In E. J. Mash & L. G. Terdal (Eds.), *Behavioral assessment of childhood disorders* (pp. 221–255). New York: Guilford.

Friman, P. C., & Christophersen, E. R. (1983). Behavior therapy and hyperactivity: A brief review of therapy for a big problem. *The Behavior Therapist, 6*, 175–176.

Fritschler, A. L. (1975). *Smoking and politics: Policy-making and the federal bureaucracy* (2nd ed.). Englewood Cliffs, NJ: Prentice-Hall.

Frodi, A. M., & Lamb, M. E. (1980). Child abusers' responses to infant smiles and cries. *Child Development, 51,* 238–241.

Frodi, A. M., Lamb, M. E., Leavitt, L. A., & Donovan, W. L. (1978). Fathers' and mothers' responses to infant smiles and cries. *Infant Behavior and Development, 1,* 187–198.

Fry, L. (1983). Women in society. In S. Spence & G. Shepherd (Eds.), *Developments in social skills training* (pp. 251–274). London: Academic.

Fuhrman, M. J., & Kendall, P. C. (in press). Cognitive tempo and behavioral adjustment in children. *Cognitive Therapy and Research.*

Fuller, G. D. (1978). Current status of biofeedback in clinical practice. *American Psychologist, 33,* 39–48.

Furman, W., & Buhrmester, D. (1982). The contributions of siblings and peers to the parenting process. In M. J. Kostelnik, A. R. Rabin, L. A. Phenice, & A. K. Soderman (Eds.), *Child nurturance: Vol. 2. Patterns of supplementary parenting* (pp. 69–100). New York: Plenum.

Furtkamp, E., Giffort, D., & Schiers, W. (1982). In-class evaluation of behavior modification knowledge: Parallel tests for use in applied settings. *Journal of Behavior Therapy and Experimental Psychiatry, 13,* 131–134.

Galassi, J. P., Frierson, H. T., & Sharer, R. (1981). Concurrent versus retrospective assessment in test anxiety research. *Journal of Consulting and Clinical Psychology, 49,* 614–615.

Garbarino, J. (1977). The human ecology of child maltreatment: A conceptual model for research. *Journal of Marriage and the Family, 39,* 721–735.

Garbarino, J. (1981). *What we know about child maltreatments.* Unpublished manuscript.

Gardner, J. M. (1972). Selection of nonprofessionals for behavior modification programs. *American Journal of Mental Deficiency, 76,* 680–685.

Gardner, J. M., & Giampa, F. L. (1971). The attendant behavior check list: Measuring on-the-ward behavior of institutional attendants. *American Journal of Mental Deficiency, 75,* 617–622.

Garfield, S. L. (1978). Research on client variables in psychotherapy. In S. L. Garfield & A. E. Bergin (Eds.), *Handbook of psychotherapy and behavior change* (2nd ed)., pp. 191–232). New York: Wiley.

Garfield, S. L. (1983). Effectiveness of psychotherapy: The perennial controversy. *Professional Psychology: Research and Practice, 14,* 35–43.

Garner, D. M., & Bemis, K. M. (1982). A cognitive–behavioral approach to anorexia nervosa. *Cognitive Therapy and Research, 6,* 123–150.

Garrison, S. R., & Stolberg, A. L. (1983). Modification of anger in children by affective imagery training. *Journal of Abnormal Child Psychology, 11,* 115–130.

Garrow, J. S. (1978). *Energy balance and obesity in man* (2nd ed.). Amsterdam: Elsevier.

Garrow, J. S. (1981). *Treat obesity seriously: A clinical manual.* London: Churchill Livingstone.

Garrow, J. S., & Gardiner, G. T. (1981). Maintenance of weight loss in obese patients after jaw wiring. *British Medical Journal, 282,* 858–859.

Gartner, A. (1971). *Paraprofessionals and their performances: A survey of education, health and social service programs.* New York: Praeger.

Gast, D. L., & Nelson, C. M. (1977). Legal and ethical considerations for the use of timeout in special education settings. *Journal of Special Education, 11,* 457–467.

Gaudin, J. M., & Pollane, L. (1983). Social networks, stress and child abuse. *Children and Youth Services Review, 5,* 91–102.

Gaylin, W. (1982). The "competence" of children: No longer all or none. *Journal of the American Academy of Child Psychiatry, 21,* 153–162.

Gaylord-Ross, R. J., & Pitts-Conway, V. (1983). Social behavior development in integrated secondary autistic programs. In N. Certo, N. Haring, & R. York (Eds.), *Public school integration of the severely handicapped: Rational issues and progressive alternatives* (pp. 197–219). Baltimore: Paul H. Brookes.

Gelder, M., Bancroft, J., Gath, D. H., Johnston, D. W., Mathews, A., & Shaw, P. (1973). Specific and non-specific factors in behaviour therapy. *British Journal of Psychiatry, 123,* 445–462.

Geller, E. S. (1981). Evaluating energy conservation programs: Is verbal report enough? *Journal of Consumer Research, 8,* 331–335.

Genuth, S. M., Castro, J. H., & Vertes, V. (1974). Weight reduction in obesity by outpatient semistarvation. *Journal of the American Medical Association, 230,* 987–991.

Giles, T. R. (1983a). Probable superiority of behavioral interventions I Traditional comparative outcome. *Journal of Behavior Therapy and Experimental Psychiatry, 14,* 29–32.

Giles, T. R. (1983b). Probable superiority of behavioral intervention. II. Empirical status of the equivalence of therapies hypothesis. *Journal of Behavior Therapy and Experimental Psychiatry, 14,* 189–196.

Giles-Sims, J. (1983). *Wife battering: A systems theory approach.* New York: Guilford.

Glasgow, R. E., Klesges, R. C., Godding, P. R., & Gegelman, R. (1983a). Controlled smoking, with or without carbon monoxide feedback, as an alternative for chronic smokers. *Behavior Therapy, 14,* 386–397.

Glasgow, R. E., Klesges, R. C., & Vasey, M. W. (1983b). Controlled smoking for chronic smokers: An extension and replication. *Addictive Behaviors, 8,* 143–150.

Glass, G. V., McGaw, B., & Smith, M. L. (1981). *Meta-analysis in social research.* Beverly Hills, CA: Sage.

Goldbourt, U., & Medalie, J. H. (1977). Characteristics of smokers, nonsmokers, and ex-smokers among 10,000 adult males in Israel. *American Journal of Epidemiology, 105,* 75–86.

Goldfried, M. R. (Ed.). (1982). *Converging theories in the practice of psychotherapy.* New York: Springer.

Goldfried, M. R. (1983). The behavior therapist in clinical practice. *The Behavior Therapist, 6,* 45–46.

Goldfried, M. R., & Davison, G. C. (1976). *Clinical behavior therapy.* New York: Holt, Rinehart & Winston.

Goldfried, M. R., & Robins, C. (1983). Self-schemas, cognitive bias, and the processing of therapeutic experiences. In P. C. Kendall (Ed.), *Advances in cognitive–behavioral research and therapy* (Vol. 2), New York: Academic.

Goldin, P. (1969). A review of children's reports of parent behaviors. *Psychological Bulletin, 71,* 222–236.

Goldstein, A. (1982). Agoraphobia: Treatment successes, treatment failures, and theoretical implications. In D. Chambless & A. Goldstein (Eds.), *Agoraphobia* (pp. 183–214). New York: Wiley.

Gomez-Schwartz, B. (1978). Effective ingredients in psychotherapy: Prediction of outcome from process variables. *Journal of Consulting and Clinical Psychology, 46,* 1023–1035.

Goodman, K. (1983). A behavior analyst in international development. *The Behavior Therapist, 6,* 193–194.

Gordon, T. (1975). *Parent effectiveness training.* New York: Wyden.

Gordon, T., Kannel, W. B., Dawber, T. R., & McGee, D. (1975). Changes associated with quitting cigarette smoking: The Framingham Study. *American Heart Journal, 90,* 322–328.

Gortmaker, S. L., Walker, D. K., Jacobs, F. H., & Ruch-Ross, H. (1982). Parental

smoking and the risk of childhood asthma. *American Journal of Public Health,*
72, 574–579.

Graham, L. E. II, Taylor, C. B., Hovell, M. F., & Siegel, W. (1983). Five-year follow-up
to a behavioral weight loss program. *Journal of Consulting and Clinical Psychology, 51,* 322–323.

Graziano, A. M., & Bythell, D. L. (1983). Failures in child behavior therapy. In E. B. Foa
& P. M. G. Emmelkamp (Eds.), *Failures in behavior therapy* (pp. 406–424). New
York: Wiley.

Graziano, A. M., & Katz, J. N. (1982). Training paraprofessionals. In A. S. Bellack,
M. Hersen, & A. E. Kazdin (Eds.), *International handbook of behavior modification
and therapy* (pp. 207–229). New York: Plenum.

Graziano, A. M., & Mooney, K. C. (1982). Behavioral treatment of "nightfears" in
children: Maintenance improvement at 2½- to 3-year follow-up. *Journal of Consulting and Clinical Psychology, 50,* 598–599.

Greenberg, L. S. (1983a). Psychotherapy process research. In C. E. Walker (Ed.), *Handbook of clinical psychology* (pp. 169–204). Homewood, IL: Dow Jones–Irwin.

Greenberg, L. S. (1983b). Toward a task analysis of conflict resolution in Gestalt therapy.
Psychotherapy: Theory, Research, and Practice, 20, 190–201.

Greenberg, L. S., & Webster, M. C. (1982). Resolving decisional conflict by Gestalt
two-chair dialogue: Relating process to outcome. *Journal of Counseling Psychology, 29,* 468–477.

Greenblatt, M., Becerra, R. M., & Serafetinides, E. A. (1982). Social networks and mental
health: An overview. *American Journal of Psychiatry, 139,* 977–984.

Greene, B. F., & Neistat, M. D. (1983). Behavior analysis in consumer affairs: Encouraging dental professionals to provide consumers with shielding from unnecessary x-ray exposure. *Journal of Applied Behavior Analysis, 16,* 13–27.

Greene, B. F., Rouse, M., Green, R., & Clay, C. (1984). Behavior analysis in consumer
affairs: Retail and consumer response to publicizing food price information.
Journal of Applied Behavior Analysis, 17, 3–22.

Greenwood, C. R., Walker, H. M., Todd, N. M., & Hops, H. (1981). Normative and
descriptive analysis of preschool free play social interaction rates. *Journal of
Pediatric Psychology, 6,* 343–367.

Gresham, F. M. (1983). Social skills assessment as a component of mainstreaming
placement decisions. *Exceptional Children, 49,* 331–336.

Griest, D. L., Forehand, R., & Wells, K. C. (1981). Follow-up assessment of parent
behavioral training: An analysis of who will participate. *Child Study Journal,
11,* 221–229.

Griest, D. L., & Wells, K. C. (1983). Behavioral family therapy with conduct disorders in
children. *Behavior Therapy, 14,* 37–53.

Griffith, R. G. (1983). The administrative issues: An ethical and legal perspective.
In S. Axelrod & J. Apsche (Ed.), *The effects of punishment on human behavior*
(pp. 317–338). New York: Academic.

Gross, A. M. (1982). Self-management training and medication compliance in children
with diabetes. *Child and Family Behavior Therapy, 4*(2/3), 47–55.

Gross, A. M., & Ekstrand, M. (1983). Increasing and maintaining roles of teacher praise:
A study using public posting and feedback fading. *Behavior Modification, 7,*
126–135.

Gross, R. T., & Fremouw, W. J. (1982). Cognitive restructuring and progressive relaxation
for treatment of empirical subtypes of speech-anxious subjects. *Cognitive Therapy
and Research, 6,* 429–436.

Grunberg, N. E. (1982). The effects of nicotine and cigarette smoking on food consumption and taste preferences. *Addictive Behaviors, 7,* 317–331.

Grunberg, N. E., Bowen, D. J., & Morse, D. E. (in press). Effects of nicotine on body weight and food consumption in rats. *Psychopharmacology*.

Grunberg, N. E., & Morse, D. E. (in press). Cigarette smoking and food consumption in the United States. *Journal of Applied Social Psychology*.

Guidano, V. F., & Liotti, G. (1983). *Cognitive processes and emotional disorders*. New York: Guilford.

Gurman, A. S. (1978). Contemporary marital therapies: A critique and comparative analysis of psychodynamics, systems and behavioral approaches. In T. Paolino & B. McCrady (Eds.), *Marriage and marital therapy from three perspectives* (pp. 445–556). New York: Brunner/Mazel.

Gust, S. W., Pickens, R. W., & Pechacek, T. F. (1983). Relation of puff volume to other topographical measures of smoking. *Addictive Behaviors, 8*, 115–119.

Gwinup, G. (1975). Effect of exercise alone on the weight of obese women. *Archives of Internal Medicine, 135*, 676–680.

Hafner, R. J. (1976). Fresh symptom emergence after intensive behaviour therapy. *British Journal of Psychiatry, 129*, 378–383.

Hafner, R. J. (1977). The husbands of agoraphobic women and their influence on treatment outcome. *British Journal of Psychiatry, 131*, 289–294.

Hafner, R. J., & Ross, M. W. (1983). Predicting the outcome of behaviour therapy for agoraphobia. *Behaviour Research and Therapy, 21*, 375–382.

Haggerty, R. J. (1977). Changing lifestyles to improve health *Preventive Medicine, 6*, 276–209.

Hahlweg, K., Revenstorf, D., & Schindler, L. (1982). Treatment of marital distress: Comparing families and modalities. *Advances in Behaviour Research and Therapy, 4*, 57–74.

Haley, W. E. (1983). A family–behavioral approach to the treatment of the cognitively impaired elderly. *The Gerontologist, 23*, 18–20.

Hamburg, D. A. (1982). Health and behavior [Editorial]. *Science, 217*, 399.

Hamilton, J. L. (1972). The demand for cigarettes: Advertising, the health scare, and the cigarette advertising ban. *Review of Economics and Statistics, 54*, 401–411.

Hamilton, M. (1960). A rating scale for depression. *Journal of Neurology, Neurosurgery and Psychiatry, 23*, 56–62.

Hamilton, S. B., & Waldman, D. A. (1983). Self-modification of depression via cognitive–behavioral intervention strategies: A time series analysis. *Cognitive Therapy and Research, 7*, 99–106.

Hammen, C. L., & Krantz, S. (1976). Effect of success and failure on depressive cognitions. *Journal of Abnormal Psychology, 85*, 577–586.

Hampson, R. B., & Tavormina, J. B. (1980). Relative effectiveness of behavioral and group training with foster mothers. *Journal of Consulting and Clinical Psychology, 48*, 294–295.

Handleman, J. S., & Harris, S. L. (1983a). A comparison of one-to-one versus complete instruction autistic children. *Behavioral Disorders, 9*, 22–26.

Handleman, J. S., & Harris, S. L. (1983b). Generalization across institutional settings by autistic children. *Child and Family Behavior Therapy, 5*(1), 73–83.

Hannafin, M. J., & Witt, J. C. (1983). System intervention and the school psychologist: Maximising interplay among roles and functions. *Professional Psychology, 14*, 128–136.

Harman, D., & Brim, O. G. (1980). *Learning to be parents: Principles, programs and methods*. Beverly Hills, CA: Sage.

Harrell, T. H., & Ryon, N. B. (1983). Cognitive–behavioral assessment of depression: Clinical validation of the Automatic Thoughts Questionnaire. *Journal of Consulting and Clinical Psychology, 51*, 721–725.

Harris, G. M., & Johnson, S. B. (1983). Coping imagery and relaxation instructions in a covert modeling treatment for test anxiety. *Behavior Therapy, 14,* 144–157.

Harris, K. R. (1982). Cognitive-behavior modification: Application with exceptional students. *Focus on Exceptional Children, 15*(2), 1–16.

Harris, M. G., Hallbauer, E. S. (1973). Self-directed weight control through eating and exercise. *Behaviour Research and Therapy, 11,* 523–529.

Harris, S. L. (1983). *Families of the developmentally disabled: A guide to behavioral intervention.* New York: Pergamon.

Harris, S. L., & Ferrari, M. (1983). Developmental factors in child behavior therapy. *Behavior Therapy, 14,* 54–72.

Hartman, L. M., & Cashman, F. E. (1983). Cognitive–behavioral and psychopharmacological treatment of delusional symptoms: A preliminary report. *Behavioural Psychotherapy, 11,* 50–61.

Hatzenbuehler, L. C., & Schroeder, H. E. (1982). Assertiveness training with outpatients: The effectiveness of skill and cognitive procedures. *Behavioural Psychotherapy, 10,* 234–252.

Hayes, S. C. (1981). Single case experimental design and empirical clinical practice. *Journal of Consulting and Clinical Psychology, 49,* 193.

Haynes, S. G., Feinleib, M., & Kannel, W. B. (1980). The relationship of psychosocial factors to coronary heart disease in the Framingham study. III. Eight year incidence of coronary heart disease. *American Journal of Epidemiology, 111,* 37–58.

Hazzard, A., Christensen, A., & Margolin, G. (1983). Children's perceptions of parental behaviors. *Journal of Abnormal Child Psychology, 11,* 49–60.

Heads, T. B. (1978). Ethical and legal considerations in behavior therapy. In D. Manholin (Ed.), *Child behavior therapy* (pp. 416–433). New York: Gardner.

Heather, N., & Robertson, I. (1981). *Controlled drinking.* London: Methuen.

Hechtman, L., & Weiss, G. (1983). Long-term outcome of hyperactive children. *American Journal of Orthopsychiatry, 53,* 532–541.

Hedges, L. V. (1982). Estimation of effect size from a series of independent experiments. *Psychological Bulletin, 92,* 490–499.

Herjanic, B., & Reich, W. (1982). Development of a structured psychiatric interview for children: Agreement between child and parent on individual symptoms. *Journal of Abnormal Child Psychology, 10,* 307–323.

Herr, S. S., Arons, S., & Wallace, R. E. (1983). *Legal rights and mental health care.* Lexington, MA: Lexington Books (Heath).

Hetherington, R. W. (1982). Quality assurance and organizational effectiveness in hospitals. *Health Service Research, 17,* 185–201.

Higgins, R. L., Frisch, M. B., & Smith, D. (1983). A comparison of role-played and natural responses to identical circumstances. *Behavior Therapy, 14,* 158–169.

Hinerman, P. S. (1983). *Teaching autistic children to communicate.* Rockville, MD: Aspen Systems Corporation.

Hinshaw, S. P., Henker, B., & Whalen, C. (1984). Self-control in hyperactive boys in anger-inducing situations: Effects of cognitive–behavioral training and of methylphenidate. *Journal of Abnormal Child Psychology, 12,* 55–77.

Hirayama, T. (1981). Nonsmoking wives of heavy smokers have a higher risk of lung cancer: A study from Japan. *British Medical Journal, 282,* 163–165.

Hochheimer, J. L. (1981). Reducing alcohol abuse: A critical review of educational strategies: In M. H. Moore & D. R. Gerstein (Eds.), *Alcohol and public policy* (pp. 89–98). Washington, DC: National Academy Press.

Hodges, E. G. (1971). Crime prevention and the indeterminate sentence law. *American Journal of Psychiatry, 128,* 291–295.

Hodges, K., Kline, J., Stern, L., Cytryn, L., & McKnew, D. (1982). The development of a child assessment interview for research and clinical use. *Journal of Abnormal Child Psychology, 10,* 173–189.

Holden, A. E., O'Brien, G. T., Barlow, D. H., Stetson, D., & Infantino, A. (1983). Self-help manual for agoraphobia: A preliminary report of effectiveness. *Behavior Therapy, 14,* 545–556.

Holden, G. W. (1983). Avoiding conflict: Mothers as tacticians in the supermarket. *Child Development, 54,* 233–240.

Holland, E. L., & McLaughlin, T. F. (1982). Using public posting and group consequences to manage student behavior during supervision. *Journal of Educational Research, 76,* 29–34.

Hollingshead, A. B., & Redlich, F. C. (1958). *Social class and mental illness.* New York: Wiley.

Hollon, S. D., & Beck, A. T. (1979). Cognitive therapy of depression. In P. C. Kendall & S. D. Hollon (Eds.), *Cognitive–behavioral interventions: Theory, research, and procedures* (pp. 153–204). New York: Academic.

Hollon, S. D., & Kendall, P. C. (1980). Cognitive self-statements in depression: Development of an Automatic Thoughts Questionnaire. *Cognitive Therapy and Research, 4,* 383–395.

Holmes, N., Hemsley, R., Rickett, J., & Likierman, H. (1982). Parents as cotherapists: Their perceptions of a home-based behavioral treatment for autistic children. *Journal of Autism and Developmental Disorders, 12,* 331–342.

Holroyd, K. A., & Andrasik, F. (1982a). A cognitive–behavioral approach to recurrent tension and migraine headache. In P. C. Kendall (Ed.), *Advances in cognitive-behavioral research and therapy* (Vol. 1, pp. 276–320). New York: Academic.

Holroyd, K. A., & Andrasik, F. (1982b). Do the effects of cognitive therapy endure?: A two-year follow-up of tension headache sufferers treated with cognitive therapy or biofeedback. *Cognitive Therapy and Research, 6,* 325–334.

Horenstein, D., Houston, B. K., & Holmes, D. S. (1973). Clients', therapists', and judges' evaluations of psychotherapy. *Journal of Consulting Psychology, 20,* 149–153.

Horn, W. F., Chatoor, I., & Conners, C. K. (1983). Additive effects of dexedrine and self-control training: A multiple assessment. *Behavior Modification, 7,* 383–402.

Houston, B. K., Fox, J. E., & Forbes, L. (in press). Trait anxiety and children's state anxiety, cognitive behaviors, and performance under stress. *Cognitive Therapy and Research.*

Howard, A. N., Grant, A., Edwards, O., Littlewood, E. R., & McLean Baird, I. (1978). The treatment of obesity with a very-low-calorie liquid formula diet: An inpatient outpatient comparison using skimmed milk as the chief protein source. *International Journal of Obesity, 3,* 321–332.

Huber, J. W., & Altmaier, E. M. (1983). An investigation of the self-statement systems of phobic and nonphobic individuals. *Cognitive Therapy and Research, 7,* 355–362.

Hunter, J. E., Schmidt, F. L., & Jackson, G. B. (1982). *Meta-analysis: Cumulating research findings across studies.* Beverly Hills, CA: Sage.

Hurd, P. D., Johnson, C. A., Pechacek, T., Bast, L. P., Jacobs, D. R., & Luepker, R. V. (1980). Prevention of cigarette smoking in seventh grade students. *Journal of Behavioral Medicine, 3,* 15–28.

Hutchings, J. (1982). Child abuse: Applying a behavioural model. *Behavioural Approaches with Children, 6*(4), 3–19.

Isaacs, C. D., Embry, L. H., & Baer, D. M. (1982). Training family therapists: An experimental analysis. *Journal of Applied Behavior Analysis, 15,* 505–520.

Ivanic, M. J., Reid, D. H., Iwata, B. A., Faw, S. D., & Page, T. J. (1981). Evaluating a supervision program for developing and maintaining therapeutic staff–resident interactions during institutional care routines. *Journal of Applied Behavior Analysis, 14,* 95–107.

Jacobson, N. S., Follette, W. C., & McDonald, D. W. (1982). Reactivity to positive and negative behavior in distressed and nondistressed married couples. *Journal of Consulting and Clinical Psychology, 50,* 706–714.

Jannoun, L., Munby, M., Catalan, J., & Gelder, M. (1980). A home-based treatment program for agoraphobia: Replication and controlled evaluation. *Behavior Therapy, 11,* 294–305.

Jansson, L., & Ost, L. (1982). Behavioral treatments for agoraphobia: An evaluative review. *Clinical Psychology Review, 2,* 311–337.

Jason, L. A. (1984). Developing undergraduates' skills in behavioral interventions. *Journal of Community Psychology, 12,* 130–139.

Jason, L. A., & Burrows, B. (1983). Transition training for high school seniors. *Cognitive Therapy and Research, 7,* 79–92.

Jason, L. A., & Glenwick, D. S. (in press). Behavioral community psychology: A review of recent research and applications. In M. Hersen, R. M. Eisler, & P. M. Miller (Eds.), *Progress in behavior modification* (Vol. 17). New York: Academic.

Jenkins, C. D., Zyzanski, S. J., & Rosenman, R. H. (1976). Risk of new myocardial infarction in middle-aged men with manifest coronary heart disease. *Circulation, 53,* 342–347.

Jenkins, W. O., DeValera, E. K., & Mueller, J. S. (1977). Behavioral Evaluation, Treatment, and Analysis (BETA) system in the prediction of criminal and delinquent behavior. *Quarterly Journal of Corrections, 1,* 44–50.

Jensen, J. E. (1983, March 23). [Letter to Drs. Mark and Linda Sobell from Subcommittee on Investigations and Oversight, Committee on Science and Technology, House of Representatives, U.S. Congress].

Johnson, D. W., Maruyama, G., Johnson, R. T., Nelson, D., & Skon, L. (1981). Effects of cooperative, competitive, and individualistic goal structures on achievement: A meta-analysis. *Psychological Bulletin, 89,* 47–62.

Jones, E. E., & Nisbett, R. E. (1972). The actor and the observer: Divergent perceptions of the causes of behavior. In E. E. Jones, D. E. Kanouse, H. H. Kelley, R. E. Nisbett, S. Valins, & B. Weiner (Eds.), *Attribution: Perceiving the causes of behavior* (pp. 79–94). Morristown, NJ: General Learning Press.

Jones, M. L., Czyzewski, M. J., Otis, A. K., & Hannah, G. T. (1983). Shaping social policy: Developing a national social policy information network. *The Behavior Therapist, 6,* 149–151.

Jones, R. G. (1968). *A factored measure of Ellis' irrational belief system, with personality and maladjustment correlates.* Unpublished doctoral dissertation, Texas Technological College.

Kanfer, F. H., & Phillips, J. S. (1970). *Learning foundations of behavior therapy.* New York: Wiley.

Kanfer, F. H., & Saslow, G. (1969). Behavioral diagnosis. In C. M. Franks (Ed.), *Behavior therapy: Appraisal and status.* New York: McGraw-Hill.

Kannel, W. B., & Dawber, T. R. (1972). Atherosclerosis as a pediatric problem. *Journal of Pediatrics, 80,* 544–554.

Katahan, M., Pleas, J., Thackery, M., & Wallston, K. A. (1982). Relationship of eating and activity self-reports to follow-up weight maintenance in the massively obese. *Behavior Therapy, 13,* 521–528.

Katzell, R. A., & Guzzo, R. A. (1983). Psychological approaches to productivity improvement. *American Psychologist, 38,* 468–472.

Kazdin, A. E. (1978a). Conceptual and assessment issues raised by self-efficacy theory. *Advances in Behaviour Research and Therapy, 1,* 177–185.

Kazdin, A. E. (1978b). *History of behavior modification: Experimental foundations of contemporary research.* Baltimore: University Park Press.

Kazdin, A. E. (1980a). *Behavior modification in applied settings* (Rev. ed.). Homewood, IL: Dorsey.

Kazdin, A. E. (1980b). *Research design in clinical psychology.* New York: Harper & Row.

Kazdin, A. E. (1981). Acceptability of child treatment techniques: The influence of treatment efficacy and adverse side effects. *Behavior Therapy, 12,* 493–506.

Kazdin, A. E. (1982a). History of behavior modification. In A. S. Bellack, M. Hersen, & A. E. Kazdin (Eds.), *International handbook of behavior modification and therapy* (pp. 3–32). New York: Plenum.

Kazdin, A. E. (1982b). Single-case experimental designs. In P. C. Kendall & J. N. Butcher (Eds.), *Handbook of research methods in clinical psychology* (pp. 461–490). New York: Wiley.

Kazdin, A. E. (1982c). Symptom substitution, generalization, and response variation: Implications for psychotherapy. *Psychological Bulletin, 91,* 349–365.

Kazdin, A. E. (1983). Psychiatric diagnosis, dimensions of dysfunction, and child behavior therapy. *Behavior Therapy, 14,* 73–99.

Kazdin, A. E., French, N. H., Unis, A. S., Esveldt-Dawson, K., & Sherick, R. B. (1983). Hopelessness, depression, and suicidal intent among psychiatrically disturbed inpatient children. *Journal of Consulting and Clinical Psychology, 51,* 504–510.

Kazdin, A. E., & Wilson, G. T. (1978). *Evaluation of behavior therapy: Issues, evidence and research strategies.* Cambridge, MA: Ballinger.

Keane, T. M. (1983). Behavior therapy in the media. *The Behavior Therapist, 6,* 91.

Keefe, F. J., & Block, A. R. (1982). Development of an observation method for assessing pain behavior in chronic low back pain patients. *Behavior Therapy, 13,* 363–375.

Kelly, G. A. (1955). *The psychology of personal constructs.* New York: Norton.

Kelly, J. A. (1983). *Treating child-abusive families: Intervention based on skills-training principles.* New York: Plenum.

Kelly, R. J. (1982). Behavioral reorientation of pedophiles: Can it be done? *Clinical Psychology Review, 2,* 387–408.

Kemp, D. R. (1983). Assessing human rights committees: A mechanism for protecting the rights of institutionalized mentally retarded persons. *Mental Retardation, 21,* 13–16.

Kendall, P. C. (1977). On the efficacious use of self-instructional procedures with children. *Cognitive Therapy and Research, 1,* 331–341.

Kendall, P. C. (1978). Anxiety: States, traits,—situations? *Journal of Consulting and Clinical Psychology, 46,* 280–288.

Kendall, P. C. (1981). Cognitive–behavioral interventions with children. In B. B. Lahey & A. E. Kazdin (Eds.), *Advances in clinical child psychology* (Vol. 4, pp. 53–90). New York: Plenum.

Kendall, P. C. (1982a). Behavioral assessment and methodology. In C. M. Franks, G. T. Wilson, P. C. Kendall, & K. D. Brownell, *Annual review of behavior therapy: Theory and practice* (Vol. 8, pp. 39–81). New York: Guilford.

Kendall, P. C. (1982b). Cognitive processes and procedures in behavior therapy. In C. M. Franks, G. T. Wilson, P. C. Kendall, & K. D. Brownell, *Annual review of behavior therapy* (Vol. 8, pp. 120–155). New York: Guilford.

Kendall, P. C. (1983). Methodology and cognitive–behavioural assessment. *Behavioural Psychotherapy, 11,* 285–301.

Kendall, P. C. (1984a). Behavioral assessment and methodology. In G. T. Wilson, C. M. Franks, K. D. Brownell, & P. C. Kendall, *Annual review of behavior therapy: Theory and practice* (Vol. 9, pp. 39–94). New York: Guilford.

Kendall, P. C. (1984b). Social cognition and problem-solving: A developmental and child-clinical interface. In B. Gholson & T. Rosenthal (Eds.), *Applications of cognitive–developmental theory* (pp. 115–148). New York: Academic.

Kendall, P. C. (1984c). Cognitive–behavioral interventions with children: Further needs. *The Behavior Therapist, 7*, 169–171.

Kendall, P. C., & Bemis, K. M. (1983). Thought and action in psychotherapy: The cognitive–behavioral approaches. In M. Hersen, A. E. Kazdin, & A. S. Bellack (Eds.), *The clinical psychology handbook* (pp. 565–592). New York: Pergamon.

Kendall, P. C., & Braswell, L. (1982). On cognitive–behavioral assessment: Model, measures, and madness. In C. D. Spielberger & J. N. Butcher (Eds.), *Advances in personality assessment* (Vol. 1, pp. 35–82). Hillsdale, NJ: Erlbaum.

Kendall, P. C., & Braswell, L. (1984). *Cognitive–behavioral therapy for impulsive children.* New York: Guilford.

Kendall, P. C., & Finch, A. J. (1979). Developing nonimpulsive behavior in children: Cognitive–behavioral strategies for self-control. In P. C. Kendall & S. Hollon (Eds.), *Cognitive–behavioral interventions: Theory, research, and procedures* (pp. 37–79). New York: Academic.

Kendall, P. C., & Fischler, G. L. (1984). Behavioral and adjustment correlates of problem-solving: Validational analyses of interpersonal cognitive problem-solving measures. *Child Development, 55*, 879–892.

Kendall, P. C., & Hollon, S. D. (1981). Assessing self-referent speech: Methods in the measurement of self-statements. In P. C. Kendall & S. D. Hollon (Eds.), *Assessment strategies for cognitive–behavioral interventions* (pp. 85–118). New York: Academic.

Kendall, P. C., & Hollon, S. D. (1983). Calibrating the quality of therapy: Collaborative archiving of tape samples from therapy outcome trials. *Cognitive Therapy and Research, 7*, 199–204.

Kendall, P. C., & Koehler, C. (in press). Outcome evaluation in child behavior therapy: Methodological and conceptual issues. In P. Bornstein & A. E. Kazdin (Eds.), *Handbook of child behavior therapy.* Homewood, IL: Dow Jones-Irwin.

Kendall, P. C., & Kriss, M. (1983). Cognitive–behavioral interventions. In C. E. Walker (Ed.), *Handbook of clinical psychology* (Vol. 2, pp. 1069–1110). Homewood, IL: Dow Jones-Irwin.

Kendall, P. C., Lerner, R. M., & Craighead, W. E. (1984). Human development and intervention in childhood psychopathology. *Child Development, 55*, 71–82.

Kendall, P. C., & Maruyama, G. (in press). Meta-analysis: On the road to synthesis of knowledge? *Clinical Psychology Review.*

Kendall, P. C., & Morison, P. (1984). Integrating cognitive and behavioral procedures for the treatment of socially isolated children. In A. Meyers & W. E. Craighead (Eds.), *Cognitive behavior therapy with children* (pp. 261–288). New York: Plenum.

Kendall, P. C., & Norton-Ford, J. D. (1982). Therapy outcome research methods. In P. C. Kendall & J. N. Butcher (Eds.), *Handbook of research methods in clinical psychology* (pp. 429–460). New York: Wiley.

Kent, R. N., & O'Leary, K. D. (1976). A controlled evaluation of behavior modification with conduct problem children. *Journal of Consulting and Clinical Psychology, 44*, 586–596.

Kent, R. N., & O'Leary, K. D. (1977). Treatment of conduct problem children: BA and/or PhD therapists. *Behavior Therapy, 8*, 653–658.

Keogh, B. K., & Barkett, C. J. (1980). An educational analysis of hyperactive children's achievement problems. In C. K. Whalen & B. Henker (Eds.), *Hyperactive children: The social ecology of identification and treatment* (pp. 259–282). New York: Academic.

Kern, J. M. (1982a). The comparative external and concurrent validity of three role-plays for assessing heterosocial performance. *Behavior Therapy, 13,* 666-680.

Kern, J. M. (1982b). Predicting the impact of assertive, empathic–assertive, and non-assertive behavior: The assertiveness of the assertee. *Behavior Therapy, 13,* 486-498.

Kern, J. M., Miller, C., & Eggers, J. (1983). Enhancing the validity of role-play tests: A comparison of three role-play methodologies. *Behavior Therapy, 14,* 482-492.

Kettlewell, P. W., & Kausch, D. F. (1983). The generalization of the effects of a cognitive-behavioral treatment program for aggressive children. *Journal of Abnormal Child Psychology, 11,* 101-114.

Kiesler, C. A. (1982). Mental Hospitals and alternative care: Noninstitutionalization as potential public policy for mental patients. *American Psychologist, 37,* 349-360.

Kiesler, C. A. (1983). Social psychological issues in studying consumer satisfaction with behavior therapy. *Behavior Therapy, 14,* 226-236.

Kiesler, D. J. (1966). Some myths of psychotherapy research and the search for a paradigm. *Psychological Bulletin, 65,* 110-136.

Kiesler, D. J. (1971). Experimental designs in psychotherapy research. In A. E. Bergin & S. L. Garfield (Eds.), *Handbook of psychotherapy and behavior change.* New York: Wiley.

Kielser, D. J. (1980). Psychotherapy process research: Viability and directions in the 1980s. In W. DeMoor & H. R. Wijngaarden (Eds.), *Psychotherapy: Research and training.* Amsterdam: Elsevier/North-Holland Biomedical Press.

Kirigin, K. A., Braukmann, C. J., Atwater, J. D., & Wolf, M. M. (1982). An evaluation of teaching-family (Achievement Place) group homes for juvenile offenders. *Journal of Applied Behavior Analysis, 15,* 1-16.

Kirk, J. W. (1983). Behavioural treatment of obsessional–compulsive patients in routine clinical practice. *Behaviour Research and Therapy, 21,* 57-62.

Kirsch, I., & Wickless, C. V. (1983). Concordance rates between self-efficacy and approach behavior are redundant. *Cognitive Therapy and Research, 7,* 179-187.

Kirschenbaum, D. S. (1983). Toward more behavioral early intervention programs: A rationale. *Professional Psychology: Research and Practice, 14,* 159-169.

Klein, D. F., Zitrin, C. M., Woerner, M. G., & Ross, D. C. (1983). Treatment of phobias. *Archives of General Psychiatry, 40,* 139-145.

Klein, M., Mathieu, P., Kiesler, D., & Gendlin, E. (1969). *The Experiencing Scale.* Madison: Wisconsin Psychiatric Institute.

Klein, S., Frank, P., & Jacobs, J. (1980). Token economy program for developing independent living skills in geriatric inpatients. *Psychosocial Rehabilitation Journal, 4,* 1-11.

Kleitsch, E., Whitman, T. L., & Santos, J. (1983). Increasing verbal interaction among elderly socially isolated mentally retarded adults: A group language training procedure. *Journal of Applied Behavior Analysis, 16,* 217-233.

Knowles, J. (1977). The responsibility of the individual. *Daedalus, 106,* 57-80.

Koegel, R. L., Rincover, A., & Egel, A. L. (Eds.). (1982). *Educating and understanding autistic children.* San Diego: College Hill Press.

Kolko, D. J., Parrish, J. M., & Wilson, F. E. (in press). Obstacles to appointment keeping in a child behavior management clinic. *Child and Family Behavior Therapy.*

Koplan, J. P., Powell, K. E., Sikes, R. K., Shirley, R. W., & Campbell, C. C. (1982). An epidemiologic study of the benefits and risks of running. *Journal of the American Medical Association, 248,* 3118-3121.

Kovacs, M. (1980). Rating scales to assess depression in school-aged children. *Acta Paedopsychiatrica, 46,* 305-315.

Krantz, S., & Hammen, C. (1979). Assessment of cognitive bias in depression. *Journal of Abnormal Psychology, 88,* 611–619.

Krapfl, J. E., & Gasparotto, G. (1982). Behavioral systems analysis. In L. W. Frederiksen (Ed.), *Handbook of organizational behavior management* (pp. 21–38). New York: Wiley.

Krasner, L., & Houts, A. C. (1984). A study of the "value" systems of behavioral scientists. *American Psychologist, 39,* 840–850.

Kuiper, N. A., & MacDonald, M. R. (1983). Reason, emotion, and cognitive therapy. *Clinical Psychology Review, 3,* 297–316.

Ladd, G. W., & Keeney, B. P. (1983). Intervention strategies and research with socially isolated children: An ecological-systems perspective. *Small Group Behavior, 14,* 176–185.

Lader, M. H., & Mathews, A. M. (1968). A physiological model of phobic anxiety and desensitization. *Behaviour Research and Therapy, 6,* 411–421.

Ladouceur, R. (1983). Participant modeling with or without cognitive treatment for phobias. *Journal of Consulting and Clinical Psychology, 51,* 942–944.

Lambert, M. J. (Ed.). (1983). *Psychotherapy and patient relationships.* Homewood, IL: Dorsey.

Landman, J. T., & Dawes, R. (1982). Psychotherapy outcome: Smith and Glass' conclusions stand up under scrutiny. *American Psychologist, 37,* 504–516.

Langer, E., & Abelson, W. (1974). A patient by any other name: Clinician group differences in labeling bias. *Journal of Consulting and Clinical Psychology, 42,* 4–9.

Larson, D., Attkisson, C., Hargreaves, W., & Nguyen, T. (1979). Assessment of client patient satisfaction: Development of a general scale. *Evaluation and Program Planning, 2,* 197–207.

Lauer, R. M., & Clarke, W. R. (1980). Immediate and long-term prognostic significance of childhood blood pressure levels. In R. M. Lauer & R. B. Shekelle (Eds.), *Childhood prevention of atherosclerosis and hypertension* (pp. 281–290). New York: Raven.

Lauer, R. M., Conner, W. E., Leaverton, P. E., Reiter, M. A., & Clarke, W. R. (1975). Coronary heart disease risk factors in school children. *Journal of Pediatrics, 86,* 697–706.

Lauer, R. M., & Shekelle, R. B. (Eds.). (1980). *Childhood prevention of atherosclerosis and hypertension.* New York: Raven.

Laws, R. D., & Holmen, M. L. (1978). Sexual response faking by pedophiles. *Criminal Justice and Behavior, 5,* 343–356.

Lazarus, A. A. (1963). The results of behaviour therapy in 126 cases of severe neurosis. *Behaviour Research and Therapy, 1,* 65–78.

Lazarus, A. A. (1971). *Behavior therapy and beyond.* New York: McGraw-Hill.

Lazarus, A. A. (1981). *The practice of multimodal therapy.* New York: McGraw-Hill.

Lazarus, A. A., & Fay, A. (1982). Resistance or rationalization? A cognitive–behavioral perspective. In P. L. Wachtel (Ed.), *Resistance: Psychodynamic and behavioral approaches* (pp. 115–132). New York: Plenum.

LeBow, J. (1982). Consumer satisfaction with mental health treatment. *Psychological Bulletin, 91,* 244–259.

LeBow, M. D. (1984). *Child obesity: A new frontier of behavior therapy.* New York: Springer.

Lebowitz, M. D., & Burrows, B. (1976). Respiratory symptoms related to smoking habits of family adults. *Chest, 69,* 48–50.

Lee, C. (1983a). *Conceptual and methodological issues in self-efficacy theory.* Unpublished doctoral dissertation, University of Adelaide, South Australia, Australia.

Lee, C. (1983b). Self-efficacy and behaviour as predictors of subsequent behaviour in an assertiveness training programme. *Behaviour Research and Therapy, 21*, 225–232.

Lee, C. (in press-a). Accuracy of efficacy and outcome expectations in predicting performance in a simulated assertiveness task. *Cognitive Therapy and Research.*

Lee, C. (in press-b). Efficacy expectations and outcome expectations as predictors of performance in a snake-handling task. *Cognitive Therapy and Research.*

Levendusky, P. G., Berglas, S., Dooley, C. P., & Landau, R. J. (1983). Therapeutic contract programme: Preliminary report on a behavioural alternative to the token economy. *Behaviour Research and Therapy, 21*, 137–142.

Levenkron, J. C., Cohen, J. D., Mueller, H. S., & Fisher, E. B. (1983). Modifying the Type A coronary-prone behavior pattern. *Journal of Consulting and Clinical Psychology, 51*, 192–204.

Levine, J (1983). Is deinstitutionalization the answer for the chronic mentally ill? [Review of J. A. Talbott's *The chronic mentally ill: Treatment, programs, systems*]. *Contemporary Psychology, 28*, 20–22.

Levy, R. I., & Moskowitz, J. (1982). Cardiovascular research: Decades of progress, a decade of promise. *Science, 217*, 121–129.

Ley, P. (1981). Professional non-compliance: A neglected problem. *British Journal of Clinical Psychology, 20*, 151–154.

Ley, P. (1982a). Psychology in medicine. In S. Canter & D. Canter (Eds.), *Psychology in practice* (pp. 41–59). New York: Wiley,

Ley, P. (1982b). Studies of recall in medical settings. *Human Learning, 1*, 223–233.

Liberman, R. P. (1979). Social and political challenges to the development of behavioral programs in organizations. In P. O. Sjoden, S. Bates, & W. S. Dockens (Eds.), *Trends in behavior therapy* (pp. 369–398). New York: Academic.

Liberman, R. P. (1980). [Review of G. L. Paul & R. J. Lentz's *Psychosocial treatment for chronic mental patients*]. *Journal of Applied Behavior Analysis, 13*, 367–381.

Lichtenstein, E. (1982). The smoking problem: A behavioral perspective. *Journal of Consulting and Clinical Psychology, 50*, 804–819.

Liebowitz, M. R., & Klein, D. (1982). Agoraphobia: Clinical features, pathophysiology, and treatment. In D. Chambless & A. Goldstein (Eds.), *Agoraphobia* (pp. 153–182). New York: Wiley.

Lindner, P. G., & Blackburn, G. L. (1976). An interdisciplinary approach to obesity utilizing fasting modified by protein-sparing therapy. *Obesity/Bariatric Medicine, 5*, 198–216.

Linehan, M. M., Goodstein, J. L., Nielsen, S. L., & Chiles, J. A. (1983). Reasons for staying alive when you are thinking of killing yourself: The Reasons for Living Inventory. *Journal of Consulting and Clinical Psychology, 51*, 276–286.

Linehan, M. M., & Nielsen, S. L. (1981). Assessment of suicide ideation and parasuicide: Hopelessness and social desirability. *Journal of Consulting and Clinical Psychology, 49*, 773–775.

Linehan, M. M., & Nielsen, S. L. (1983). Social desirability: Its relevance to the measurement of hopelessness and suicidal behavior. *Journal of Consulting and Clinical Psychology, 51*, 141–143.

Link, B. (1982). Mental patient status, work, and income: An examination of the effects of a psychiatric label. *American Sociological Review, 47*, 202–215.

Link, B. (1983). Reward system of psychotherapy: Implications for inequities in service delivery. *Journal of Health and Social Behavior, 24*, 61–69.

Link, B., & Milcarek, B. (1980). Selection factors in the dispensation of therapy: The Matthew effect in the allocation of mental health resources. *Journal of Health and Social Behavior, 21*, 279–290.

Linn, R. (1976). *The last chance diet*. Secaucus, NJ: Lyle Stuart.

Lipsky, M. J., Kassinove, H., & Miller, N. J. (1980). Effects of rational–emotive therapy, rational role reversal, and rational–emotive imagery on the emotional adjustment of community mental health center patients. *Journal of Consulting and Clinical Psychology, 48*, 366–374.

Lohr, J. M., & Bonge, D. (1982). The factorial validity of the Irrational Beliefs Test: A psychometric investigation. *Cognitive Therapy and Research, 6*, 225–230.

London, P. (1983). Science, culture and psychotherapy: The state of the art. In M. Rosenbaum, C. M. Franks, & Y. Jaffe (Eds.), *Perspectives on behavior therapy in the eighties* (pp. 17–32). New York: Springer.

Lovaas, O. I., Ackerman, A. B., & Taubman, M. T. (1983). An overview of behavioral treatment of autistic persons. In M. Rosenbaum, C. M. Franks, & Y. Jaffe (Eds.), *Perspectives on behavior therapy in the eighties* (pp. 287–308). New York: Springer.

Luria, A. R. (1982). *Language and cognition*. New York: Wiley.

Lutzker, J. R. (1984). Project 12-Ways: Treating child abuse and neglect from an ecobehavioral preference. In R. F. Dangel & R. A. Polster (Eds.), *Parent training: Foundations of research and practice* (pp. 260–295). New York: Guilford.

Lutzker, J. R., McGimsey, J. F., McRae, S., & Campbell, R. V. (1983). Behavioral parent training: There's so much more to do. *The Behavior Therapist, 6*, 110–110.

MacDonald, M. L. (1983). Behavioral consultation in geriatric setting. *The Behavior Therapist, 6*, 172–174.

Maher, B. (1983). The education of health psychologists: Quality counts, numbers are dangerous. *Health Psychology, 2*(Suppl.), 37–47.

Maher, C. A. (1981). Improving the delivery of special education and related services in public schools. *Journal of Organizational Behavior Management, 3*, 29–44.

Maher, C. A. (1982). Performance feedback to improve the planning and evaluation of instructional programs. *Journal of Organizational Behavior Management, 3*, 33–40.

Mahoney, M. J. (1977). Reflections on the cognitive–learning trend in psychotherapy. *American Psychologist, 32*, 5–13.

Mahoney, M. J. (1980). Psychotherapy and the structure of personal revolutions. In M. J. Mahoney (Ed.), *Cognition and clinical science* (pp. 157–180). New York: Plenum.

Mahoney, M. M., & Kern, J. M. (1983). Variations in role-play tests of heterosocial performance. *Journal of Consulting and Clinical Psychology, 51*, 141–152.

Mandler, G. (1982). The construction of emotion in the child. In C. E. Izard (Ed.), *Measuring emotions in infants and children*. Cambridge, England: Cambridge University Press.

Mansell, J., Felce, D., De Kock, V., & Jenkins, J. (1982). Increasing purposeful activity of severely and profoundly mentally-handicapped adults. *Behaviour Research and Therapy, 20*, 593–604.

Mansell, J., Jenkins, J., Felce, D., & De Kock, V. (1984). Measuring the activity of severely and profoundly mentally handicapped adults in ordinary housing. *Behaviour Research and Therapy, 22*, 23–29.

Marks, I. M. (1978). Behavioral psychotherapy of adult neurosis. In S. L. Garfield & A. E. Bergin (Eds.), *Handbook of psychotherapy and behavior change* (2nd ed., pp. 493–547). New York: Wiley.

Marks, I. M. (1981). *Cure and care of the neuroses*. New York: Wiley.

Marks, I. M., & Gelder, M. (1965). A controlled retrospective study of behaviour therapy in phobic patients. *British Journal of Psychiatry, 111*, 561–573.

Marks, I. M., Gray, S., Cohen, D., Hill, R., Mawson, D., Ramm, E., & Stern, R. S. (1983). Imipramine and brief therapist-aided exposure in agoraphobics having self-exposure homework. *Archives of General Psychiatry, 40*, 153–162.

Marks, I. M., & Mathews, A. (1979). Brief standard self-rating for phobic patients. *Behaviour Research and Therapy, 17*, 263-267.

Marks, I. M., Stern, R. S., Mawson, D., Cobb, J., & McDonald, R. (1980). Clomipramine and exposure for obsessive-compulsive rituals. I. *British Journal of Psychiatry, 136*, 1-25.

Marlatt, G. A. (1983). The controlled drinking controversy: A commentary. *American Psychologist, 38*, 1097-1110.

Marlatt, G. A., & Gordon, J. R. (1980). Determinants of relapse: Implications for the maintenance of behavior change. In P. O. Davidson & S. M. Davidson (Eds.), *Behavioral medicine: Changing health lifestyles* (pp. 410-452). New York: Brunner/Mazel.

Marshall, W. L., & Gauthier, J. (1983). Failures in flooding. In E. Foa & P. M. G. Emmelkamp (Eds.), *Failures in behavior therapy* (pp. 82-103). New York: Wiley.

Martin, J. E., & Dubbert, P. M. (1982). Exercise applications and promotion in behavioral medicine: Current status and future directions. *Journal of Consulting and Clinical Psychology, 50*, 1004-1017.

Martin, L. (1974). Some thoughts on mainstreaming. *Exceptional Children, 41*, 150-153.

Marzillier, J. S., & Winter, K. (1983). Limitations of the treatment for social anxiety. In E. Foa & P. M. G. Emmelkamp (Eds.), *Failures in behavior therapy* (pp. 104-120). New York: Wiley.

Mash, E. J. (in press). Families with problem children. In A. Doyle, D. Gold, & D. Moscavitz (Eds.), *Children in families under stress*. San Francisco: Jossey-Bass.

Mash, E. J., & Johnston, C. (1982). A comparison of the mother-child interactions of younger and older hyperactive and normal children. *Child Development, 53*, 1371-1381.

Mash, E. J., & Johnston, C. (1983a). Parental perceptions of child behavior problems, parenting, self-esteem, and mothers' reported stress in younger and older hyperactive and normal children. *Journal of Consulting and Clinical Psychology, 51*, 86-99.

Mash, E. J., & Johnston, C. (1983b). The prediction of mothers' behavior with their hyperactive children during play and task situations. *Child and Family Behavior Therapy, 5*(2), 1-14.

Mash, E. J., & Johnston, C. (1983c). Sibling interactions of hyperactive and normal children and their relationship to reports of maternal stress and self-esteem. *Journal of Clinical Child Psychology, 12*, 91-99.

Matarazzo, J. D. (1980). Behavioral health and behavioral medicine: Frontiers for a new health psychology. *American Psychologist, 35*, 807-817.

Matarazzo, J. D. (1982). Behavioral health's challenge to academic, scientific, and professional psychology. *American Psychologist, 37*, 1-14.

Matarazzo, J. D. (1983). Education and training in health psychology: Boulder or bolder? *Health Psychology, 2*, 73-113.

Mathews, A. M., Gelder, M. G., & Johnston, D. W. (1981). *Agoraphobia: Nature and treatment*. New York: Guilford.

Mathews, A. M., Johnston, D. W., Lancashire, M., Munby, M., Shaw, P. M., & Gelder, M. G. (1976). Imaginal flooding and exposure to real phobic situations: Treatment outcome with agoraphobic patients. *British Journal of Psychiatry, 129*, 362-371.

Matson, J. L., & DiLorenzo, T. M. (1984). *Punishment and its alternatives: A new perspective for behavior modification*. New York: Springer.

Matuzas, W., & Glass, R. M. (1983). Treatment of agoraphobia and panic attacks. *Archives of General Psychiatry, 40*, 220-222.

Mavissakalian, M., & Michelson, L. (1983a). Agoraphobia: Behavioral and pharmacological treatment. N = 49. *Psychopharmacology Bulletin, 19*, 116–118.

Mavissakalian, M., & Michelson, L. (1983b). Self-directed in vivo exposure practice in behavioral and pharmacological treatments of agoraphobia. *Behavior Therapy, 14*, 506–519.

Mavissakalian, M., Michelson, L., & Dealy, R. S. (1983a). Pharmacological treatment of agoraphobia: Imipramine versus imipramine with programmed practice. *British Journal of Psychiatry, 143*, 348–355.

Mavissakalian, M., Michelson, L., Greenwald, D., Kornblith, S., & Greenwald, M. (1983b).Cognitive–behavioral treatment of agoraphobia: Paradoxical intention versus self-instructional training. *Behaviour Research and Therapy, 21*, 75–86.

Mayer, G. R., Butterworth, T., Nafpaktitis, M., & Sulzer-Azaroff, B. (1983). Preventing school vandalism and improving discipline: A three-year study. *Journal of Applied Behavior Analysis, 16*, 355–369.

McAlister, A. L., Perry, C., Killen, J., Slinkard, L. A., & Maccoby, N. (1980). Pilot study of smoking, alcohol, and drug abuse prevention. *American Journal of Public Health, 70*, 719–721.

McAlister, A. L., Perry, C., & Maccoby, N. (1979). Adolescent smoking: Onset and prevention. *Pediatrics, 63*, 650–658.

McArdle, W. D., Katch, F. I., & Katch, V. L. (1981). *Exercise physiology: Energy, nutrition, and human performance.* Philadelphia: Lea & Febiger.

McFall, R. M. (1982). A review and reformulation of the concept of social skills. *Behavioral Assessment, 4*, 1–33.

McFatter, R. M. (1982). Purposes of punishment: Effects of utilities of criminal sanctions on perceived appropriateness. *Journal of Applied Psychology, 67*, 255–267.

McGuire, T. G., & Frisman, L. K. (1983). Reimbursement policy and cost-effective mental health care. *American Psychologist, 38*, 935–940.

McIntyre, K. O., Lichtenstein, E., & Mermelstein, R. J. (1983). Self-efficacy and relapse in smoking cessation: A replication and extension. *Journal of Consulting and Clinical Psychology, 51*, 632–633.

McIntyre, T. J., Bornstein, P. H., Isaacs, C. D., Woody, D. J., Bornstein, M. T., Clucas, T. J., & Long, G. (1983). Naturalistic observation of conduct disordered children: An archival analysis. *Behavior Therapy, 14*, 375–385.

McLoughlin, C. S., & Sametz, L. (1983). Knowledge of trainees in school psychology about children's legal rights. *Psychological Reports, 52*, 286.

McMahon, R. J., & Forehand, R. L. (1983). Consumer satisfaction in behavioral treatment of children: Types, issues, and recommendations. *Behavior Therapy, 14*, 209–225.

McNair, D. M., & Kahn, R. J. (1981). Imipramine compared with a benzodiazeprine for agoraphobia. In D. F. Klein & J. E. Rabkin (Eds.), *Anxiety: New research and changing concepts.* New York: Raven.

McNamara, J. R., & Andrasik, F. (1982). Recidivism follow-up for residents released from a forensic psychiatry behavior change treatment program. *Journal of Psychiatric Treatment and Evaluation, 4*, 423–426.

McNamara, J. R., & Blumer, C. A. (1982). Role playing to assess social competence: Ecological validity considerations. *Behavior Modification, 6*, 519–549.

Meehl, P. (1954). *Clinical versus statistical prediction.* Minneapolis: University of Minnesota Press.

Mehlman, S. K., Baucom, D. H., & Anderson, D. (1983). Effectiveness of cotherapists versus single therapists and immediate versus delayed treatment in behavioral marital therapy. *Journal of Consulting and Clinical Psychology, 51*, 258–266.

Meichenbaum, D. H. (1977). *Cognitive behavior modification: An integrative approach.* New York: Plenum.

Meichenbaum, D. H., & Cameron, R. (1982). Cognitive behavior modification: Current issues. In G. T. Wilson & C. M. Franks (Eds.), *Contemporary behavior therapy: Conceptual and empirical foundations* (pp. 310–338). New York: Guilford.

Meichenbaum, D. H., & Gilmore, J. (1982). Resistance: From a cognitive–behavioral perspective. In P. Wachtel (Ed.), *Resistance: Psychodynamic and behavioral approaches* (pp. 133–156). New York: Plenum.

Meichenbaum, D. H., & Goodman, J. (1971). Training impulsive children to talk to themselves: A means of developing self-control. *Journal of Abnormal Psychology, 77,* 115–126.

Meyers, A. W., & Cohen, R. (1984). Cognitive–behavioral interventions in educational settings. In P. C. Kendall (Ed.), *Advances in cognitive–behavioral research and therapy* (Vol. 3, pp. 131–167). New York: Academic.

Meyers, A. W., & Craighead, W. E. (Eds.). (1984). *Cognitive behavior therapy with children.* New York: Plenum.

Meyers, A. W., Thackwray, D. E., Johnson, C. B., & Schleser, R. (1983). A comparison of prompting strategies for improving appointment compliance of hypertensive individuals. *Behavior Therapy, 14,* 207–274.

Michael, J. L. (1980). Flight from behavior analysis. *The Behavior Therapist, 3,* 1–22.

Michael, J. M. (1982). The second revolution in health. Health promotion and its environmental base. *American Psychologist, 37,* 936–941.

Michelson, L., DiLorenzo, T. M., Calpin, J. P., & Ollendick, T. H. (1982). Situational determinants of the behavioral assertiveness role-play test for children. *Behavior Therapy, 13,* 724–734.

Miller, N. E. (1983a). Behavioral medicine: Symbiosis between laboratory and clinic. *Annual Review of Psychology, 34,* 1–31.

Miller, N. E. (1983b). Some main themes and highlights of the National Working Conference on Education and Training in Health Psychology. *Health Psychology, 2*(Suppl.), 11–14.

Miller, R. C., & Berman, J. S. (1983). The efficacy of cognitive behavior therapies: A quantitative review of the research evidence. *Psychological Bulletin, 94,* 39–53.

Miller, W. R. (1983a). Controlled drinking: A history and critical review. *Journal of Studies on Alcohol, 10,* 152–163.

Miller, W. R. (1983b). Motivational interviewing with problem drinkers. *Behavioural Psychotherapy, 11,* 147–172.

Miller, W. R., & Baca, L. M. (1983). Two-year follow-up of bibliotherapy and therapy-directed controlled drinking training for problem drinkers. *Behavior Therapy, 14,* 441–448.

Miller, W. R., & Hester, R. K. (1980). Treating the problem drinker: Modern approaches. In W. R. Miller (Ed.), *The addictive behaviors: Treatment of alcoholism, drug abuse, smoking, and obesity* (pp. 11–142). New York: Pergamon.

Mills, K. C., McCarty, D., Ward, J., Minuto, L., & Patzynski, J. (1983). A residence hall tavern as a collegiate alcohol abuse prevention activity. *Addictive Behaviors, 8,* 105–108.

Milne, D. L. (1982). A companion of two methods of teaching behaviour modification to mental handicap nurses. *Behavioural Psychotherapy, 10,* 54–64.

Mintz, J. (1983). Integrating research evidence: A commentary on meta-analysis. *Journal of Consulting and Clinical Psychology, 51,* 71–75.

Mischel, W. (1968). *Personality and assessment.* New York: Wiley.

Mischel, W. (1982). A cognitive-social learning approach to assessment. In T. V. Merluzzi,

C. R. Glass, & M. Genest (Eds.), *Cognitive assessment* (pp. 479–501). New York: Guilford.

Missel, P., & Sommer, G. (1983). Depression and self-verbalization. *Cognitive Therapy and Research, 7,* 141–148.

Moffitt, T. E. (1983). The learning theory model of punishment: Implications for delinquency deterrence. *Criminal Justice and Behavior, 10,* 131–158.

Monroe, S. M., Bellack, A. S., Hersen, M., & Himmelhoch, J. M. (1983). Life events, symptom course, and treatment outcome in unipolar depressed women. *Journal of Consulting and Clinical Psychology, 51,* 604–615.

Montagu, A. (1983). *Growing young.* New York: McGraw-Hill.

Moon, J. R., & Eisler, R. M. (1983). Anger control: An experimental comparison of three behavioral treatments. *Behavior Therapy, 14,* 493–505.

Moos, R. H., & Finney, J. W., (1983). The expanding scope of alcoholism treatment research. *American Pyschologist, 38,* 1036–1044.

Morris, R. J., & Brown, D. K. (1983). Legal and ethical issues in behavior modification with retarded persons. In J. L. Matson & F. Andrasik (Eds.), *Treatment issues and innovations in mental retardation* (pp. 61–95). New York: Plenum.

Morris, R. J., & Kratochwill, T. R. (Eds.). (1983). *The practice of child therapy.* New York: Pergamon.

Morris, R. J., & Magrath, K. H. (1983). The therapeutic relationship in behavior therapy. In M. J. Lambert (Ed.), *Psychotherapy and patient relationships* (pp. 145–189). Homewood, IL: Dorsey.

Mosteller, F. M., & Bush, R. R. (1954). Selected quantitative techniques. In G. Lindzey (Ed.), *Handbook of social psychology: Vol. 1. Theory and method* Reading, MA: Addison-Wesley.

Munby, M., & Johnston, D. W. (1980). Agoraphobia: The long-term follow-up of behavioural treatment. *British Journal of Psychiatry, 137,* 418–427.

Murphy, G. (1982). Sensory reinforcements in the mentally handicapped and autistic child: A review. *Journal of Austism and Developmental Disorders, 12,* 265–278.

Murphy, G. E., Simons, A. D., Wetzel, R. D., & Lustman. (1984). Cognitive therapy and pharmacotherapy: Singly and together in the treatment of depression. *Archives of General Psychiatry, 41,* 33–41.

Nathan, P. E. (1983). Failures in prevention: Why we can't prevent the devastating effect of alcoholism and drug abuse. *American Psychologist, 38,* 459–467.

National Academy of Sciences. (1981). *Report of the Committee on Indoor Air Pollutants, National Research Council.* Washington, DC: National Academy Press.

National Institute on Alcohol Abuse and Alcoholism. (1982). *Report to the United States Congress on federal activities on alcohol abuse and alcoholism FY 1980.* Rockville, MD: Author.

Neef, N. A., Shafer, M. S., Egel, A. L., Cataldo, M. F., & Parrish, J. M. (1983). The class specific effects of compliance training with "do" and "don't" requests: An analogue analysis and classroom application. *Journal of Applied Behavior Analysis, 16,* 81–89.

Neisworth, J. T., & Madle, R. A. (1982). Retardation. In A. S. Bellack, M. Hersen, & A. E. Kazdin (Eds.), *International handbook of behavior modification and therapy* (pp. 853–889). New York: Plenum.

Nelson, R. O. (1983). Behavioral assessment: Past, present, and future. *Behavioral Assessment, 5,* 195–206.

Nevid, J. S. (1983). Hopelessness, social desirability, and construct validity. *Journal of Consulting and Clinical Psychology, 51,* 139–140.

Newberger, E. H., Newberger, C. M., & Hampton, R. L. (1983). Child abuse: The current theory base and future research needs. *Journal of the American Academy of Child Psychiatry, 22,* 262–268.

Newman, R. K., & Simpson, R. L. (1983). Modifying the least restrictive environment to facilitate the integration of severely emotionally disturbed children and youth. *Behavioral Disorders, 8,* 103–112.

Nicholson, R. A., & Berman, J. S. (1983). Is follow-up necessary in evaluating psychotherapy? *Psychological Bulletin, 93,* 261–278.

Nisbett, R., & Ross, L. (1980). *Human inference: Strategies and shortcomings of social judgement.* Englewood Cliffs, NJ: Prentice-Hall.

Nisbett, R., & Wilson, T. (1977). Telling more than we can know: Verbal reports on mental processes. *Psychological Review, 84,* 231–259.

Nomellini, S., & Katz, R. C. (1983). Effects of anger control training on abusive parents. *Cognitive Therapy and Research, 7,* 57–68.

Norcross, J. C., & Prochaska, J. O. (1982). A national survey of clinical psychologists: Affiliations and orientations. *The Clinical Psychologist, 35,* 1–8.

Norcross, J. C., & Wogan, M. (1983). Relationship of behavior therapists' characteristics, activities, and clients to reported practices in therapy. *Professional Psychology: Research and Practice, 14,* 44–56.

Norman, W. H., Miller, I. W., & Klee, S. H. (1983). Assessment of cognitive distortion in a clinically depressed population. *Cognitive Therapy and Research, 7,* 133–140.

Norton, G. R., Allen, G. E., & Hilton, J. (1983). The social validity of treatments for agoraphobia. *Behaviour Research and Therapy, 21,* 393–399.

Novaco, R. W. (1975). *Anger control.* Lexington, MA: Heath.

O'Brien, R. M., Dickinson, A. M., & Rosow, M. P. (Eds.). (1982). *Industrial behavior modification: A management handbook.* New York: Pergamon.

O'Dell, S. L. (1982). Enhancing parent involvement training: A discussion. *The Behavior Therapist, 5,* 9–13.

O'Dell, S. L., Tarler-Benlolo, L., & Flynn, J. M. (1979). An instrument to measure knowledge of behavioral principles as applied to children. *Journal of Behavior Therapy and Experimental Psychiatry, 10,* 29–34.

O'Donnell, C. R., & Tharp, R. G. (1982). Community intervention and the use of multidisciplinary knowledge. In A. S. Bellack, M. Hersen, & A. E. Kazdin (Eds.), *International handbook of behavior modification and therapy* (pp. 291–318). New York: Plenum.

O'Farrell, T. J., & Keuthen, N. J. (1983). Readability of behavior therapy self-help manuals. *Behavior Therapy, 14,* 449–454.

O'Farrell, T. J., Keuthen, N. J., Connors, G. J., & Upper, D. (1983). Age-related differences among psychiatric inpatients. *International Journal of Behavioral Geriatrics, 2,* 30–37.

O'Farrell, T. J., Sewitch, T. S., & Cutter, H. S. G. (1980). Participants' assessment of a training institute in behavior therapy. *Journal of Behavior Therapy and Experimental Psychiatry, 11,* 161–172.

O'Hara, M. W., & Rehm, L. P. (1983). Hamilton Rating Scale for Depression: Reliability and validity of judgements of novice raters. *Journal of Consulting and Clinical Psychology, 51,* 318–319.

Oldridge, N. B., Donner, A. P., Buck, C. W., Jones, N. L., Andrew, G. M., Parker, J. O., Cunningham, D. A., Kavanaugh, T., Rechnitzer, P. A., & Sutton, J. R. (1983). Predictors of dropout from cardiac exercise rehabilitation: Ontario Exercise–Heart Collaborative Study. *American Journal of Cardiology, 51,* 70–74.

O'Leary, K. D. (1980). Pills or skills for hyperactive children. *Journal of Applied Behavior Analysis, 13,* 191–204.

O'Leary, K. D. (1984). *The image of behavior therapy: It is time to take a stand. Behavior Therapy, 15*, 219–233.

O'Leary, K. D., & Carr, E. G. (1982). Childhood disorders. In G. T. Wilson & C. M. Franks (Eds.), *Contemporary behavior therapy: Conceptual and empirical foundations* (pp. 445–504). New York: Guilford.

O'Leary, K. D., & Wilson, G. T. (1975). *Behavior therapy: Application and outcome.* Englewood Cliffs, NJ: Prentice-Hall.

O'Leary, K. D., & Wilson, G. T. (in press). *Behavior therapy: Application and outcome* (2nd ed.). Englewood Cliffs, NJ: Prentice-Hall.

Ollendick, T. H., & Hersen, M. (Eds.). (1984a). *Child behavioral assessment: Principles and procedures.* New York: Pergamon.

Ollendick, T. H., & Hersen, M. (1984b). An overview of child behavioral assessment. In T. H. Ollendick & M. Hersen (Eds.), *Child behavioral assessment: Principles and procedures* (pp. 3–19). New York: Pergamon.

O'Malley, S. S., Suh, C. S., & Strupp, H. H. (1983). The Vanderbilt Psychotherapy Process Scale: A report on the scale development and a process-outcome study. *Journal of Consulting and Clinical Psychology, 51*, 581–586.

Orton, I. K., Beiman, I., LaPointe, K., & Lankford, A. (1983). Induced states of anxiety and depression: Effects on self-reported affect and tonic psychophysiological response. *Cognitive Therapy and Research, 7*, 233–244.

Ossip-Klein, D. J., Martin, J. E., Prue, D. M., & Davis, C. J. (1983). Assessment of smoking topography generalization across laboratory, clinical, and naturalistic settings. *Addictive Behaviors, 8*, 11–18.

Öst, L. G., & Götestam, K. G. (1976). Behavioral and pharmacological treatments for obesity: An experimental comparison. *Addictive Behaviors, 1*, 331–338.

Palgi, A., Bistrian, B. R., Greenburg, I., & Blackburn, G.L. (1982). *Significant weight loss (over 40 pounds) and prolonged maintenance (2–7 years) with medical treatment of obesity.* Unpublished manuscript, Harvard University.

Parloff, M. B. (1983). Who will be satisfied by "consumer satisfaction" evidence? *Behavior Therapy, 14*, 242–246.

Patterson, R. L. (Ed.). (1982). *Overcoming deficits of aging: A behavioral approach.* New York: Plenum.

Patterson, R. L., & Eberly, D. H. (1983). Social and daily living skills. In P. M. Lewinsohn & L. Teri (Eds.), *Clinical geropsychology: New directions in assessment and treatment* (pp. 116–138). New York: Pergamon.

Patterson, R. L., & Jackson, G. M. (1981). *Behavioral approaches to gerontology.* In L. Michelson, M. Hersen, & S. M. Turner (Eds.), *Future perspectives in behavior therapy* (pp. 293–313). New York: Plenum.

Pattison, E. M., Sobell, M. B., & Sobell, L. C. (1977). *Emerging concepts of alcohol dependence.* New York: Springer.

Paul, G. L. (1967). Strategies in outcome research in psychotherapy. *Journal of Consulting Psychology, 31*, 109–118.

Pechacek, T. F. (1979). Modification of smoking behavior. In *Smoking and health: A report of the Surgeon General* (DHEW Publ. No. (PHS) 79-50066) (pp. 213–228). Washington, DC: U.S. Government Printing Office.

Peele, S. (1983, April). Through a glass darkly. *Psychology Today*, pp. 38–42.

Pendery, M. L., Maltzman, I. M., & West, L. J. (1982). Controlled drinking by alcoholics?: New findings and a reevaluation of a major affirmative study. *Science, 217*, 169–174.

Perloff, R., & Nelson, S. D. (1983). Economic productivity and the behavioral sciences: An introduction. *American Psychologist, 38*, 451–453.

Perry, C., Killen, J., Telch, M., Slinkard, L. A., & Danaher, B. G. (1980). Modifying smoking behavior of teenagers: A school-based intervention. *American Journal of Public Health, 70,* 722–724.

Peterson, C., Semmel, A., von Baeyer, C., Abramson, L. Y., Metalsky, G. I., & Seligman, M. E. P. (1982). The Attributional Style Questionnaire. *Cognitive Therapy and Research, 6,* 287–300.

Petrunik, M. (1982). The politics of dangerousness. *International Journal of Law and Psychiatry, 5,* 225–253.

Piersel, W. C., & Gutkin, T. B. (1983). Resistance to school-based consultation: A behavioral analysis of the problem. *Psychology in the Schools, 20,* 311–320.

Polansky, N., Chalmers, M. A., Buttenwieser, E., & Williams, D. P. (1979). The isolation of the neglectful family. *American Journal of Orthopsychiatry, 49,* 149–152.

Poppen, R. (1983). Clinical practice and biofeedback research: Are the data really necessary? *The Behavior Therapist, 6,* 145–148.

Pressley, M. (1979). Increasing children's self-control through cognitive interventions. *Review of Educational Research, 49,* 319–370.

Pressley, M., Reynolds, W. M., Stark, K. D., & Gettinger, M. (1983). Cognitive strategy training and children's self-control. In M. Pressley & J. R. Levin (Eds.), *Cognitive strategy training: Psychological foundations* (pp. 216–264). New York: Springer-Verlag.

Prinz, R. J., Roberts, W. A., & Hartman, E, (1980) Dietary correlates of hyperactive behavior in children. *Journal of Consulting and Clinical Psychology, 48,* 760–769.

Prue, D. M., Frederiksen, L. W., & Bacon, A. (1978). Organizational behavior management: An annotated bibliography. *Journal of Organizational Behavior Management, 1,* 216–257.

Prue, D. M., Krapfl, J. E., & Martin, J. E. (1981). Brand fading: The effects of gradual changes to low tar and nicotine cigarettes on smoking rate, carbon monoxide and thiocyanate levels. *Behavior Therapy, 12,* 400–416.

Puska, P., Vartiainen, E., Pallonen, U., Ruotsalainen, P., Tuomilheto, J., Koskela, K., Lahtinen, A., & Norppa, J. (1981). The North Karelia Youth Project: A community-based intervention study on CVD risk factors among 13- to 15-year-old children: Study design and preliminary findings. *Preventive Medicine, 10,* 133–148.

Quattrochi-Tubin, S., & Jason, L. A. (1983). The influence of introversion–extraversion on activity choice and satisfaction among the elderly. *Personality and Individual Differences, 1,* 17–22.

Quayle, D. (1983). American productivity: The devastating effect of alcoholism and drug abuse. *American Psychologist, 38,* 454–458.

Quilitch, H. R. (1975). A comparison of three staff-management procedures. *Journal of Applied Behavior Analysis, 8,* 59–66.

Rachman, S. (1983a). Behavioural medicine, clinical reasoning and technical advances. *Canadian Journal of Behavioural Science, 15,* 318–333.

Rachman, S. (Ed.). (1983b). Fear and courage among military bomb disposal operators. *Advances in Behaviour Research and Therapy, 4,* 99–165.

Rachman, S. (1983c). Irrational thinking, with special reference to cognitive therapy. *Advances in Behaviour Research and Therapy, 5,* 63–88.

Rachman, S. (1983d). The modification of agoraphobic avoidance behaviour: Some fresh possibilities. *Behaviour Research and Therapy, 21,* 567–574.

Rachman, S. (1983e). Obstacles to the successful treatment of obsessions. In E. Foa & P. M. G. Emmelkamp (Eds.), *Treatment failures in behavior therapy* (pp. 35–57). New York: Wiley.

Rachman, S., Cobb, J., Grey, S., MacDonald, D., Mawson, D., Sartory, G., & Stern, R.

(1979). The behavioural treatment of obsessional–compulsive disorders, with and without clomipramine. *Behaviour Research and Therapy*, *17*, 467–478.

Rachman, S., & Hodgson, R. (1980). *Obsessions and compulsions*. Englewood Cliffs, NJ: Prentice-Hall.

Rachman, S., & Philips, C. (1975). *Psychology and medicine*. London: Temple Smith.

Rachman, S., & Wilson, G. T. (1980). *The effects of psychological therapy*. Oxford: Pergamon.

Rapoff, M. A., & Christophersen, E. R. (1982). Compliance of pediatric patients with medical regimens: A review and evaluation. In R. B. Stuart (Ed.), *Adherence, compliance and generalization in behavioral medicine* (pp. 79–124). New York: Brunner/Mazel.

Rapport, M. D., Murphy, A., & Bailey, J. S. (1982). Ritalin versus response cost in the control of hyperactive children: A within-subject comparison. *Journal of Applied Behavior Analysis*, *15*, 205–216.

Reich, W., Herjanic, B., Welner, Z., & Gandhy, P. R. (1982). Development of a structured psychiatric interview for children: Agreement on diagnosis comparing child and parent interviews. *Journal of Abnormal Child Psychology*, *10*, 325–336.

Reid, D. H., & Whitman, T. L. (1983). Behavioral staff management in institutions: A critical review of effectiveness and acceptability. *Analysis and Intervention in Developmental Disabilities*, *3*, 131–149.

Reisinger, J. J. (1982). Unprogrammed learning of differential attention by fathers of oppositional children. *Journal of Behavior Therapy and Experimental Psychiatry*, *12*, 203–208.

Reisinger, J. J., & Lavigne, J. V. (1980). An early intervention model for pediatric settings. *Professional Psychology*, *11*, 582–590.

Repace, J. L., & Lowery, A. H. (1980). Indoor air pollution, tobacco smoke, and public health. *Science*, *208*, 464–472.

Reynolds, W. M., & Stark, K. D. (1983). Cognitive behavior modification: The clinical application of cognitive strategies. In M. Pressley & J. R. Levin (Eds.), *Cognitive strategy research: Psychological foundations*. New York: Springer-Verlag.

Rhode, G., Morgan, D. P., & Young, K. R. (1983). Generalization and maintenance of treatment gains of behaviorally handicapped students from resource rooms to regular classrooms using self-evaluation procedures. *Journal of Applied Behavior Analysis*, *16*, 171–188.

Rice, L. N., Koke, C., Greenberg, L. S., & Wagstaff, A. (1979). *Manual for client voice quality*. Toronto: York University Counseling and Development Center.

Rickel, A. U., Eshelman, A. K., & Loigman, G. A. (1983). Social problem solving training: A follow-up study of cognitive and behavioral effects. *Journal of Abnormal Child Psychology*, *11*, 15–28.

Robertson, J., Wendiggensen, P., & Kaplan, I. (1983). Towards a comprehensive treatment for obessional thoughts. *Behaviour Research and Therapy*, *21*, 347–356.

Rodin, J. (1983). Welcome to the participants of the National Working Conference on Education and Training in Health Psychology. *Health Psychology*, *2*(Suppl.), 49–51.

Romanczyk, R. G., & Lockshin, S. (1981). *How to create a curriculum for autistic and other handicapped children*. Lawrence, KS: H&H Enterprises.

Rorer, L. G. (1983). "Deep" RET: A reformulation of some psychodynamic explanations of procrastination. *Cognitive Therapy and Research*, *7*, 1–10.

Rosenbaum, M. (1980). A schedule for assessing self-control behaviors: Preliminary findings. *Behavior Therapy*, *11*, 109–121.

Rosenbaum, M., Franks, C. M., & Jaffe, Y. (Eds.). (1983). *Perspectives on behavior therapy in the eighties*. New York: Springer.

Rosenthal, R. (1983a). Assessing the statistical and social importance of the effects of psychotherapy. *Journal of Consulting and Clinical Psychology, 51,* 4–13.

Rosenthal, R. (1983b). Meta-analysis: Toward a more cumulative social science. In L. Bickman (Ed.), *Applied social psychology annual* (Vol. 4). Beverly Hills, CA: Sage.

Rosenzweig, S. (1983). Mental hospital deinstitutionalization: Reservations. *American Psychologist, 38,* 349.

Ross, A. O. (1980). *Psychological disorders of children: A behavioral approach to theory, research, and therapy* (2nd ed.). New York: McGraw-Hill.

Ross, D. M., & Ross, S. A. (1976). *Hyperactivity: Research, theory, and action.* New York: Wiley.

Ross, D. M., & Ross, S. A. (1982). *Hyperactivity: Current issues, research, and theory* (2nd ed.). New York: Wiley.

Ross, H. L. (1982). *Deterring the drinking driver: Legal policy and social control.* Lexington, MA: Lexington Books (Heath).

Ross, S. M., & Gottfredson, D. K. (1983). *Cognitive self-statements in depression: Findings across clinical populations.* Paper presented at the annual meeting of the Association for Advancement of Behavior Therapy, Washington, DC.

Ross, S. M., Todt, E., & Rindflesh, M. (1983). *Interrelationships between measures of binge-eating severity, depression and dysfunctional cognitions.* Paper presented at the annual meeting of the Association for Advancement of Behavior Therapy, Washington, DC.

Routh, D. K., & Perlman, J. L. (1982). The clinical uses of punishment: Bane or boon? In D. K. Routh (Ed.), *Learning, speech and the complex effects of punishment: Essays honoring George J. Wischer* (pp. 181–211). New York: Plenum.

Ruggles, T. R., & LeBlanc, J. M. (1982). Behavior analysis procedures in classroom teaching. In A. S. Bellack, M. Hersen, & A. E. Kazdin (Eds.), *International handbook of behavior modification and therapy* (pp. 959–996). New York: Plenum.

Runyan, C. W., DeVellis, R. F., DeVellis, B. M., & Hochbaum, G. M. (1982). Health psychology and the public health perspective: In search of the pump handle. *Health Psychology, 1,* 169–180.

Rush, A. J., Beck, A. T., Kovacs, M., & Hollon, S. (1977). Comparative efficacy of cognitive therapy and pharmacotherapy in the treatment of depressed outpatients. *Cognitive Therapy and Research, 1,* 17–37.

Rush, A. J., & Shaw, B. (1983). Failures in treating depression by cognitive behavior therapy. In E. Foa & P. M. G. Emmelkamp (Eds.), *Failures in behavior therapy* (pp. 217–228). New York: Wiley.

Ryan, V., & Gizynski, M. (1971). Behavior therapy in retrospect: Patients' feelings about their behavior therapists. *Journal of Consulting and Clinical Psychology, 37,* 1–9.

Sacco, W. P. (1982). Statistical power considerations in the use of cost-effectiveness analysis. *Professional Psychology, 13,* 752–775.

Sachs, J. S. (1983). Negative factors in brief psychotherapy: An empirical assessment. *Journal of Consulting and Clinical Psychology, 51,* 557–564.

Safire, W. (1981). *William Safire on language.* New York: Avon.

Safran, J. D., & Greenberg, L. S. (1982). Cognitive appraisal and reappraisal: Implications for clinical practice. *Cognitive Therapy and Research, 6,* 251–258.

Sajwaj, T., Schnelle, J. F., McNees, M. P., & McConnell, S. (1983). Organizational behavior management in a community mental health center: The development of a staff performance assessment system. *Behavioral Assessment, 5,* 245–261.

Sametz, L., McLoughlin, C. S., & Streib, V. L. (1983). Children's constitutional rights: Interpretations and implications. *Psychology in the Schools, 20,* 175–183.

Sanders, M. R. (1982). The generalization of parent responding to community settings:

The effects of instructions, plus feedback, and self-management training. *Behavioural Psychotherapy, 10,* 10–14.

Sanders, M. R., & Dadds, M. R. (1982). The effects of planned activities and child management procedures in parent training: An analysis of setting generality. *Behavior Therapy, 13,* 452–461.

Sanders, M. R., & Glynn, T. (1981). Training parents in behavioral self-management: An analysis of generalization and maintenance. *Journal of Applied Behavior Analysis, 14,* 223–237.

Sarason, S. B. (1981). An asocial psychology and a misdirected clinical psychology. *American Psychologist, 36,* 827–836.

Sarason, S. B., Davidson, K. S., Lighthall, F. F., Waite, R. R., & Ruebush, B. K. (1960). *Anxiety and elementary school children.* New York: Wiley.

Sarbin, T., Taft, R., & Bailey, D. (1960). *Clinical inference and cognitive theory.* New York: Holt.

Satterfield, J. H., Satterfield, B. T., & Cantwell, D. P. (1981). Three year multimodality treatment study of 100 hyperactive boys. *Journal of Pediatrics, 98,* 650–655.

Schaffer, N. D. (1983). The utility of measuring the skillfulness of therapeutic techniques. *Psychotherapy: Theory, research, and practice, 20,* 330–336.

Schmidt, W. (1980). Effects of alcohol consumption on health. *Journal of Public Health Policy, 1,* 25–40.

Schnelle, J. F., & Traughber, B. (1983). A behavioral assessment system applicable to geriatric nursing facility residents. *Behavioral Assessment, 5,* 231–243.

Schnelle, J. F., Traughber, B., Morgan, D. G., Embry, J. E., Binion, A. F., & Coleman, A. (1983). Management of geriatric incontinence in nursing homes. *Journal of Applied Behavior Analysis, 16,* 235–241.

Schoggen, P. (1983). Behavior settings and the quality of life. *Journal of Community Psychology, 11,* 144–157.

Schreibman, L. (1983). Are we forgetting the *parent* in parent training? *The Behavior Therapist, 6,* 107–109.

Schreibman, L., Koegel, R. L., Charlop, M., & Egel, A. J. (1982). Autism. In A. S. Bellack, M. Hersen, & A. E. Kazdin (Eds.), *International handbook of behavior modification and therapy* (pp. 891–915). New York: Plenum.

Schreibman, L., & Mills, J. I. (1983). Infantile autism. In T. H. Ollendick & M. Hersen (Eds.), *Handbook of child psychopathology* (pp. 123–149). New York: Plenum.

Schreibman, L., O'Neill, R. E., & Koegel, R. L. (1983). Behavioral training for siblings of autistic children. *Journal of Applied Behavior Analysis, 16,* 129–138.

Schuele, J. G., & Wiesenfeld, A. R. (1983). Automatic response to self-critical thoughts. *Cognitive Therapy and Research, 7,* 189–194.

Schutz, R. P., Vogelsberg, R. T., & Rusch, F. R. (1980). A behavioral approach to integrating individuals into the community. In A. R. Novak & L. W. Heal (Eds.), *Integration of developmentally disabled individuals into the community* (pp. 107–119). Baltimore: Paul H. Brookes.

Schwartz, G. (1983). Conference consensus regarding the status of health psychology: National Working Conference on Education and Training in Health Psychology. *Health Psychology, 2*(Suppl.), 9.

Schwartz, M., Friedman, R., Lindsay, P., & Narrol, H. (1982). The relationship between conceptual tempo and depression in children. *Journal of Consulting and Clinical Psychology, 50,* 488–490.

Scott, M. (1980). Ecological theory and methods for research in special education. *Journal of Special Education, 14,* 279–294.

Seligman, M. E. P., & Johnston, J. (1973). A cognitive theory of avoidance learning.

In J. McGuigan & B. Lumsden (Eds.), *Contemporary approaches to conditioning and learning.* New York: Wiley.

Selman, R. L. (1980). *The growth of interpersonal understanding: Developmental and clinical analyses.* New York: Academic.

Seltzer, C. C., & Mayer, J. (1970). An effective weight control program in a public school system. *American Journal of Public Health, 60,* 679–689.

Sgroi, S. M. (1982). *Handbook of clinical intervention in child sexual abuse.* Lexington, MA: Lexington Books (Heath).

Shapiro, D. A., & Shapiro, D. (1983). Comparative therapy outcome research: Methodological implications of meta-analysis. *Journal of Consulting and Clinical Psychology, 51,* 42–53.

Sharpley, C. F., & Sharpley, A. M. (1981). Contingent versus non-contingent rewards in the classroom: A review of the literature. *Journal of School Psychology, 19,* 250–259.

Sheehan, D. V. (1982). Current concepts in psychiatry. *New England Journal of Medicine, 307,* 156–158.

Sheehan, D. V., Ballenger, J., & Jacobsen, G. (1980). Treatment of endogenous anxiety with phobic, hysterical, and hypochondriacal symptoms. *Archives of General Psychiatry, 37,* 51–59.

Sheldon-Wildgen, J., & Risley, T. R. (1982). Balancing client's rights: The establishment of human-rights and peer-review committees. In A. S. Bellack, M. Hersen, & A. E. Kazdin (Eds.), *International handbook of behavior modification and therapy* (pp. 263–289). New York: Plenum.

Sher, K. J., Frost, R. O., & Otto, R. (1983). Cognitive deficits in compulsive checkers: An exploratory study. *Behaviour Research and Therapy, 21,* 357–363.

Showdown on smoking: To smoke or not to smoke has changed from a simple question of health and habit to an explosive issue of civil rights and social etiquette. (1983, June 6). *Newsweek,* pp. 24–25.

Simons, A. D., Garfield, S. L., & Murphy, G. E. (1984). The process of change in cognitive therapy and pharmacotherapy for depression. *Archives of General Psychiatry, 41,* 45–51.

Singer, J. E., & Krantz, D. S. (1982). Perspectives on the interface between psychology and public health. *American Psychologist, 37,* 955–960.

Skinner, B. F. (1983). Intellectual self-management in old age. *American Psychologist, 38,* 239–244.

Skinner, B. F., & Vaughan, M. (1983). *Enjoy old age.* New York: Norton.

Sloan, V. J., Jason, L. A., & Bogat, G. A. (in press). *Child Study Journal.*

Sloane, R. B., Staples, F. R., Cristol, A. H., Yorkston, N. J., & Whipple, K. (1975). *Psychotherapy versus behavior therapy.* Cambridge, MA: Harvard University Press.

Smith, D. (1982). Trends in counseling and psychotherapy. *American Psychologist, 37,* 802–810.

Smith, M. L., & Glass, G. V. (1977). Meta-analysis of psychotherapy outcome studies. *American Psychologist, 32,* 752–760.

Smith, M. L., Glass, G., & Miller, T. (1980). *The benefits of psychotherapy.* Baltimore: Johns Hopkins University Press.

Smith, T. (1982). *Critque of rational–emotive therapy.* Unpublished manuscript.

Smith, T. W. (1983). Change in irrational beliefs and the outcome of rational–emotive psychotherapy. *Journal of Consulting and Clinical Psychology, 51,* 156–157.

Snyder, J., & Brown, K. (1983). Oppositional behavior and non-compliance in preschool children: Environmental correlates and skills deficits. *Behavioral Assessment, 5,* 333–348.

Sobell, M. B., & Sobell, L. C. (1973a). Alcoholics treated by individualized behaviour therapy: One year treatment outcome. *Behaviour Research and Therapy, 11,* 599–618.

Sobell, M. B., & Sobell, L. C. (1973b). Individualized behavior therapy for alcoholics. *Behavior Therapy, 4,* 49–72.

Sobell, M. B., & Sobell, L. C. (1978). *Behavioral treatment of alcohol problems: Individualized therapy and controlled drinking.* New York: Plenum.

Sobell, M. B., & Sobell, L. C. (1984). The aftermath of heresy: A response to Pendery et al.'s (1982) critique of "Individualized Behavior Therapy for Alcoholics." *Behaviour Research and Therapy, 22,* 413–440.

Solomon, L. J., Brehony, K. A., Rothblum, E. D., & Kelly, J. A. (1982). Corporate managers' reactions to assertive social skill exhibited by males and females. *Journal of Organizational Behavior Management, 4*(3/4), 49–63.

Solomon, K., & Hart, R. (1978). Pitfalls and prospects in clinical research on antianxiety drugs: Benzodiazepines and placebo—a research review. *Journal of Clinical Psychiatry, 4,* 823–831.

Sours, H. E., Frattali, V. P., Brand, C. D., Feldman, R. A., Forbes, A. L., Swanson, R. C., & Paris, A. L. (1981). Sudden death associated with very-low-calorie weight reduction regimens. *American Journal of Clinical Nutrition, 34,* 453–461.

Spence, S., & Shepherd, G. (Eds.). (1983). *Developments in social skills training.* London: Academic.

Spengler, J. D., & Sexton, K. (1983). Indoor air pollution: A public health perspective. *Science, 221,* 9–17.

Spivack, G., & Shure, M. B. (1974). *Social adjustment of young children.* San Francisco: Jossey-Bass.

Stalgaitis, S. J., Meyers, A. W., & Krisak, J. (1982). A social learning theory model for reduction of correctional officer stress. *Federal Probation, 47,* 33–41.

Stalonas, P. M., Johnson, W. G., & Christ, M. (1978). Behavior modification for obesity: The evaluation of exercise, contingency management, and program adherence. *Journal of Consulting and Clinical Psychology, 46,* 463–469.

Stamler, J. (1980). Improved life styles: Their potential for the primary prevention of atherosclerosis and hypertension in childhood. In R. M. Lauer & R. B. Shekelle (Eds.), *Childhood prevention of atherosclerosis and hypertension* (pp. 3–36). New York: Raven.

Stampfl, T. G. (1983). Exposure treatment for psychiatrists [Review of J. C. Boulougouris's *Learning theory approaches to psychiatry*]. *Contemporary Psychology, 28,* 527–529.

Steinbrueck, S. M., Maxwell, S. E., & Howard, G. S. (1983). A meta-analysis of psychotherapy and drug therapy in the treatment of unipolar depression with adults. *Journal of Consulting and Clinical Psychology, 51,* 856–863.

Stern, J. S. (1984). Is obesity a disease of inactivity? In A. J. Stunkard & E. Stellar (Eds.), *Eating and its disorders.* New York: Raven.

Steuer, J. L., & Hammen, C. L. (1983). Cognitive–behavioral group therapy for the depressed elderly: Issues and adaptations. *Cognitive Therapy and Research, 7,* 285–296.

Stevens, G., & Gardner, S. (1983). A study of attitudes toward hyperkinesis using Q methodology. *Behavioral Disorders, 8,* 9–18.

Stockwell, G. (1982). Editorial. *Behavioural Psychotherapy, 10,* 215–216.

Stone, G. C. (1983). Summary of recommendations of the National Working Conference on Education and Training in Health Psychology. *Health Psychology, 2*(Suppl.), 15–18.

Storandt, M. (1983). Psychology's response to the graying of America. *American Psychologist, 38,* 323–326.

Strain, P. S., Kerr, M. M., & Ragland, E. V. (1979). Effects of peer-mediated social initiations and prompting/reinforcements procedures on the social behavior of autistic children. *Journal of Autism and Developmental Disorders, 9,* 41-54.

Strain, P. S., Lambert, D. L., Kerr, M. M., Stagg, V., & Lenkner, D. A. (1983). Naturalistic assessment of children's compliance to teachers' requests and consequences for compliance. *Journal of Applied Behavior Analysis, 16,* 243-249.

Strupp, H. H. (1977). Reformulation of the dynamics of therapists' contributions. In A. S. Gurman & A. M. Razin (Eds.), *Effective psychotherapy* (pp. 1-22). New York: Pergamon.

Strupp, H. H., & Hadley, S. W. (1979). Specific versus nonspecific factors in psychotherapy. *Archives of General Psychiatry, 36,* 1125-1136.

Stuart, R. B. (1971). A three-dimensional approach for the treatment of obesity. *Behaviour Research and Therapy, 9,* 177-186.

Stuart, R. B. (Ed.). (1982a). *Adherence, compliance and generalization in behavioral medicine.* New York: Brunner/Mazel.

Stuart, R. B. (1982b). A natural history of health behavior decision-making. In R. B. Stuart (Ed.), *Adherence, compliance and generalization in behavioral medicine* (pp. 3-27). New York: Brunner/Mazel.

Stuart, R. B., & Guire, K. (1978). Some correlates of the maintenance of weight loss through behavior modification. *International Journal of Obesity, 2,* 225-235.

Suedfeld, P. (1982). Environmental factors influencing maintenance of lifestyle change. In R. B. Stuart (Ed.), *Adherence, compliance and generalization in behavioral medicine* (pp. 125-144). New York: Brunner/Mazel.

Sulzer-Azaroff, B., & Pollack, M. J. (1982). The modification of child behavior problems in the home. In A. S. Bellack, M. Hersen, & A. E. Kazdin (Eds.), *International handbook of behavior modification and therapy* (pp. 917-958). New York: Plenum.

Swan, G. E., & MacDonald, M. O. (1978). Behavior therapy in practice: A national survey of behavior therapists. *Behavior Therapy, 9,* 799-807.

Talbott, J. A. (Ed.). (1981). *The chronic mentally ill: Treatment, programs, systems.* New York: Human Sciences.

Talbott, J. A. (1983). Foreword. In S. S. Herr, S. Arons, & R. E. Wallace, *Legal rights and mental health care* (pp. xi-xiii). Lexington, MA: Lexington Books (Heath).

Tanabe, G. (1982). The potential for public health psychology. *American Psychologist, 37,* 942-944.

Taylor, D. W. (1979). A test of the health belief model in hypertension. Cited in Ralpoff, M. A., & Christopherson, E. R. (1982). Compliance of pediatric patients with medical regimens. In R. B. Stuart (Ed.), *Adherence, Compliance and generalization in behavioral medicine* (pp. 79-124). New York: Brunner/Mazel.

Taylor, F. G., & Marshall, W. L. (1977). Experimental analysis of a cognitive-behavioral therapy for depression. *Cognitive Therapy and Research, 1,* 59-72.

Taylor, H. L., Buskirk, E. R., & Remington, R. D. (1973). Exercise in controlled trials of the prevention of coronary heart disease. *Federation Proceedings, 32,* 1623-1627.

Teasdale, J. D. (1978). Self-efficacy: Toward a unifying theory of behavioural change? *Advances in Behaviour Research and Therapy, 1,* 211-215.

Teasdale, J. D. (1983). Negative thinking in depression: Cause, effect, or reciprocal relationship? *Advances in Behaviour Research and Therapy, 5,* 3-26.

Teasdale, J. D., & Fennell, M. J. V. (1982). Immediate effects on depression of cognitive therapy interventions. *Cognitive Therapy and Research, 6,* 343-352.

Telch, M. J. (1981). The present status of outcome studies: A reply to Frank. *Journal of Consulting and Clinical Psychology, 49,* 472-475.

Telch, M. J. (1982). *A comparison of behavioral and pharmacological approaches to the treatment of agoraphobia.* Unpublished doctoral dissertation, Stanford University.

Telch, M. J., Teaman, B. H., & Taylor, C. B. (1983). Antidepressant medication in the treatment of agoraphobia: A critical review. *Behaviour Research and Therapy*, *21*, 505–518.

Thompson, J. K., Jarvie, G. J., Lahey, B. B., & Cureton, K. J. (1982). Exercise and obesity: Etiology, physiology, and intervention. *Psychological Bulletin*, *91*, 55–79.

Threlkeld, R. M., & DeJong, W. (1983). Hiring the disabled: An attempt to influence behavioral intention through a media presentation. *Rehabilitation Psychology*, *28*, 105–114.

Tobacco Institute (1982, November 8). What happens to smoke in the air? [Advertisement]. *Newsweek*.

Tryon, G. S. (1983). Pleasures and displeasures of full time private practice. *The Clinical Psychologist*, *36*, 45–48.

Tuma, J. M., & Cohen, R. (1981). *Pediatric psychology: An investigation of factors relative to practice and training*. Unpublished manuscript, Louisiana State University, Baton Rouge.

Tuma, J. M., & Pratt, J. M. (1982). Clinical child psychology practice and training: A survey. *Journal of Clinical Child Psychology*, *11*, 27–34.

Tuomilheto, J., Koskela, K., Puska, P., Bjorkqvist, S., & Salonen, J. (1978). A community anti-smoking programme: Interim evaluation of the North Karelia project. *International Journal of Health Education*, *21*(Suppl.), 1–15.

Turkat, I. D., & Feuerstein, M. (1978). Behavior modification and the public misconception. *American Psychologist*, *22*, 194.

Turkewitz, H., & O'Leary, K. D. (1981). An apparent outcome study of behavioral marital therapy and community therapy. *Journal of Marital and Family Therapy*, *7*, 159–169.

Turnbull, A. P. (1983). Parent–professional interactions. In M. E. Snell (Ed.), *Systematic instruction of the moderately and severely handicapped child* (24th ed., pp. 18–43). Columbus, OH: Charles E. Merrill.

Tversky, A., & Kahneman, D. (1974). Judgement under uncertainty: Heuristics and biases. *Science*, *185*, 1124–1131.

Tversky, A., & Kahneman, D. (1981). The framing of decisions and the psychology of choice. *Science*, *211*, 453–458.

Tymchuk, A. J. (1983). Interventions with parents of the mentally retarded. In J. L. Matson & J. A. Mulick (Eds.), *Handbook of mental retardation* (pp. 369–380). New York: Pergamon.

United States Department of Health, Education and Welfare. (1979a). *Healthy people: The Surgeon General's report on health promotion and disease prevention* (DHEW Publ. No. (PHS) 79-55071). Washington, DC: U.S. Government Printing Office.

United States Department of Health, Education and Welfare. (1979b). *Healthy people: The Surgeon General's report on health promotion and disease prevention: Background papers* (DHEW Publ. No. (PHS) 79-55071A). Washington, DC: U.S. Government Printing Office.

United States Department of Health, Education and Welfare. (1979c). *Smoking and health: A report of the Surgeon General* (DHEW Publ. No. (PHS) 79-50066). Washington, DC: U.S. Government Printing Office.

United States Department of Health and Human Services. (1983). *The health consequences of smoking: Cardiovascular disease. A report of the Surgeon General*. Washington, DC: U.S. Government Printing Office.

Urbain, E. S. (1983). *Building self-image: A cognitive–behavioral group manual for adolescents*. St. Paul, MN: Wilder Child Guidance Center.

Vaillant, G. E. (1983). *The natural history of alcoholism: Causes, patterns, and paths to recovery.* Cambridge, MA: Harvard University Press.

Vaillant, G. E., & Milofsky, E. S. (1982). The etiology of alcoholism: A prospective viewpoint. *American Psychologist, 37,* 494–503.

Van Den Pol, R. A., Reid, D. H., & Fugua, R. W. (1983). Peer training of safety-related skills to institutional staff: Benefits for trainers and trainees. *Journal of Applied Behavior Analysis, —,* 139–158.

Van Itallie, T. B. (1978). Liquid protein mayhem. *Journal of the American Medical Association, 240,* 144–145.

Vardin, P. A., & Brody, I. N. (1979). Introduction. In P. A. Vardin & I. N. Brody (Eds.), *Children's rights: Contemporary perspectives* (pp. xv–xvii). New York: Teachers College Press.

Vertes, V., Genuth, S. M., & Hazelton, I. M. (1977). Supplemental fasting as a large scale outpatient program. *Journal of the American Medical Association, 238,* 2151–2153.

Viney, W., Waldman, D. A., & Barchilon, J. (1982). Attitudes toward punishment in relation to beliefs in free-will and determinism. *Human Relations, 35,* 939–950.

Voeltz, L. M. (1980). Children's attitudes toward handicapped peers. *American Journal of Mental Deficiency, 84,* 455–464.

Voeltz, L. M. (1982). Effects of structured interactions with severely handicapped peers on children's attitudes. *American Journal of Mental Deficiency, 86,* 380–390.

Voeltz, L. M., Evans, I. M., Derer, K. R., & Hanashiro, R. (1983). Targeting excess behavior for change. A clinical decision model for selecting priority goals in educational contests. *Child and Family Behavior Therapy, 5*(3), 17–36.

Vogt, T. M. (1983). Effects of parental smoking on medical care utilization by children. *American Journal of Public Health, 74,* 30–34.

Voors, A. W., Foster, T. A., Frerichs, R. R., Webber, L. S., & Berenson, G. S. (1976). Studies of blood pressure in children, ages 5–14 years in a total biracial community: The Bogalusa Heart Study. *Circulation, 54,* 319–327.

Wachtel, P. L. (1977). *Psychoanalysis and behavior therapy: Toward an integration.* New York: Basic Books.

Wachtel, P. L. (Ed.). (1982a). *Resistance: Psychodynamic and behavioral approaches.* New York: Plenum.

Wachtel, P. L. (1982b). What can dynamic therapies contribute to behavior therapy? *Behavior Therapy, 13,* 594–609.

Wack, J. T., & Rodin, J. (1982). Smoking and its effect on body weight and the systems of caloric regulation. *American Journal of Clinical Nutrition, 35,* 366–380.

Wadden, T. A., Stunkard, A. J., & Brownell, K. D. (1983a). Very low calorie diets: Their efficacy, safety, and future. *Annals of Internal Medicine, 99,* 675–684.

Wadden, T. A., Stunkard, A. J., Brownell, K. D., & Dey, S. C. (1984). The treatment of moderate obesity by behavior modification and very-low-calorie diets. *Journal of Consulting and Clinical Psychology, 52,* 692–694.

Wadden, T. A., Stunkard, A. J., Brownell, K. D., & Van Itallie, T. B. (1983b). The Cambridge Diet: More mayhem? *Journal of the American Medical Association, 250,* 2833–2844.

Wahler, R. G., & Afton, A. D. (1980). Attentional processes in insular and non-insular mothers: Some differences in their summary reports about child problem behavior. *Child Behavior Therapy, 2,* 25–41.

Wahler, R. G., & Fox, J. J. (1981). Setting events in applied behavior analysis: Toward a conceptual and methodological expansion. *Journal of Applied Behavior Analysis, 14,* 327–338.

Wahler, R. G., & Graves, M. (1983). Setting events in social networks: Ally or enemy in child behavior therapy. *Behavior Therapy, 14,* 19–36.

Walker, L. E. (1979). *The battered woman.* New York: Harper & Row.

Wallander, J. L., Curran, J. P., & Myers, P. E. (1983). Social calibration of the SSIT: Evaluating social validity. *Behavior Modification, 7,* 423–445.

Warner, K. E. (1977). The effects of the anti-smoking campaign on cigarette consumption. *American Journal of Public Health, 67,* 645–650.

Warner, K. E. (1981). Cigarette smoking in the 1970's: The impact of the anti-smoking campaign on consumption. *Science, 211,* 729–731.

Warner, K. E., & Murt, H. A. (1983). Premature deaths avoided by the anti-smoking campaign. *American Journal of Public Health, 73,* 672–677.

Watson, D., & Friend, R. (1969). Measurement of social-evaluative anxiety. *Journal of Consulting and Clinical Psychology, 33,* 448–457.

Weiner, M. L. (1983). The ego activation method: An *in vivo* cognitive therapy integrating behavioral and psychodynamic approaches. *Cognitive Therapy and Research, 7,* 11–16.

Weiss, B. (1983). Behavioral toxicology and environmental health science: Opportunity and challenge for psychology. *American Psychologist, 38,* 1174–1187.

Weiss, S. M. (1982). Health psychology: The time is now. *Health Psychology, 1,* 81–91.

Weiss, S. M. (1983). Planning the National Working Conference on Education and Training in Health Psychology. *Health Psychology, 2*(Suppl.), 19–25.

Weissberg, R. P., Cowen, E. L., Lotyczewski, B. S., & Gesten, E. L. (1983). The primary mental health project: Seven consecutive years of program outcome research. *Journal of Consulting and Clinical Psychology, 51,* 100–107.

Willems, E. P. (1983). Training for ecobehavioral technology. In M. Rosenbaum, C. M. Franks, & Y. Jaffe (Eds.), *Perspectives on behavior therapy in the eighties* (pp. 416–429). New York: Springer.

Wexler, D. A., & Rice, L. N. (Eds.). (1974). *Innovations in client-centered therapy.* New York: Wiley.

Whalen, C. K. (1983). Hyperactivity, learning problems, and the attentive deficit disorders. In T. H. Ollendick & M. Hersen (Eds.), *Handbook of psychopathology* (pp. 151–199). New York: Plenum.

Whalen, C. K., & Henker, B. (Eds.). (1980). *Hyperactive children: The social ecology of identification and treatment.* New York: Academic.

Whang, P. L., Fletcher, R. K., & Fawcett, S. B. (1982). Training counseling skills: An experimental analysis and social validation. *Journal of Applied Behavior Analysis, 15,* 325–334.

Wherry, J. N. (1983). Some legal considerations and implications for the use of behavior modification in the schools. *Psychology in the Schools, 20,* 46–51.

White, J., & Froeb, H. (1980). Small airways dysfunction in nonsmokers chronically exposed to tobacco smoke. *New England Journal of Medicine, 302,* 720–723.

Whitman, T. L., Scibak, J. W., Butler, K. M., Richter, R., & Johnson, M. R. (1982). Improving classroom behavior in mentally retarded children through correspondence training. *Journal of Applied Behavior Analysis, 15,* 545–564.

Wilkinson, C. B., & O'Connor, W. A. (1982). Human ecology and mental illness. *American Journal of Psychiatry, 139,* 985–990.

Williams, C. L., Arnold, C. B., & Wynder, E. L. (1977). Primary prevention of chronic disease beginning in childhood: The Know Your Body Program: Design of study. *Preventive Medicine, 6,* 344–357.

Williams, C. L., & Wynder, E. L. (1976). Preventive medicine: A blind spot. *Journal of the American Medical Association, 236,* 2196–2197.

Williamson, D. A., Moody, S. C., Granberry, S. W., Lethernon, V. R., & Blouin, D. C. (1983). Criterion-related validity of a role-play social skills test for children. *Behavior Therapy, 14,* 466–481.

Wilmore, J. H., & McNamara, J. J. (1974). Prevalence of coronary heart disease risk factors in boys, 8 to 12 years of age. *Journal of Pediatrics, 84*, 527–533.

Wilson, G. T. (1978). Methodological considerations in treatment outcome research on obesity. *Journal of Consulting and Clinical Psychology, 46*, 687–702.

Wilson, G. T. (1980). Behavior therapy for obesity. In A. J. Stunkard (Ed.), *Obesity* (pp. 325–344). Philadelphia: W. B. Saunders.

Wilson, G. T. (1982a). Clinical issues and strategies in the practice of behavior therapy. In C. M. Franks, G. T. Wilson, P. C. Kendall, & K. D. Brownell (Eds.), *Annual review of behavior therapy: Theory and practice* (Vol. 8, pp. 305–345). New York: Guilford.

Wilson, G. T. (1982b). Fear reduction methods and the treatment of anxiety disorders. In C. M. Franks, G. T. Wilson, P. C. Kendall, & K. D. Brownell (Eds.), *Annual review of behavior therapy: Theory and practice* (Vol. 8, pp. 82–119). New York: Guilford.

Wilson, G. T. (1982c). How useful is meta-analysis in evaluating the effects of different psychological therapies? *Behavioural Psychotherapy, 10*, 221–231.

Wilson, G. T. (1983). *Cognitive processes and procedures in the clinical use of exposure treatment.* Unpublished manuscript, Rutgers University.

Wilson, G. T. (1984a). Clinical issues and strategies in the practice of behavior therapy. In G. T. Wilson, C. M. Franks, K. D. Brownell, & P. C. Kendall (Eds.), *Annual review of behavior therapy: Theory and practice* (Vol. 9, pp. 309–343). New York: Guilford.

Wilson, G. T. (1984b). Fear reduction methods and the treatment of anxiety disorders. In G. T. Wilson, C. M. Franks, K. D. Brownell, & P. C. Kendall (Eds.), *Annual review of behavior therapy: Theory and practice* (Vol. 9, pp. 95–131). New York: Guilford.

Wilson, G. T. (1984c). *Theoretical orientations of graduates of schools of professional psychology.* Unpublished manuscript, Rutgers University.

Wilson, G. T. (in press-a). Behavior therapy for bulimia. In K. D. Brownell & J. Foreyt (Eds.), *Physiology, psychology, and treatment of the eating disorders.* New York: Basic Books.

Wilson, G. T. (in press-b). Limitations of meta-analysis in clinical psychology. *Clinical Psychology Review.*

Wilson, G. T., & Evans, I. M. (1976). Adult behavior therapy and the therapist–client relationship. In C. M. Franks & G. T. Wilson, *Annual review of behavior therapy: Theory and practice* (Vol. 4, pp. 771–792). New York: Brunner/Mazel.

Wilson, G. T., & Franks, C. M. (Eds.). (1982). *Contemporary behavior therapy: Conceptual and empirical foundations.* New York: Guilford.

Wilson, G. T., Hannon, A. E., & Evans, I. M. (1968). Behavior therapy and the therapist–patient relationship. *Journal of Consulting and Clinical Psychology, 32*, 103–109.

Wilson, G. T., & O'Leary, K. D. (1980). *Principles of behavior therapy.* Englewood Cliffs, NJ: Prentice-Hall.

Wilson, G. T., & Rachman, S. J. (1983). Meta-analysis and the evaluation of psychotherapy outcome: Limitations and liabilities. *Journal of Consulting and Clinical Psychology, 51*, 54–64.

Wilson, P. H., Goldin, J. C., & Charbonneau-Powis, M. (1983). Comparative efficacy of behavioral and cognitive treatments of depression. *Cognitive Therapy and Research, 7*, 111–124.

Wine, J. (1971). Test anxiety and direction of attention. *Psychological Bulletin, 76*, 92–104.

Wine, J. (1980). Cognitive-attentional theory of test anxiety. In I. Sarason (Ed.), *Test anxiety: Theory, research and application.* Hillsdale, NJ: Erlbaum.

Winett, R. A. (1983). [Comment on Matarazzo's "Behavioral health's challenge to academic, scientific, and professional psychology"]. *American Psychologist, 38,* 120–121.

Winett, R. A., Hatcher, J. W., Fort, T. R., Leckliter, J. N., Love, S. Q., Riley, A. W., & Fishback, J. F. (1982a). The effects of videotape modeling and daily feedback on residential electricity conservation, home temperature and humidity, perceived comfort, and clothing worn: Winter and summer. *Journal of Applied Behavior Analysis, 15,* 381–402.

Winett, R. A., Neale, M. S., & Williams, K. R. (1982b). The effects of flexible work schedules on urban families with young children: Quasi-experimental ecological studies. *American Journal of Community Psychology, 10,* 49–64.

Winkler, R. C. (1983). The contribution of behavioral economics to behavior modification. In M. Rosenbaum, C. M. Franks, & Y. Jaffe (Eds.), *Perspectives on behavior therapy in the eighties* (pp. 397–415). New York: Springer.

Winkler, R. C., & Winett, R. A. (1982). Behavioral interventions in resource conservation. *American Psychologist, 37,* 421–455.

Wise, E. H., & Haynes, S. N. (1983). Cognitive treatment of test anxiety: Rational restructuring versus attentional training. *Cognitive Therapy and Research, 7,* 69–78.

Wolfe, D. A. (1983, August). *Early intervention methods for child abuse prevention.* Paper presented at the annual meeting of the American Psychological Association, Anaheim, CA.

Wolfe, D. A., Fairbank, J. A., Kelly, J. A., & Bradlyn, A. S. (1983) Child abusive parents' physiological responses to stressful and nonstressful behavior in children. *Behavioral Assessment, 5,* 363–371.

Wolpe, J. (1958). *Psychotherapy by reciprocal inhibition.* Stanford, CA: Stanford University Press.

Wolpe, J. (1973). *The practice of behavior therapy.* New York: Pergamon.

Wolpe, J., & Lazarus, A. A. (1966). *Behavior therapy techniques.* New York: Pergamon.

Woo, R., Garrow, J. S., & Pi-Sunyer, F. X. (1982a). Effect of exercise on spontaneous calorie intake in obesity. *American Journal of Clinical Nutrition, 36,* 470–477.

Woo, R., Garrow, J. S., & Pi-Sunyer, F. X. (1982b). Voluntary food intake during prolonged exercise in obese women. *American Journal of Clinical Nutrition, 36,* 478–484.

Woods, P. A., & Cullen, C. (1983). Determinants of staff behaviour in long-term care. *Behavioural Psychotherapy, 11,* 4–17.

Woods, P. A., & Guest, E. (1980). Toilet training the severely retarded: The importance of evaluation. *Nursing Times, 72*(12), 53–56.

Worland, J., Carney, R. M., Weinberg, H., & Milch, R. (1982). Dropping out of group behavioral parent training. *Behavioral Counseling Quarterly, 2,* 37–41.

Yang, M. U., & Van Itallie, T. B. (1976). Composition of weight loss during short-term weight reduction: Metabolic responses of obese subjects to starvation and low calorie ketogenic and nonketogenic diets. *Journal of Clinical Investigation, 58,* 722–730.

Yates, S. M., & Aronson, E. (1983). A social psychological perspective on energy conservation in residential buildings. *American Psychologist, 38,* 435–444.

Yeaton, W. H., & Sechrest, L. (1981). Critical dimensions in the choice and maintenance of successful treatments: Strength, integrity, and effectiveness. *Journal of Consulting and Clinical Psychology, 49,* 156–167.

Yulevich, L. (1981). *Punishment: A concept that is no longer necessary.* Unpublished manuscript.

Zajonc, R. B. (1980). Feeling and thinking: Preferences need no inferences. *American Psychologist, 35*, 151–175.

Zangwill, W. M. (1983). An evaluation of a parent training program. *Child and Family Behavior Therapy, 5*(4), 1–16.

Zatz, S., & Chassin, L. (1983). Cognitions of test-anxious children. *Journal of Consulting and Clinical Psychology, 51*, 526–534.

Zeiss, A., & Jones, S. O. (1983). Behavioral treatment of depression: Examining treatment failures. In E. Foa & P. M. G. Emmelkamp (Eds.), *Failures in behavior therapy* (pp. 197–216). New York: Wiley.

Zeiss, A., Lewinsohn, P., & Munoz, R. (1979). Nonspecific improvement effects in depression using interpersonal skills training, pleasant activities scheduling or cognitive training. *Journal of Consulting and Clinical Psychology, 47*, 427–439.

Zinner, S. H., Levy, P. S., & Kass, E. H. (1971). Familial aggregation of blood pressure in children. *New England Journal of Medicine, 284*, 401–408.

Zitrin, C. M. (1981). Combined pharmacological and psychological treatment of phobias. In M. Mavissakalian & D. H. Barlow (Eds.), *Phobia*. New York: Guilford.

Zitrin, C. M., Klein, D. F., & Woerner, M. G. (1978). Behavior therapy, supportive psychotherapy, imipramine and phobias. *Archives of General Psychiatry, 35*, 307–316.

Zitrin, C. M., Klein, D. F., & Woerner, M. G. (1980). Treatment of agoraphobia with group exposure in vivo and imipramine *Archives of General Psychiatry, 37*, 63–72.

Zitrin, C. M., Klein, D. F., Woerner, M. G., & Ross, D. C. (1983). Treatment of phobias: I. Comparison of imipramine hydrochloride and placebo. *Archives of General Psychiatry, 40*, 125–139.

Zuroff, D. C., Colussy, S. A., & Wielgus, M. S. (1983). Selective memory and depression: A cautionary note concerning response bias. *Cognitive Therapy and Research, 7*, 223–232.

AUTHOR INDEX

367

SUBJECT INDEX